CONTEMPORARY MISSION THEOLOGY

The American Society of Missiology Series, published in collaboration with Orbis Books, seeks to publish scholarly works of high merit and wide interest on numerous aspects of missiology—the study of Christian mission in its historical, social, and theological dimensions. Able presentations on new and creative approaches to the practice and understanding of mission will receive close attention from the ASM Series Committee.

American Society of Missiology Series, No. 53

CONTEMPORARY MISSION THEOLOGY

*Engaging the Nations: Essays in Honor of
Charles E. Van Engen*

Edited by
Robert L. Gallagher and Paul Hertig

ORBIS BOOKS
Maryknoll, New York 10545

ORBIS BOOKS
Maryknoll, New York 10545

Fathers and Brothers
MARYKNOLL™
TOGETHER IN GOD'S MISSION OF MERCY

Founded in 1970, Orbis Books endeavors to publish works that enlighten the mind, nourish the spirit, and challenge the conscience. The publishing arm of the Maryknoll Fathers and Brothers, Orbis seeks to explore the global dimensions of the Christian faith and mission, to invite dialogue with diverse cultures and religious traditions, and to serve the cause of reconciliation and peace. The books published reflect the views of their authors and do not represent the official position of the Maryknoll Society. To learn more about Maryknoll and Orbis Books, please visit our website at www.maryknollsociety.org.

Library of Congress Cataloging in Publication Data

Names: Gallagher, Robert L., author, editor. | Hertig, Paul, 1955- author, editor. | Engen, Charles Edward van.
Title: Contemporary mission theology: engaging the nations: essays in honor of Charles E. van Engen / edited by Robert L. Gallagher & Paul Hertig.
Description: New York: Orbis Books, 2017. | Series: The American Society of Missiology series | Includes bibliographical references and index.
Identifiers: LCCN 2016032201 | ISBN 9781626982116 (pbk.)
Subjects: LCSH: Missions—Theory. | Missions. | Engen, Charles Edward van.
Classification: LCC BV2070 .C74 2017 | DDC 266—dc23 LC
record available at https://lccn.loc.gov/2016032201

Dedicated to Charles E. Van Engen,
A Master Teacher and Mentor

Jean and Charles Van Engen

Contents

Part 3
Mission Theology in Context

Part 4
Mission Theology and the Church

Part 5
Mission Theology and Church History

Preface to the American Society of Missiology Series

The purpose of the American Society of Missiology Series is to publish—without regard for disciplinary, national, or denominational boundaries—scholarly works of high quality and wide interest on missiological themes from the entire spectrum of scholarly pursuits relevant to Christian mission, which is always the focus of books in the Series.

By mission is meant the effort to effect passage over the boundary between faith in Jesus Christ and its absence. In this understanding of mission, the basic functions of Christian proclamation, dialogue, witness, service, worship, liberation, and nurture are of special concern. And in that context questions arise, including, how does the transition from one cultural context to another influence the shape and interaction between these dynamic functions, especially in regard to the cultural and religious plurality that comprises the global context of Christian life and mission.

The promotion of scholarly dialogue among missiologists, and among missiologists and scholars in other fields of inquiry, may involve the publication of views that some missiologists cannot accept, and with which members of the Editorial Committee themselves do not agree. Manuscripts published in the Series, accordingly, reflect the opinions of their authors and are not understood to represent the position of the American Society of Missiology or of the Editorial Committee. Selection is guided by such criteria as intrinsic worth, readability, coherence, and accessibility to a range of interested persons and not merely to experts or specialists.

The ASM Series, in collaboration with Orbis Books, seeks to publish scholarly works of high merit and wide interest on numerous aspects of missiology—the scholarly study of mission. Able presentations on new and creative approaches to the practice and understanding of mission will receive close attention.

THE ASM SERIES COMMITTEE
Jonathan J. Bonk
Angelyn Dries, O.S.F.
Scott W. Sunquist

Foreword

Scott W. Sunquist

The volume you hold in your hand is a rich repository of mission theology. This is a rare book, commendable for its lucid outline and diverse representation as well as for its content. The book guides us from biblical and theological foundations of mission, through the church and mission history, into contemporary issues in mission. Some of the best mission scholars today handle beautifully each of the topics.

This volume holds together so well because it follows the life and scholarship of an important missiologist: Charles E. Van Engen. Raised in Mexico of missionary parents, Van Engen was educated in the United States and the Netherlands. His missionary and educational vocation has taken him throughout the world, yet mostly in southern California and Latin America. This volume represents the world both in its topics as well as in the amazing array of authors.

Van Engen's scholarship has also been wide ranging. He has written and taught on the Bible and mission (*Announcing the Kingdom: The Story of God's Mission in the Bible*), the theology of mission (*Mission-on-the-Way: Issues in Mission Theology*), the city (*God So Loves the City*), and the church and mission (*God's Missionary People: Rethinking the Purpose of the Local Church*), in addition to most of the other topics covered in this volume. In all of these areas, his scholarship is forward looking, careful, and engaging.

Van Engen's book *God's Missionary People* (translated into ten languages) looked forward to the missional-church concept before mission became an adjective.[1] In that single volume, he set the tone for much of the later discussions about the church that broke away from the traditional Reformation "marks of the church." *God's Missionary People* pulls together the work of great theologians and ecumenical leaders of the past to show how they (Karl Barth, John Mackay, and others) recognized the missionary nature of the church. Furthermore, the book functions as a guide to understanding the church together with how to lead a church with this missional understanding. In the last chapter, Van Engen even coined the expression "missional administration of the local church."

---

1. Charles E. Van Engen, *God's Missionary People: Rethinking the Purpose of the Local Church* (Grand Rapids: Baker Academic, 1991).

In this nicely balanced treatment of *Contemporary Mission Theology,* the legacy continues with the best of Dutch missiology, mixed with a Latin American context and North American scholarship. Students will continue to interact with the taproot of this tradition—Chuck Van Engen—and now see the extension of this scholarship through not only engaging the legacy but also *Engaging the Nations.*

Preface

C. Douglas McConnell

A textbook on mission theology informed by the scholarship of Charles E. Van Engen is an important resource. As you will quickly discover, this compendium of articles by such a diverse group of scholars will provide the necessary complement to the recent works of Christopher J. H. Wright, Scott W. Sunquist, Michael W. Goheen, and others, some of whom contributed to this volume. Serious students of the mission of God have enjoyed insights from these scholars. In this volume from trusted colleagues we can consider various perspectives of mission theology, which represents a unique discipline within the wider conversations of missiology and theology. It is particularly gratifying to know that the contributors offered these articles out of respect for Chuck Van Engen, my friend and colleague.

You may read more about Chuck's life and work in his biographical chapter. Understandably, there is much to say about Chuck. He is one of those people about whom friends and acquaintances rarely employ the descriptor "shy." His gregarious nature combines with wit and intellect to make him a most memorable person. It has been my privilege to be a friend and colleague of Chuck, or Carlitos, depending on the context, since the early 1990s. We served together on the faculty of Fuller Theological Seminary in Pasadena, California, for fifteen of his twenty-seven years at Fuller. I knew him as a fellow professor, his dean, and most recently his provost. In truth, it is much easier to be a fellow professor!

Without a doubt, Chuck is one of those great academics that you turn to when the times call for wise counsel. When the School of World Mission (SWM) was in the midst of the spiritual dynamics discoveries, for example, the faculty turned to Chuck to be the needed replacement of Arthur F. Glasser upon his retirement. Van Engen brought a discerning voice that combined the biblical and theological scholarship needed at the time. His experience as a missionary, including the range of phenomena so interesting to SWM students and faculty alike, was just the right touch for the job.

Another important example is Chuck's approach to a biblical theology of mission during the period surrounding the coming of the third millennium. There were so many strategic plans, and even newly launched movements, that it presented more a cacophony than a Holy Spirit–led symphony. One last example, very meaningful to me as provost, came while working on the new curriculum. There was a need for the theologians from the schools of Theology and Intercultural Studies to pull together a course that was global in its scope while holding to the best theological traditions, all the while maintaining the evangelical moorings of our seminary. Along with other key colleagues, Chuck worked diligently, even participating in a working group retreat, to ensure we met the deadline.

Chuck Van Engen is above all a teacher and mentor, witnessed by the impressive list of scholars mentored in their doctoral studies. His impact is extensive; if only noting the doctoral theses he directly influenced, you would have to multiply each of those by about 250 pages, submitted an average of three times before the defense of each thesis. You would need a calculator! Should you care to contact any of these scholars, they would readily attest to Chuck's patient supervision of each of them. Interestingly, many scholars desire to limit the number of mentees under their tutelage due to the pressures of their academic careers and the demands of each doctoral student. Not so with Van Engen. In fact, at a time when he had more doctoral students than anyone in our seminary, he conceived of and launched the Latin American Christian Ministries program with the help of a group of dedicated colleagues—some have doctorates mentored by Van Engen—adding more students to his load. His rationale for such a selfless commitment was that the mission of God needed many more thoughtful leaders. The resulting program is amazing in its ambitious design. This volume seems to provide both logic and validity to that vision.

As you can imagine, writing a preface for one who has given so much to our beloved seminary upon his retirement leaves me in a quandary. I am blessed to have been his colleague and sad at the thought that my friend will not be attending our frequent academic meetings. Along with you, I will return to this volume often, both in forming thoughtful reflection and in refreshing my memory prior to teaching or writing. I hope you can vicariously share in the benefit of working next to such an outstanding person. Each contributor to this volume shares the same respect for our great friend and colleague Chuck Van Engen.

Biography of
Charles E. Van Engen

In 1983, Chuck, Jean, and their children found themselves in Holland, Michigan, for nine months due to Chuck's need to undergo arthroscopic repair of his knees. While there, the Western Theological Seminary (WTS) invited him to help them design the program and the courses that would become a full-time faculty position in missiology. As a result of his work Chuck was urged to consider accepting the position himself. After much soul searching, Chuck and Jean made the very difficult decision to leave Chuck's birthplace and ministry locale of Chiapas and move to Holland, Michigan.

Chuck taught a number of missiology courses at Western and eventually converted his course on relational evangelism into a book, *You Are My Witnesses* (1992). In addition, his course on applied missiology for the local congregation became *God's Missionary People: Rethinking the Purpose of the Local Church* (1991). This latter book now exists in translations in ten languages and was a precursor to what later works published by the Gospel and Our Culture Network called the "missional church." During the three years that Chuck taught at Western he also served as secretary-treasurer of the Midwest Fellowship of Professors of Mission.

In the spring of 1987, while Chuck and Jean were in Pasadena for Chuck to teach a course as an adjunct professor in the School of World Mission (SWM), Paul Pierson as dean, along with the SWM faculty, invited him to join them. At the time, Chuck and Jean knew they would be leaving Western, and Chuck accepted the position in SWM. The family moved to California in July 1988.

MISSIOLOGY AT FULLER THEOLOGICAL
SEMINARY (1988–2015)

When Chuck arrived at Fuller in the fall of 1988, Arthur F. Glasser, in the process of retiring, graciously handed all his courses over to Chuck along with a request to create new courses in biblical theology of mission, church growth missiology, missiology as a discipline, mission theology, and Latin American studies. This involved Chuck working closely with Dean S. Gilliland (Contextualization) and C. Peter Wagner (Church Growth), along with the rest of the SWM faculty. Donald A. McGavran still had an office and a presence in the SWM faculty. He enthusiastically welcomed Chuck.

Very soon, Chuck gained a reputation at Fuller Seminary as the professor whose classes began with hearty singing and prayer. His greatest joy at Fuller was teaching, mentoring, and encouraging students—women and men—in their mission and ministry formation. He ended up teaching more than fifteen different courses at Fuller in SWM, in the School of Theology master's programs, in the DMin program, the Korean missiology program, and in what is now the Center for Hispanic/Latino Church Studies. In 1994, the seminary honored Chuck with the C. Davis Weyerhaeuser Award for Excellence. In May of 1996, he became the Arthur F. Glasser Chair of Biblical Theology of Mission in SWM. His inaugural address was entitled "Mission of, in, and on the Way," based on Luke 9. In the late 1990s he was asked to work with colleagues from the School of Theology and the School of Psychology to create Fuller's Faculty Senate, which he chaired twice.

Along with his love of teaching, and in addition to his own writing, such as *Mission on the Way: Issues in Mission Theology* (Grand Rapids: Baker Books, 1996) and his editorship of *The State of Missiology Today: Global Innovations in Christian Witness* (Downers Grove, IL: IVP Academic, 2016), he considered it a joy and privilege to work with others in writing and publishing. By way of example, early in his time at Fuller, Chuck asked Paul E. Pierson and Dean S. Gilliland to help him compile a book as a tribute to Arthur F. Glasser, his predecessor, colleague, and mentor, titled *The Good News of the Kingdom: Mission Theology for the Third Millennium* (Maryknoll, NY: Orbis Books, 1993). The congratulatory list at the back of the original bound volume of the work is a truly amazing who's-who of mission thought and missiology around the world: all friends of Glasser. Once the book was available, Art insisted on sitting in Chuck's garage writing a note and signing every one of several hundred volumes sent to each of those on the congratulatory list.

Thus began one of Chuck's contributions to SWM, a series of Festschrifts, volumes collected in honor of a colleague that also serve as snapshots of an area of missiology at a particular time in history. During his time in SWM, later known as the School of Intercultural Studies (SIS), Chuck created and/ or edited volumes in honor of Paul Pierson (*Missiological Education for the Twenty-first Century: The Book, the Circle and the Sandals*, edited with Dudley Woodberry and Eddie Elliston, 1996); Wilbert Shenk (*Evangelical, Ecumenical, and Anabaptist Missiologies in Conversation*, edited with James R. Krabill and Walter Sawatsky, 2006); and Charles Kraft (*Paradigm Shifts in Christian Witness: Insights from Anthropology, Communication, and Spiritual Power*, edited with Darrell Whiteman and J. Dudley Woodberry, 2008). He also assisted with and participated in Festschrifts for Dean Gilliland (*Appropriate Christianity*, ed. Charles H. Kraft, 2005) and Dudley Woodberry (*Toward Respectful Understanding and Witness among Muslims: Essays in Honor of J. Dudley Woodberry*, Evelyne Reisacher, gen. ed., with Joseph Cumming and Dean Gilliland, 2012).

One of Chuck's greatest joys at Fuller was walking alongside PhD students in SWM. On two occasions this interaction led to two extended multiquarter seminars that eventuated in publications: *God So Loves the City: Seeking a Theology for Urban Mission* (ed. with Jude Tiersma Watson, 1994); and

Footprints of God: Mission Of, In, and On the Way (ed. with Nancy Thomas and Robert L. Gallagher, 1999). Alongside those projects, Chuck also enjoyed working on collaborative publication projects with colleagues in and outside of Fuller. That was the case with *Evangelical Dictionary of World Missions* (A. Scott Moreau, gen. ed., with Harold Netland, 2000). After four quarters of team teaching with Dan Shaw, they published *Communicating God's Word in a Complex World: God's Truth or Hocus-Pocus*, 2003. Also in 2003, Chuck helped create and edit a Festschrift in honor of his friend Jerald D. Gort, longtime assistant to Johannes Verkuyl and a member of the faculty of the Free University of Amsterdam, who had helped Chuck and Jean so very much during their time in Amsterdam (*Fullness of Life for All: Challenges for Mission in the Early 21st Century*, ed. with Inus Daneel and Hendrik Vroom, 2003).

Chuck also represented SWM in the larger world of professional scholarly missiology by actively participating in the Association of Professors of Mission (secretary-treasurer, 1988–1996), the American Society of Missiology (a number of presentations), the Academy of Evangelism in Higher Education, and the American Society of Church Growth (president, 1999–2001). Over the course of his years at Fuller, he has taught missiology at the Overseas Ministry Study Center (OMSC) in New Haven, Connecticut, as well as in Germany, Denmark, India, Brazil, Korea, and numerous countries throughout Latin America.

OFFICER OF THE GENERAL SYNOD OF THE REFORMED CHURCH IN AMERICA (1996–2000)

While teaching full time at Fuller, much to Chuck's surprise, the General Synod of the Reformed Church in America (RCA) elected him to be its vice-president in 1996. Tradition dictates that the vice-president becomes the president the next year and then moderator of the General Program Council (the administrative program group that leads the denomination) the year after that. During his presidential year, due to Chuck's insistence, the RCA approved holding "Mission 2000," the largest mission gathering in the RCA's history. Over 1,600 people met on Long Island, New York, in June of 2000 to celebrate God's mission locally and globally through the RCA to the world. These church and ecumenical activities served as background years later when he became a member of the Theology Commission of the Lausanne Movement (2006–2010) in preparation for Lausanne III, which met in Cape Town, South Africa, in the fall of 2010.

FOUNDER OF LATIN AMERICAN CHRISTIAN MINISTRIES (2000 TO THE PRESENT)

Beginning in 1999, Pablo A. Deiros from Argentina, a professor at Fuller Seminary, and Chuck began to share with each other their concerns regarding the need to provide additional theological and missiological formation for those serving as faculty members in Bible schools and seminaries throughout Latin America. No accredited doctoral programs existed in Latin America, and few could afford to come to the United States or to Europe to study. Most scholars stopped their education after receiving their master's degree. Following this initial conversation, in consultation with other colleagues and through much prayer, Chuck and Jean, Pablo Deiros, and Paul Pierson founded Latin American Christian Ministries, Inc. (LACM) in 2000. Its stated purpose is "to provide teaching and church leadership mentoring skills, programs and resources for Christian ministries and pastors in Latin America." This non-profit organization has become the initiator and foundational support for the Latin American Doctoral Program in Theology (LADPT).

Organized as a multisite and multidenominational community of Latin American scholars working together in a graduate school of theology, the program is directed by Latin Americans, taught by Latin Americans, and offered to leaders in Latin America. Applicants must hold a master's degree and fulfill strict entrance requirements. A foundational value of the program is that students will not need to leave for any extended time the Bible schools, seminaries, churches, or mission agencies where they are ministering, in order to carry out upper-level theological and missiological studies.

Officially launched in Londrina, Brazil, in February 2004, as of September 2015, there were over 70 active doctoral candidates studying in this PhD-level graduate program. They represent more than 20 Latin American countries and over 30 churches, denominations, and mission agencies. They are taught and mentored by a core faculty of 16 and an additional adjunct faculty of over 30 Latin American scholars. Eight have graduated from the program with their PhD degrees and three others are in the process of graduation. This program appears to be one of the first programs of its kind to be approved and accredited at a university level by a Latin American government. In June 2008, the Association of Theological Schools accepted the LADPT as an unaccredited affiliate member.

Flowing from his involvement in Latin America, Chuck helped edit or wrote several books in Spanish: *La iglesia latinoamericana: Su vida y su mission* (ed. with Alberto Roldán and Nancy Thomas, 2011); *Principios de compañerismo misionero en Chiapas* (2014); and *Misión y comisión: Historias de mi tierra* (2015).

CONCLUSION

In September 2015, Chuck became senior professor at Fuller, and he and Jean moved to Holland, Michigan. They continue to spend much of their time leading LACM (Chuck as CEO and president) and supporting the doctoral program. When asked whom he would name as his "gurus" in missiology, Chuck responded with the names of Helen Barrett Montgomery, Roland Allen, J. H. Bavinck, Hendrik Kraemer, Johannes Verkuyl, Donald McGavran, Arthur Glasser, Orlando Costas, Lesslie Newbigin, Ralph Winter, Paul Hiebert, and Chuck Kraft. Drawing inspiration from them, he is a mission thinker, teacher, mentor, mission mobilizer, servant, and encourager. When asked how he would sum up his life and career thus far, he answered, "My greatest joy has been to invest time in the lives of people who will in turn invest their lives in others."

Contributors

Christina Tellechea Accornero is currently the CEO of *V3 Coaching* in Indianapolis, Indiana, where she coaches individuals and corporate groups to advance their value, voice, and vision through training, seminars, webinars, and personal coaching. Chris has published essays in several books, including *First Steps to Ministry*, *God So Loves the City*, and *Gospel Bearers, Gender Barriers*.

Gerald H. Anderson (PhD, Boston University) is director emeritus of the Overseas Ministries Study Center in New Haven, Connecticut, former editor of the *International Bulletin of Missionary Research* (1977–2000), and a member of the International Advisory Board of *Bibliographia Missionaria* (Rome). He has published widely on the theology of mission, and was editor of the *Biographical Dictionary of Christian Missions* (1999).

Adam D. Ayers is an assistant professor of Anthropology at Vanguard University, and pastor of Faith Worship Community in Costa Mesa, California. He holds an MA in biblical studies (Vanguard University), and a PhD in intercultural studies (Fuller Theological Seminary). Founder of *Stoa Ministries International*, Adam has published widely on social boundaries and religious behavior.

Antonio Carlos Barro is founder of and professor at South American Theological Seminary in Londrina, Brazil. A Presbyterian minister, he earned an MA in missiology (Reformed Theological Seminary), and a ThM and PhD in intercultural studies (Fuller Theological Seminary).

Jorge Henrique Barro, a Presbyterian minister with a ThM in mission and a PhD in intercultural studies from Fuller Theological Seminary, is president of the Latin American Theological Fellowship, professor at South American Theological Seminary (Londrina, Brazil), and an evaluator with the Brazilian Ministry of Education for Theological Schools.

Stephen B. Bevans is a priest in the Catholic missionary congregation of the Society of the Divine Word (S.V.D.), and since 1986 has taught at Catholic Theological Union in Chicago as emeritus professor of mission and culture. He holds the STL (Pontifical Gregorian University, Rome), and MA and PhD degrees (University of Notre Dame). Among his many books are *Models of Contextual Theology* (2002) and, with Roger P. Schroeder, *Constants in Context* (2004) and *Prophetic Dialogue* (2011).

Stephen E. Burris is founding editor of the journal *New Urban World*, CEO of Urban Loft Publishers, and senior editor of the *International Journal of Urban Transformation*. A pastor of the Golden Valley Church, San Bernardino, California, he has served cross-culturally in Zimbabwe.

Pablo A. Deiros is vice president of the International Baptist Theological Seminary in Buenos Aires, Argentina. He has authored more than sixty books, teaches at Fuller Theological Seminary (Pasadena, California), and with Charles E. Van Engen, was cofounder of the Latin American Doctoral Program (PRODOLA). He has a ThM (International Baptist Theological Seminary, Buenos Aires) and a PhD in history (Southwestern Baptist Theological Seminary).

Robert L. Gallagher (PhD, Fuller Theological Seminary) is the department chair, director of the master of arts program in intercultural studies, and associate professor of intercultural studies at Wheaton College Graduate School in Chicago, where he has taught since 1998. His publications include the co-editing of *Footprints of God* (MARC, 1999), *Mission in Acts: Ancient Narratives in Contemporary Contexts* (Orbis Books, 2004), and *Landmark Essays in Mission and World Christianity* (Orbis Books, 2009).

Sarita D. Gallagher (PhD, Fuller Theological Seminary) is associate professor of religion at George Fox University in Newberg, Oregon. She served as a missionary with CRC Churches International in Papua New Guinea and Australia, and teaches courses in biblical theology, intercultural studies, world religions, and world Christianity. Her publications include *Abrahamic Blessing: A Missiological Narrative of Revival in Papua New Guinea* (Pickwick, 2014).

Michael W. Goheen (PhD, Utrecht) is theological director and scholar-in-residence at the Missional Training Center in Phoenix, Arizona, and professor of mission and theology at Redeemer Seminary, Dallas, Texas. He has authored and edited nine books, including *The Drama of Scripture* (with Craig Bartholomew, Baker, 2004), *A Light to the Nations* (Baker, 2011), and *An Introduction to Christian Mission Today* (InterVarsity Press, 2014).

Jerald D. Gort is emeritus associate professor of missiology and theology of religion at the Faculty of Theology, Free University of Amsterdam. He has published in the areas of mission studies, ecumenics, and theology of religion, and is cofounder and coeditor of the Amsterdam academic series Currents of Encounter, which has published fifty-five volumes.

David Hartono, PhD in intercultural studies (Fuller Theological Seminary), was a Central Committee member of the Communion of Churches in Indonesia, general chairman of the Communion of Churches in Indonesia (Western Kalimantan Province), pastor at New Life Community Church (RCA), and president of the executive committee of the Council for Pacific and Asian American Ministry (CPAAM) of the Reformed Church in America (RCA).

Paul Hertig is professor of global studies at Azusa Pacific University. He has integrated the fields of Bible and mission throughout his teaching career, and has published twenty essays along with the following books: *Matthew's Narrative Use of Galilee in the Multicultural and Missiological Journeys of Jesus; Mission in Acts: Ancient Narratives in Contemporary Context;* and *Landmark Essays in Mission and World Christianity*—the latter two coedited with Robert L. Gallagher.

Young Lee Hertig is senior lecturer at Azusa Pacific University, Azusa, California, and cofounder and executive director of the Innovative Space for Asian American Christianity (ISAAC) and Asian American Women on Leadership (AAWOL) in Los Angeles, California. She holds three masters of arts degrees in counseling psychology, theology, and anthropology, together with a PhD in intercultural studies (Fuller Theological Seminary). She has published widely on spirituality, sustainability, and diversity from a Yinist intersectional perspective.

Jan A. B. Jongeneel is reverend emeritus in the Netherlands Reformed Church and in the Minahasa Evangelical Christian Church (Indonesia), visiting professor of Yale Divinity School, and honorary emeritus professor of missiology at Utrecht University. He has authored various books, including a *Missiological Encyclopedia* (2 volumes), *Experiences of the Spirit: Conference on Pentecostal and Charismatic Research in Europe at Utrecht University 1989,* and *Jesus Christ in World History: His Presence and Representation in Cyclical and Linear Settings* (2009).

J. Andrew Kirk has taught courses on six continents, and has recently authored *What Is Mission? Theological Explorations; Mission under Scrutiny; The Future of Reason, Science, and Faith; Mission as Dialogue; Civilizations in Conflict? Islam, the West, and Christian Faith;* and *The Church and the World.* Kirk is currently a senior research fellow at the International Baptist Theological Study Centre in Amsterdam.

J. N. J. (Klippies) Kritzinger is an emeritus professor of missiology at the University of South Africa (UNISA), where he taught from 1981 to 2015, and was the editor of *Missionalia: Southern African Journal of Missiology* until 2009. He worked with Nico Smith to establish the inner-city congregation of Melodi ya Tshwane (1992–2015), and since 2003, has served in management of the Northern Theological Seminary in Pretoria (URCSA).

C. Douglas McConnell is professor of leadership and intercultural studies in the School of Intercultural Studies and provost emeritus at Fuller Theological Seminary. Prior to Fuller Seminary, McConnell spent fifteen years in Australia and Papua New Guinea, was associate professor and chair of the Department of Intercultural Studies and Evangelism at Wheaton College Graduate School, and International Director of Pioneers.

Mary Motte, PhD, is a missiologist and member of an international missionary institute, the Franciscan Missionaries of Mary (F.M.M.). She is director of the Mission Resource Center of the U.S. province with responsibilities for mission research, ecumenical relations, and ongoing education sessions related to mission and the spirituality of the foundress of the F.M.M.

Mary Thiessen Nation has a PhD in intercultural studies (Fuller Theological Seminary) and trains ministers and missionaries to embrace an embodied Christian spirituality, and to learn holistic biblical responses to crises, conflict, and trauma. Mary and her husband, Mark, served with Mennonite Mission Network in London, England, for six years prior to moving to Harrisonburg, Virginia, where she is currently an affiliate professor at Eastern Mennonite Seminary.

vanThanh Nguyen is a Catholic missionary of the Society of the Divine Word (S.V.D.), holder of the Francis Xavier Ford, M.M., Chair of Catholic Missiology, and professor of New Testament studies at Catholic Theological Union in Chicago, Illinois. His publications include *Peter and Cornelius: A Story of Conversion and Mission* (2012), *Stories of Early Christianity* (2013), and is co-editor of *God's People on the Move: Biblical and Global Perspectives on Migration and Mission* (2014).

Bokyoung Park is an ordained minister of the Presbyterian Church of Korea. She serves as a professor of missiology at Presbyterian University and Theological Seminary (PUTS) in Seoul, Korea. After finishing her M Div at PUTS, she earned a PhD in intercultural studies at Fuller Theological Seminary, and has authored several books in Korean including *Women and Mission* (2005), *Introduction to Contemporary Missiology* (2008), *Women, God's Mission and Church* (2013), and *Holistic Evangelical Missiology* (2016).

DeLonn L. Rance is the founding director of Intercultural Doctoral Studies, chair of the Global Missions Department, and associate professor of intercultural studies at the Assemblies of God Theological Seminary in Springfield, Missouri. He was also the founding dean of the School of Theology and Missions at the Universidad Cristiana de las Asambleas de Dios in El Salvador, and is presently a missiologist for both the Assemblies of God World Fellowship and the Pentecostal World Fellowship.

Shawn B. Redford specializes in biblical theology of mission and missiological hermeneutics, having taught at Fuller Theological Seminary where he received his PhD. He currently teaches at the Africa International University, Nairobi Evangelical Graduate School of Theology (AIU-NEGST), and in remote areas in Kenya while serving with CMF International.

Mossai T. Sanguma is the founder of the Protestant University of the Ubangi in the Democratic Republic of Congo, and the former president of the Evangelical Community in the Ubangi and Mongala (CEUM). He now serves as the chair of the Mission Department at Université Protestante au Congo (UPC), vice coordinator of the Francophone Missiologist Network in Africa, and editor of *Réconciliation: Gage pour la reconstruction.*

Roger P. Schroeder's major publications include two works with Stephen B. Bevans, S.V.D.: *Constants in Context* (Orbis Books, 2004), and *Prophetic Dialogue* (Orbis Books, 2011). He is also the author of *What Is the Mission of the Church?* (Orbis Books, 2008). Schroeder is a member of the Catholic missionary order of the Society of the Divine Word (S.V.D.), with whom he served as a missionary in Papua New Guinea for six years.

Kyung Lan Suh teaches mission theology at Fuller Theological Seminary, having earned her PhD in intercultural studies (Fuller Theological Seminary). She served for twenty years as a youth pastor, director of education, mission pastor, and pastoral administrator at the Orange Korean CRC in California.

Scott W. Sunquist is the dean of Fuller Theological Seminary's School of Intercultural Studies and professor of world Christianity. He taught at Pittsburgh Theological Seminary as professor of world Christianity, having previously served as a missionary in the Republic of Singapore, where he was a lecturer in church history, ecumenics, and Asian Christianity at Trinity Theological College, and an ordained minister of the Presbyterian Church (U.S.A.), pastoring the Covenant Presbyterian Church in Singapore.

Jude Tiersma Watson, PhD, is an associate professor of urban mission in the School of Intercultural Studies at Fuller Theological Seminary, and serves on the executive committee for the Fuller Youth Institute. Jude and her husband, John, are elders with InnerCHANGE/CRM, a Christian Order among the Poor. Jude has lived in the Westlake immigrant neighborhood in central Los Angeles for over twenty years.

Introduction

Paul Hertig

Our studies at Fuller Theological Seminary (in the 1980s and 1990s) pressed our biblical and missiological thinking beyond previous comprehension, largely because of our connections with our doctoral mentor, Charles E. Van Engen. The first time we met Chuck at a School of Intercultural Studies function, he spoke of God's desire to engage the nations for Christ. He combined the winsome passion of a Pentecostal Latino with the philosophic intellect of a Reformed European. What amazed us about Chuck—as we attended every course that he offered, worked as his research assistants, and even participated in teaching some of his courses—was his ability to take complex ideas and reduce them to understandable concepts. There were many times, stumped in the progress of our dissertations, that within minutes of sitting in his office and explaining our dilemma, he unfolded the solution in a straightforward manner, leaving us grateful to benefit from a master teacher and mentor.

In this volume of essays honoring Chuck Van Engen and his influences, we explore the theme of God's engagement of the nations, organizing it around Chuck's integrative fields in the discipline of missiology, and based on the structure of his seminal work, *Mission on the Way: Issues in Mission Theology* (Baker Books, 1996). Each section of our book, with three chapters in each section, lays out various fields of Van Engen's missiology, appropriately concluding with his own chapter, in which he establishes a missiological framework to explore a futuristic road map for this millennium.

PRELIMINARY ESSAYS

In "The Emergence of Mission Theology," Jan A. B. Jongeneel provides a sweeping historical perspective of mission theology that includes Christianity in a minority position from the New Testament period onward, and in a majority position from the time of Constantine the Great in the Roman Empire onward. In "A New Missionary Age," Gerald H. Anderson emphasizes that faithfulness in mission will be measured in terms that reflect the total quality of our discipleship, where survival and justice for all God's people accompany salvation. These two giants in the field of missiology provide solid historical and theological foundations for this profound and contemporary study of mission theology.

PART 1: MISSION THEOLOGY AND THE BIBLE

Michael W. Goheen, in "The Biblical Story of Narrative Theology," argues that a missional hermeneutic does not simply trace a particular theme of mission throughout the biblical story; instead, mission is an indispensable lens and central plot of the biblical story. David Hartono, in "Contextual Christology: Carrying the Great Commission with Joy," probes Paul's contextual Christology of becoming all things to all people and explores the contextual nature of Jesus's Incarnation and postresurrection appearances. Stephen E. Burris, in "Mission Theology in the City: Sowing Urban Seeds of *Shalom*," stresses transformation and reconciliation in response to the ministry of Jesus, which includes serving the oppressed, exploited, enslaved, hungry, sick, poor, orphaned, widowed, imprisoned; and, as signposts of the kingdom of God, sowing seeds of *shalom* whenever and wherever we have opportunity.

PART 2: MISSION THEOLOGY AND CHURCH BELIEFS

Stephen B. Bevans, S.V.D., and Roger P. Schroeder, S.V.D., in "Missionary Ecclesiology: Evangelical, Ecumenical, and Catholic Developments in 'Engaging the Nations,'" establish that the church is organized not for its own sake but for the sake of mission. J. Andrew Kirk, in "Missionary Theology: Roland Allen and Vincent Donovan Rediscovered," analyzes the efforts of these two missiologists to apply Paul's missionary methods in Christian communities cross-culturally with the goal of producing truly indigenous churches, independent of support from abroad. With a premise that to know God is to represent God on earth, embody compassion and justice, and in particular, to defend and protect the weak and vulnerable, in "Mission Theology and the Nature of God," J. N. J. (Klippies) Kritzinger emphasizes that the life of a Christian community should be a faithful and impactful performance of the Christian message in a particular context.

PART 3: MISSION THEOLOGY IN CONTEXT

"Carlitos de Las Casas: A Theologian Made in Latin America," by Antonio Carlos Barro and Jorge Henrique Barro, examines Charles Van Engen's landmark book *God's Missionary People* and its contextual contribution to missiology in Latin America. In "Recovering Reconciliation as God's Mission: Its Implications for North and South Korea," Kyung Lan Suh emphasizes that restorative justice requires truth, conversion, and forgiveness to reconcile North and South Korea. In "Redeeming Mission Theology in Africa: A Congolese Perspective toward Resolving Ethnic Conflict," Mossai T. Sanguma demonstrates that mission was confused by nationalists, paternalists, and imperialists during the colonial era and needs to shift in Africa to a redeeming mission full of forgiveness, reconciliation, and freedom, which comes from the heart of a merciful God.

PART 4: MISSION THEOLOGY AND THE CHURCH

In "Matthew's Experience of Discipleship and the Great Commission," Paul Hertig explores how Matthew's calling to discipleship lays the foundation for the experiential learning component and reciprocity implicit and explicit in the Great Commission. In "Missionary Churches in Acts: A Model of Intercultural Engagement with the Nations," vanThanh Nguyen, S.V.D., examines the missionary churches in Acts so that committed Christians today will find inspiration, through the earliest witnesses, to continue in the missionary enterprise of the church. Adam D. Ayers, in "Group Identities and Boundaries during the Pauline Mission," considers how group definitions may be exercised to integrate others as "we." To bridge the "historical gap," rather than interpret "them," we all participate together in reading the text, since "they" are not "them," but "they" are "we."

PART 5: MISSION THEOLOGY AND CHURCH HISTORY

In "Historic Perspectives on Catholic Mission Theology," Mary Motte, F.M.M., explores incarnational spaces and lived experiences of solidarity with the poor, relating to the world from below, and discovering relationships that reach beyond faith, culture, language, and economy. Pablo A. Deiros, in "Historical Perspectives on Protestant Mission Theology: Striving toward a New Model for a Postmodern Context," applies the theory of scientific models to the development of Christian mission represented (1) at the International Missionary Conference held at Edinburgh in 1910, and (2) through the prevailing mission theology of the majority world. He draws conclusions on the debate of present pluralistic and globalized models. Exploring "Historic Perspectives of Pentecostal Mission Theology," DeLonn L. Rance reviews the historical context that birthed the missiology of the indigenous church, redefines the principles of the indigenous church for the twenty-first century, identifies indigenous church core values, and concludes with a personal narrative of the intersection of missiology and praxis.

PART 6: MISSION THEOLOGY AND RELIGIOUS PLURALISM

In "Good News for All People: Engaging Luke's Narrative Soteriology of the Nations," Robert L. Gallagher explores Christ's salvation in the narratives of Luke's Gospel, and in doing so, examines God's engagement of the nations. Sarita D. Gallagher, in "Interfaith Education and the *Missio Dei*: A Case Study in the Pacific Northwest," inspects the missiological outcomes of a christo-centric model of interfaith engagement in an academic setting with the premise that sharing the gospel of Christ remains central to Christian witness. Yet, at the heart of Christ's imperative, is loving our neighbors in the midst of religious diversity and theological difference. In "Interreligious Dialogue and Convivence: Missional Challenge and Charge for Today," Jerald D. Gort reviews historical and contemporary attitudes of Christianity toward other religions, discusses the concept of contextualization and certain insights of postmodernism that are germane to dialogue and then, against this background, sketches out four constitutive modes of interreligious dialogue.

PART 7: MODERNITY AND POSTMODERNITY IN MISSION THEOLOGY

Emboldened by the connection between quantum physics and Taoism, Young Lee Hertig, in "Mission Theology and Stewardship of the Earth," coins the term *Yinist* (an Asian American epistemology of belonging that moves beyond the existing feminist discourses), and amid emerging womanist and *mujerista* approaches responds to modernity's disconnection of humanity from the rest of God's creation, a position buoyed and rooted in evangelical Christian faith. In contrast to social norms, Bokyoung Park, in "Korean Women Missionaries: Agents of God's Mission," shows how Korean women's contributions in missions have not only increased in the past three decades but have also challenged the missionary community by raising feminist consciousness. In a narrative approach, she explores how Korean women missionaries have contributed to the *missio Dei* within the context of Korean mission history. In "Mission Theology and Postmodern Social Networks," Shawn B. Redford demonstrates how social networks can release human potential while diminishing levels of control, structure, resources, empowerment, and personal glory—allowing those engaged in God's mission to demonstrate human frailty, trust, and solidarity with the Holy Spirit's missional leadership—toward resourceful and God-directed mission practices.

PART 8: MISSION THEOLOGY AND MINISTRY FORMATION

In "Engaging the Nations in Los Angeles: A Spirituality of Accompaniment," Jude Tiersma Watson looks specifically at the nations that have moved to central Los Angeles and includes an integrating theme of a spirituality of accompaniment as a means of mission. She includes God's big-picture narrative that embraces the people in her neighborhood as well as the story of the larger globalizing forces impacting urban neighborhoods. In "Carrying Heavy Stories: Discerning What the Body Carries," Mary Thiessen Nation explains through life stories and Scripture that trauma affects the physical body, that each experience of trauma warrants attention to the whole person, including the spiritual aspects, and that our bodies were created to carry the gospel. Christina Tellechea Accornero, in "Reaping Missionary Leaders in the College Years," observes that a convergence happens during college that cultivates leadership preparation and launching for those who will be the future leaders of our missional enterprises. She explores a leadership development model through stories and conversations.

CONCLUSION: SEEKING WAYS FORWARD IN MISSION THEOLOGY

Charles E. Van Engen responds to the essays in this volume and perceptively describes five paradigm shifts in "Seeking Ways Forward in Mission Theology": (1) exploration of mission thinking focused on discovering new cultures, new peoples, and new languages outside Western Europe; (2) expansion of mission agencies and denominations to include theological and missiological richness of the new civilizations and cultures they encountered; (3) enculturation during a time of decolonization, and the rise of the nation-states around the globe that spawned an emphasis on national churches that began to determine their own structures, leadership, priorities, and destinies; (4) the Exodus paradigm (during this era, the search for liberation in various contexts around the world became the topic of missiological reflection, calling for a liberating engagement of the socioeconomic and political realities of nation-states); (5) the Exile paradigm, in which Christian persons, groups of people, churches, and mission agencies engage one another and their contexts as pilgrims in a foreign land in the midst of the largest mass migration of peoples in the history of the earth.

The Emergence of Mission Theology

Jan A. B. Jongeneel

The dissertation of Charles E. Van Engen, supervised by professors Johannes Verkuyl and Jan Veenhof at the Free University of Amsterdam, described, analyzed, and evaluated the mission theology of one specific school: the Church Growth Movement of Donald A. McGavran, Arthur F. Glasser, and congenial thinkers.[1] The present contribution, based on encyclopedic knowledge of mission studies in the nineteenth and twentieth centuries, intends to extend the scope of Van Engen's dissertation, both in time and in space.[2] In this way, I want to honor Van Engen as a good friend and as a colleague with in-depth experience in Latin America.

The term "mission theology" emerged in the nineteenth century, yet doing mission and a working mission theology are much older. They actually are as old as the Bible, specifically the New Testament. This chapter distinguishes between the emergence of doing mission and mission theology in the setting of Christianity in a minority position (from the New Testament period onward), and doing them from a majority position (from the time of Constantine the Great in the Roman Empire onward). It also pays attention to the religious and postreligious contexts in which Christian missions and mission theologies have operated in the past and are operating today. In other words, mission theology is emerging in the context of (1) pre-Christian cyclical belief systems, (2) post-Christian linear Islam, and (3) post-Christian largely linear secularism (since the Enlightenment era). At the end, I will make some final observations, referring once again to Van Engen.

MISSION THEOLOGY AS OLD AS THE BIBLE

The emergence of mission theology is much older than the theory of the Church Growth Movement, developed by McGavran in the wake of the Tambaram Conference (1938), which extensively dealt with "the growing

---

1. Charles E. Van Engen, *The Growth of the True Church: An Analysis of the Ecclesiology of Church Growth Theory* (Amsterdam: Rodopi, 1981), 515-17.
2. Jan A. B. Jongeneel, *Philosophy, Science, and Theology of Mission in the 19th and 20th Centuries: A Missiological Encyclopedia*, 2 vols. (Frankfurt am Main: Peter Lang, 1995–97).

church."[3] In the nineteenth century Edward White wrote about "missionary theology,"[4] and Gustav Warneck, founding father of "missiology" (German: *Missionswissenschaft*)" as an academic discipline, about "mission theology" (German: *Missionstheologie*).[5] They coined these terms and later generations followed in one way or another. There is no doubt, however, that mission theology emerged long before these terms circulated.

The seventeenth-century Netherlands reformed theologian Gisbertus Voetius was the first scholar who developed a "comprehensive Protestant theology of missions."[6] Several Roman Catholic missiologists, though, preceded him. In fact, we can go back to the New Testament era and describe Jesus as a missionary,[7] and the apostle Paul as a mission theologian.[8] There are even biblical scholars who go back to the Old Testament, viewing it as the birthplace of mission theology. One of them, the Jesuit Yves Raguin, wrote about "the missionary theology of the Old Testament."[9]

Although scholars continue to debate the absence or presence of missionary patterns in the Old Testament, it is obvious that the New Testament is rooted in the Old Testament, and that some Old Testament missionary concepts influenced the New Testament profile of doing mission. The missionary view of Deutero-Isaiah, for instance, that Israel is destined to be "a light to the nations" (Isa. 42:6, 49:6), is affirmed by Simeon in the temple, having the baby Jesus in his arms (Luke 2:32; cf. Acts 13:47).[10] *Christian* mission and mission theology, however, exist only after Peter and the other disciples concluded that nobody else other than Jesus of Nazareth was the promised Messiah, destined to be the light to the nations.

THE EMERGENCE OF MISSION THEOLOGY IN MINORITY SETTINGS

Mission theology first developed in minority settings from the time of the New Testament onward. Buddhism emerged as a missionary religion, as did Christianity some centuries later. Both religions started as peaceful minority movements. Yet, after the conversion of King Asoka (ca. 300–232 BCE) to

---

3. International Missionary Council, *Tambaram Series,* 7 vols. (Oxford: Oxford University Press, 1939), vol. 2: "The Growing Church."

4. Edward White, *Missionary Theology: Considered in Its Two Doctrines of Endless Misery, and a Post-Millennial Advent of Christ* (London: Stock, 1869).

5. Gustav Warneck, "Die Missionslehre als 'Kerygtik," *Allgemeine Missions-Zeitschrift* 4 (1877): 443-58.

6. Jan A. B. Jongeneel, "The Missiology of Gisbertus Voetius: The First Comprehensive Protestant Theology of Missions," *Calvin Theological Journal* 26 (1991): 47-79.

7. Oswald E. Brown, *Jesus as a Missionary* (Nashville: Missionary Training School, 1905).

8. Gustav Warneck, *Evangelische Missionslehre: Ein missionstheoretischer Versuch* (Gotha: Perthes, 1892), vol. I, 194-251: "Die Missionstheologie des Paulus."

9. Yves Raguin, *La théologie missionaire de l'Ancien Testament* (Paris: Seuil, 1947).

10. Robert Martin-Achard, *A Light to the Nations: A Study of the Old Testament Conception of Israel's Mission to the World* (Edinburgh: Oliver and Boyd, 1962; French original, 1959).

Buddhism and the Emperor Constantine the Great (died 337) to Christianity, they became powerful, at least in some settings—with positive and negative consequences for their missionary work. Both religions differ because not only is Christianity a monotheistic religion, but also, from the very beginning, it aimed to reach "all nations" (Matt. 28:19).

Until the influence of Constantine the Great on the church and its mission at home and abroad, Christianity functioned in a minority position. After the conversion of Constantine, the church in Asia outside the Roman Empire remained in that position. The mission and mission theology of the church of the East (also known as the Nestorians) and Monophysites[11] outside this empire were congenial with the mission and mission theology of the apostles and evangelists who also lived in a minority position, and shaped their mission theory and practice as powerless messengers.

Doing mission and mission theology from a minority position was, both historically and systematically, the rule. The early church (before the conversion of Emperor Constantine) and the church of the East emerged as unprotected missionary bodies. They preached the gospel as a message of cross bearing in conformity with the suffering Christ, who did not become king on earth, but in heaven (from the resurrection onward). Justin Martyr in the West and Nestorian laypeople spreading "the luminous religion" of Jesus in central Asia, Mongolia, and China were eminent witnesses of doing mission and mission theology from a minority position.

In today's world, most Asian Christians still live as minorities and do their mission from a powerless position. In their midst emerged mission theologians whose thoughts and acts were characterized not by "silver or gold" (Acts 3:6), but by a powerlessness that appealed to the powerful name of Jesus Christ, crucified and resurrected. Kosuke Koyama of Japan emerged as the spokesperson of all contemporary Asian mission theologians in a minority position. He coined a short, yet sharp formula to clarify the nature of proclaiming from a minority perspective. He propagated what he called "the crucified mind," that is, the mind shaped by the foolishness and weakness of God, the Father of Jesus Christ, as the authentic source and guideline of Christian witness. This was over against "the crusading mind," the mind shaped by the medieval crusades rooted in the *corpus christianum*. In other words, we need "mission as cross bearing" over against "mission as crusade."[12] In today's Japan and most other Asian nations, Christian mission theology is alive as a minority theology, facing both cyclical religions, such as Shinto, Taoism, Buddhism, and Hinduism, and the linear Islam. Many of these nations have a large number of first-generation Christians, of whom some have become leaders of the missionary movement and mission theologians.

---

11. Monophysitism asserted that in the person of Jesus Christ there was only one, divine nature rather than two natures, divine and human, as asserted at the Council of Chalcedon in 451.

12. Kosuke Koyama, "What Makes a Missionary? Toward Crucified Mind, Not Crusading Mind," in *Crucial Issues in Mission Today*, ed. Gerald H. Anderson and Thomas F. Stransky (New York: Paulist Press, 1974), 117-32.

THE EMERGENCE OF MISSION THEOLOGY
IN MAJORITY SETTINGS

After the conversion of Constantine the Great to Christianity, power politics started to affect the life of the church in the Roman Empire and its mission at home and abroad. Doing mission and mission theology from a majority position was, and still is, the exception. However, in the course of the Middle Ages, the exception became the rule, at least in Europe. The frame of the Roman Empire largely shaped the missionary writings of great theologians such as John Chrysostom and Augustine of Hippo. Augustine emphasized the unity of the Catholic Church (Latin and Greek as *lingua franca*) over against the Donatists along the north coast of Africa who wanted to make the church indigenous (and use local languages). In northern Europe, Willibrord and Boniface were great missionaries, each in his own way supported by the power structure of the Christianized Roman Empire.

Although the innovative orders of friars, primarily the Franciscans and the Dominicans, while protected by the Christianized Roman Empire, started to do mission outside the *corpus christianum*, they still emerged as members of Western organizations. Therefore, they also represent a second type of mission and mission theology after the powerless early church. Although Protestant church and mission leaders had an antipathy to Rome, they were willing to learn from the missionary teachings and experiences of the medieval Catholic orders, and even from the Jesuits. They shaped their own Protestant form of *corpus christianum*, stipulating that the *pax Christi* and the *pax Neerlandica* and subsequently the *pax Brittannica* could easily go hand in hand.

Johannes van den Berg observed that evangelical leaders such as William Carey and William Wilberforce "bracketed together 'civilization' and 'the spread of the Gospel,' 'moral instruction' and 'the diffusion of the blessings of Christianity.'"[13] They and other Protestant church leaders, mission theologians, and overseas missionaries started to think and behave as victors. They did not view the intertwining of foreign mission with Western colonization as problematic. There still might be some contemporary Western mission theologians who view the Christianized West (primarily Great Britain and the United States) as "God's chosen people," and "the peculiar possession of the Messiah" to do the will of God on earth and evangelize the entire human community.[14] For example, people with great optimism about the possibilities of converting the whole earth dominated the World Missionary Conference at Edinburgh in 1910. The often-quoted slogan of John R. Mott, "the evangelization of the world in this generation," was the programmatic summary of the nineteenth- and early-twentieth-century "glorious" mission theologies.

---

13. Johannes van den Berg, *Constrained by Jesus' Love: An Inquiry into the Motives of the Missionary Awakening in Great Britain in the Period between 1698 and 1815* (Utrecht: J. H. Kok, 1956), 192.

14. Jan A. B. Jongeneel, *Jesus Christ in World History: His Presence and Representation in Cyclical and Linear Settings* (Frankfurt am Main: Peter Lang, 2009), 333-34.

World War I alarmed Christian theologians and reminded them to be cautious. They raised the question as to what extent was Continental Europe Christian, given the fact that the "Christian Germans" started to fight against the "Christian French." Karl Barth was a sharp critic who developed a "theology of crisis," which did not share the optimism of the Edinburgh conference. Hendrik Kraemer's *Christian Message in a Non-Christian World* translated Barth's insights into a global mission theology, which replaced optimism by "(biblical) realism."[15] He stated that the non-Christian world existed in the West as well as in Asia and Africa. The West was not the elected messenger to the majority world because the West also needs conversion.[16] Henri Godin and Yves Daniel were even more critical than Kraemer. In the middle of World War II, they raised the question as to whether France was "a mission country." That is, was France in need of Christian evangelization?[17] After the Second World War, mission scholars such as Johannes C. Hoekendijk, my predecessor in Utrecht University, distanced themselves as much as possible from the medieval *corpus christianum* and its continuation in modern times (Christendom and "chosen nations").[18]

After Barth and Kraemer, Western mission theology divided into two groups of theologians and missionaries. On the one hand, there were people who did not object to the traditional intertwining of Westernization and Christianization, and consequently viewed the territorial expansion of Christianity as the ultimate goal of mission.[19] On the other hand, there were scholars who were critical of established Western Christianity and its missionary enterprise. Balanced mission theologians can only bridge this gap by separating the good from the bad in Western mission history, emphasizing that the *corpus christianum* was both a blessing and a curse. The introduction of monogamy, Sunday as the common free day (since Constantine the Great), and the Christian era (since Pope Gregory I) certainly belong to the former category. Yet, conversion by force, the crusades, and the Inquisition fit in to the latter. Further, it is necessary to raise the question whether the nineteenth-century concept of the Christianization of cultures can be viewed as a mission goal as legitimate as the classic goals of the conversion of individuals, the planting of churches, and doxology as articulated by Voetius in the middle of the seventeenth century.[20]

---

15. Hendrik Kraemer, *The Christian Message in a Non-Christian World* (Bangalore: Centre for Contemporary Christianity, 2009) (reprint, with an introduction by Jan A. B. Jongeneel and new appendixes).

16. Ibid., 16-17.

17. Henri Godin and Yves Daniel, *La France, pays de mission?* (Paris: Cerf, 1943).

18. Johannes C. Hoekendijk, *The Church Inside Out* (Philadelphia: Westminster Press, 1966).

19. Cf. Kenneth S. Latourette, *A History of the Expansion of Christianity*, 7 vols. (New York: Harper and Brothers, 1937–45).

20. Gisbertus Voetius, *Politica ecclesiastica*, 3 vols. (Amsterdam: J. à Waesberg, 1663–76). Cf. Jongeneel, "The Missiology of Gisbertus Voetius," 63-68.

THE EMERGENCE OF MISSION THEOLOGY
IN PRECHRISTIAN CYCLICAL RELIGIOUS SETTINGS

Having noted the difference between the emergence of doing mission and mission theology in the setting of Christianity in a minority versus a majority position, I will now focus attention on the religious and postreligious contexts in which Christian missions and mission theologies have operated in the past and their relevance today. First, I will explore mission theology emerging in the context of pre-Christian cyclical belief systems in which cyclical religions are those that view time and ages as recurring.

The Nestorians and Monophysites were the first Christians who encountered the adherents of the cyclical religions of Asia and Africa, and did missionary work in their midst. In modern times, their pattern of doing mission underwent total transformation. True sons of the Roman Catholic Church discovered new routes and new worlds. The arrival of the Italian Christopher Columbus in the Bahama Islands (1492) and the Portuguese explorer Vasco da Gama in South India (1498), together with the circumnavigation of the globe by the Portuguese aristocrat Ferdinand Magellan (1522), renewed the adage of Emperor Constantine: "By this sign [the sign of the cross] you shall conquer." Columbus's journal stated firmly, "I conceive . . . the principal wish of our most serene King [to be] the conversion of these people to the holy faith of Christ."[21]

After the time of Columbus and da Gama, both Roman Catholic and Protestant missionaries applied their "glorious" mission theology to the fields in Asia and Africa where they encountered the adherents of primal religions and other cyclical religions possessing holy books: Hinduism, Buddhism, Taoism, and Shintoism. In the twentieth century, some of them started to view the cycle or wheel (symbol of Buddhism) as the prime challenge of past and present Christian missions. Western theologians Hendrik Berkhof and J. E. Lesslie Newbigin thoroughly reflected on the cyclical view of time and history as the greatest missionary challenge. Berkhof stated optimistically, "The forces which were born out of [the Christian] faith . . . have won the world, and have also liberated, or are liberating the people of Asia and Africa from the cycle of their existence."[22] In addition, Newbigin emphasized that preaching the gospel in ancient cultures such as India and China "is giving an irreversible direction to that which was static or merely cyclical."[23]

Indigenous theologians became the successors of Western scholars such as Berkhof and Newbigin. During the twentieth century, they took the lead in shaping mission and mission theology in the East and South. In India, "Third

---

21. John R. Hale et al., *Age of Exploration* (New York: Time Life Books, 1967), 13.

22. Hendrikus Berkhof, *Christ the Meaning of History* (London: SCM Press, 1966), 35. The Dutch version of this study appeared before the Newbigin publication mentioned in the next footnote.

23. J. E. Lesslie Newbigin, "The Gathering Up of History in Christ," in *Missionary Church in East and West,* ed. Charles C. West and David M. Paton (London: SCM Press, 1959), 83.

World theology" emerged before World War II. First-generation Christians such as Vengal Chakkarai and Pandipeddi Chenchiah became mission leaders. Chakkarai used the Hindu concept of *avatar* to explain the unique Christ event, stating that Jesus Christ is a nonrecurring *avatar*. The evangelist Saddhu Sundar Singh, who originated from a mixed Sikh and Hindu background, accompanied them. In addition, converts from Buddhism became leaders in the missionary movement and mission studies, especially those from the Korean peninsula, including my former PhD candidates Kim Kyoung Jae and Kim Ig-Jin.[24]

Christianity is not the only world religion with global networks and developing transatlantic activities. In recent history, it faces the emerging missionary awareness of the cyclical religions, leading to the foundation of their global networks. Since the World's Parliament of Religions in Chicago (1893), the Ramakrishna movement began Hindu mission in the West. After World War II, Buddhists founded their World Fellowship of Buddhists. Today Christian mission theologies in East and West need to respond properly to these emerging missionary fellowships, each with its own in-depth missionary concepts and programs.

In the setting of cyclical religions in Asia and elsewhere, majority-world theologians emphasize that the Christian message and mission must focus on the goal (Greek: *telos*). M. M. Thomas, a member of the Mar Thoma Syrian Church, discussed this topic in evaluating the Hindu viewpoints of Swami Vivekananda as leader of the Ramakrishna movement. Thomas stated,

No doubt, the cyclic concept has a great deal of validity. Nature repeats its day and night and the seasons. The wheel of birth, growth, and death is characteristic of individuals and civilizations and perhaps of worlds. The Christian understanding of historical and cosmic process need not to deny the reality of the cycles of nature and life. But it stands or falls with the doctrine of the ultimate divine purpose of that process.[25]

In a slightly different way, Koyama highlighted this point. He chose the image of the spiral as a way of transcending the dichotomy of the cycle and the line, defining the spiral as a circular movement within the frame of the (dominant) linear view of history.[26]

---

24. Kim Kyoung Jae, *Christianity and the Encounter of Asian Religions: Method of Correlation, Fusion of Horizons, and Paradigm Shifts in the Korean Grafting Process* (Zoetermeer: Boekencentrum, 1994); Kim Ig-Jin, *History and Theology of Korean Pentecostalism: Sunbogeum (Pure Gospel) Pentecostalism* (Zoetermeer: Boekencentrum, 2003).

25. M. M. Thomas, *The Acknowledged Christ of the Indian Renaissance* (London: SCM Press, 1969).

26. Kosuke Koyama, "Will the Monsoon Rain Make God Wet? An Ascending Spiral View of History," in *What Asian Christians Are Thinking: A Theological Source Book*, ed. Douglas J. Elwood (Quezon City: New Day Publishers, 1978), 131-44.

THE EMERGENCE OF MISSION THEOLOGY
IN POSTCHRISTIAN LINEAR SETTINGS

I will now explore the mission theology emerging in the context of post-Christian linear Islam before finally viewing post-Christian secularism since the Enlightenment era. Mission theology developed differently in contexts with a linear rather than a cyclical view of time.

In modern times, Christian mission took advantage of the discoveries of da Gama, Columbus, and Magellan. One of the motives to discover new routes to India was to avoid the Muslims as intermediaries between East and West. The discoverers wanted to cooperate with the legendary Prester John "to make a great world alliance of the faithful, through which at last the power of the Muslims would be brought to the ground."[27] Compared with the mission theologians before 1500 CE, modern mission theologians look at Islam differently. After the failure of the medieval crusades, early mission theologians were confident that the Christian navies of Spain, Portugal, and other European nations could make Islam a peripheral and negligible religion. Nineteenth-century mission theologian Albert Schweitzer more or less ignored Islam. In his book on global Christianity, he restricted himself to less than a page in considering Islam as a world religion.[28] In the twentieth century, great Western mission theologians such as Zwemer and Kraemer brought new ways of approaching Islam.

In encountering Muslims, doing mission and mission theology from a majority position is helpful, yet it will never surpass the significance of the powerless witness of Christians living in the house of the Islamic (dar al-Islam). In medieval Bagdad, the Nestorian patriarch Timothy I preached the gospel to the third Abbasid caliph. Timothy declared, "Muhammad is worthy of all praise, by all reasonable people, O my Sovereign. . . . Muhammad separated his people from idolatry and polytheism, and attached them to the cult and the knowledge of one God, beside whom there is no other God. . . . Finally, Muhammad taught about God, His Word, and His Spirit; and since all the prophets had prophesied about God, His Word, and His Spirit, Muhammad walked in the path of all the prophets."[29] This quote clarifies that the patriarch wanted to avoid antagonism, and at the same time desired to be faithful to the triune God, using the Qur'an's description of Jesus Christ as Allah's Word (*Kalam*) and Allah's Spirit (*Roh*). The attitude of medieval Western Christians was the opposite of Timothy's approach. They engaged in the crusades, which had a negative effect on the relations between Muslims and Christians. Paul Marshall pointed to the endurance of these negative

---

27. Stephen C. Neill, *A History of Christian Missions* (Harmondsworth: Penguin Books, 1979), 120.

28. Albert Schweitzer, *Christianity and the Religions of the World* (New York: Doubleday, 1923).

29. Samir Khalil Samir S.J., "Alphonse Mingana, 1878–1937, and His Contribution to Early Christian-Muslim Studies." Lecture at First Woodbrooke Mingana Symposium. Selly Oak Colleges, Birmingham, UK, May 25, 1990, 29.

effects until today. He declares, "Many Christians in the Middle East who had no part in the crusades, and also suffered under them, nevertheless bear the legacy of centuries of hatred and frequently have the epithet 'crusader' spat in their faces."[30]

Since the Middle Ages, Islam has been the second major challenge for mission and mission theology following that of the pre-Christian cyclical belief systems. The Muslim World League (1980) and other worldwide Muslim organizations are challenging Christianity on six continents. In and beyond these networks some self-confident Muslims stipulate that Islam is humanity's final religion, which is destined to rule the entire world. Christians who live outside the house of Islam need to come into that house. First-generation Christians from Muslim backgrounds are indispensable to rethink Christian mission to those of the Islamic faith, both theoretically and practically.

In post–World War II Africa, a new type of mission theology emerged, developed by first-generation Christians such as Tokunboh Adeyemo of Nigeria and Lamin Sanneh of Gambia. Both converted scholars wrote from the viewpoint of "a crucified mind." The former did not view Islam as a threat, but as a threefold challenge to Christianity: the Muslim theocratic vision of life and society, sense of community (*ummah*), and commitment to missions. He believed that Christians could meet these challenges by absolute surrender to Christ, total obedience to his commandment of love, and Christ-like compassion for people who do not believe in Jesus as Lord and Savior.[31] Sanneh emphasized the translatability of God's Word in Christianity over against Islam. "Scriptural translation is the vintage mark of Christianity, whereas for Islam, universal adherence to a non-translatable Arabic Qur'an remains its characteristic feature. This has major consequences for how we see mission and . . . conversion."[32]

THE ENLIGHTENMENT AND ITS SECULAR OFFSPRING

The third and final challenge is secularism, initially promoted by David Hume and other Enlightenment philosophers. They transformed Christian faith in God's revelation into a rational belief and became nominal members. Similar to Islam, secularism is a post-Christian movement with its features of continuity and discontinuity with Christian belief and ethos. Continuity appears in maintaining the linear view of time and history. Most Enlightenment philosophers, and in their wake evolutionists, communists, and many existentialists, view the universe as having a beginning and an end. The existentialist Karl Jaspers confessed in his

---

30. Paul Marshall, *Their Blood Cries Out: The Worldwide Tragedy of Modern Christians Who Are Dying for Their Faith* (Dallas: Word Publishing, 1997), 215.

31. Christina M. Breman, *The Association of Evangelicals in Africa: Its History, Organization, Members, Projects, External Relations, and Message* (Zoetermeer: Boekencentrum, 1996).

32. Lamin Sanneh, *Translating the Message: The Missionary Impact on Culture* (Maryknoll, NY: Orbis Books, 1992), 211.

book on world history, "My outline is based on an article of faith: that mankind has one single origin and one goal."[33]

Since the Enlightenment, European Christianity has been declining because of the claims of the Enlightenment and the resultant development of secular worldviews. In the eighteenth and nineteenth centuries, there was a renewal in Christian apologetics to face the new realities. Moreover, since the middle of the nineteenth century, committed Christians engaged in "home mission" (German: *innere Mission*) to stop the increasing group of intellectuals and laypeople leaving the church. Home missions developed a strategy that for a while was effective. Nevertheless, in the end it did not avert the trend of church members leaving the church en masse. In the twentieth century, this exodus accelerated in several European nations. Friedrich Gogarten, linked with Barth, was one of the first twentieth-century theologians who wanted to be positive regarding the development of Western culture. He accepted the secularization process, while rejecting secularism as ideology. However, others viewed this distinction as artificial in the fight of conservative Christians against the secularization process as a fight against windmills.[34] In addition, Harvey Cox in *The Secular City*, viewed secularization as a necessity.[35]

In the last few decades, the naïve optimism of secularization has passed. No thoughtful scholar believes that the entire human community will end up as a secular, atheistic/agnostic community. Promising developments inside world Christianity (especially the growth of majority-world Christianity), the growth of Islam, and the renaissance of various cyclical religions in Asia and their offspring in the West such as Theosophy, New Age, and New Religious Movements, which depend on Hindu and/or Buddhist patterns of thinking and lifestyle, have partly caused this recent change in outlook.

The churches responded to the ongoing de-Christianization of Europe with programs of re-Christianization. In his encyclical *Redemptoris missio*, Pope John Paul II talked about "reevangelization" and "the new evangelization." European churches earnestly pray and hope that new mission theologies and mission practices will emerge and stem the flood of secularism. To overcome the contemporary "decline of Christendom in Western Europe,"[36] there is a desperate need for the witness of first-generation European Christians originating from secularism and communism, similar to the cases of Christians encountering the adherents of the cyclical religions and the Islamic world. Professional missiologists need to listen carefully to former atheists and agnostics such as Gabriel Marcel in France, C. S. Lewis in the United Kingdom, and Aleksandr Solzhenitsyn in Russia. The Anglican theologian Alister McGrath also belongs to this category of first-generation Christians in the West. It is a pity to observe that contemporary mission scholars neglect their honest contributions to

---

33. Karl Jaspers, *The Origin and Goal of History* (New Haven: Yale University Press, 1959).

34. Arend T. Van Leeuwen, *Christianity in World History* (London: Edinburgh House Press, 1965).

35. Harvey Cox, *The Secular City* (London: Macmillan, 1965).

36. Hugh McLeod and Werner Ustorf, eds., *The Decline of Christendom in Western Europe, 1750–2000* (Cambridge: Cambridge University Press, 2003).

proclaim God in Christ over against the claims of the Enlightenment and its offspring. Moreover, it is a pity to see that none of the former atheists/agnostics seems to have become a mission leader or a mission theologian. Consequently, the emergence of former Hindus, Buddhists, and Muslims as leading mission theologians seems to exist without any emergence of former atheists/agnostics contributing to the rethinking and reshaping of the Christian mission in a secular environment.

FINAL OBSERVATIONS

At the very beginning of his academic career, Van Engen committed himself to bring the human community in touch with Jesus Christ as Lord over all. He proclaims, "This is the message which the Church of Jesus Christ, his Body, must learn to speak today in word and deed, expressing the deepest conviction that the unity, peace, and justice of a just and participatory society is only to be achieved in the context of the reign of Jesus Christ in all, through all, and over all, individually and corporately."[37] This summarizes the entire academic career of Van Engen.

Since the days of the apostles and evangelists Christian mission and mission theology have emerged in a variety of settings and ways. This introduction only discussed their emergence in minority and majority contexts, as well as in the settings of the pre-Christian cyclical religions and post-Christian Islam and secularism. We can and must supply other innovative insights. Some scholars look at their emergence in the context of migration, modernity, postmodernity, or ecology, and others at their emerging in specific groups of people: women and *Dalit* ("oppressed" in Hindi, referring to the caste of the untouchables). Other missiologists plea for narrative and/or intercultural mission theology. Last, but not least, Van Engen paid special attention to the emergence of mission theology in the cities.[38] All these different types of doing mission and mission theology are very helpful as long as they serve the ultimate goal of bringing the human community to its final destination: the goal of the glorification of the triune God (doxology), and a full life for all in harmony, peace, hope, and love.

---

37. Van Engen, *The Growth of the True Church*, 510-11.
38. Charles E. Van Engen and Jude Tiersma, eds., *God So Loves the City: Seeking a Theology for Urban Mission* (Monrovia, CA: MARC, 1994).

A New Missionary Age

Gerald H. Anderson

I acquired the title of my essay, *A New Missionary Age*, from the encyclical *Redemptoris missio* (Mission of the Redeemer, *RM*), issued by Pope John Paul II in 1991.[1] In it he said, "The moment has come to commit all the Church's energies to a new evangelization and to the mission *ad gentes*" (*RM* 3). In addition, he concluded, "I see the dawning of a new missionary age, which will become a radiant day bearing an abundant harvest, if all Christians, and missionaries and young Churches in particular, respond with generosity and holiness to the calls and challenges of our time" (*RM* 92). This encyclical, in my judgment, represents the most important, comprehensive, balanced, encouraging, and challenging official statement of mission theology since the Second Vatican Council. For me, it is an evangelical statement of enormous significance for all Christians. It is noteworthy that Pope Francis recently referred to John Paul II as "a great missionary of the church."

A few years ago, I was lecturing at a large evangelical Protestant seminary in Seoul, Korea, in a class of 162 students that began at 6:30 a.m. One morning I read to the class some quotations from the Lausanne Covenant, of which Billy Graham was the chair. Also I read some quotations from the Ecumenical Affirmation on Mission and Evangelism from the World Council of Churches, and then—without telling them the source—I read some quotations from *Redemptoris missio,* and I asked them, "Who do you think said that?" One student put up his hand and said, "Billy Graham." When I told them it was really Pope John Paul II, they were quite surprised, to put it mildly. I trust that John Paul II would not have been displeased if he heard that some of the students mistook him for Billy Graham. I will return to *Redemptoris missio* in a moment, but first let me give some background for the context of mission in the global religious scene today.

BACKGROUND

It is widely recognized that in terms of numbers Christianity is now predominantly a so-called majority-world religion since its center of gravity

---

1. The writer delivered this address on the occasion of his receiving an honorary Doctor of Missiology Degree from the Pontifical Urbaniana University in Rome (November 14, 2013).

has shifted to the non-Western world, from the Northern to the Southern Hemisphere, resulting in what Philip Jenkins has described as the "browning" of world Christianity.[2] Reflecting this shift, Mark A. Noll, at the University of Notre Dame, has pointed out that "this past Sunday it is possible that more Christian believers attended church in China than in all of so-called 'Christian Europe.'" He continues, "This past Sunday more Anglicans attended church in each of Kenya, South Africa, Tanzania, and Uganda than did Anglicans in Britain and Canada, and Episcopalians in the United States combined. This past Sunday there were more Roman Catholics at worship in the Philippines than in any single country of Europe, including . . . Italy, Spain, or Poland."[3] In fact, there are more Catholics in Manila than in Holland. Moreover, the Catholic Church in the Philippines baptizes more people every year than in France, Spain, Italy, and Poland combined. We became aware during the visit of Pope Francis that Brazil has more Catholics than Italy, France, and Spain combined. Also, he observed during his visit, it is the continent "where the majority of the world's Catholics live."

On the one hand, we celebrate the fact that the number of Christians in the world has increased dramatically over the last one hundred years, from approximately 550 million to 2.5 billion. That is the good news. The bad news is that despite this increase, however, the percentage of Christians in the total population of the world has actually decreased by 1.5 percent over the last 100 years, from 34.5 percent to 33 percent today, despite the sacrificial service and support of missionaries and churches of all types in all parts of the world.[4] So world Christianity has increased, yet not grown in the last one hundred years. People are "coming in the front door" of the church in Africa and "going out the back door" in Europe.

Moreover, there are actually far more non-Christians in the world today than when Jesus was on earth. In Jesus's time, there were approximately 250 million people on earth. Today the population of the world is 7.5 billion, and 2.5 billion persons claim to be Christian. Therefore, there are at least 5 billion people who have either never heard the gospel, or have heard it and rejected it. Considering numbers alone, there are nineteen times more non-Christians today than when the risen Christ commissioned his disciples to "Go and make disciples of all nations" (Matt. 28:19). These statistics indicate there must be significant changes in the way we see the task of the church in its mission. The mission field today obviously includes the West. For instance, we have 100 million unchurched people in the United States, which makes it one of the largest mission fields in the world. It also means that we in the West have much to learn from Christians in other parts of the world where the church is growing.

---

2. Philip Jenkins, *The Next Christendom: The Coming of Global Christianity* (New York: Oxford University Press, 2002), 193.

3. Mark A. Noll, *The New Shape of World Christianity* (Downers Grove, IL: InterVarsity Press, 2009), 20-21.

4. See Todd M. Johnson and Peter F. Crossing, "Status of Global Mission, 2013, in the Context of AD 1800–2025," *International Bulletin of Missionary Research* 37, no. 1 (2013): 33.

When Bishop Lesslie Newbigin returned to England after a lifetime of missionary service in India, where he was bishop of Chennai when he left, he became the pastor of a church with eighteen members, scheduled to close. The church was located near a prison in Birmingham. He was seventy years old, and he quickly came to realize that this pastorate was "much harder than anything I met in India. There is a cold contempt," he said, "for the Gospel [here] which is harder to face than opposition." And this led him to conclude that the West was "the most difficult missionary frontier in the contemporary world . . . one of which the churches have been—on the whole—so little conscious." He became convinced that "England is a pagan society and the development of a truly missionary encounter with this very tough form of paganism is the greatest intellectual and practical task facing the church."[5]

A recent analysis of church attendance in Great Britain (including England, Wales, and Scotland, but not Northern Ireland) reported that in 2010 there was 5.7 percent of the population in church on an average Sunday. In addition, it projected that this will decline by almost half to 2.8 percent church attendance in 2030.[6] Our churches in the West are now in a new missionary situation, and we can no longer consider our cultures as gospel friendly. As John Paul II said in *Tertio millenio adveniente,* "The more the West is becoming estranged from its Christian roots, the more it is becoming missionary territory" (*TMA* 57). For these and other reasons, Europe may be the Dark Continent of the twenty-first century.

I like to remind people that Palestine is on the western edge of Asia. Therefore, I would claim that Jesus was an Asian, all of the early disciples were Asians, and the church was born in Asia. The Incarnation, the crucifixion, the resurrection, the Great Commission—all of this happened in Asia. Wonderfully, Asian churches today are recovering their Asian identity and the Asian rice-roots of the gospel. Philip Jenkins says this shift "constitutes a religious and cultural revolution quite comparable to the Reformation of the sixteenth century, though on a far vaster scale."[7] As a church historian, I would say that the most exciting chapter in the history of Christianity is the chapter presently in progress. Let me give just a few examples to illustrate why I believe this is true.

In 1900, there were only 8 million Christians in Africa south of the Sahara; in 2013, there are 500 million Christians in Africa. Bishop Stephen Neill once said this shift represents the greatest change in the profile of world Christianity in a thousand years. As further evidence of this turning point in church history, we can also mention the following:

In 1900, there were only 1.2 million Christians in China, and in 1949 when the Communists took over there were 5 million Christians. Today it is

---

5. Lesslie Newbigin, *Unfinished Agenda: An Updated Autobiography* (Eugene, OR: Wipf & Stock, 2009), 249.

6. Peter Brierley, *God's Questions: Vision, Strategy and Growth* (Tonbridge, Kent: ADBC Publishers, 2010), 159.

7. Emily Eakin and Felicia R. Lee, "On Target and Off in 2002; . . . and In with the Underrated," *New York Times,* December 28, 2002, B7.

estimated that there are 80 to 100 million Christians in China, with 16,500 new converts every day.[8]

One other striking example of this shift is South Korea. One hundred years ago, Seoul had a population of 125,000, with two tiny Protestant churches and a few Catholic churches. Today Seoul has ten million people and thousands of Protestant and Catholic churches. For years, I had been hearing and reading about the dynamic growth and vitality of the churches in South Korea. However, I only fully appreciated the situation when I witnessed it firsthand. When I was in Seoul, I observed that everything about the churches in South Korea was huge; and shall I say, aggressive, in a good sense. There are now 22,000 Korean Protestant missionaries serving outside of Korea, and a substantial number of Korean Catholic missionaries also (I do not know the exact number).

Before going to Korea, I received a request by email from the dean of the seminary, who was my host, asking if I would be willing to speak to her Sunday school class of women at one of the Presbyterian churches in the center of Seoul. I told her I would be happy to do that. What she did not tell me was that there were 650 women in the class. It turned out that her church is one of the largest Presbyterian churches in Seoul, having over 50,000 members, with 24 ministers and 6 services on Sunday plus an evening service. On the following Sunday, just before I left Seoul, I preached at one of the early services at this church, where 5,000 attended. When I told them that my wife and I attend the First Presbyterian Church in New Haven, Connecticut, which has 230 members, they said, "What's the problem?"

MISSION TODAY

The scope of mission today is the whole church, with the whole gospel, for the whole person, in the whole world—stretching from Buenos Aires, to Burundi, to Bangladesh, to Beijing, to Berlin, to Boston, and Birmingham, England. Within this global context, I want to mention one of the factors that will increasingly be a defining mark of church and mission in many parts of the world. It is the reality that Christians in many parts of the non-Western world find themselves living under conditions of persecution, violence, and authoritarian governments.

In his recent book, *The Global War on Christians*, John L. Allen, Jr., says, "Christians today indisputably are the most persecuted religious body on the planet."[9] Another recent book titled *Christianophobia: A Faith under Attack*, by Rupert Shortt, claims, "More Christians than people of any other faith group now live under threat."[10] These are the conditions in numerous countries, and in some situations the intolerance and persecution affects persons of other religious

---

8. David B. Barrett, Todd M. Johnson, and Peter F. Crossing. "Missiometrics 2008: Reality Checks for World Christian Communions," *International Bulletin of Missionary Research* 32, no. 1 (2008): 28-29.

9. John L. Allen, Jr., *The Global War on Christians: Dispatches from the Front Lines of Anti-Christian Persecution* (New York: Image Books, 2013), 1.

10. Rupert Shortt, *Christianophobia: A Faith under Attack* (Grand Rapids: Eerdmans, 2013).

faiths as well as Christians. Therefore, there are plenty of case studies of how
churches and missions are carrying out their understanding of discipleship
and witness under duress. One need only mention India, Pakistan, Indonesia,
Malaysia, Myanmar, North Korea, China, Afghanistan, most countries of
the Middle East and Persian Gulf, Sudan, Somalia, Ethiopia, Zanzibar, and
Nigeria, to name just a few places where the words of the Creed, "He suffered
under Pontius Pilate," have taken on special meaning for Christians. There were
approximately 100,000 Christian martyrs in 2013.[11] These persons died *because*
they were Christians, and the majority of them were local indigenous believers.
Once again, we are realizing that the blood of the martyrs is the seed of the
church.

Considering the recent persecution of Christians, we may conclude that
increasingly, faithfulness and effectiveness in Christian mission are measured
as much by the *quality* of our discipleship as by the *quantity* of disciples
produced by our missionary endeavors. To put it another way: God will measure
our faithfulness in mission in larger terms that reflect the total quality of our
discipleship, where the issues are not only salvation but also survival and justice
for all God's people.

The church in mission today faces serious challenges, both external and
internal. These include persecution, secularism, resurgent world religions,
communism, totalitarian regimes, and postmodern skepticism. These external
factors and forces, however, are a lesser threat to the church in mission. The
church has dealt with these in the past and has prevailed. It will continue to
overcome them, although in some situations it will be at great human cost of
struggle, suffering, and sacrifice, even martyrdom. The most serious threat to
the church's mission today comes not from outside the church, but from inside
the church itself, from a rampant, radical theological relativism that denies the
unique, ultimate, and universal claims of the gospel. Once again, Jesus poses the
question, "Who do you say I am?" The church today hears many opinions and
options other than Peter's confession.

In *Redemptoris missio*, John Paul II pointed to this problem when he spoke of
"widespread indifferentism . . . based on incorrect theological perspectives . . .
characterized by a religious relativism which leads to the belief that 'one religion
is as good as another'" (*RM* 36). This theological virus is widespread. It infects
many churches. In this sense, an ecumenical virus has reached global epidemic
proportions.

THEOLOGY OF RELIGIONS

I have often said that no issue in missiology is more important, more
difficult, more controversial, or more divisive than the theology of religions,
which David J. Bosch said "is the epitome of mission theology."[12] This is where

11. Johnson and Crossing, "Status of Global Mission, 2013," 33.
12. David J. Bosch, *Transforming Mission: Paradigm Shifts in Theology of Mission* (Maryknoll,
NY: Orbis Books, 1991), 477.

conflicting truth claims among world religions challenge Christians to articulate their understanding of the relationship between God's redemptive activity in Jesus Christ and people of other faiths.

In Scripture and in the history of Christian doctrine, there are two major traditions regarding the relationship of God's redemptive activity in Jesus Christ and with people of other faiths.[13] One tradition, while recognizing the uniqueness and universality of Jesus Christ, emphasizes the *continuity* of God's revealing and redeeming activity in Christ with God's activity among all people everywhere. It views Christian faith as the climax of a divine revelation, says F. C. Grant, that began long before human history ("he chose us in Christ before the foundation of the world," Eph. 1:4) and has been available to everyone, thus emphasizing the initiative of prevenient grace.[14] Jesus Christ in this view is crucial, normative, and definitive, but not exclusive. What is true of Jesus Christ in a focal way is pervasively true of the whole cosmos. He is the key or clue to the rest of God's activity.

In this tradition, the Word of God did not end with the historic person of Jesus, yet it is not apart from Christ in the Spirit. There is much biblical and patristic testimony to support this tradition. John's Gospel affirms that the same light that was in Jesus enlightens everyone (John 1:1-9), for "Christ is all and in all" (Col. 3:11). Paul said that a thousand years before the birth of Jesus, "Christ" was with the Israelites in their wanderings in Sinai (1 Cor. 10:4 RSV). In addition, Acts 14 assures us that God "did not leave himself without witness" among all the nations, even among those who had no knowledge of the biblical revelation (Acts 14:16-17). In this view, the *logos spermatikos* is active everywhere, sowing seeds of truth, and preparing the way for the gospel, "For the grace of God has appeared, bringing salvation to all" (Tit. 2:11).

This position appears in the Dogmatic Constitution on the Church (*Lumen gentium*) of Vatican II. The document states, "Those also can attain to everlasting salvation who through no fault of their own do not know the gospel of Christ or his Church, yet sincerely seek God and, moved by grace, strive by their deeds to do his will, as it is known to them through the dictates of conscience" (*LG* 16).

This theological tradition was clearly reflected in John Paul II's 1979 encyclical on human redemption (*Redemptor hominis*)—his first encyclical (a papal letter sent to all bishops of the Roman Catholic Church). In it, he relates the redemption in Christ to everyone, without exception. He stated,

---

13. See Gerald H. Anderson, "Theology of Religions and Missiology: A Time of Testing," in *The Good News of the Kingdom: Mission Theology for the Third Millennium*, ed. Charles Van Engen, Dean S. Gilliland, and Paul Pierson (Maryknoll, NY: Orbis Books, 1993), 200-208; and Gerald H. Anderson, "Prevenient Grace in World Mission," in *World Mission in the Wesleyan Spirit,* ed. Darrell L. Whiteman and Gerald H. Anderson (Franklin, TN: Providence House Publishers, 2009), 43-52.

14. See the response by F. C. Grant to the "Dogmatic Constitution on Divine Revelation," in *The Documents of Vatican II*, ed. Walter M. Abbott (New York: Herder & Herder/Association Press, 1966), 129.

The human person—every person without exception—has been redeemed by Christ; because Christ is in a way united to the human person—every person without exception—even if the individual may not realize this fact. "Christ, who died and was raised up for all"—for every human being and for all human beings—"can through His Spirit offer man the light and the strength to measure up to his supreme destiny" (*RH* 14).

While this papal statement is grounded in biblical and patristic testimony, the explicit, unqualified emphasis that "every person without exception—has been redeemed by Christ," and that Christ is already united to "every person without exception—even if the individual may not realize this fact," raised certain questions, especially for mission theology. For example, it is not clear whether "redeemed by Christ" implies or is synonymous with "everlasting salvation." If the redemption of humanity is a *fait accompli*, for each person "without any exception whatever," then why is there any urgency or need for persons of another faith or no faith to hear the gospel, to proclaim their faith in Jesus Christ, join in the visible church via baptism, and to partake of the sacraments?

In his encyclical letter on the Holy Spirit, *Dominum et vivificantem*, issued on May 18, 1986, John Paul II expanded on this view when he said (in paragraph 53):

We cannot limit ourselves to the two thousand years, which have passed since the birth of Christ. We need to go further back, to embrace the whole of the action of the Holy Spirit even before Christ—from the beginning, throughout the world, and especially in the economy of the Old Covenant. For this action has been exercised, in every place and at every time, indeed in every individual, according to the eternal plan of salvation, whereby this action was to be closely linked with the mystery of the Incarnation and Redemption, which in its turn exercised its influence on those who believed in the future coming of Christ. This is attested to especially in the Letter to the Ephesians (1:3-14). Grace, therefore, bears within itself both a Christological aspect and a pneumatological one, which becomes evident above all in those who expressly accept Christ: "In him (in Christ) you . . . were sealed with the promised Holy Spirit, which is the guarantee of our inheritance, until we acquire possession of it" (Eph. 1:13f.).

But, still within the perspective of the great Jubilee, we need to look further and go further afield, knowing that "the wind blows where it wills," according to the image used by Jesus in his conversation with Nicodemus (cf. John. 3:8). The Second Vatican Council, centered primarily on the theme of the Church, reminds us of the Holy Spirit's activity also "outside the visible body of the Church." The Council speaks precisely of "all people of good will in whose hearts grace works in an unseen way. For, since Christ died for all, and since the ultimate vocation of man is in fact one, and divine, we ought to believe that the Holy Spirit in a manner known only to God offers to everyone the possibility of being associated with this Pascal mystery." (Quoted from *Gaudium et spes* 22)

The implications of this position appeared a few weeks later, at the conclusion of the Day of Prayer for Peace, held in Assisi on October 27, 1986, when John Paul II said, "The pilgrimage to Assisi has taught us anew to be aware of the common origin and common destiny of humankind. Let us see in it an anticipation of what God would like the developing history of humanity to be: a fraternal journey in which we accompany one another toward the transcendent goal which he sets for us."

The other tradition of theology of religions emphasizes a radical *discontinuity* between the realm of Christian revelation, beginning with God's prevenient grace, and the whole range of non-Christian religious experience. In this view, God has spoken to humanity only in the person of Jesus Christ and "there is salvation in no one else" (Acts 4:12). This tradition—emphasizing Christ's saying in John 14:6 that "no one comes to the Father but by me," (RSV)— is the narrow, exclusivist tradition, which is equally, if not more strongly represented in Scripture and in the history of Christian doctrine.

These two streams of teaching and tradition are hard to reconcile; they seem almost contradictory. Yet, we often find them almost side-by-side in the New Testament. For instance, in John's Gospel, the author tells us that Jesus was "the true light that enlightens every man" (1:4, 9 RSV). Yet, in the same passage John claims, "The light shines in the darkness" (not everything was light!), and it was only to those "who believed in his name, he gave power to become children of God" (1:12 RSV). John 3 tells us that God sent his only Son into the world "that the world might be saved through him. He who believes in him is not condemned; he who does not believe is condemned" (RSV). In John 10 Jesus says, "I am the door, if anyone enters by me, he will be saved" (v. 9), but there are "other sheep that are not of this fold; I must bring them also. . . . So there shall be one flock, one shepherd" (v. 16 RSV). In John 14:2, Jesus says, "In my Father's house are many mansions," (NKJV) which some pluralists quote to suggest that there are many religions of salvific value in the kingdom of God. In that same chapter, however, Jesus also said, "I am the way, and the truth, and the life; no one comes to the Father, but by me" (John 14:6 RSV).

My point is that both of these streams are part of the Christian tradition. Both have support in Scripture and patristic teaching. Both affirm God's prevenient grace among all people. The history of Christian missions well represents both. It is imperative that we maintain both of these traditions in Christian thought in some sort of creative tension. That is difficult to do when those from one tradition offer continuity with doubtful uniqueness, and those from the other side offer uniqueness without continuity. Our theological understanding needs to appreciate mission and religious pluralism in uniqueness *with* continuity.[15]

---

15. This formulation was first suggested by Edmund Soper in *The Philosophy of the Christian World Mission* (Nashville: Abingdon-Cokesbury Press, 1943), 225-27.

Moreover, that brings us back to *Redemptoris missio*, because I believe it demonstrates the creative tension I have described, when it says, "It is necessary to keep these two truths together [what I have called two traditions], namely, the real possibility of salvation in Christ for all mankind, and the necessity of the Church for salvation. Both of these truths help us to understand the *one mystery of salvation*, so that we come to know God's mercy and our own responsibility" (9).

On the one hand, *Redemptoris missio* affirms that "for all people—Jews and Gentiles alike—salvation can only come from Jesus Christ" (*RM* 5). Proclamation is "the permanent priority of mission" (*RM* 44), and the aim of proclamation is conversion, which means, "accepting, by a personal decision, the saving sovereignty of Christ and becoming his disciple. The church calls all people to this conversion" (*RM* 46). And "no one can enter into communion with God except through Christ, by the work of the Holy Spirit" (*RM* 5). At the same time it says,

> Today, as in the past, many people do not have an opportunity to come to know or accept the Gospel revelation or to enter the Church. The social and cultural conditions in which they live do not permit this, and frequently they have been brought up in other religious traditions. For such people salvation in Christ is accessible by virtue of a grace, which, while having a mysterious relationship to the Church, does not make them formally part of the Church, but enlightens them in a way, which is accommodated to their spiritual and material situation. This grace comes from Christ; it is the result of his Sacrifice and is communicated by the Holy Spirit. It enables each person to attain salvation through his or her free cooperation. . . . We are obliged to hold that the Holy Spirit offers everyone the possibility of sharing this Paschal Mystery in a manner known to God. (*RM* 10)

A certain ambiguity is present here that is difficult to explain, other than to acknowledge that God's grace operates in mysterious ways known only to God.

It is one thing to acknowledge that God's prevenient grace is present and active among people of other faiths, but the more difficult question is whether Christ is present in non-Christian religions as such, and whether we consider they offer ways of salvation. It is one thing to recognize that Christ is present with people of other faiths; it is quite another to say that this provides salvific efficacy to other faiths, and that people of other faiths may be saved in their religions or even *through* their religions. I recall many years ago asking D. T. Niles from Sri Lanka whether non-Christians could be saved in and through their own religions without explicit faith in Christ. His reply was, "If they are saved, they are saved because of what Christ has done for them."

Redemptoris missio states, "Whatever the Spirit brings about in human hearts and in the history of peoples, in cultures and religions serves as a preparation for the Gospel and can only be understood in reference to Christ, the Word who took flesh by the power of the Spirit" (*RM* 29). In addition, according to John Paul

II in *Tertio millennio adveniente,* "The Incarnate Word is thus the fulfillment of the yearning present in all the religions of mankind: this fulfillment is brought about by God himself and transcends all human expectations. It is the mystery of grace" (*TMA* 6).[16]

At this point let me say that to my knowledge, there has never been published in any language a comprehensive objective study of the Christian theology of religions throughout the history of the church. I mention this here with the hope that perhaps I might challenge someone to undertake such a project.

INTERRELIGIOUS DIALOGUE

In this "New Missionary Age," while proclamation is "the permanent priority of mission" (*RM* 44), *Redemptoris missio* also says, "Inter-religious dialogue is a part of the Church's evangelizing mission. . . . Dialogue is not in opposition to the mission *ad gentes* and is one of its expressions" (*RM* 55). Unfortunately, there is a certain polarization today between mission and dialogue, where some advocates of dialogue deny the validity of mission because they believe that evangelistic missionary work will interfere with interreligious dialogue. This antimission attitude is ironic because the genesis and impetus for interreligious dialogue came from the missionary movement.

There is also skepticism about interreligious dialogue from some advocates of mission and evangelism because they believe that dialogue may lead to compromise and syncretism. One missionary said he would be willing to die for the sake of evangelism, yet he would not die for the cause of dialogue. I would say to that missionary, "Why not?" Mission and dialogue are both valid means of expressions of Christian witness, each with its own authentic integrity. It is important that we affirm them together, in the unity of the church's witness.

Because of my involvement in interreligious dialogues (and trialogues), I think I have a deeper understanding of my own Christian faith. One caveat, however, is that I do not think of dialogue as a tool or strategy for evangelism. Some non-Christians are reluctant to participate in dialogue, as they suspect evangelism is our motive. Of course, it is my hope and prayer that everyone will ultimately come to faith in Jesus Christ. That is not, however, my motive in dialogue. Rather, interfaith dialogue is an opportunity to listen and learn, as well as to speak and share what we believe, to develop relationships of understanding and respect, and in some situations to find issues of common concern where we might cooperate. As stated in *Redemptoris missio,* "The Church sees no conflict between proclaiming Christ and engaging in interreligious dialogue. Instead, she feels the need to link the two in the context of her mission *ad*

---

16. Two other important documents for comparison on this subject that were issued during the same decade are *Christianity and the World Religions,* by the International Theological Commission, approved by Cardinal Joseph Ratzinger on September 30, 1996, and the Declaration "Dominus Iesus: On the Unicity and Salvific Universality of Jesus Christ and the Church," from the Congregation for the Doctrine of the Faith and ratified by Pope John Paul II on June 16, 2000.

gentes. These two elements must maintain both their intimate connection and their distinctiveness; therefore they should not be confused, manipulated or regarded as identical, as though they were interchangeable" (*RM 55*).[17] While interreligious dialogue is a risky enterprise, it will have a necessarily important role in "The New Missionary Age," an age of increasing religious pluralism.

CONCLUSION

We conclude where we began, with *Redemptoris missio*, where John Paul II said, "God is preparing a great springtime for Christianity," and "the missionary task must remain foremost, for it concerns the eternal destiny of humanity and corresponds to God's mysterious and merciful plan" (*RM 86*). Thanks be to God, and to God be the glory!

---

17. See the important essays and insights in William R. Burrows, ed., *Redemption and Dialogue: Reading* Redemptoris Missio *and Dialogue and Proclamation* (Maryknoll, NY: Orbis Books, 1993). See also the document on "Christian Witness in a Multi-Religious World: Recommendations for Conduct," jointly issued in June 2011 by the World Council of Churches, the Pontifical Council for Inter-religious Dialogue of the Roman Catholic Church, and the World Evangelical Alliance, which begins, "Mission belongs to the very being of the church," and calls for careful study of the issues of mission and interreligious dialogue, the building of trust and cooperation among people of all religions, and the promotion of religious freedom everywhere. See *International Bulletin of Missionary Research* 35, no. 4 (2011): 194-96.

Part 1

Mission Theology and the Bible

Chapter 1

The Biblical Story of Narrative Theology

Michael W. Goheen

Almost two decades ago in a chapter entitled "The Importance of Narrative Theology," Charles E. Van Engen urged readers to consider "narrative theology as viewed from an evangelical perspective" as a "creative and fruitful way" to do missional theology.[1] It is notable that he published these words in 1996. Five years later, Gabriel Fackre would lament, "The missing evangelical voice impoverishes the current theological conversation about narrative."[2] He remarks that evangelicals were just beginning to clear their throats, raise their hands, and weigh in on the issue of narrative theology.

Chuck Van Engen, an early pioneer in narrative theology and mission, co-edited *Footprints of God,* with the subtitle *A Narrative Theology of Mission.* He was the primary author in concert with Arthur Glasser in *Announcing the Kingdom: The Story of God's Mission in the Bible.* His doctoral training at the Free University of Amsterdam under Johannes Verkuyl and Jan Veenhof, who stand in the Dutch Calvinist tradition of reading the Bible as one redemptive-historical story, helped him see the importance of narrative theology. Yet the primary reason we see this theme weaving its way throughout his lectures and writing is a commitment to Scripture. The Bible is foremost a story of the mission of God in and through God's people and centered on the person of Jesus Christ. In honoring Chuck for his academic work and contribution, it is appropriate to revisit the importance of narrative theology for mission.

A MESSIANIC AND MISSIONAL READING OF SCRIPTURE

We do not start with narrative and mission but with Jesus. He leads us to a narrative reading of Scripture with mission at the center.[3] At the close of Luke's

---

1. Charles E. Van Engen, *Mission on the Way: Issues in Mission Theology* (Grand Rapids: Baker, 1996), 44.

2. Gabriel Fackre, "Narrative Theology from an Evangelical Perspective," in *Faith and Narrative,* ed. Keith E. Yandell (Oxford: Oxford University Press, 2001), 188.

3. We may not allow narrative as a general theological category, as important as it is, to eclipse Jesus. "Jesus is prior to the story," says Stanley Hauerwas ("The Church as God's New Language,"

Gospel, the resurrected Jesus met with the disciples and "opened their minds so that they could understand the Scriptures" (24:45). To employ a contemporary theological category, Jesus gives them a hermeneutical key to understand the story of the Old Testament Scriptures. That key is disclosed in his subsequent words: "This is what is written: The Messiah will suffer and rise from the dead on the third day, and repentance for the forgiveness of sins will be preached in his name to all nations, beginning at Jerusalem" (24:46-47). In these words, Jesus offers a twofold hermeneutical key.[4] The first is messianic: the Messiah will suffer and rise from the dead on the third day. The second is missional: his people will preach repentance for the forgiveness of sins in his name to all nations. The grammar of Jesus's words is clear: he refers to both Christ *and* the subsequent mission of the church. Together they form a key to interpret the Old Testament story.

The Old Testament story is one of restoration and renewal. God set out on the long road of redemption to restore the whole creation and the whole of human life. Jesus stood with the other Jews of his day in reading the Old Testament as a story awaiting an ending. That story finds its climactic point in Jesus the Messiah who accomplishes this salvation. The work of the Messiah fulfills "what is written," especially his death and resurrection. However, the Old Testament story is also one of the restoration and renewal *of all nations through God's chosen people.* The whole Old Testament story has in view from the outset the salvation of all nations, indeed, of the entire creation through a chosen people. God's particularistic means in choosing Abraham and Israel have a universal goal in the salvation of all nations. The Old Testament awaits an ending, not only in how salvation will be accomplished (in the Messiah), but also how that salvation will include all nations (in mission). The mission of God through the church to the ends of the earth fulfills "what is written."

These words of Jesus invite a twofold response. The first reads the Old Testament story with a messianic and missional lens. The second looks forward and reads the New Testament with this same lens. In other words, if we are to read the Bible aright we must recognize not only the centrality of Christ, but also the essential missional thread that weaves its way through the whole Scripture. Thus, Jesus's words demand a narrative theology—if we understand that to mean reading the Bible as one unfolding story of salvation. In addition, mission is central to that story and so requires a missional hermeneutic.

A missional hermeneutic is not simply a matter of tracing of the theme of mission throughout the biblical story the way we might trace the theme of work, for example. It is seeing mission as an indispensable lens since it is part of the central plot of the biblical story. Richard Bauckham alerts us of this in his definition of a "missionary hermeneutic," as "a way of reading the Bible

---

in *Scriptural Authority and Narrative Interpretation,* ed. Garret Green [Philadelphia: Fortress Press, 1987], 188). Yet, the gospel writers reveal Jesus in a story of his life, death, and resurrection, which is the climactic point of a bigger story of universal history narrated in the Old Testament. Therefore, Jesus himself points us to narrative.

4. Christopher J. H. Wright, *The Mission of God: Unlocking the Bible's Grand Narrative* (Downers Grove, IL: InterVarsity Press, 2006), 30, 41.

for which mission is the hermeneutical key. . . . A missionary hermeneutic of this kind would not be simply a study of the theme of mission in the biblical writings, but a way of reading *the whole of Scripture* with mission as its central interest and goal."[5] Bauckham identifies two approaches in biblical scholarship favorable for developing a missional hermeneutic: narrative and canonical.

Thus, if we are to find our light for mission in Scripture it becomes advisable and essential to attend to the narrative shape of Scripture. In this essay, I highlight four reasons that narrative is essential for mission: it is the only way we can understand the authority of Scripture; it roots mission in the mission of God; it reveals that mission flows from a missional ecclesiology; and it equips the church for its missionary encounter with culture.

STORY AND THE AUTHORITY OF SCRIPTURE

We seek an appropriation of narrative theology. So, what does that mean? Evangelicalism is a multifaceted phenomenon, and this can mean a number of things; but crucial in evangelicalism is the authority of Scripture since the Bible is the Word of God. Therefore, an evangelical approach to narrative theology and mission will ask about the nature of Scripture and its authority.[6]

N. T. Wright claims, "The whole point of Christianity is that it offers a story which is the story of the whole world."[7] Those are strong words indeed— Scripture narrates *the whole point of Christianity* as a true story of the whole world! Wright drives to the very core of the Christian faith and the very nature of Scripture. Jesus is the heart of the Christian faith and the center of the story, the fullest revelation of God and his purpose for the whole world. Yet, that revelation comes to us in a historical narrative of his life, death, and resurrection revealing and accomplishing God's purpose for the whole world. Jesus, the climax of a cosmic story narrated in the Old Testament, fulfills the narrative that begins with creation and accomplishes the restoration of the whole creation. Jesus stands squarely in the middle of a story of universal history, revealing the true story of the world.

A Hindu scholar who taught world religions in an Indian university clearly understood Christianity as a truth narrative, and once said to Lesslie Newbigin:

> I can't understand why you missionaries present the Bible to us in India as a book of religion. It is not a book of religion—and anyway we have plenty of books of religion in India. We don't need any more! I find in your Bible a unique interpretation of universal history, the history of the whole

---

5. Richard Bauckham, "Mission as Hermeneutic for Scriptural Interpretation," 1. Unpublished lecture given at Cambridge in November 1999.

6. N. T. Wright, "How Can the Bible Be Authoritative?" *Vox Evangelica* 21 (1991): 7-32; N. T. Wright, *The New Testament and the People of God* (Minneapolis: Fortress Press, 1992), 139-43; see also Richard Bauckham, *Scripture and Authority Today* (Cambridge: Grove Books, 1999), especially chapter 4, "The Authority of the Biblical Story."

7. Wright, *New Testament and the People of God*, 41-42.

of creation and the history of the human race. And therefore a unique interpretation of the human person as a responsible actor in history. That is unique. There is nothing else in the whole religious literature of the world to put alongside it.[8]

Newbigin told me that this scholar believed that it was ludicrous for anyone to claim to know the meaning of universal history. Even more absurd is the claim that a single human being in history reveals its meaning. The Indian scholar was astonished that Christians who accept the authority of Scripture would minimize the Bible and reduce it to another book of religion. Unique in the religious literature of the world, the Bible contains the true story of the world and the meaning of human life!

With the vicissitudes of mission today, it is essential to return to the Bible to get our bearings. David J. Bosch, commenting on the importance of Scripture in this new era of mission, says, "If we want the missionary enterprise to be authentic and our reflections on mission to be relevant" we will need "to pay even more serious attention to this branch of missiology" than previously. He observes that in times past, theologians formed a biblical foundation of mission by gleaning certain "missionary texts" from the Old and New Testament to undergird the contemporary missionary enterprise.

Undoubtedly, "behind this entire approach lay the assumption that one already knew what 'mission' was and now only had to prove that it was mandated by Scripture" and that "in looking for a biblical foundation for mission, missionary advocates as a matter of course took it for granted that it was *the enterprise they knew and were engaged in* that had to be justified biblically." Bosch contends that isolated passages of Scripture should not determine mission, but "the thrust of the central message of Scripture. In other words, either mission—properly understood—lies at the heart of the biblical message, or it is so peripheral to that message that we need not be overly concerned with it." He advocates a missional reading of Scripture in which we read Scripture "*as a whole.*"[9] To understand mission in the Bible means we must attend to the Bible as a redemptive-historical whole in which we find mission as a central theme.

STORY AND THE MISSION OF GOD

Bosch's brief analysis points to something else. It is only as we read the Bible as a whole that we can understand *what mission really is*. He notes that a colonial framework shaped our understanding of mission for several centuries. Theologians constructed a biblical foundation for mission with a selection of

---

8. Lesslie Newbigin, *A Walk Through the Bible* (Louisville, KY: Westminster John Knox Press, 1999), 4.

9. David J. Bosch, "Reflections on Biblical Models of Mission," in *Toward the 21st Century in Christian Mission*, ed. James M. Phillips and Robert T. Coote (Grand Rapids: Eerdmans, 1993), 175-78.

texts that supported that vision. A return to reading Scripture as a redemptive-historical whole will correct selective proof texting and help us wrestle with authentic mission. At least two important theological themes have emerged through a narrative reading of Scripture that are essential for understanding the nature of mission: the *missio Dei* and the missionary nature of the church.

The Second World War dismantled the colonial framework for mission. This became clear by the early 1950s, and Christians convened the Willingen Conference to draft a new theological framework for mission. The well-known *missio Dei* emerged as the unifying structure. There were at least two understandings of the *missio Dei* present in Willingen: a more traditional understanding that was christocentric and gave full recognition to the church as the primary agent in God's mission and a more secular understanding that emphasized the work of the Spirit in the world.[10] As all traditions gradually embraced the *missio Dei* of the church, it was the traditional understanding that rightly found favor in evangelical circles.

Two observations on this brief history highlight the importance of narrative for the emergence of the *missio Dei* in mission theology. First, the understanding of God's mission arose during a time when the biblical theology movement was in its ascendancy.[11] The biblical theology movement stressed three things: a theological interpretation of Scripture that features God as the primary actor in the biblical drama; the unity of Scripture in which all else finds its place; and the importance of history—God's mighty acts *in history*—as the medium of revelation. A biblical-theological approach provided the framework that enabled the notion of the *missio Dei* to emerge at Willingen.

A second observation highlights the importance of narrative for the *missio Dei*. As mission thinkers seized a biblical-theological framework for God's mission, it opened the way for many biblical, theological, missiological, and ecclesiological insights to find consistent and systematic expression in a theology of mission.[12] In his introduction to the Willingen conference report, Norman Goodall says that it was "recognized that in the fields of biblical and theological studies there had been taking place, for some years, movements that were proving deeply significant for all who sought a fuller apprehension of the Christian faith. At the same time, it was felt that these studies and movements of thought had not become related, with sufficient explicitness, to the missionary calling of the Church."[13]

---

10. See further Michael W. Goheen, "The Future of Mission in the World Council of Churches: The Dialogue between Lesslie Newbigin and Konrad Raiser," *Mission Studies* 21, no. 1 (2004): 97-111.

11. Ellen Flessemen-van Leer, *The Bible: Its Authority and Interpretation in the Ecumenical Movement*, Faith and Order Paper 99 (Geneva: World Council of Churches, 1980), 1.

12. Rodger Bassham, "Seeking a Deeper Theological Basis for Mission," *International Review of Mission* 67 (1978): 331-37.

13. Norman Goodall, ed., *Missions under the Cross: Addresses Delivered at the Enlarged Meeting of the Committee of the International Missionary Council at Willingen, in Germany, 1952; with Statements Issued by the Meeting* (London: Edinburgh, 1953), 10f.

The mission of God understood in narrative terms drew together biblical, theological, missiological, and ecclesiological gains from the twentieth century into a coherent vision for mission. The narrative story brought insights from the *biblical and theological* guild into fruitful connection with mission: for example, the already-not-yet nature of the kingdom; the relationship between salvation history and world history; the work of the Spirit as primarily missionary; and salvation as comprehensive restoration of creation. It also paved the way for many *missiological* convictions that had been gaining strength over the past three or four decades to find consistent expression. For example, the unreal distinctions between older and younger churches, between home base and mission field, and between domestic and foreign missions; the relationship between church and mission; the West as a mission field; the integral relationship between evangelism and social involvement; and unity and mission. The consistent formulation of these convictions in a new framework played a major role in dealing a deathblow to the colonial framework for mission. Finally, many *ecclesiological* insights from the twentieth century found a place in the *missio Dei*: for example, the missionary nature of the church; the pilgrim church; new and more flexible forms of ministry; and the importance of the laity in mission of the church.

As we cast an eye back over the lists in the previous paragraph, we find many insights taken for granted in our understanding of mission. One factor, theologically speaking, for bringing together a coherent theology of mission arose from the dominance of the biblical theology movement, providing a narrative framework for the *missio Dei* in which these insights found a home.

Today most mission thinkers would begin with the mission of God in framing a biblical understanding of mission. Yet, as happens with all important and useful concepts, there is the danger that we might uproot them from their original soil. In the present climate, it is important to stress a *narrative* formulation of the *missio Dei*. There is a danger that the metaphor present at Willingen (the Father sends the Son, the Son sends the Spirit, the Son sends the church in the power of the Spirit) might become a schema or formula disconnected from the biblical narrative. Then the *missio Dei* is in danger of many unbiblical interpretations. Another more subtle danger among evangelicals is minimizing the Old Testament and its crucial importance for mission.[14]

STORY AND THE MISSIONAL CHURCH

The narrative framework of Scripture gives us another important insight to understand the nature of mission: the fundamental identity of the people of God is missional. Many kinds of words and actions expressive of our missionary vocation will flow from that missional identity. As with the *missio Dei*, a missionary understanding of the church grew in the soil of a biblical-theological reading of Scripture.

---

14. See David J. Bosch, *Transforming Mission: Paradigm Shifts in Theology of Mission* (Maryknoll, NY: Orbis Books, 1991).

Narrative theologians recognize that story is especially effective in shaping the identity of a person or people. Indeed, it is primarily by tracing the story of God's people in their role in the biblical story that we understand our missional identity.[15] Wilbert Shenk rightly says, "The Bible does not offer a definition of the church or provide us with a doctrinal basis for understanding it. Instead, the Bible relies on images and narrative to disclose the meaning of the church."[16]

To understand the missional identity of the church we must attend carefully to the Old Testament. In the Old Testament God forms the fundamental identity of his people in relationship to the nations. At an important juncture of redemptive history, the movement from God's universal dealings with all humankind (Gen. 1–11) to a particular focus on Abraham and Israel, God promises a restoration, a blessing of creational life to Abraham so that he might be a channel of that blessing to the nations (Gen. 12:2-3; 18:18-19). Blessed to be a blessing: that is the fundamental identity stamped on God's people at the outset. Exodus tells the story of the formation of this people. The book portrays God's people in terms of a people who are redeemed from idolatry to serve the living God (Exod. 1–18), who are bound to God in covenant (Exod. 19–24), and who know the presence of God in their midst (Exod. 25–40). At the center of the Exodus narrative is the vocation given to Israel at Sinai: they are to be a display people "for the whole earth belongs to me" (Exod. 19:3-6). Calling Israel to be a holy people who fulfill the priestly vocation of bringing blessing to the nations (cf. Num. 6:22-27), God immediately gives Israel the law so that it might live out an attractive lifestyle before the nations (cf. Deut. 4:5-8). He then places Israel in the land to display what it means to be in covenant with God. Being visible to the nations is part of their very identity. In spite of God's gifts of a temple, kings, prophets and more, Israel fails. Once a light, they are overcome by the darkness of pagan idolatry. However, the prophets declare that God will not abandon the promise to bring blessing to all nations through Israel. God promises to gather and renew the people of God to fulfill their calling (Ezek. 36:16-28).

Jesus follows: "That God has chosen and sanctified his people to make it a contrast-society in the midst of the other nations was for Jesus the self-evident background of all his actions." In Jesus, we see God's "eschatological action . . . to restore or even re-establish his people, in order to carry out definitively and irrevocably his plan of having a holy people in the midst of the nations."[17] This gives us a perspective on the ministry of Jesus. He gathers the lost sheep of Israel in order to form them for their missional calling. His death, resurrection, and gift of the Spirit complete the work needed to bring life and renewal to Israel to carry out that task. Nevertheless, his work is not only for Israel. Intended for all nations, the cross ends the old age dominated by evil. The resurrection

---

15. Michael W. Goheen, *A Light to the Nations: The Missional Church in the Biblical Story* (Grand Rapids: Baker, 2011).

16. Wilbert Shenk, "Foreword," in John Driver, *Images of the Church in Mission* (Scottsdale, PA: Herald Press, 1997), 9.

17. Gerhard Lohfink, *Jesus and Community: The Social Dimension of the Christian Faith*, trans. John P. Galvin (Philadelphia: Fortress Press, 1982), 123.

inaugurates a new creation. Gathered and renewed, Israel goes to the nations (Matt. 28:18-20; Luke 24:45-49).

The book of Acts narrates how God fulfills the promise of the prophets to gather Israel into God's eschatological salvation and then the nations. In the earliest chapters of Acts the gathering of Israel initiated by Jesus continues. Many believe, yet many refuse and are broken off (Rom. 11:17-21). Then the engrafting of the Gentiles commences, beginning in and from Antioch, as Paul and his companions establish a witness to the gospel in places where people have never heard the Good News. In this mission, the people of God take a new form as a noncentralized, multi-ethnic community that must embody the Good News amid all the cultures of the world. The book of Acts ends abruptly, a literary technique that issues an invitation for its readers to participate in the ongoing story, and make known the Good News to the ends of the earth. We can capture the meaning of mission in this narrative with two important distinctions made by Lesslie Newbigin that have become important for many mission theologians: the differences between missionary dimension and missionary intention; and mission and missions.

During the middle of the twentieth century, the scope of mission broadened significantly to include the identity of the church and all its work. Some were concerned that this broadening view of mission might eclipse the more specific evangelistic and missionary task of the church. While there was an appreciation of the emerging comprehensive scope of mission, it also had the potential to smother intentional evangelistic activities.

In this context, Newbigin makes the distinction "between mission as a *dimension* of the Church's whole life, and mission as the primary *intention* of certain activities." Everything the church does has a missionary dimension. "But not everything the Church does has a missionary intention." Missionary intention includes certain activities that are "an action of the Church in going out beyond the frontiers of its own life to bear witness to Christ as Lord among those who do not know Him, and when the overall *intention* of that action is that they should be brought from unbelief to faith."[18]

In a second distinction, Lesslie Newbigin notes that throughout the nineteenth and early twentieth centuries, mission was reduced to cross-cultural missions—the taking of the gospel from the Christian West to the non-Christian non-West. Things changed: the non-Western church grew and the church in the West receded. This new situation along with the broadening view of mission altered cross-cultural missions. Newbigin believed it was essential "to identify and distinguish the specific foreign missionary task within the total Mission of the Church."[19]

18. Lesslie Newbigin, *One Body, One Gospel, One World* (London: William Carling and Co., 1958). 43-44.

19. Lesslie Newbigin, "Mission and Missions," *Christianity Today* 4, no. 2 (August 1, 1960): 911.

Thus, he distinguishes between mission and missions (with an "s").[20] Mission is the calling of the church to declare the gospel as it participates in God's mission. Missions are particular enterprises within that total mission "which have the primary intention of bringing into existence a Christian presence in a milieu where previously there was no such presence or where such presence was ineffective."[21] Thus, missions remain an important and essential part of the ongoing mission of the church in places and to peoples who have not heard the Good News.[22] Newbigin points to the church at Antioch (Acts 13:1-3) as a missional church also concerned with missions.

These helpful distinctions indicate that Newbigin defines mission in narrative terms. Mission involves the presence of a distinctive people, witness to Christ in the public square, evangelism, missions, witness in word and deed, and much more. All of these various components of mission find their proper place in the missional vocation of the church.

STORY AND A MISSIONARY ENCOUNTER

If faithful, the church takes a missionary posture in any cultural context with the meeting of ultimate and comprehensive stories—the biblical story and the cultural story. A missionary encounter requires that the church live fully in the biblical story and contextualize the gospel in its culture in a way that is faithful to that story. This will involve a critical participation that embraces the creational good while opposing the destructive idolatry that can exist in any culture. Thus, central to the church's mission is an offer of the gospel as a counter-story as the true way of life, a call for radical conversion, an invitation to understand and live in the world in the light of the gospel.

Tireless in calling the Western church back to a missionary encounter with its culture, [23] Lesslie Newbigin believed that the Western church was an "advanced case of syncretism."[24] A missionary encounter occurs when the church believes the Bible to be the true story of the world, and embodies and proclaims its comprehensive claims as a witness in the face of the dominant cultural narrative.

---

20. David J. Bosch also makes a distinction between mission and missions but in a different way. Mission is the mission of God while missions are human activities of the church that participate in God's mission. See *Transforming Mission*, 391.

21. Lesslie Newbigin, "Cross-currents in Ecumenical and Evangelical Understandings of Mission," *International Bulletin of Missionary Research* 6, no. 4 (1982): 142-51,149.

22. I try to articulate and develop the importance of this distinction for today in the last chapter of my book *Introducing Christian Mission Today: Scripture, History, and Issues* (Downers Grove, IL: InterVarsity Press, 2014).

23. Using different language both N. T. Wright and Richard Bauckham make the same point. Wright, *The New Testament and the People of God*, 132; Wright, *The Bible for the Postmodern World* (Grand Rapids: Baker, 2003), 9-12; Bauckham, *Bible and Mission: Christian Witness in a Postmodern World* (Grand Rapids: Baker, 2001), especially chapter 4.

24. Lesslie Newbigin, *A Word in Season: Perspectives on Christian World Mission* (Grand Rapids: Eerdmans, 1994), 23.

Newbigin charges that the reverse has taken place: the Western church has allowed the biblical story to be absorbed into the more comprehensive cultural story.

An essential ingredient in reversing syncretism in the West is to recover Scripture as a true grand story. "I do not believe that we can speak effectively of the Gospel as a word addressed to our culture unless we recover a sense of the Scriptures as a canonical whole, as the story which provides the true context for our understanding of the meaning of our lives—both personal and public."[25] If we fragment the story of the Bible into bits, we can easily domesticate the reigning cultural story. When we only have bits—moral bits, systematic-theological bits, devotional bits, historical-critical bits, narrative bits, and homiletical bits—there is no comprehensive grand narrative. The all-embracing cultural story accommodates the Bible bits, and it becomes *that* story that shapes our lives. Australian sociologist John Carroll, who is not a professing Christian, rightly observes, "The waning of Christianity as practiced in the West is easy to explain. The Christian churches have comprehensively failed in their one central task—to retell their foundation story in a way that might speak to the times."[26]

Thus reading the Bible's unfolding story will enable the church in the West, but also in other parts of the world, to be faithful to its missional calling as a contrast people who embody and announce the gospel in the midst of a culture that finds its center in something other than Jesus.

CONCLUSION

There are many questions surrounding narrative theology. It means different things to different people. In this essay I have been primarily speaking of narrative in terms of what N.T. Wright calls a "worldview-story," or what others have called a metanarrative.[27] With the terminology of "worldview-story" Wright wants to speak of narrative developing from the very shape of the Bible that must become the ultimate and comprehensive worldview in which we live our lives. From this standpoint, it is clear that narrative will be crucial for anyone who takes biblical authority and mission seriously—an enduring mark of the evangelical tradition. I am grateful for Chuck Van Engen's commitment to the biblical story and to the centrality of mission in that narrative. May that legacy capture the church of the twenty-first century. Our faithfulness depends on it.

---

25. Lesslie Newbigin, "'Response to the Word of God?,' John Coventry, S.J.,'" *The Gospel and Our Culture Newsletter* 10, no. 2 (1991): 2.

26. John Carroll, *The Existential Jesus* (Brunswick, Australia: Scribe Publications, 2008).

27. Wright, *New Testament and the People of God*, 124. Bauckham defines metanarrative as "a narrative about the whole of reality that elucidates the meaning of the whole of reality" and ascribes this to the Bible (*Bible and Mission*, 12).

Chapter 2

Contextual Christology:
Carrying the Great Commission with Joy

David Hartono

Evangelicals affirm that the risen Christ is the foundation of our faith and hope; he is also the basis of our missional endeavors. "And if Christ has not been raised, our preaching is useless and so is your faith. . . . And if Christ has not been raised, your faith is futile; you are still in your sins" (1 Cor. 15:14, 17).[1] In addition, if Christ has risen from the dead, who then do we say he is? Jesus put this very question before his disciples: "Who do people say the Son of Man is?" and, "Who do you say I am?" (Matt. 16:13, 15). Peter replied to him and said, "You are the Christ, the Son of the living God," and Jesus responded, "Blessed are you, Simon the son of Jonah, for this was not revealed to you by man, but by my Father in heaven" (Matt. 16:13-17).

When the Sanhedrin tried Jesus, he remained silent when people accused him of many things. However, when the High Priest asked him, "Are you the Christ, the Son of the Blessed One?" Jesus replied, "I am . . . And you will see the Son of Man sitting at the right hand of the Mighty One and coming on the cloud of heaven" (Mark 14:53-65). In this instance, Jesus testified that he was the Christ, the Son of the Blessed One. He also indirectly stated that he would rise from the dead and conquer the power of death. Jesus, the answer to the question of Christology and the foundation of our faith and hope, plays a vital role as a guiding force for the orthopraxis of Christian mission in a global setting.

After a careful reflection of our book title, *Contemporary Mission Theology: Engaging the Nations*, the vision set forth by the editors is evident: to consider effective mission in an era of great global challenges. Churches and Christians worldwide should not aspire to strive for uniformity in doing mission, but rather unity in close partnership. This would allow churches from different parts of the world to grapple with the problems they are facing with a theological and contextual grounding. At this intersection, the preeminent importance of Christology becomes apparent, and puts forward its absolute central position in any mission praxis and mission theology.

---

1. All scriptural quotations are from the New International Version.

However, the task of engaging the nations and exploring the contours of mission theology with a global perspective is not easy. We must discern how to engage with other worldviews respectfully, given differences in culture, civilization, and religious faith.[2] The challenge is to understand the intercultural relationship between the received texts (the Bible) and the incarnate text (Jesus Christ) as revealed in the received texts. For example, one should not assume that Asian and European churches have had an identical articulation of biblical texts concerning Christology. This observation becomes apparent when studying the Taiping Revolution in China (1850–1864)[3] since most contemporary Western missionaries and churches regard the Taiping Heavenly Kingdom's (*Taiping Tianguo*) contextual Christology as heretical.[4]

The question I posed at the beginning of this essay guides the organization of this paper: if Christ has risen from the dead, who then do we say he is? It is a question worthy of our deepest consideration. This essay proceeds with five reflective thematic topics: (1) the centerpiece of Christology; (2) the intent of Christology; (3) probing the intent and the principle of Paul's contextual Christology; (4) the importance of Christology; and (5) revisiting the Great Commission. Let us now address how to engage people with Christ in order to advance *missio Dei* and *missio Christi* in the world.[5]

THE CENTERPIECE OF CHRISTOLOGY:
NO OTHER NAME—THE FINALITY OF CHRIST JESUS

Evangelicals should not shy away from acknowledging the validity of using the Scripture as their primary source of absolute authority. The Scripture affirms the finality of Christ Jesus. Opposition to the Christian mission is not new. Anyone who reads the gospels, the Acts of the Apostles, and the Pauline Epistles can notice the harsh opposition to Jesus, to his teachings, his ministry, his disciples, and his followers. Jesus has summed this up by saying, "They will treat you this way because of my name, because they do not know the one who sent me" (John 15:21). Those who opposed him disdained the core of Jesus's self-identification and, as a corollary to that, could not accept the core of the Christian gospel: that there is no other name but Jesus Christ and that he is God.

The validity of that claim hinged on the fulfillment of his prophecy that he would rise from the dead on the third day (Mark 8:31). It is unthinkable that

---

2. See David Hartono, "Paul's Contextual Christology as a Preferred Model for Creedal Churches" (PhD diss., Fuller Theological Seminary, School of World Mission, 1996), 5-9.

3. See Franz Michael and Chung Li Chang, *The Taiping Rebellion: History and Documents,* 3 vols. (Seattle, WA: University of Washington Press, 1971–72).

4. Kenneth Scott Latourette questioned the Christian origin of the Taiping Revolution. See *A History of Christian Mission in China* (New York: Macmillan, 1929).

5. Karl Barth first described mission as derived from the nature of God, utilizing the term *missio Dei.* See David J. Bosch, *Transforming Mission: Paradigm Shifts in Theology of Mission* (Maryknoll, NY: Orbis Books, 1991), 390-93.

a person who had a group of mostly uneducated followers could hang on a cross, and then reshape and direct public opinion that he had indeed risen from the dead.[6] If the historicity and truth of Christ's resurrection were false, there would have been no chance for the continuation of the Christian faith (see Matt. 27–28; Acts 1–28). He is indeed the only Savior of the world (Matt. 12:14; Mark 14:60-64; Luke 22:66-71; John 10:29-33).

Despite fierce opposition and persecution, first-century Christians were still eager to share the Good News with their neighbors and greater communities. Many of them were eyewitnesses of Jesus's resurrection and appearance (1 Cor. 15:3-9). For them, propagating the Good News and engaging in mission were privileges in a joyful enterprise given by God. However, after the passage of over two thousand years, present-day Christians can no longer rely on the claim of being eyewitnesses to the historical events of Jesus's crucifixion and resurrection. Rather, they are guardians of accumulated Christian traditions. Therefore, opponents of Christian faith argue that since present-day Christians can no longer claim to be eyewitnesses, they lost the ground to claim that their faith in Christ was absolute. In 1893, at the forum of the Parliament of World Religions held in Chicago, Hindu and Buddhist scholars challenged the finality of Christ, specifically: Narendranath Datta of India (otherwise known as Swami Vivekananda), Dharmapala of Sri Lanka, and Soyen Shaku of Japan.[7] Their positions were consistent with the postmodern mind-set that there are no absolutes and that relativism reigns supreme.

Additionally, over 120 years ago, Martin Kahler (1835-1912) sparked a debate on the historicity of Jesus Christ. He proposed that there was a dichotomy between the historical Jesus (*historisch Jesus*) and the Christ of faith (*geschichtlich Christ*).[8] This highly speculative intellectual treatment on the historicity of Jesus Christ had a detrimental impact on the spread of the gospel and the Christian world mission by separating history and faith. Truly, the historical resurrection of Jesus is the basis for the primacy and finality of Christ. This is the *conditio sine qua non* for Christians engaging in world mission. Moreover, the core message of the gospel has to be soundly grounded in the Bible, a testament to the redemptive activity of God, wrought in Jesus Christ (John 20:31).

In response to this divine action, Christians should proclaim that in Christ, God has reconciled "the world to Himself, not imputing their trespasses to them, and has committed to us the word of reconciliation" (2 Cor. 5:19). Charles Van Engen posits that Christians should do so in word and in deed, with a spirit of humility to love people of other faiths and ideologies.[9] Yet, if

---

6. See Michael Green, *Evangelism in the Early Church* (Grand Rapids: Eerdmans, 2003); Rodney Stark, *The Triumph of Christianity* (New York: Harper Collins, 2011).

7. See Wilfred Cantwell Smith, *The Meaning and End of Religion* (New York: Macmillan, 1962); also John Nicol Farquhar, *Modern Religious Movement in India* (New York: Macmillan, [1915 [repr., 2009]).

8. James D. G. Dunn and Scot McKnight, eds., *The Historical Jesus in Recent Research* (Winona Lake, IN: Eisenbrauns, 2005), 67-84 (on Martin Kahler).

9. See Charles Van Engen, *Mission on the Way: Issues in Mission Theology* (Grand Rapids: Baker Books, 1996), 26.

Christian churches deny the absolute supremacy and finality of Jesus Christ, then in essence, Christian faith is empty and meaningless, and churches will lose their value to exist.

Classical Christology is a systematization of the Scripture's teachings about Jesus Christ. In essence, the doctrinal teaching that confesses that Jesus is Christ (Acts 2:36, 5:42; Rom. 10:9; Phil. 2:11; 1 John 5:1). As debates about Christology and interpretation of biblical texts pertaining to the Lordship of Jesus Christ continue, so will the debate over the function of doctrine also persist.[10] Since the spread of the Christian faith to continents outside Europe, is it possible that the receivers of the gospel can fully understand what they hear within their respective cultural contexts?[11] Can new believers in Christ from countries that received the gospel relatively later accurately formulate contextual theology? In addition, can dominant creedal or confessional churches accept these global theologies? This leads us to a discussion of the legitimacy of the praxis of the contextualization of Christology.[12]

THE INTENT OF CHRISTOLOGY: CHRIST IN LIVING CONTEXT

It would be unfortunate if seminary treated Christology as a solely intellectual discipline. Christology should not form division in the church but serve as a unifier. When known and glorified by people as Lord, then Jesus will draw people of all races and cultures to himself (John 12:32). It is in this context that the praxis of the contextualization of theology plays an important role.

However, contextualization is a complex and complicated theological praxis. The first stage is the presentation and reception of theology to those living in different contexts of culture, language, semiology, and worldview. The second stage is the expression and sharing of faith within the nuances of the receivers' own cultural understandings. I propose that the global community of believers who live within diverse cultural contexts and church traditions should have to deem a good model of contextual theology legitimate and acceptable.

The Taiping Revolution in China was a unique revolutionary moment, the first major revolt in Chinese history led by people who professed the Christian faith. In the end, the Qing Dynasty crushed the Taiping Revolution. Many factors contributed to their defeat, and significant among them were the movement's endogenous power struggles, moral decay, and corruption. Besides these, one of the contributing factors to the downfall of the Taiping Revolution was the opposition of Western missionaries who regarded Taiping contextual

---

10. Gerald H. Anderson and Thomas F. Stransky, eds., *Christ's Lordship and Religious Pluralism* (Maryknoll, NY: Orbis Books, 1981).

11. See Dean S. Gilliland, ed., *The Word Among Us: Contextualizing Theology for Mission Today* (Dallas: Word Publishing, 1989), 13.

12. See Charles Van Engen, "The New Covenant Knowing God in Context," in *The Word Among Us*, ed. Dean S. Gilliland (Dallas: Word Publishing, 1989), 74-100.

Christology as heretical and asked their respective governments to aid the Qing Dynasty in crushing the Taiping Revolution.

What lessons might there be for missiologists on the enormity of human loss and political upheaval during the Taiping Revolution? According to John C. Gregory, "the Scripture of the Old and New Testament are their standard of faith now as they were at the commencement of the movement," and, "As long as they receive them as the Word of God we have reasonable grounds of hope that their errors will gradually be corrected."[13]

In short, political catastrophe and personal wrongs impeded the maturity of a Chinese contextualization praxis in the nineteenth century. Despite that early end to the expansion of indigenous Christian thought in China, the diversity of theological thought and its implications still deserve some consideration. Scholar William A. P. Martin's words may be true: "The complete collapse of the Taiping government meant that China lost the golden opportunity of her thousands years of history to witness the existence of a government based on Christian teachings."[14]

PROBING THE INTENT AND THE PRINCIPLE OF PAUL'S CONTEXTUAL CHRISTOLOGY

Paul, as a great missionary and a master of the praxis of contextualization, shed light for later generations of missiologists to ponder the validity of their own praxis within the framework of community confession. Epistemologically, a confession of faith cannot stand outside of the dialectical interaction between faith and culture, and it thereby cannot assume the role of "dogmatic judge." Rather, it should function as a common link between different kinds of contextualized theologies and accepted theologies. Across spatial and temporal divides, it serves as a bridge between one theology and another.[15] Let us look at Paul's writings that shed some light on this issue.

As a former Pharisee (Phil. 3:5-6), Paul held a rigid view on the authority of the Old Testament. However, his conversion, missionary speeches, and writings provide evidence that he did not strictly adhere to contemporaneous rabbinical interpretations of the Old Testament. Rather, he developed a unique christocentric theology by reinterpreting Old Testament texts while maintaining a continuous relationship with it. Paul's postconversion understanding was that the person of Jesus Christ fulfilled God's promise of the coming of Messiah. More than any other New Testament writer, Paul used the Old Testament

---

13. John C. Gregory, "British Missionary Reaction to the Taiping Movement in China," *Journal of Religious History* 2 (1963): 204-18. See Vincent Shih, *The Taiping Ideology: It Sources, Interpretation and Influence* (Seattle, WA: University of Washington Press, 1967).

14. William A. P. Martin, *The Circle of Cathay* (New York: Revell, 1900), 142.

15. See Jürgen Moltmann, "The Confession of Jesus Christ: A Biblical Theological Consideration," in *An Ecumenical Confession of Faith?* ed. Hans Küng and Jürgen Moltmann (New York: Seabury Press, 1979), 13-19.

to establish and strengthen his christocentric theology. Hence, his contextual Christology strongly affirmed the christocentric soteriology that God's salvation is obtainable by grace through faith alone. In the truest sense, Jesus, true God and man, fulfills the promise of the Messiah.

Paul's contemplation of the person and work of Jesus Christ is the dominant feature in his Christology: by grace through faith, humanity and God are reconciled in Jesus Christ (Eph. 2:8-9). It is worth noting that Paul's prevalent mention of the formulas "in Christ," "with Christ," or "through Christ" points to the exclusiveness of Christian faith, comprising a unique feature of Pauline Christology. Furthermore, Paul's missional and pastoral contexts determined his theological reflection to a large degree. Sometimes he encountered divergent opinions from various communities. When this happened, he always turned to the unsearchable riches of Jesus Christ.[16] The controversies he faced led him to a deeper understanding of Christ.[17] This fact further enhances the relevance of studying Paul's contextual Christology.

Paul's key principle in contextualization, "I have become all things to all people so that by all possible means I might save some" (1 Cor. 9:22), deserves a close look. Foundational to this principle was his joy that by God's grace he had experienced conversion when on his way to Damascus to persecute Christians. On the road to Damascus, Jesus Christ appeared to him in glory: "About noon, O king, I saw a light from heaven brighter than the sun, blazing around me and my companions" (Acts 26:13). Because of this encounter with the risen Lord, he accepted the fact that Jesus is Lord and the promised Messiah. Since then, Paul, called to be the apostle to the Gentiles, had a genuine desire to preach the Good News to all people, Jews and Gentiles alike (Acts 26:17). He understood that in Christ they are one (Gal. 3:27-28).[18]

Living in pluralistic, urban societies, there may have been more leniency toward divergent views, since "in the Mediterranean world in which Paul lived, subject to the all-overriding interests of the Roman state, each ethnic and cultic group was permitted and even expected to live according to its traditions."[19] This was the sociocultural climate of the *Pax Romana* society in Paul's time, where religious extremism and political correctness were seemingly absent.

What then is the exact meaning of the phrase "I have become all things to all people?" Some scholars posit that the phrase might convey Paul's "apostolic opportunism."[20] Other scholars, such as Joseph B. Lightfoot, maintain that the phrase is "the key to all seeming inconsistencies in different representations of his conduct."[21] It is possible to interpret this phrase in the light of missional contextual adaptation. I emphasize that Paul did not modify the changeless

---

16. W. G. Kümmel, *The Theology of the New Testament,* trans. John E. Steely (New York: Abingdon, 1973), 139.

17. See William Barclay, *The Mind of St. Paul* (London: SCM, 1973).

18. For further study, see F. F. Bruce, *Paul: Apostle of the Free Spirit* (Exeter: Paternoster, 1977).

19. See Henry L. Ellison, "Paul and the Law—All Things to All Men," in *Apostolic History and the Gospel,* ed. W. W. Gasque and Ralph Martin (Exeter: Paternoster, 1970), 197.

20. Henry Chadwick, "All Things to All Men," *New Testament Studies* 1 (1954–1955): 261-75.

21. Joseph B. Lightfoot, *St. Paul's Epistle to the Galatians* (Lynn, MA: Hendrickson, 1981).

gospel to meet his missionary aims (Gal. 1:8). As Günther Bornkamm argues, the principle of "I have become all things to all people" is not Paul's attempt to remove "the σκάνδαλον [ensnaring] character of his message." Rather, Paul varied the language of his message and varied his method of presenting and explaining the gospel, according to the situational context of his audience.[22] For Paul, the principle "I have become all things to all people" may mean the renunciation of certain liberties in a given situation, in order to gain more converts than if he had not made himself "a slave to all" (1 Cor. 9:19).[23]

THE CONTEXTUAL NATURE OF CHRIST JESUS'S INCARNATION AND POSTRESURRECTION APPEARANCE

In a general survey of literature pertaining to Christological discussion, there is emphasis on the work and the person of Christ Jesus. It follows either a deductive methodology that begins with the second person of the Godhead to the incarnate Christ Jesus, or an inductive methodology that begins from the humanity of Jesus to the Godhead's second person in Holy Trinity. The third methodology is a synthetic approach of the aforementioned methodologies— that is, the holistic Christ Jesus who is both God and perfect man.[24]

This essay delivers a fourth approach that encourages Christians of all nations to engage in world mission and to construct a contextual theology with a global perspective. It is a Christology in practice. Evangelical Christians should hold absolute belief in the historical fact that Jesus Christ the risen Lord is the core, the centerpiece, the very foundation and the indispensable element of the gospel message. Without him, there is no Good News, and there will be no Christian church, no Christian faith, and no Christian world mission. With this in mind, contextual theology is not simply a buzzword but a critical principle for both occidental evangelical confessional theologians and for majority-world theologians who develop indigenous contextual theology. Dean S. Gilliland states that the good thing about contextualization is that it safeguards against the imperialism of theology.[25]

The Incarnation of the second person of the Holy Trinity is the culmination of the fulfillment of God's eternal plan. God enacted salvation by entering humanity (John 1:1-4, 14; 3:13), and actualized it through the virgin birth of

---

22. Günther Bornkamm, "The Missionary Stance of Paul in 1 Corinthians 9 and in Acts," in *Studies in Luke–Acts,* ed. L. E. Keck and J. L. Martyn (London: SPCK, 1968), 194-207.

23. Archibald Robertson and Alfred Plummer, *First Epistle of Paul to the Corinthians* (Edinburgh: T&T Clark, 1929). See also George Hendry, "Christology," in *A Dictionary of Christian Theology* (London: SCM, 1969), 51-64; Frederick W. Grosheide, *Commentary on the Epistle to the Corinthians,* trans. A. W. Heathcate and P. J. Allcock (London: Epworth Press, 1962).

24. See Wolfhart Pannenberg, *Jesus, God and Man,* trans. L. L. Wilkins and D. A. Priebe (Philadelphia: Westminster, 1968), 63-73; Daniel P. Fuller, *The Easter Faith and History* (London: Tyndale, 1968), 50-77, 112-40; Hendry, "Christology."

25. Dean S. Gilliland, "Contextual Theology as Incarnational Mission," in *The Word Among Us* (1989), 13.

Jesus Christ in Bethlehem (Matt. 1:18-25; Luke 2:8-20). It is interesting to note the discourse of Jesus Christ with Jews: "Your father Abraham rejoiced at the thought of seeing my day; he saw it and was glad . . . before Abraham was born, I am!" (John 8:56-57).[26] Paul further elaborated that Christ Jesus, "who being in very nature God, did not consider equality with God something to be grasped" (Phil. 2:6).[27] Those who believe in him will be granted grace, faith, and power to become his children, and will be born again by the Holy Spirit (Eph. 2:8; John 1:12; 3:3-5). Jesus himself stated that a person could not see and enter the kingdom of God without being born again (John 3:3, 5). A corollary is that people can only know Jesus in his context, in his way, in his domain. These three phrases mean that those who were called by him should live after God's own heart, and live within God's will (cf. 1 Sam. 13:14; Rom. 12:2). To live in his context, in his way, and in his domain is a requirement that applies to everyone, Gentiles and Jews alike. These verses lend clarity to help us understand the new dynamic relationship of God and humanity in the christocentric context. Christology lies at the contours of mission theology in a global perspective.

The postresurrection appearance of Jesus Christ to his disciples and to Paul has its contextual dimension, including a "customized" approach to each person according to the person's contextual need. Jesus appeared to his disciples and female followers by showing them the crucified body. Yet, to Paul he appeared in glory and identified himself with the persecuted church (John 20:10-29; 21:1-11; Acts 26:1-23).[28] The Old Testament describes divine glory as fiery. Paul, who was well versed in scriptures, knew that, thus, Christ Jesus's appearance in glory radically changed Paul's perception of Jesus. He acknowledged him as Christ, the Messiah.[29] Christ Jesus appeared in different settings so that people who lived in different contexts would come to know him at a deeper, more personal level. However, one thing that remains unchanged in his appearance was his finality and power over death. This understanding gives us joy and certainty that engaging the nations in constructing contextual mission theology with a global perspective is a doable praxis.

---

26. In John 8:56-57, Jesus does not claim preexistence but deity; see Andreas J. Kostenberger, *John*, Baker Exegetical Commentary on the New Testament (Grand Rapids: Baker Academic, 2008), 273; Rudolph Schnackenburg, *The Gospel According to Saint John*, trans. C. Hastings et al., 3 vols. (New York: Crossroad, 1990), 2:220. See also Stephen Motyer, *"Your Father the Devil?" A New Approach to John and "the Jews"* (Carlisle: Paternoster, 1997), 159; Herman Ridderbos, *The Gospel According to John*, trans. J. Vriend (Grand Rapids: Eerdmans, 1997), 322-23.

27. Some scholars question that the meaning of verse 6 refers to total equality of Christ and God. See C. A. Wanamaker, "Philippians 2:6-11: Son of God or Adamic Christology?" in *New Testament Studies* 33 (1987): 187. However, Moïses Silva's comments are more poignant, "Theological inferences drawn from grammatical nuances (and in a quasi-poetical passage to boot) seldom are worth considering seriously." See his *Philippians*, Baker Exegetical Commentary on the New Testament (2d ed.; Grand Rapids: Baker Academic, 2005), 114.

28. Darrell Bock posits, "[T]his passage shows that there was a real external event," rather than just a mere vision. See his *Acts*, Baker Exegetical Commentary on the New Testament (Grand Rapids: Baker Academic, 2007), 716-17. Also, see F. F. Bruce, *The Book of the Acts: New London Commentary on the New Testament* (London: Marshall, Morgan & Scott, 1977), 491.

29. See Kim Seyoon, *The Origin of Paul's Gospel* (Tübingen: Mohr, 1984).

UNLEASHING THE DYNAMIC POWER OF CHRIST JESUS'S TEACHINGS IN THE GREAT COMMISSION

As previously discussed, those who engage in Christian world mission should have a strong conviction in the finality of Christ Jesus. Thus, the contours of missiology in global perspectives should not restrict themselves to a discussion of contextual theology *per se*, but to *modus operandi* as well. Che Bin Tan refers to cross-cultural situations in which people "read and understand the Bible from their own cultural perspective and can therefore misunderstand and distort its message."[30] He further elaborates the differences in epistemology according to cultural context, arguing that in China, "philosophical thinking never begins with epistemology or ontology, for the Chinese mind-set is not interested in abstract but in concrete."[31] Although the circumstances vary from region to region, one point remains constant: cultural context is key.

Doing mission and presenting the gospel should take a serious account not only of local cultural and religious environments but their educational, political, and economic strata as well. How do missionaries present the gospel cross-culturally? These aforementioned factors demand a nonuniform theological propositional approach in presenting the gospel. This understanding will enhance and deepen the sense of necessity of contextualization praxis.

Generally, majority-world people are interested in knowing if they will receive dynamic power and strength to live in a world full of challenges. Will new faith in Christ Jesus help them experience dynamic hope, love, and peace that they have not experienced before (1 Cor. 13:13; John 14:27)?[32] Proclaiming the gospel means to bring people into the awareness of Jesus's promise: "I have come that they may have life, and have it to the full" (John 10:10). It is his intent that people who believe in him should obtain the fullness of life.

Before his ascension, the Lord Jesus gave all of his followers the Great Commission, which crossed the temporal divide of past, present, and future until his second coming. "Then Jesus came to them and said: 'All authority in heaven and on earth has been given to me. Therefore go and make disciples of all nations, baptizing them in the name of the Father and of the Son and of the Holy Spirit, and teaching them to obey everything that I have commanded you. And surely I am with you always, to the very end of the age'" (Matt. 28:18-20).

CONCLUSION

In conclusion, let me suggest three key points to our Christological discussion. First, Christ said that the Father vested all authority in heaven and on earth in

---

30. Che Bin Tan, "Constructing a Theology of Mission for the Chinese Church," in *The Good News of the Kingdom: Mission Theology for the Third Millenium*, ed. Charles Van Engen, Dean S. Gilliland, and Paul Pierson (Maryknoll, NY: Orbis Books, 1993), 228.

31. Ibid., 231.

32. See Charles Van Engen, "The Relationship of Bible and Mission in Mission Theology," in *The Good News of the Kingdom*, 253-63.

him. Therefore, Christians should realize that they have been empowered with Christ's authority to go and make disciples of all nations with a spirit of humility and love. They shall present the gospel and bear witness for Christ Jesus in every culture and in every region of the world with power and confidence. In simpler terms, they shall do mission and evangelism with power. The opposite of this is a lack of confidence, which occurs when one fails to put one's trust in Christ Jesus, in whom God has vested full authority. Jesus commissioned his followers to make disciples of all nations in love and in humility. It is almost certain that a lack of conviction in doing mission was the dominant reason for the decline of enthusiasm in mainline Protestant churches in their world missions, and the decline of their church membership.[33]

Second, baptism in the name of the Father, the Son, and the Holy Spirit in the first-century context was an anathema for Jewish people. Did not the Jewish leaders condemn Jesus to death because of his claim to be God? Thus, a willing reception of baptism in the name of the triune God in the first-century context was equivalent to signing a "covenant of death." Either a person believed totally in Christ Jesus or they did not. This is the radical challenge of the Great Commission that Christians have long overlooked.

Finally, what does Jesus mean when he asked his followers to do "all things he had commanded them?" Is what he had "commanded them" equivalent to all things he had taught them? A study of Christology should revisit Jesus's sayings in the Gospel accounts, as they form the core of the apostolic teachings. He assures all of his believers that in carrying the Great Commission he will be with them until the end of the earth. Therefore, an understanding of the importance of Christology is especially pressing for churches and all believers who are yearning to engage the nations in world missions. Let us carry out the Great Commission with joy!

---

33. See Rodney Stark, *The Triumph of Christianity* (New York: HarperCollins, 2011), 410-11; Michael Gryboski, "PC USA Decline in Churches and Members Continued in 2013," *Christian Post*, June 2, 2014.

Chapter 3

Mission Theology in the City:
Sowing Urban Seeds of Shalom

Stephen E. Burris

I first met Charles E. Van Engen in 1993. He was the Associate Professor of Theology of Mission and Latin American Studies, and I was the In-Service Director at the Fuller School of World Mission. We worked closely on his Biblical Foundations of Mission course to prepare it for online education. That experience fed my already keen desire to see more theological work in mission studies, even as the School of World Mission was transitioning from a church-growth model to a more holistic model in missions. It is also worth noting that our honoree has spent the majority of his life attempting to put together a solid theological foundation for the practice of mission. It is no accident that much of the documentation for this essay comes from him. Far too often, we placed strategic priority on pragmatism and then later, if at all, have tried to find biblical evidence supporting current and on-going practice.[1] This has been especially true in urban mission.[2] Charles Van Engen has been a strong voice advocating the priority of working out urban theology, in the context of ministry, that then informs our practice and from an interdisciplinary perspective. Chuck has continually called us back to the text of Scripture as our base for mission practice.

---

1. For a short overview of recent scholarship in this area, see Charles E. Van Engen, "Foreword," in Shawn Redford, *Missiological Hermeneutics: Biblical Interpretation for the Global Church*, American Society of Missiology Monograph Series 11 (Eugene, OR: Pickwick Publications, 2012), xi-xvii. Van Engen sets the stage when he writes, "Intuitively, we might think it obvious that one of the most basic aspects of mission theology would have to do with the relation of the Bible to mission theory and practice. Sadly, such is not the case"(xi).

2. Van Engen observes that "urban churches continue to struggle to find how to be viable missional communities of faith in the city," urging that we "search for a theology of mission that will give us new eyes for perceiving our city, inform our activism, guide our networking, and energize our hope for the transformation of our city." See Charles E. Van Engen, *Mission on the Way: Issues in Mission Theology* (Grand Rapids: Baker Books, 1996), 93, 94.

Van Engen further developed Kingdom Missiology,[3] or what Arthur F. Glasser, George Eldon Ladd, and Geoffrey W. Bromiley have called Kingdom-of-God theology for missiology; Van Engen called it a missiology of transformation.[4] This essay will focus on a missiology of transformation as an appropriate mission theology in the city. Any mission theology must take seriously *the word, the context, and the faith community* if it is to be effective and biblical.[5] It must also be dynamic and relational. This tripartite approach to urban mission is central to any kingdom missiology that seeks to transform lives and communities.[6]

As we consider the subtitle of this current book, *Engaging the Nations*, we must stress that the nations have migrated to the cities of the world. The unreached-peoples paradigm has given way to the urban paradigm of the twenty-first century. Timothy Keller has said, "We believe ministry in the center of the global cities is the highest priority for the church in the twenty-first century."[7] Each paradigm builds on the previous experiences and the urban focus is no different.[8] Therefore, a mission theology in the city must include lessons we have learned from the past that are applicable for the present and future that we develop in specific contexts. Stephen B. Bevans states, "Theology is only *theology* when it begins to make sense to particular people at particular times and in particular places."[9]

---

3. Van Engen specifically calls this a "Trinitarian kingdom-oriented missiology" and states, "a covenantal/kingdom mission theology would take seriously the role of refugees, women, the poor, the marginalized, the weak, and the foolish in understanding a biblical hermeneutic of the Church's participation in God's mission." See Charles E. Van Engen, "Preface," in *The Good News of the Kingdom: Mission Theology for the Third Millennium,* ed. Charles Van Engen, Dean S. Gilliland, and Paul Pierson (Maryknoll, NY: Orbis Books, 1993), xiii, 258.

4. Charles E. Van Engen, "Toward a Missiology of Transformation," in *Transformation: A Unifying Vision of the Church's Mission,* ed. Luis K. Bush; 2005 Forum for World Evangelization (Thailand, September 2004), 96-106. "The phrase *spiritual transformation* reflects our desire to help people love God with all of their mind, heart, soul, and strength. We use the phrase *societal transformation* to refer to the work of helping people learn to love their neighbors as themselves (Matt. 22:37-9)." See Eric Swanson and Sam Williams, *To Transform a City: Whole Church, Whole Gospel, Whole City* (Grand Rapids: Zondervan, 2010), 44.

5. Van Engen refers to this as the tripartite nature of theology in "Constructing a Theology of Mission for the City," in Charles Van Engen and Jude Tiersma, *God So Loves the City: Seeking a Theology for Urban Mission* (Monrovia, CA: MARC, 1994), 249-55.

6. Harvie Conn called this a trialogue in Harvie Conn and Manuel Ortiz, *Urban Ministry: The Kingdom, The City and the People of God* (Downers Grove, IL: IVP Academic, 2001).

7. Timothy Keller, *Center Church: Doing Balanced, Gospel-Centered Ministry in Your City* (Grand Rapids: Zondervan, 2012), 21.

8. "We speak of a paradigm shift because we now know that in its construction a new paradigm will always draw from prior knowledge as well as create new perspectives and understanding. The shift involves continuity with past knowledge while it also offers new insight that is discontinuous with the known. This is also the case with our understanding of God's mission and the construction of missiology as a discipline." See Charles Van Engen, "Preface," in *Paradigm Shifts in Christian Witness: Insights from Anthropology, Communication, and Spiritual Power,* ed. Charles E. Van Engen, Darrell L. Whiteman, and J. Dudley Woodberry (Maryknoll, NY: Orbis Books, 2008), xv.

9. Stephen B. Bevans, *An Introduction to Theology in Global Perspective* (Maryknoll, NY: Orbis Books, 2011), 25. He goes on to state that there is "no such thing as a kind of generic theology" (52). Cf. Stephen B. Bevans and Roger P. Schroeder. *Constants in Context: A Theology of Mission for Today* (Maryknoll, NY: Orbis Books, 2004).

The place of the city in God's plan of redemption has become increasingly clearer. As has been well documented by others,[10] the city has played a major role throughout history. I have selected four snapshots that represent God's concern for the city, its people, and its future. This will provide a foundation upon which to draw some conclusions regarding a mission theology in the city. Van Engen provides the thesis statement for this essay. "Like a sponge is permeated with water, so our mission is to offer new life to the women and men of our world of the twenty-first century in which all of their life, every aspect of life, all arenas of life are permeated with the presence of God the Father, Son and Holy Spirit. And the rich and powerful of this world need to be transformed; they need to be converted, just as much as the poor and the weak."[11]

BABYLONIAN CAPTIVITY

Jeremiah 29:4-11 gives amazing instructions to those in exile and captivity. They are to see the time in Babylon as an opportunity to have families, build houses, plant gardens, and give sons and daughters in marriage, and other regular and normal functions of life in the city. Jeremiah 29:7 is a perspective changer, "But seek the welfare (*shalom*) of the city where I have sent you into exile, and pray to the Lord on its behalf, for in its welfare you will find your welfare."[12] This is not just about captivity and exile any longer, or those hauled off to Babylon against their will enduring whatever the captors have in store for them. Rather, God has sent them to this specific place for a purpose. They are to seek the welfare of the city, and as the city prospers, so will the exiles; indeed, God has plans for their welfare, which includes a future and a hope.[13] Jeremiah instructs the exiles to see this time as an opportunity to seek goodness (*shalom*) in the city of their captors. *Shalom* may already be present in some form. Our first task may be to find where God is already at work—despite conditions that

---

10. Cf. Ray Bakke, *A Theology as Big as the City* (Downers Grove, IL: IVP Academic, 1997); Robert C. Linthicum, *City of God, City of Satan: A Biblical Theology of the Urban Church* (Grand Rapids: Zondervan, 1991); Conn and Ortiz, *Urban Ministry*; Keller, *Center Church*; Sean Benesh, *View from the Urban Loft: Developing a Theological Framework for Understanding the City* (Eugene, OR: Resource Publications, 2011); and Roger Greenway, *Discipling the City: A Comprehensive Approach to Urban Mission* (Grand Rapids: Baker Book House, 1992).

11. Van Engen, "Toward a Missiology of Transformation," 103.

12. All Scripture references are from the NRSV version of the Bible.

13. Van Engen calls this a missiology of hope when he writes, "First, a missiology of hope means that Christians care, and care so deeply that they will risk hoping for the new. . . . Secondly, a missiology of hope means that Christians dare to believe that together they can change the world. . . . God's reign comes when people accept Jesus as Lord—and in obedience begin to see God's will being done 'on earth as it is in heaven' (Matt 6:10). This involves structural and societal change as well as personal transformation. It involves the whole person, not only the spiritual aspects. It involves all of life, not only the ecclesiastical. . . . This missiology of hope is deeply and creatively transformational, for it seeks to be a sign of the present and coming Kingdom of God." See Charles Van Engen, "Faith, Love, and Hope: A Theology of Mission on-the-Way," in *The Good News of the Kingdom: Mission Theology for the Third Millennium*, ed. Charles Van Engen, Dean S. Gilliland, and Paul Pierson (Maryknoll, NY: Orbis Books, 1993), 260-61.

seem to suggest otherwise, as though God has forsaken the city. Often our job is to connect with God where *shalom* is evident; this window into the mission theology for the city is still just as relevant today. Although many of our cities appear to be forsaken, Robert Linthicum clearly suggests that God is present even though it looks like the city belongs to Satan.[14]

In the West, especially in North America, "white flight" refers to people who moved to the suburbs to escape the city. Most people who had choices moved to the suburbs, and so did the church. In time, they vilified the city and failed to recognize the presence of *shalom*. All the necessary goods and services were close by in the shopping malls and strip malls that sprang up. Today that has expanded to include online shopping with front-door delivery. As a result, the privileged abandoned the church and people in the city. Christians did not see the city as a place where God was present or where God had placed them and therefore saw little need to seek the welfare of the city. Israel forgot Jeremiah's call almost entirely. The suburbs seemed safer, the schools better, and they could live with their own kind of people. In far too many cases, the churches left behind were weak or they closed, unable to meet the growing needs of those who lived in the city.[15] Hope was lost. "What hope is there for communities that have lost their way, their way of life, their coherence, their *hope*?"[16]

This view of the city is dramatically different from the picture Jeremiah paints. Jeremiah makes two clear points. First, seek the welfare of the city. Make it your home, live there, have families, and plant gardens. Second, the captives (God's covenant people) are where God put them and where God wants them for the next seventy years. These two points are missing in much of the strategizing that goes on in churches today. The focus is mostly inward and benefits those who are already attending "our" church. We need a paradigm shift for the churches in the suburbs to take appropriate action in the city of which they are now a distant part. David J. Bosch said it this way, "The church's first missionary responsibility is not to change the world, but to change herself."[17] This analysis is important as we look to the future with its increasing urbanization.

---

14. Cf. Linthicum, *City of God, City of Satan*.

15. Van Engen states, "Either churches in the city recreate themselves into modified social agencies responding to the inner city poor's 'inadequacies' by 'doing for' them, but seldom empowering them, or they become fortresses primarily interested in their own survival. . . . They also too seldom see themselves as agents of God's kingdom for the city's holistic transformation through the proactive empowerment of marginalized persons in the city." See Van Engen, *God So Loves the City*, 273.

16. N. T. Wright, *Surprised by Hope: Rethinking Heaven, the Resurrection, and the Mission of the Church* (New York: HarperOne, 2008), 5.

17. It is worth noting that there is evidence that some churches are "reverse migrating" back to the city. These courageous churches are selling their buildings in the suburbs, and moving to a location in the city whether it is a storefront, a house, a lodge, or some other location. They have elected to go into an often difficult and hostile environment to be salt and light, leaven, mustard seed, and *shalom* to the city.

"THE NAZARETH MANIFESTO"

Luke 4:16-21 reflects the calling of the church. Jesus's first public statement focuses on the poor, captives, blind, oppressed, prisoners, and even alludes to the year of jubilee.[18] When John the Baptist wanted confirmation that Jesus was the Messiah in Matthew 11:3-5, he asks, "Are you the one who is to come, or are we to wait for another?" Jesus answers, "Go and tell John what you hear and see: the blind receive their sight, the lame walk, the lepers are cleansed, the deaf hear, the dead are raised, and the poor have good news brought to them." This is especially significant today with over a billion people in our world living in desperate conditions, where sex trafficking is a multibillion dollar business, and it is estimated that there are over 30 million slaves—60,000 in the United States,[19] where medical care, clean water, adequate housing, and other basic human rights are lacking or inadequate. Jesus shows that his ministry, in addition to the call to "seek and to save the lost" (Luke 19:10), includes the oppressed, exploited, and otherwise marginalized people. This must be central to a mission theology in the city because "the coming of the Kingdom is to provide a tangible manifestation of God's attitude toward poverty and injustice. His people will grapple with the injustice that brings exploitation and poverty and will be particularly concerned to help the poor and suffering. It is on this basis that the poor can rejoice."[20]

The absurd dichotomy between "social action" and "evangelism" neglects solid theological reflection and proper exegesis of what Jesus taught, the apostles modeled, and the first-century church practiced. It was not then and it cannot be now.[21] Luke reveals Jesus's ministry with healing, exorcizing evil spirits, raising the dead, and feeding the hungry. The "kingdom" parables show a tangible theme of the kingdom of God in the "not-yet" form now, and in the final and complete form at the *parousia*.

Van Engen puts this in the context of Jesus as prophet, priest, and king as he sums up the holistic mission of Christ and therefore the church.

At the very least, its *prophetic role* involves the Church in calling for and working toward justice, toward shalom, toward righteousness and peace in human relationships and in social structures. The church's *priestly role* must, by the same token, involve its sacramental presence, its call for

---

18. Jesus's quote from Isaiah concludes with the "year of the Lord's favor" (4:21).

19. Max Fisher, "This map shows where the world's 30 million slaves live. There are 60,000 in the U.S." See *Washington Post* (October 17, 2013), accessed online.

20. Arthur F. Glasser, with Charles E. Van Engen, Dean S. Gilliland, and Shawn B. Redford, *Announcing the Kingdom: The Story of God's Mission in the Bible* (Grand Rapids: Baker Academic, 2003), 216.

21. "The Greek words *sōzō* and *sōtēria* were used interchangeably in the New Testament for healing, yet are almost always translated "salvation," in which spiritual salvation was strongly assumed. Influenced by this false dichotomy, translators made a choice, which worked to cement it for some. These words are not limited to spiritual salvation, but also mean salvation from economic oppression, psychological oppression, as well as physical and social healing." See Stephen E. Burris and Kendi Howells Douglas, *River of God: An Introduction to World Mission* (Eugene, OR: Wipf & Stock, 2012), 1.

reconciliation of people with God, each other, and themselves (2 Cor. 5), and an offering of the redemption found in Jesus Christ to all who will come. The Church's *kingly role* calls the Church to take seriously its role in nation building, in bringing harmony to chaos, in calling for government, which cares for its people, and in organizing itself for the proclamation of the gospel of freedom and grace in Jesus Christ.[22]

We thus need to reexamine our priorities, programs, giving, staffing, and the use of our ministry opportunities to get in step with Jesus and his mission statement in Luke 4:16-21.

TO THE LEAST OF THESE

Jesus also talks about the sheep and the goats in Matthew 25:31-46. He directly ties doing good to "the least of these" as doing it to him. The hungry, the thirsty, the stranger, the sick, the naked, and the prisoner—the least of these: "As servants they are judged by what they did or did not do for those in their world who were obviously in need."[23] There is not any evidence whatsoever that this basis of judgment has changed over the past twenty centuries. The basis for the division between the sheep and the goats is the person's compassionate response to the needs of helping the poor, feeding the hungry, giving the thirsty something to drink, welcoming strangers, giving clothes to the naked, taking care of the sick, and visiting prisoners. Perhaps it is time to revisit and rethink the significant passage from Ezekiel 16:48-9: "As I live, says the Lord God, your sister Sodom and her daughters have not done as you and your daughters have done. This was the guilt of your sister Sodom: she and her daughters had pride, excess of food, and prosperous ease, but did not aid the poor and needy." These sobering words should speak loudly to a Western church that continues to consume at inordinate and unsustainable levels while sisters and brothers in the majority world and in cities all over the world lack the basic sustenance of life.[24]

SOWING SEEDS OF *SHALOM*

People use the parable of the sower, Matthew 13:1-23 (also Mark 4:1-20; Luke 8:4-15), in some curious and creative ways. Some in the missions' community justify targeting the more "receptive" mission fields, usually listed as receptive homogeneous units, which later became known as unreached peoples, and to keep a lighter missionary presence in the more "resistant" fields. Van Engen noticed this when he wrote,

---

22. Charles Van Engen, *God's Missionary People: Rethinking the Purpose of the Local Church* (Grand Rapids: Baker Book House, 1991), 124.

23. Ibid., 95.

24. Cf. Ash Barker, *Slum Life Rising: How to Enflesh Hope within a New Urban World* (Melbourne: UNOH Publications, 2012).

The parable speaks of the fact that Jesus presented his message *to everyone alike*, but that some were willing to hear and others were not. The difference in soils may have something to tell us about receptivity. But if this is so, it will *not* tell us to concentrate on the good soil. That may be good farming but it is totally extraneous to the text of the parable. . . . In other words, if something is crystal clear about this parable, it is the *indiscriminate* sowing of the seed, not the selective proclamation of the Gospel. But there are four other very important lessons that I believe Jesus wanted the disciples to learn. First, the farmer sows indiscriminately, *in spite of knowing that the responses will vary*. The farmer understands his field, and he knows (in fact expects) differences in response. Secondly, the response of the seed is not to the sower, but rather consists in growing, developing, and giving fruit—it is response to the Word, to the Kingdom, and to God. Thirdly, notice in Jesus' explanation of the parable (Matt. 13:19-23), there are a variety of agents that create heightened resistance in addition to the conditions of the field. . . . Fourth, there is a background to this parable that deals with God's *providence*.[25]

Jesus used this basic agricultural illustration to show that sowing seeds is essential business of the kingdom, regardless of the outcome of the sowing or even the field planted. Paul taught us that God gives the increase—our job is to sow seeds (1 Cor. 3:5-6). While the world is more urban than rural—and the rate of increase in urban population is accelerating—Jesus was using an agricultural example to show that the priority of sowing seeds remains. As our fields have changed from agrarian to urban, we may need to modify or discard sowing methods that worked well in rural areas as we encounter the intricacies of the city. Seeds of *shalom* are scattered all over the city, including its slums, favelas, shanty towns, squalor communities, and squatter neighborhoods. Each seed of *shalom* is planted, grows, and has an impact even as light dispels darkness, salt preserves meat, and yeast leavens bread. Therefore, Christians sow seeds and encourage transformation in the city. This incarnational expression may take on many forms and activities. We start where people are hurting and we foster reconciliation and hope. Yet, one principle is discernible—we sow seeds of *shalom* and seek the welfare of the city wherever God has called us to serve.

Our mission theology in the city must incorporate sowing seeds of *shalom*. This most primary of human interactions, at the foundation of Jewish society in the Old Testament and Jesus's teaching on the kingdom of God in the New Testament, is imperative in our world today. *Shalom* brings wholeness, justice, restoration, reconciliation, and peace into relationships and structures corrupted by sin, and affects the lives of people. *Shalom* is required now more than ever. This is why Jeremiah instructs captives in Babylon to "seek the welfare of the

---

25. Charles Van Engen, "Reflecting Theologically about the Resistant." A paper presented to the Evangelical Missiological Society, San Francisco, CA, November 20, 1997; subsequently published in J. Dudley Woodberry, ed., *Reaching the Resistant: Barriers and Bridges to Mission* (Pasadena, CA: William Carey Library, 1998), 23-24.

city." In spite of the reality that their own city had been devastated, plundered, ransacked, burned, and left in ruins as they watched, God instructs the new slaves to seek the good of the city, home of their captors, and their home for the next seventy years. Can we do less? This is the golden rule in action, and our rapidly changing world urgently needs what we have to offer in the name of Jesus.

CONCLUSION

A mission theology of the city should encompass these four "snapshots" as we contemplate ministry in the urban centers of the world. First, as aliens and foreigners we are to seek the *shalom* of those we have the opportunity to serve. Our ultimate goal is transformation and reconciliation. The local context will arbitrate the urgent needs that the church must provide first. Second, by helping the poor, captives, blind, and oppressed we reflect the ministry of Jesus as he defined it in Luke 4. A careful study of Luke's Gospel will show the types of activities Jesus involved himself in as he went about establishing the kingdom of God on earth. We should pay close attention to those same activities as we exegete the city where God has called us to serve. Third, "the least of these" includes those specifically mentioned in Luke 4, but also appears to include everyone left that is not specifically in that list, thereby focusing on all who are oppressed, exploited, enslaved, hungry, sick, poor, orphaned, widowed, and in prison. We live in a messy world that sin has corrupted. The world desperately needs the people of God working to make a difference. Fourth, as the sower sows, so we sow seeds of *shalom* whenever and wherever we have opportunity. As sowers, we should not preselect those who appear to be the most receptive, but, rather, we are the signposts of the kingdom of God and we bring that kingdom to life in a world that seriously needs life and hope.

To borrow from Van Engen: as we move further into the twenty-first century, we need a kingdom missiology of transformation and reconciliation that emanates from a deeply personal, biblical, and corporate *faith* in Jesus Christ (the king), is lived out in the body of Christ as an ecumenical fellowship of love (the central locus of Christ's reign), and offers *hope* for the total transformation of God's world (as a sign of the present in-breaking of the coming kingdom of God).[26] So where do we start? I include here the astute insight of Christopher J. H. Wright as pointing the way:

Where do we start? The language of the "priority of evangelism" implies that the only proper starting point must always be evangelistic proclamation. Priority means it is the most important, most urgent, the thing to be done first, and everything else must take second, third or fourth place. But the difficulty with this is that (1) it is not always possible or desirable in the immediate situation, and (2) it does not even reflect

---

26. Van Engen, "Faith, Love, and Hope," 253–54.

the actual practice of Jesus. . . . But ultimately we must not rest content until we have included within our own missional response the wholeness of God's missional response to the human predicament—and that of course includes the good news of Christ, the cross and resurrection, the forgiveness of sin, the gift of eternal life that is offered to men and women through our Witness to the gospel and the hope of God's new creation. Mission may not always begin with evangelism. But mission that does not ultimately include declaring the Word and the name of Christ, the call to repentance, and faith, and obedience has not completed its task. It is defective mission, not holistic mission."[27]

The context will tell us the most imperative or ultimate need. Our task, in partnership with the Holy Spirit, is to seek the good among those whom we serve. We may build bridges of love by giving a cup of cold water in Jesus's name, feeding the hungry, giving clothes to the naked, securing medical treatment for the sick, helping the dying to do so with dignity, and all the while being the hands and feet of Jesus that extend his kingdom on earth. Kingdom missiology includes transformation and reconciliation—of people and societies. Transformation and reconciliation is the goal of a mission theology in the city.

Transformation takes place one person and one community at a time. It begins with an individual and moves through communities much like yeast leavens bread. This is what Jesus says the kingdom is, yeast, a mustard seed, small yet powerful, subversive at times, but with enough potential to take over a garden or a loaf of bread, a kitchen, a house, a neighborhood, a community, a city, even a world. It is the renewing of the mind at the street level. Rather than viewing the enormous need that exists in the world today, it is far better to start by bringing *shalom* into the community that is immediately available to us. In that ministry context we can work toward a world made right, a world where all individuals and institutions, families and people, regardless of their social standing, as well as the whole creation, are joined together leading to the praise of the Lamb, who alone is worthy of our praise, and makes all things new.[28]

27. Christopher J. H. Wright, *The Mission of God: Unlocking the Bible's Grand Narrative* (Downers Grove, IL: IVP Academic, 2006), 318-19.
28. Burris and Howells Douglas, *River of God*, 13.

Part 2

Mission Theology and Church Beliefs

Chapter 4

Missionary Ecclesiology: Evangelical, Ecumenical, and Catholic Developments in "Engaging the Nations"

Stephen B. Bevans, S.V.D., and
Roger P. Schroeder, S.V.D.

At the end of his article "Church" in the *Evangelical Dictionary of World Missions*, Charles Van Engen quotes from Lesslie Newbigin's classic work on the church, *The Household of God*. Newbigin writes: "Just as we must insist that a church which has ceased to be a mission has lost the essential character of a church, so we must also say that a mission which is not at the same time truly a church is not a true expression of the divine apostolate. An unchurchly mission is as much a monstrosity as an unmissionary church."[1]

In many ways, these lines by perhaps the most influential thinker on mission in the twentieth century encapsulate Chuck Van Engen's work in the area of missionary or missional ecclesiology in the last three and a half decades. It is true, as the saying goes, that "the church doesn't have a mission; the mission has a church." Mission, as Wilbert R. Shenk has pointed out so ably, "must precede the church."[2] Nevertheless, the mission has a *church*. As we have expressed it in our own writings, the church is a community-in-mission.[3] In this same way, Chuck's lifelong work has been an effort to balance both communion and mission in ecclesiological reflection. To cite the title of his early but defining work in this regard, the church is *God's Missionary People*.[4]

---

1. Lesslie Newbigin, *The Household of God* (New York: Friendship Press, 1954), 169.

2. Wilbert R. Shenk, *Changing Frontiers of Mission,* American Society of Missiology Series (Maryknoll, NY: Orbis Books, 1995), 7.

3. Stephen B. Bevans and Roger P. Schroeder, *Prophetic Dialogue: Reflections on Christian Mission Today* (Maryknoll, NY: Orbis Books, 2011), 26.

4. Charles Van Engen, *God's Missionary People: Rethinking the Purpose of the Local Church* (Grand Rapids: Baker Academic, 1991).

In this chapter on missionary ecclesiology, we will survey the work of theologians, and not official church documents, as valuable as they are. First, we will survey Chuck's missionary ecclesiology in the context of several other Evangelical and Protestant efforts of missiological thinking about the church's engagement with the nations. Second, we will survey the slowly emerging missionary ecclesiology in our own Roman Catholic tradition and add a constructive step of sketching out a future project of one of us (Bevans) to write a full-blown Catholic missionary ecclesiology.

A note on the terminology "missionary" and "missional": in general, the first term is the one we prefer as Roman Catholics. "Missional" seems to be preferred in Protestant and Evangelical circles, possibly to avoid the negative connotations that the terms "mission" and "missionary" have for many members of these churches, especially in the "mainline" (Presbyterian, Lutheran, Methodist) traditions.

EVANGELICAL/PROTESTANT
MISSIONARY/MISSIONAL ECCLESIOLOGY

While Australian Catholic ecclesiologist Richard Lennan has recently characterized missionary/missional ecclesiology as a "growing body of ecclesio-logical literature,"[5] that body is already quite considerable. Already in 1998, the bibliography published at the end of the landmark book *Missional Church* cited twenty-five works under the heading of "Missional Theologies of the Church," including classic works by Karl Barth, David Bosch, Johannes Hoekendijk, and Lesslie Newbigin.[6] Protestants, evangelicals, or Anglicans wrote or edited all of these works. Searching for "missional church" today on Google yields about one million items, so this survey can hardly do full justice to the topic. We can focus, however, on several significant works, and prominent among them will be Chuck Van Engen's contribution.

God's Missionary People

Chuck's *God's Missionary People*, published in 1991, is the oldest of several ecclesiologies we will survey. It is a very systematic work, based on a discussion of how Christians must intertwine "church" and "mission" in thinking and action. The missionary vision of the church is rooted in Willingen's 1952 affirmation that "there is no participation in Christ without participation in His mission to the world."[7] Such participation, however, is not general. It can only be manifest in a concrete local community of Christians. Chapter 3 roots the

---

5. Richard Lennan, "Book Review: *Who Is the Church? An Ecclesiology for the Twenty-First Century* (Shorter Notices)," *Theological Studies* 75 (2014): 460.

6. Darrell L. Guder, ed., *Missional Church: A Vision for the Sending of the Church in North America*, The Gospel and Our Culture Series (Grand Rapids: Eerdmans, 1998), 269-71.

7. International Missionary Council, *The Missionary Obligation of the Church* (London: Edinburgh House, 1952), 3.

church biblically with a study of the Letter to the Ephesians, and in chapter 4 Chuck makes one of the most important moves in the book: reinterpreting the traditional four dimensions or marks of the church, what he calls "distinctives" or "attributes," in a dynamic, missionary way. Basing this move on discussions of the four marks by theologians such as Hans Küng, Hendrikus Berkhof, Jürgen Moltmann, and Jon Sobrino, he writes, "Maybe it is time we begin to see the four words of Nicea not as adjectives, which modify a thing we know as Church, but as adverbs which describe the missionary action of the Church's essential life in the world."[8] Thus the church's mission is envisioned as working for the world's unity, as a community that lives as a sanctifying power of forgiveness and holiness, as "a bridge-building" movement of reconciliation and healing, and as a proclaiming force rooted in the apostolic witness.[9] Each of these tasks, of course, takes place in concrete, local situations.

In subsequent chapters, Chuck speaks of the "missionary intention" of the local church as being for the world, identifying with the oppressed, preaching the gospel in both word and deed, and "yearning for numerical growth."[10] The church's "purpose" is service, building a supportive and challenging community, witnessing, and proclaiming, totally focused on the kingdom or reign of God.[11] Participating in the threefold mission of Christ as priest, prophet, and king, a missionary church embodies these as healer and liberator.[12] As the church focuses on missionary service and proclamation, it recognizes that structure needs to serve the mission and not vice versa. The *whole church* is missionary, and so within this understanding the laity are recognized as more than "Santa's helpers," and ordained persons are distinguished as "those who will equip, motivate, and mobilize the members for ministry and mission."[13]

One classical element missing in the book is reflection on the major biblical images of the church, such as people of God, body of Christ, and Temple of the Spirit. These, however, Chuck describes in his article in the *Evangelical Dictionary of World Missions* as "not still photographs but rather moving pictures, dynamic videos of the church living out its witness in the world. For example, the church is the salt of the *earth*. It is the light *of the world*. As the body of Christ, it is the physical presence of Jesus *in the world*. As a holy priesthood (1 Peter 2) the church is a priest *for the Gentiles*, who see the good works of the church and glorify God."[14]

In simple and clear language, Chuck Van Engen provides a sketch of a missionary church that is biblically based and theologically rich—all in less than two hundred pages. He manages to balance the visible and invisible aspects of the church, along with its essential communal nature, which its participation

---

8. Van Engen, *God's Missionary People*, 68.

9. Ibid. See the illustration on p. 69.

10. Ibid., 73-84.

11. Ibid., chaps. 6 and 7, 87-118.

12. Ibid., 119-30.

13. Ibid., 156.

14. Charles Van Engen, "Church," in *Evangelical Dictionary of World Missions*, ed. A. Scott Morea (Grand Rapids: Baker Academic, 2000), 193.

in God's mission calls forth. Other missionary/missional ecclesiologies will develop his fundamental insights.

From Sending to Being Sent

The book that in many ways put missionary/missional ecclesiology "on the map" was *Missional Church: A Vision for the Sending of the Church in North America*, edited by Darrell L. Guder and published in 1998. Six members of the "Gospel and Our Culture Network"—Lois Barrett, Inagrace T. Dietterich, Guder, George R. Hunsberger, Alan J. Roxburgh, and Craig Van Gelder— developed the book over a number of years. The realization that the church of North America no longer exists in a culture imbued with Christianity, yet exists in a state of mission, fueled the vision of the book. This situation reveals the true nature of the church as participant in God's mission, as "its instrument and witness."[15] *Missional Church* is an effort to reflect on how the church can move "from church with mission to missional church," from understanding itself as a sending church to a church that is sent.[16]

After analyzing North American culture and the shape of the North American church, the authors locate the church in relation to the reign of God as its representative in the world. Rather than a "vendor of services" that caters to various needs of people, the determining vision of the church—even as it responds to felt needs—is one of forming itself as a community that is a "sign and foretaste" of God's design for creation.[17] The church does not "build," "establish," or "extend" God's reign, but embodies it in its countercultural lifestyle, in continuing the preaching, teaching, and healing work of Jesus and in practices of worship, reconciliation, and discernment.[18] Leadership in the missional church equips God's people for mission. The missional church finds concrete expression in the local community, but finds universality in a universal communion that is, in a reordering of the traditional four marks, "apostolic, catholic, holy, and one—or, with Van Engen, to be proclaiming, reconciling, sanctifying, and unifying."[19]

While explicit preaching is certainly part of the vision of the book, its focus, it seems to us, is much more on the witness of the church community as a people who embody the gospel in their mutual support, countercultural witness, joyful worship, and reconciling practice. The focus is not so much on what the church does as on what it is: the quality of life that it demonstrates to the world around it. *Missional Church*'s focus on North America, however, leads it to focus less on solidarity with the poor. In addition, while the Gospel and Our Culture Network made efforts to be more inclusive and intercultural, it has had limited

---

15. Guder, ed., *Missional Church*, 5.
16. Ibid., 6. The latter phrase is the title of chap. 1, 1-17.
17. Ibid., 77-109.
18. Ibid., chaps. 5 and 6, 110-82.
19. Ibid., 255, referring to Chuck Van Engen in *God's Missionary People*.

success.[20] The book, nevertheless, is a major effort of missionary/missional ecclesiology and serves as a genuine landmark in its development.

Developments of Missionary/Missional Ecclesiology

In 2000, two of the collaborators in the *Missional Church* volume, Darrell Guder and Craig Van Gelder, each published important contributions to the development of missionary/missional ecclesiology. Guder's book is entitled *The Continual Conversion of the Church*.[21] Guder develops his ecclesiology in three sections. First, he establishes that in today's post-Christendom context, the only way the church can be faithful is to open up to contemporary understandings of mission as participation in the *missio Dei*. The church can only be a missionary church. Guder then reflects on the content or message of that mission, which is the Good News of the reign of God, preached and embodied in Jesus of Nazareth. More than either Chuck's work or *Missional Church*, Guder roots the church's mission in the mission of Jesus. The book's first section ends with a proposal that "witness" "serves as an overarching definition of the church's calling."[22] Guder's second section addresses the challenge that, although the Christian message requires contextualization, it must avoid any kind of "reductionism" that would diminish the original power of the gospel. Such reductionism was already present in the earliest years of the church, as well in both the medieval reduction of Christianity to ecclesiocentrism and the Reformation's reduction of salvation to an individual reality. Particularly the latter reduction eclipsed mission. To take up the challenge posed by the reductionist tendency of the church, Guder calls in his third part for the church's continual conversion to missionary consciousness and practice. Mission needs to shape every aspect of the church, both at the local and the institutional levels, attending to the fact that "whatever is not mission is not part of the church's vocation."[23]

Van Gelder writes on the church out of a conviction that contemporary North America is a "mission field where effective ministry requires skills in cross-cultural communication."[24] Such a missionary situation, says Van Gelder, demands a "missiological ecclesiology"[25] that recognizes the church as taking its identity from the mission of the Trinity in the world.[26] Such an ecclesiology develops in three moves. First, ecclesiology focuses on the nature of the church.

20. Some effort at focusing on other cultures is seen in the more practical follow-up volume to *Missional Church*; see Lois Y. Barrett, ed., *Treasure in Clay Jars: Patterns in Missional Faithfulness*, The Gospel and Our Culture Series (Grand Rapids: Eerdmans, 2004).

21. Darrell L. Guder, *The Continuing Conversion of the Church*, Gospel and Our Culture (Grand Rapids: Eerdmans, 2000).

22. Ibid., 2.

23. Ibid., 207.

24. Richard Mouw, "Foreword" to Craig Van Gelder, *The Essence of the Church: A Community Created by the Spirit* (Grand Rapids: Baker, 2000), 7.

25. Van Gelder, *The Essence of the Church*, 31-37.

26. Ibid., 11.

The church is "a people who are created by the Spirit to live as a missionary community."[27] In a marvelous image, Van Gelder draws on his boyhood experience of growing up on a farm in Iowa to propose that the church is "God's demonstration plot." Like small fields of corn that grew along country roads to demonstrate the effectiveness of a new breed of corn, the church community demonstrates the breaking into the world of the reign of God. "Its very presence invites the world to watch, listen, examine, and consider accepting God's reign as a superior way of living."[28] This first move also includes the church's origin in Jesus's ministry of the reign of God and a discussion of the various images of the church.[29] The second move in missiological ecclesiology is to reflect on how the church "does what it is"[30]—the shape and purpose of the church's ministry, or how the church continues Jesus's kingdom ministry. Ministry serves the mission, and flows out of it.[31] In the third place, and only at this point, does the organizational structure of the church come under consideration and reflection: "The church organizes what it does."[32] Organization supports the ministry of the church.[33] The church's organization is not for its own sake, but for the sake of mission.

Like Van Gelder, Cheryl M. Peterson writes from the North American context, and argues that, rather than searching for new programs and strategies to make the church relevant, Christians need to focus on the church's identity as such.[34] Peterson examines three models or "theological accounts"[35] of the church—the church as "word-event," as communion, and as missional—and, while she sees important aspects in all three, suggests that the missional church model is the most adequate for our contemporary post-Christendom situation. She proposes a narrative method of ecclesiology that "starts with the Spirit,"[36] focusing on the Acts of the Apostles as a kind of paradigm for a community that is led and formed by the Spirit. In Acts, the Spirit is "directing [the disciples] outside of their comfort zones, pushing them to cross religious, ethnic, and social boundaries, creating *koinonia*, and proclaiming salvation to all."[37] The church participates in the mission of the Trinity, but that mission begins, as in the actual order of God's mission, with the mission of the Spirit.[38]

---

27. Ibid., 25.

28. Ibid., 100.

29. Ibid., 73-126.

30. Ibid., 37.

31. Ibid., 127-54. For further development of this chapter, see Craig Van Gelder, *The Ministry of the Missionary Church: A Community Led by the Spirit* (Grand Rapids: Baker Books, 2007).

32. Van Gelder, *The Essence of the Church*, 37.

33. Ibid., 155-84.

34. Cheryl M. Peterson, *Who Is the Church? An Ecclesiology for the Twenty-First Century* (Minneapolis: Fortress Press, 1999), 4.

35. Ibid., 37.

36. Ibid., 105.

37. Ibid., 115.

38. Ibid., 94-95.

ROMAN CATHOLIC MISSIONARY ECCLESIOLOGY

In the five decades since the close of the Second Vatican Council in 1965, advocates of missionary ecclesiology have been somewhat of a "minority voice," especially because of the emphasis on "communion ecclesiology" as the ecclesiological perspective preferred by official Vatican sources.[39] Nevertheless, one of the most important and bold statements of the Council called for a clear missionary ecclesiology: "the pilgrim church is missionary by its very nature" (*Ad gentes* 2).[40] This idea was taken up ten years later in Paul VI's powerful apostolic exhortation *Evangelii nuntiandi* when he spoke of the church as having its deepest identity in mission and evangelization, (*Evangelii nuntiandi*, 14), and John Paul II reiterated this in the encyclical *Redemptoris missio* (e.g., 1, 2, 20). Most recently, Pope Francis has described the church as a "community of missionary disciples" (*Evangelii gaudium*, 24). In the years after the Council, however, ecclesiological emphasis focused more on the communal nature of the church—itself a significant departure from the focus on institution and hierarchy that was prevalent in the late Middle Ages and after the Council of Trent in the sixteenth century. Yet, there has indeed been a "majority voice" of several Catholic missiologists and theologians. We can only highlight a few of these scholars here, but they are indeed, as Richard Lennan has written, a "growing body."[41]

Contribution to Catholic Ecclesiology

In 2008, Richard Gaillardetz published a significant contribution to Catholic ecclesiology in his book *Ecclesiology for a Global Church: A People Called and Sent.*[42] Gaillardetz acknowledges the priority of mission in the formation of the church community. As he puts it, "Today's ecclesiologists tend to reject the view that Jesus first instituted a church and then gave it a mission. It is biblically and theologically more accurate to say that Jesus established a mission in the world, a mission in service of God's reign, and then called forth a community of disciples for the fulfillment of that mission."[43] Nevertheless, the subtitle and arrangement of his chapters still point somewhat to the traditional reversal of that perspective. His first chapter deals with the church as a people called to community. Only in his second chapter does he speak of this people as sent on mission.

---

39. See in particular "Letter to the Bishops of the Catholic Church on Some Aspects of the Church as Communion," Congregation for the Doctrine of the Faith (CDF).

40. See Richard R. Gaillardetz, "Francis: Pope of the Council," in *Elephants in the Living Room* (December 6, 2013), 3. Accessed from http://www.elephantsinthelivingroom.org.

41. Lennan, "Book Review," 460. For more detail on this "growing body," see Stephen B. Bevans, "Mission as the Nature of the Church in Roman Catholic Contexts," in *Called to Unity: For the Sake of Mission*, ed. John Gibaut and Knud Jorgensen (Eugene, OR: Wipf & Stock, 2015), 128-40.

42. Richard R. Gaillardetz, *Ecclesiology for a Global Church: A People Called and Sent* (Maryknoll, NY: Orbis Books, 2008).

43. Ibid., 166.

The contribution of his work to missionary ecclesiology, however, lies in another dimension of the book: its consciously global perspective. Gaillardetz deals specifically with mission under the rubric of the mark of "catholicity," open to both intercultural and interreligious dialogue with a particular focus on the Asian church.[44] Gaillardetz images the unity of the church in terms of a communion of local churches, exemplified in the emergence of basic ecclesial communities and imaged in turn in Africa as an extended family.[45] He discusses ministry through a reflection on both the African and the Latin American contexts, and makes a proposal for a "theology of ministry for a global church."[46] Gaillardetz develops the church's holiness in view of Latin American liberation theology, and investigates apostolicity in terms of the persistence of apostolic memory—illustrated by a basic ecclesial community in Chiapas, Mexico.[47] Gaillardetz characterizes episcopal and papal authority as a "ministry of memory," and gives examples of this ministry in such persons as Bishop Raymond Lucker of New Ulm, Minnesota, in the United States, and Bishop Samuel Ruiz of Chiapas, Mexico.[48]

While he acknowledges that his book is but "an initial and necessarily tentative venture toward a fully global ecclesiology,"[49] Gaillardetz has made an extremely important contribution. He concludes the book by sketching three particular areas that need development in such an ecclesiology: the significance, particularly in terms of cultural identity, of the local church; the need for greater diversity in ministerial structures; and the need for interreligious dialogue to shape the churches self-understanding and mission.[50] Gaillardetz takes ecclesiology into the twenty-first century.

In 2014, Australian theologian Neil Ormerod published his immensely important *Re-Visioning the Church*.[51] There is no way a short summary can do justice to Ormerod's complex thinking, deeply influenced by contemporary sociology and the thought of Bernard Lonergan and Lonergan's student Robert Doran. What follows is a very scanty summary of Ormerod's ecclesiology.

For Ormerod, ecclesiology is a kind of working out of the basic Catholic dynamic of nature and grace (in contrast, as he says, to the Protestant dynamic of sin and grace)[52] in the context of a faith community. The church, as Vatican II insisted, is both visible and invisible, human and divine (*Lumen gentium*, 8). Because of this, construction of an adequate ecclesiological reflection needs

---

44. Ibid., 68-80.

45. Ibid., 117-30.

46. Ibid., 154-71.

47. Ibid., 190-96 and 243-47.

48. Ibid., 278-81.

49. Ibid., 290.

50. Ibid., 291-94.

51. Neil Ormerod, *Re-Visioning the Church: An Experiment in Systematic-Historical Ecclesiology* (Minneapolis: Fortress Press, 2014).

52. Ormerod, *Re-Visioning the Church*, 52, 94-95, 114-15, 57. The grace/nature distinction, Ormerod says, follows Thomas Aquinas, whereas the grace/sin distinction is more consonant with the thought of Augustine.

to employ the social sciences.[53] As sociology and theology work together, the identity of the church emerges as the community that offers a healing vision and practice of grace that aims to alleviate and eventually overcome the forces of evil in society and in itself as well. In this way, the church's mission uncovers its identity or, in other words, its commitment to live and act in accordance with the Christian symbol of the reign of God.[54]

Ormerod sketches this understanding of the church in five theses. First, the church is the historical prolongation of Jesus's mission, which is, as thesis two articulates, the "advancement" of the reign of God. Third, Jesus advances the reign of God through "redemptive suffering, which overcomes evil through self-sacrificing love." In the fourth place, the church's mission advances the reign of God through its own practice of self-sacrificing love, a practice (thesis five) empowered by the love of the Holy Spirit that is poured into Christians' hearts. Ormerod states that implied in all five theses is that Christians love sacrifically since they participate in the very mission of the trinitarian God. "Just as the missions of the Son and the Spirit are prolongations of the processions of the Son and Spirit from the Father into the created order, so too the Church is the prolongation of the missions of the Son and Spirit into an unfolding human history."[55]

From this basic missionary stance Ormerod goes on to develop a theology of authority in the church, and then to investigate how the church's advancement of God's reign has taken place—or not—in the concrete history of the church. His is a major, systematic understanding of missionary ecclesiology in the Catholic tradition, the very latest in the "growing body of ecclesiological literature."

CONSTANTS IN CONTEXT

Although they are not ecclesiologies *per se*, Stephen Bevans and Roger Schroeder's works *Constants in Context* and *Prophetic Dialogue* are missiological works steeped in missionary ecclesiology.[56] The first lines of *Constants in Context*, for example, emphasize, "One of the most important things Christians need to know about the church is that *the church* is not of ultimate importance." Rather, we go on to say, "the point of the church is . . . to point beyond itself, to be a community that preaches, serves and witnesses to the reign of God," continuing the work of Jesus in the power of the Spirit.[57] Ecclesiology constitutes one of the six "constants" that mission embodies in concrete contexts, and we definitely favor the understanding of the church implied in "Type C" theology, one rooted in history and commitment to liberation.[58] The book concludes with

---

53. Ibid., 9-12, 31-32.
54. Ibid., 84.
55. All the quotations in this paragraph appear in Ormerod, *Re-Visioning the Church*, 103-13.
56. Stephen B. Bevans and Roger P. Schroeder, *Constants in Context: A Theology of Mission for Today* (Maryknoll, NY: Orbis Books, 2004); Bevans and Schroeder, *Prophetic Dialogue*.
57. Bevans and Schroeder, *Constants in Context*, 7.
58. Ibid., 65-67.

the following words: "Only by preaching, serving, and witnessing to the reign of God in bold and humble prophetic dialogue will the missionary church be constant in today's context."[59] The subsequent volume, *Prophetic Dialogue,* develops such "prophetic dialogue" more fully. A chapter anchors the book in which we trace the origins of the church to the pervading presence and mission of the Holy Spirit, which was made concrete in the person of Jesus of Nazareth and led Jesus's followers in becoming more open to the Spirit's boundary-breaking promptings toward inclusion of the Gentiles.[60]

One of us (Bevans) is planning to write a book on his missionary ecclesiology, which will be an "unpacking" of the lapidary phrase in Vatican II's Decree on Mission Activity: "the pilgrim church is missionary by its very nature" and the discharging of Pope Francis's call for a "community of missionary disciples" (*Evangelii gaudium*, 24). This ecclesiology emphasizes various aspects of the image of the church as "community-in-mission."

A first part of the ecclesiology reflects on "The Essence of the Church: A Community-in-*Mission*." The church is rooted in the overflowing life of the Trinity, which is itself a community-in-mission. God's first act of mission is creation.[61] Then, God breathes life into "earth creature" (Gen. 2:7) and anoints prophets to proclaim healing and justice (Isa. 61:1-2). The foundation of the church begins with the mission and ministry of Jesus, which was, in the words of Neil Ormerod, the advancement of the reign of God—the continuation of God's saving work from the beginning, but now imminent. After Jesus's death and resurrection, the disciples came to the amazing realization that the Spirit lavished upon Jesus, God now lavished upon them. Their mission was Jesus's mission and the church was born—born of crossing boundaries, born of mission. The church continues Jesus's mission in a trinitarian practice of "prophetic dialogue," boldly yet humbly witnessing to the gospel with which God entrusted it.[62]

A second part probes "The Mystery of the Church: A *Community*-in-Mission." The church is not simply a visible, fallible society. It is, in its deepest core, a society "imbued with the presence of God," a communion of "people made one with the unity of the Father, Son, and Holy Spirit" (*Lumen gentium*, 4). First, Bevans will describe the church in terms of three scripturally based images: the people of God, the body of Christ, and the Creation/Temple of the Holy Spirit. Second, Bevans will sketch the "dimensions" or "marks" of the church as dynamic "distinctives" (in Chuck Van Engen's words) of the church's

59. Ibid., 398.

60. Bevans and Schroeder, *Prophetic Dialogue,* 9-18.

61. See Bevans and Schroeder, *Prophetic Dialogue*, 9-18. See also Stephen B. Bevans, "Missiology as Practical Theology: Understanding and Embodying Mission as Trinitarian Practice," in *Invitation to Practical Theology: Catholic Voices and Visions,* ed. Claire E. Wolfteich (Mahwah, NJ: Paulist Press, 2014).

62. See Stephen B. Bevans, "Missiology as Prophetic Dialogue," Presentation given at the Religious Formation Conformation, Transformation of Religious Life: An Action Oriented Initiative (April–May 2012); Bevans and Schroeder, *Prophetic Dialogue*; David J. Bosch, *Transforming Mission: Paradigm Shifts in Theology of Mission* (Maryknoll, NY: Orbis Books, 1991), 489.

mission. Part two evidences, in sum, that "communion and mission enrich each other" (*Instrumentum laboris*, 36).

A third and final part outlines "The Structure of the Church: A Community of *Disciples-in-Mission*." Primarily, there is a "structure" of fundamental equality in virtue of Baptism. We are disciples—missionary disciples (*Lumen gentium*, 32; *Evangelii gaudium*, 24).[63] Rather than a sharp distinction between "laity" and "clergy," a missionary ecclesiology would focus on the various ways that Christian women and men share in the one mission of the church in its witness, service, and proclamation of the reign of God.[64] There does exist in the church a certain order that is not so much hierarchical as ministerial. The Petrine ministry of the pope is to oversee the entire church as it engages in its mission of witness, service, and proclamation of the reign of God. In the end, the church's design serves its participation in the mission of God.

CONCLUSION

This chapter endeavored to survey some of the "growing body of ecclesiological literature" that recognizes the priority of the church's mission for an understanding of the church. Chuck Van Engen recognized this several decades ago, and his influence has been great in this regard—certainly in our own ecclesiological and missiological work. Our hope is that such missionary/ missional focus will continue to contribute to the ecclesiological enterprise. The perspective from which one speaks of the church matters. In today's postmodern and postcolonial world, we believe that a church that recognizes its essential missionary nature, and organizes itself accordingly, is the most adequate way to do ecclesiology today. The church is indeed God's missionary people, "engaging the nations."

---

63. See Kathleen A. Cahalan, *Introducing the Practice of Ministry* (Collegeville, MN: Liturgical Press, 2010), 24-47.

64. See the reflections of Richard R. Gaillardetz in *The Church in the Making: Lumen Gentium, Christus Dominus, Orientalium Ecclesiarum* (Mahwah, NJ: Paulist Press, 2006), 52-55; see also Edward P. Hahnenberg, *Theology for Ministry: An Introduction for Lay Ministers* (Collegeville, MN: Liturgical Press, 2014), 107-27.

Chapter 5

Missionary Theology: Roland Allen and Vincent Donovan Rediscovered

J. Andrew Kirk

It is now just over 100 years since Roland Allen wrote one of the most noteworthy books on mission of the twentieth century.[1] Likewise, Vincent Donovan wrote a work nearly seventy years later out of his experiences in bringing the Christian message to the Masai of East Africa that has become just as significant.[2] I believe that these volumes are both still required reading in many missiology courses. Wherein lies the perennial fascination of these two authors?

Three years after ordination Allen was a missionary in northern China. After a few years, he returned to England due to ill health. Then, after only three years in charge of a parish, he resigned; his conscience would not allow him to "extend the sacraments of the Church to those who gave no evidence of faith."[3] He spent the rest of his life, first in England and later in Kenya, traveling and writing books, articles, and letters. He died in Nairobi in 1947. He maintained a passionate obsession for two interrelated aspects of the church's mission—its spontaneous expansion and the conditions that either encouraged or obstructed it.[4]

Donovan, an American Spiritan Catholic missionary, lived for a number of years in Tanzania sharing the gospel with the Masai people. His book, *Christianity Rediscovered*, was first published in 1978; its popularity is evident in the three editions and several reprints. He was writing at a time characterized by

---

1. Roland Allen, *Missionary Methods: St. Paul's or Ours: A Study of the Church in the Four Provinces* (Mansfield Centre, CT: Martino Publishing, 2011; orig. ed., 1912).

2. Vincent J. Donovan, *Christianity Rediscovered: An Epistle from the Masai* (London: SCM Press, 2001).

3. David M. Paton, *Reform of the Ministry: A Study in the Work of Roland Allen* (London: Lutterworth Press, 1968), 18.

4. See Roland Allen, *The Spontaneous Expansion of the Church and the Causes Which Hinder It* (London: World Dominion Press, 1927); David M. Paton and Charles H. Long, eds., *The Ministry of the Spirit: Selected Writings of Roland Allen* (Grand Rapids: Eerdmans, 1983).

Lamin Sanneh as a time of transition from the Christianity of a post-Christian West to a post-Western Christianity.[5]

Both Allen and Donovan, each in his own respective context, aimed to conduct a thorough reappraisal of settled missionary practice, attempting to throw off the accumulated baggage of the classical missionary approach and return to the essentials. Donovan, influenced by the writings of Allen, noted:

> [Allen's] suggestion that we could, with profit, look to the apostolic missionary method as an enlightenment and corrective to our own method was like an open door to me. Going through that door was the first step to limitless possibilities. . . . The main and general insights and questions of this remarkable man are as valid today as they were when they first stunned and disturbed the church of his day.[6]

Both men came to realize that the missionary methods used to establish Christian communities cross-culturally did not produce truly indigenous churches. Instead of churches able to maintain themselves and expand wholly with the local resources available, they had become almost completely dependent on support from abroad.

Allen became convinced that the meaning of indigenous, when applied to a local church, did not have to do so much with the incorporation of culturally and socially appropriate practices into its life as to becoming self-sustaining, self-governing, and self-extending. Missionary methods at the time of his writing were making such an aspiration impossible. Allen studied in-depth the way in which St. Paul went about the task of forming Christian communities across Asia Minor and Greece in the first century. He concluded that Paul's methods contradicted those of the modern missionary movement. This raises the question for the study and practice of mission, and the conclusions we should draw from the comparison.

Although the two authors spoke frequently about practical details concerning organization, finance, structures, enterprises, and other matters, they did so from an informed set of theological principles.[7] In this article, I wish to engage with the incipient missionary theology that is either articulated or implied in their writings. The purpose is not to return to two fascinating pieces of remote mission history with anecdotal interest in the twenty-first century, but to attempt to rediscover the missionary theology that guided them, and to engage with it critically, exploring its relevance. Donovan wrote,

> A parish priest in the United States remarked that even though *Christianity Rediscovered* was written in an African context, out of African experience,

---

5. Lamin Sanneh, "Preface to the Third Edition," in Donovan, *Christianity Rediscovered*, ix.

6. Donovan, *Christianity Rediscovered*, 27.

7. See David M. Paton, "Roland Allen: A Biographical and Theological Essay," in *Reform of the Ministry* (Cambridge: Lutterworth Press, 1968), 13-45; J. D. Payne, *Roland Allen: Pioneer of Spontaneous Expansion* (self-published), 7-8.

it was clear to him that the book was really written about the church in Europe and America. I was gratified it was that clear. I had hoped that readers would realize it. But more than that, I had hoped they would be able to take that basic thought, and apply it to the church in America and elsewhere in a way that I could never do; that somehow the same principles must apply to the church everywhere.[8]

THE STARTING POINT

Allen and Donovan attempted to reach behind the accumulation of traditions concerning cross-cultural missionary work to first principles. In seeking to communicate the meaning of the life of Jesus to tribes-people on the savannahs of East Africa, Donovan had to decide what message was essential to transmit. He talks about needing to rediscover what he calls "the naked gospel," and "what Karl Rahner describes theologically as 'the final and fundamental substance of the Christian message.'"[9] We might interpret this to mean the nonnegotiable core of the apostolic preaching of Jesus Christ, the absence of which would turn the Christian faith into some other kind of religious philosophy. Therefore, Donovan claims that his missionary work began with "no convictions beyond the one that Christianity is something of value" (to the whole world). Traditional ways of presenting God, Christ, salvation, discipleship, the church, sacraments, liturgy, and the priesthood would have to be reconsidered. They are part of the value that Christianity offers the world, yet not necessarily in the way that pioneer missionaries have offered them.

In a letter to his bishop, Donovan bemoans the present strategy of mission work among the Masai, for it had produced little or nothing in the way of solid, mature, growing Christian communities among the people. What holds back the real evangelistic work is the belief that indigenous people join church life through social projects, particularly through the provision of schools:

> I suddenly feel the urgent need to cast aside all theories and discussion, all efforts at strategy—and simply go to these people and do the work among them for which I came to Africa. I would propose cutting myself off from the schools and the hospital . . . and just go and talk to them about God and the Christian message . . . to go to people to do nothing but to talk to them about Christ.[10]

He found Allen's writings persuasive in rediscovering a fresh approach to mission:

> [Allen's] insights and questions challenged most of the missionary theories I had ever heard. . . . In any action taken in the name of the church today,

---

8. Donovan, "Preface," xvii.
9. Ibid., xix-xx.
10. Donovan, *Christianity Rediscovered*, 13-14.

one of the key criteria to measure the fitness of what is being done is the Bible. Is it biblical? Is it evangelical? Is it scriptural are questions that must be asked time and again?[11]

The remainder of Donovan's book is a description of how he sought to apply these perceptions to the task of sharing the gospel with a people largely resistant to the then-current missionary methods.

Allen's preoccupations were rather different, though in many points complementary to those that concerned Donovan. He began with the assumption that at the heart of mission was the "desire to see the multiplication of disciples, leaders, and churches across the globe."[12] This could happen, he believed, only by the church's own spontaneous expansion:

> The expansion which follows the exhorted and unorganized activity of individual members of the Church explaining to others the Gospel which they have found for themselves. . . . I mean also the expansion of the Church by the addition of new Churches.[13]

There were two main reasons why he believed that this proposal was the chief end of mission engagement. First, believers in the truth of Jesus Christ became recipients of the Spirit of Jesus. The Spirit, by nature, is missionary:

> The very heart and life of his message was that the mission of the Church is the work of the Spirit. . . . There is a summons to everyone who will hear to submit inherited patterns of Church life to the searching scrutiny of the Spirit.[14]

Allen believed that even if God had not given the Great Commission, the first Christians would still have taken the gospel to the nations:

> For the obligation depends not upon the letter, but upon the Spirit of Christ; not upon what He orders, but upon who He is, and the Spirit of Christ is the Spirit of Divine love and compassion and desire for souls astray from God.[15]

Second, the outcome of the missionary work of the apostle Paul made it plausible to believe that similar methods had the best chance of bringing similar results. Hence, Allen laid the foundations of his missionary theology by reengaging with Paul's implicit strategy during his various missionary journeys. It appears, then, that Allen began with missionary praxis and deduced his missionary theory from what he discovered from his historical investigations.

---

11. Ibid., 27.
12. Allen, *The Spontaneous Expansion*, 6.
13. Ibid., 7.
14. Lesslie Newbigin, "Foreword," in Allen, *The Spontaneous Expansion*, iii.
15. Roland Allen, *Essential Missionary Principles* (New York: Flemming H. Revell, 1913), 67.

A CRITIQUE OF EXISTING MISSIONARY PRACTICES

Allen felt a huge disparity between Paul's way of working and that of the mission endeavor of his time, a discrepancy that was not justified by a more sophisticated missionary theory or by changing circumstances since the first century. The accepted way of doing mission work among non-Christian populations in Africa, Asia, and the Pacific region at the end of the nineteenth century was to send as many missionaries from the West as could be recruited and financed to finish the task of "occupying" the whole "non-Christian world" with the gospel. This mission philosophy completed "the unfinished task" "in this generation"—to use some of the slogans made popular at the World Missionary Conference (Edinburgh 1910).[16]

Expectations for missionaries included the massive amount of resources for the purchase of "land on which to build houses and churches and schools." This, says Allen, is "our modern practice in founding a Church."[17] Founded with accouterments and finery, the mission station created suspicion among indigenous peoples that foreign Christians were willing to install exotic customs and strange institutions as surrogates of actual military conquest and political domination.

Further, the creation of educational and health establishments meant that staff had to be appointed and paid from overseas to service them. The missionaries also recruited some of the first Christians in their districts as hired helpers to do the work of teaching and evangelism, giving the impression that only professional, paid staff could advance the cause of Christian faith.[18] Before people could be trusted with leadership roles in the newly formed congregations, and before they could be relied on not to teach heresy, or allow substandard moral practices to prevail, they had to have a long period of training, often in a remote institution. This method of proceeding—having all the right systems in place—meant that there was often a long gap between the first evangelization and the second phase.[19] Due to a lack of ordained ministers, the people were deprived of the sacraments, theological education was decontextualized, natural leaders in the community were silenced, and divinely gifted teachers inhibited.[20]

This catalogue of errors in missionary work may seem to us either grossly exaggerated or long since corrected. Perhaps, it is surprising, therefore, to hear Donovan reiterating some of the same critiques from his experience seventy years later:

> The goal envisaged was not to be mission compounds or mission stations in every section. But Christian communities in every section. *Missions*

---

16. See J. Andrew Kirk, "All the Non-Christian World: Church, Mission and the Edinburgh 1910 Conference," in *The Church and the World: Understanding the Relevance of Mission* (Milton Keynes, UK: Paternoster, 2014), 150-74.

17. Allen, *Missionary Methods*, 74-75.

18. Ibid., 112.

19. Allen, *The Spontaneous Expansion*, 21-24.

20. Allen, *Missionary Methods*, 140-42.

belong to the missionaries. Christian communities belong to the people; indeed, they are the people. I had seen this choke law at work in the parts of Africa where I had been assigned, with the Christians taking up all the time of the missionaries . . . and other untouched tribes being left to some . . . indefinite plan of evangelization one hundred years from now. What these people were suggesting was that the church which sent me should have insured that its bishop . . . (declared) that they were . . . a fully-fledged, Eucharistic Christian community. There is no other area of church life comparable to it (present-day priesthood) in having parted from biblical norms in the establishment of present-day practice.[21]

All these diverse practices inhibited the spontaneous expansion of the church by refusing to entrust to the local churches full responsibility for their continuing life and growth.

PAUL'S MISSIONARY METHODS

While much has been written about Paul's evangelistic methods, for my purpose, I can concentrate only on the bare bones as it affects the arguments put forward by Allen and Donovan for a radically reconstructed approach to mission. Paul founded churches within months, if not weeks; within ten years he had established churches throughout the four provinces of Asia, Galatia, Macedonia, and Achaia.[22] In 57 CE, Paul spoke as if his work was finished, allowing him to plan a visit to the western end of the Mediterranean.

Crucial to Allen's and Donovan's vision is the fact that once Paul had appointed elders and handed on the apostolic tradition (Rom. 6:17), the churches were left to look after their own life. They were totally responsible for managing their own affairs: extending knowledge of Jesus Christ to the surrounding areas, administering the sacraments of baptism and the Lord's Supper, and raising their own finances. From the very beginning, the churches were organized to be able to reproduce themselves as mature churches. Paul addressed his letters to the Gentile churches in the following way: "To the church of God in Corinth"; "To the churches in Galatia"; "To the church of the Thessalonians." They had the same status as "the churches of God in Judea."

Having appointed elders in all the churches he planted, there is no evidence that Paul ever returned to ordain more. From that moment on, these leaders were responsible for appointing further leaders in newly established churches, admitting people to membership of the *ekklesia tou Theou* through baptism, and celebrating the thanksgiving meal in the local Christian communities. Paul,

---

21. Donovan, *Christianity Rediscovered*, 32, 80, 99-100, 120.

22. Henry Whitehead states, "In about six months he had founded the Church, taught the converts the necessary elements of the faith, ordained a ministry and made provision for the administration of the sacraments. Then St Paul passes on elsewhere, and the Church is left to grow in the power of the Holy Spirit" ("Introduction," in Allen, *Missionary Methods*, viii).

meanwhile, left the churches as soon as a solid core of believers was established, and moved on to a new area of work. Thus, once the church was formed, and the work of evangelization finished, Paul handed over the church to the local leaders.

APPLICATION

Theological Method

Both Donovan and Allen believed in the necessity of theological reflection originating from experience. Donovan wrote,

> I was to learn that any theology or theory that makes no reference to previous missionary experience . . . is a dead and useless thing. . . . If a theology did emerge from my work, it would have to be a theology growing out of the life and experience of the pagan peoples of the savannahs of East Africa.[23]

Similarly Allen wrote,

> As the complement of experience, doctrine renews its youth from age to age; but divorced from experience it is nothing more than the statement of an intellectual theory. . . . Doctrine, accepted either as an intellectual satisfaction, or as an authoritative pronouncement, divorced from experience, has no power in itself.[24]

Nevertheless, they were both strongly convinced that experience required review by the standard of apostolic teaching given once-for-all in the literature of the New Testament. The missionary methods that Allen advocated arose out of his reading of Paul's understanding of the way of Christ, the activity of the Spirit, and the nature of the church and its ministry. That is why he turned from the contemporary patterns of missionary organization of his time to the approach adopted by Paul. That is why he drew theological conclusions from his discovery of Paul's methods. By his own confession, Donovan noted his influence from Allen.[25] Although neither man engaged specifically with the complexities of the relationship between gospel and culture, they were mindful of the need to allow the gospel to flourish within the specific circumstances of the evangelized. Donovan expressed himself in this way:

> The way that people might celebrate the central truths of Christianity; the way they would distribute the goods of the earth and live out their daily lives; their spiritual, ascetical expression of Christianity, if they should

---

23. Donovan, *Christianity Rediscovered*, 22.
24. Allen, *The Spontaneous Expansion*, 51.
25. Donovan, *Christianity Rediscovered*, 27.

accept it; their way of working out the Christian responsibility of the social implications of the gospel—all these things . . . would be *a cultural response to a central, unchanging, supracultural, uninterpreted gospel.*[26]

In spite of Donovan's emphasis that new converts should work out the implications of salvation for themselves, he insisted that certain customs had to be reformed. Thus, he challenged the Masai to leave behind their tribal concept of God, the one who loved them yet hated their enemies; who loved the rich, yet hated the poor; who loved the good people, yet hated the evil ones:

> There is no God like that. There is only the God who loves us no matter how good or evil we are, the God you have worshipped without really knowing him, the truly unknown God—the High God.[27]

Equally, Donovan castigated many Western Christians for their belief in the tribal "God" of Western civilization and the "American Dream." The church had become more like Mars and Venus (the gods of war and sensuality) than the "[one] Father, from whom every family in heaven and on earth takes its name (Eph. 3:14-15)."

Intriguingly, Allen interpreted the indigenous nature of local churches in ways quite distinct from those emphasized in more recent mission thinking. Though he was not particularly interested in how the Christian faith could interact with the thought forms, customs, and symbols of local cultures, and social arrangements; he was, however, passionate about local churches becoming self-supporting, self-governing, and self-propagating. The one true mark of an indigenous church was that the resident converts should believe in the power of the Spirit of Jesus who is freely given to all who through faith enter the sphere of God's grace, and should apply that gospel locally. This should underpin their whole missionary theology. Furthermore, indigenous leaders should believe in the power of the *Holy* Spirit to teach new converts the truth of Jesus (Eph. 4:17-21), causing them to refrain from laying down strict ethical codes of practice. Allen emphasized the importance of the leadership reflecting underlying principles of moral behavior, drawing examples from Paul's letters (especially 1 Corinthians), rather than imposing standards of conduct from the sending churches.[28]

Fascinated that the Masai language lacks a future tense, Donovan linked that to the obvious lack of any "expectant future in their community." Through theological reflection he concluded that because only in the Jewish and Christian faith does "a Messianic hope first break upon mankind . . . I doubt if it is possible for any pagan culture to take part in true human development."[29]

---

26. Ibid., 25 (emphasis added).
27. Ibid., 36.
28. See Allen, *The Spontaneous Expansion*, 60-75 ("The Christian Standard of Morals").
29. Donovan, *Christianity Rediscovered*, 39.

Missionary Methods

In the final chapter of his book, Donovan attempts a definition of missionary work. It is that work "undertaken by a *gospel oriented community of transcultural vision, with a special mandate, charism, and responsibility of spreading and carrying that gospel to the nations of the world, with a view to establishing the church of Christ.*"[30] For Donovan, the gospel is a supracultural, unchanging message of Good News destined for all cultures. He gives a list of essential prerequisites of a pioneering Christian approach to the people of any culture: to enable the believers to expand the gospel into a creed and way of life after baptism, to enable them to pray as Christians, and to leave them the Bible, so that they can use it as a living letter in their lives. Donovan also insisted that the local church engage in future mission work involved with the wider church and world in unity, charity, and justice. He encouraged missionaries to teach the local believers that their reception of baptism is the acceptance of a total responsibility for mission, trust in the Spirit given at baptism, and use the power and gifts given to the community by the Spirit. The final step, "and the most important lesson we will ever teach them—is to leave them."[31]

For Allen, the crucial test of successful pioneer missionary work is to leave behind an independent church—by definition, one not dependent on a steady flow of second-generation missionaries from overseas, on local full-time workers paid from outside, or one burdened with the upkeep of institutions established by missionaries. Above all, an independent, local church has resources, as the body of Christ, to foster the life of the Spirit within the community, and further the work of God's mission.

Allen's greatest campaign was to persuade bishops to ordain elders from among the first converts of the local church; then the church would be able to administer the gospel sacraments of baptism and the Eucharist without having to call on the services of ministers from outside the community. He even recommended that local churches give authorization to ordain elders themselves without the necessity of a long period of formal training in special establishments remote from the local scene.

Nevertheless, in spite of this general principle of local clergy for local churches, Allen did allow for a financially supported itinerant ministry. He recognized that just as those appointed as presbyters in local churches were not expected to exercise their ministry full-time, paid for by the congregation, so there was a band of specially chosen apostolic collaborators. For instance, Timothy, Titus, Luke, Silvanus (Silas), Epaphras, and Apollos traveled between the churches.[32] Their task was to maintain the links between the different communities, building unity, and offering resources for problems that arose among those following

---

30. Ibid., 158 (emphasis original).

31. Ibid., 133.

32. Eckhard Schnabel affirms, "Of the approximately one hundred names that are connected with Paul . . . thirty-eight are co-workers of the apostle," in *Paul the Missionary* (Downers Grove, IL: InterVarsity, 2008), 249; and nearly 20 percent were women (ibid., 251).

Christ from a pagan background.[33] We are unaware of how these early apostolic collaborators received financial support. Whether, for example, like Paul, they were self-employed, having a trade while on their journeys, or whether they received provision from the churches where they ministered, or by the churches in which they became Christians. Paul accepted financial help from the church in Philippi (Phil. 4:15-19), yet not from the church in Corinth (1 Cor. 9:18; 2 Cor. 11:7-9). He did enunciate the principle, however, that "those who preach the gospel should receive their living from the gospel" (1 Cor. 9:14). This precept appeared to apply to the itinerant missionaries alone (1 Cor. 9:5).

Missionary Theology

What can we deduce from Paul's missionary practice that illuminates his missionary theology? Was the practice wholly circumstantial, dependent on the incidental nature of the earliest missionary enterprises, or does it flow from Paul's theological understanding of the nature of evangelism and the church, which was its outcome? Allen and Donovan believed that the latter was the case. For both of them (Donovan following Allen), the church is, by definition, a body of those indwelt by the Spirit of Christ who are fully equipped to continue the work of evangelism in their locality.

This implies that making known the message about Jesus, Savior and Lord, to the non-Christian world was the supreme missionary task undertaken by Christ's apostles and their converts. The fruit of this enterprise was a body of believers in Jesus, chosen, redeemed, sealed with the Holy Spirit to "the praise of his [God the Father] glorious grace" (Eph. 1:3-14). Contrary to the majority of mission theology over the last sixty years, the church is central to the purposes of God. This is the unmistakable burden of the letter to the Ephesians. The church is the Body and Bride of Christ, and the Temple of the Holy Spirit. The goal of mission is that all ethnic, social, cultural, and gender barriers are eliminated—communities of the kingdom where God dwells by his Spirit (Eph. 2:22). Communities of faith should continually grow in love, until they attain the whole measure of the fullness of Christ (Eph. 4:12-16), without stain or wrinkle of any other blemish, holy and blameless (Eph. 5:27).

If this is truly the supreme task of the church, to reproduce itself as a living agent of the Spirit of Jesus in the world, to the praise of God and the healing of the nations, two fundamental theological questions arise. First, what is the essence of the church? Second, can evangelism and church planting encompass the whole missionary calling of the people of God? Allen (and Donovan), I believe, have given their answer to the first question:

In the New Testament I find . . . the church at Antioch, the church of the Thessalonians, the church which is at Corinth, the church in somebody's house. I read of the churches in Galatia, the churches of Asia, the churches of Judea. These "churches" were local groups of Christians fully equipped

---

33. See Paton, *Reform of the Ministry*, 37.

with ministers and sacraments . . . self-supporting, self-governing, and self-extending.[34]

In light of the passages quoted from Ephesians, and in accordance with his own views, Allen might have mentioned a fourth self, namely, self-equipping. The local church has been given the full list of the gifts of grace so that it may carry out its missionary calling with all the resources it requires (1 Cor. 12 and Eph. 4).

This account of the church raises important issues for the contemporary church. There are, for example, major questions about the unity of the church in the light of countless separate denominations, and maintaining a purity of doctrine and practice within and between churches. These are questions already raised in the Pauline mission. Allen and Donovan have sought to respond to them by laying emphasis on the responsibility of the local church to attend to its own affairs by listening to what the Spirit is saying to the churches through prophetic utterance, and the written word of God. The itinerant ministers also have a role in maintaining "the unity of the Spirit in the bond of peace" (Eph. 4:3).

With regard to the second question, the answer is also complex. In a chapter entitled "Civilization and Enlightenment," Allen reflects on the social dimension of Christian mission. He appears to be quite skeptical about the amount of effort given to creating, developing, and sustaining institutions for the improvement of the physical and educational circumstances of poor and oppressed people. There were a number of reasons for this attitude. First, he was afraid that the indigenous culture would see social reform as a paternalistic and authoritarian attempt on the part of foreigners to impose their version of civilization on a population that did not understand what they were doing. In addition, he was concerned that a disproportionate emphasis on education would detract from the energy needed to establish new churches. He believed that neither education nor social reform ever produced any lasting conversion to Christ. This understanding is also a constant refrain in Donovan's assessment of mission work in East Africa.

With this argument, Roland Allen introduced a theological note that has been subsequently debated. That is, belief in Christ is the one thing needed. Out of that conviction, health, enlightenment, and reform will grow in due time. If intellectual, moral, and social advance receive primary consideration, before the acceptance of Christ, then faith in Christ is not the foundation. Missionaries should teach people to seek first the kingdom of God and its righteousness, and not Western enlightenment. Only in Christ, Allen asserted, is the promise of progress, not in our intellectual life or moral and social doctrines. The cause of all progress is spiritual renewal by the Spirit of Christ. Otherwise, we are only treating the secondary causes of problems. He concluded that Paul rejected any means of propagating faith that would distract people from a Christian belief founded in the power of God.

---

34. Allen, *The Spontaneous Expansion*, 28.

Allen did consider, though, that Christian ideals and their consequent social conditions were possible for non-Christians, apart from Christ. Yet, non-Christians cannot create Christian social progress. The danger inherent in Christian social action, divorced from its explicit roots in the gospel of Jesus Christ, is to build on another foundation.[35] Thus, Allen was inherently suspicious of the "social gospel":

> He [Allen] perceived that those who were keenest on the institutional work of the church—schools, colleges, hospitals—were not infrequently those who had doubts about the evangelistic work of the Church, either on grounds of theological liberal Protestantism, or because they doubted if the Church would ever get anywhere in its struggle with the massive force of ancient religious systems like Hinduism.[36]

Allen's attitude to what today we would call "integral mission" arose from his own experience. The warnings are still relevant, though his theological judgment may be deemed too narrow. He has not paid enough attention, for instance, to the way in which the Christian faith, acting as salt and light throughout societies and cultures, has changed the landscape.

CONCLUSION

Working in all kinds of ways for a greater measure of justice and peace is not alien to the work of evangelization, but a consistent manifestation of it. In light of the spread of local churches throughout the world, able to take on responsibility both for church planting and engagement in issues of justice, the original question raised by Allen and Donovan remains: what is the nature of pioneer, cross-cultural missionary vocation? Their writings still offer significant insight, even in the changed world of the twenty-first century.

---

35. Ibid., 79-94.
36. Paton, *Reform of the Ministry*, 43-44.

Chapter 6

Mission Theology and the Nature of God

J. N. J. (Klippies) Kritzinger

Experience in both mission and missiology has taught us that nobody stands at a universal "Archimedes point" from which the whole world can be moved. Context and culture shape all our insights. My experiences as a white South African Christian, a missiology lecturer at the University of South Africa, and an ordained minister in the Uniting Reformed Church in Southern Africa shape my approach. My doctoral studies on South African black theology[1] and my ministry experience in an African Reformed church have made me acutely aware of the challenges that racism, sexism, ethnocentrism, and xenophobia present to the church. It is from this vantage point that I think and write.

MISSION THEOLOGY: A DIMENSION OF MISSION PERFORMANCE

In this essay I use the term "mission theology" in the way that Charles Van Engen explained it: a discipline that asks "deeper questions" about mission, its main concerns being "the basic presuppositions and underlying principles which determine, from the standpoint of the Christian faith, the motives, message, methods, strategy, and goals of the Christian world mission."[2] For me these "basic presuppositions and underlying principles" of mission practice that constitute mission theology are mainly exegetical and systematic theological reflection that include context analysis, theology, strategy, and spirituality. These interact continuously in the exercise of mission by a Christian community.

Knowing God is a transformative experience, leading to conversion, commitment, and action. It is not interesting or abstract information, which leaves people's lives untouched. God's self-revealing acts in history draw people

---

1. J. N. J. Kritzinger, "Black Theology: Challenge to Mission" (D.Th. diss., University of South Africa, 1988).

2. Charles E. Van Engen, *Mission on the Way: Issues in Mission Theology* (Grand Rapids: Baker, 1996), 17-18.

into a living relationship with God, creating a faith community called to praise God and to live a life of witness that embodies God's will for society. Truth needs *action*, not merely belief or confession, in harmony with an African philosophy: "Truth is simultaneously participatory and interactive. It is active, continual, and discerning perception leading to action."[3] To know God is to represent God on earth, embody God's compassion and justice, and, in particular, to defend and protect the weak and vulnerable. The life of a Christian community should therefore be a faithful and impactful *performance* of the Christian message in a particular context.

KNOWING GOD

In my title, the phrase "the nature of God" also needs explanation. Theological reflection on the nature of God needs to clarify its methods and sources. The approach that I adopt is critical realism, which charts a way between naïve realism and constructivism. In other words, there is a reality in our communication with God, and it is not just a projection of our imagination. Yet, there is not a one-to-one correspondence between the living God and our statements about God. Critical realism admits (epistemologically) the inherent inadequacy of all human knowledge of God, while affirming that it does convey truthful information to mediate an authentic relationship with God.

Again, as our theology of mission stems from the nature of God, we must first recognize the means through which we understand the nature of God. Six key dimensions of this epistemology that inform this chapter follow: (1) This approach is relational as we receive and celebrate truth with others. (2) Knowledge of God is a matter of spiritual discernment and is guided and corrected by the Spirit. (3) We are able to find truth through the imagination as well as the rational mind. (4) An understanding of God is provisional and eschatological. (5) This approach is acutely aware of power relations, and factors of culture, gender, race, and economic class. Lastly, (6) God is never an *object* of human knowledge, yet is always the God of mystery. This epistemology requires humility since the adjective "critical" in critical realism does not refer to criticizing but criticizable: always open to criticism and correction.

SOURCES OF KNOWING GOD

The *Belgic Confession* speaks of two "books" as the means through which God is known. That is, "the creation, preservation, and government of the universe," and God's "holy and divine Word."[4] In a mission theology, the first

---

3. Mogobe B. Ramose, *African Philosophy Through* Ubuntu (Harare: Mond Books, 2002), 50.

4. Christian Reformed Church in North America, *Belgic Confession: Service Book, Part Six* (Grand Rapids: Board of Publications of the Christian Reformed Church in North America, 1983), VI-4.

of these books "in which all creatures, great and small, are as letters to make us ponder the invisible things of God: his eternal power and his divinity"[5] is particularly pertinent. The reason is due to the affirmation of God's "general revelation" to all people, which is a key deterrent against forms of mission that claim to bring God to people for the first time. We need to affirm that God has "not left himself without a witness" (Acts 14:17), and respect all cultures, religions, and worldviews. The *Belgic Confession* adds, however, that God "makes himself known to us more openly" through the Bible, making it the most important source of knowing God and of developing a mission theology.

Since bitter experiences in South Africa have shown how the Bible can be abused for the purpose of an oppressive ideology, it is necessary to adopt a hermeneutic of suspicion, always asking out of which practices a particular interpretation emerges, and what "performance" of the Christian faith it engenders. At the same time, we need a hermeneutic of trust toward the message of Scripture as the book of the church, and toward colleagues who (together with us) are trying to discern God's guidance from it for mission today. We need to listen particularly to previously silenced and excluded voices, to foster a global conversation of contextual interpretations.[6] This hermeneutic celebrates the variety of biblical metaphors and stories, as well as the plurality of interpretations of Scripture, to foster an intercultural "hermeneutic of coherence" that embraces contextual performances of Scripture across the world.[7]

THE NATURE OF GOD

The nature of God's engagement with the world shapes the performance of Christian mission in fundamental ways. The chapter will now focus on the mission of the triune God as creator, redeemer, and perfector, by first exploring the meaning of a triune interpretation of mission.[8]

How does a trinitarian understanding of God shape Christian mission? The Second Vatican Council states:

> The Church on earth is by its very nature missionary since, according to the plan of the Father, it has its origin in the mission of the Son and the Holy Spirit. The plan flows from "fountain-like love," the love of God the

---

5. Ibid.

6. Kirsteen Kim, "Missiology as Global Conversation of (Contextual) Theologies," *Mission Studies* 23, no. 3 (2004): 349-65.

7. James V. Brownson, "Speaking the Truth in Love: Elements of a Missional Hermeneutic," in *The Church Between Gospel and Culture: The Emerging Mission in North America*, ed. George R. Hunsberger and Craig Van Gelder (Grand Rapids: Eerdmans, 1996), 239.

8. Karl Barth (1928) used these three perspectives (*Gesichtspunkte*) to structure his Tambach lecture of 1919 on "the Christian in Society": *regnum naturae, regnum gratiae* and *regnum gloriae*. See K. Barth, "The Christian's Place in Society," in *The Word of God and The Word of Man*, trans. D. Horton (London: Hodder & Stoughton, 1928), 272-327; and J. N. J. Kritzinger, "The Christian in Society: Reading Barth's Tambach Lecture (1919) in Its German Context," *Hervormde Teologiese Studies* 63, no. 4 (2007): 1663-90.

Father. As the principle without principle from whom the Son is generated, and from whom the Holy Spirit proceeds through the Son, God in his great and merciful kindness freely creates us, and moreover, graciously calls us to share in his life and glory.[9]

We call this understanding of mission—flowing out of the trinitarian life of God—*missio Dei*, and it has significant implications for mission theology.

> God invites us into the life-giving mission of the Triune God, and empowers us to bear witness to the vision of abundant life for all in the new heaven and earth. How and where do we discern God's life-giving work that enables us to participate in God's mission today?[10]

A number of features stand out. First, God's mission is about *life*: The triune God is the living and life-giving God. A denial of life is a rejection of the God of life.[11] Second, Christians need to *discern* how and where the triune God is at work in life-giving ways in society, and then *join* God in that life-giving work. This highlights the centrality of discernment, which some have called "the first act of mission."[12] It also enshrines spirituality as the "beating heart" of mission performance yet raises the question of criteria for discerning the work of the Spirit.[13] Kirsteen Kim proposes, "The Holy Spirit is not present only where there is explicit Christian confession, but where there is a likeness of Christ."[14] Thus, it is *Christ-likeness* that Christians seek to discern as they identify the work of God. Third, the notion of empowerment for witness places the spotlight on the work of the Holy Spirit as the breath of life who evokes a transformative spirituality in Christian communities.[15]

Another implication of God's trinitarian being is that God did not need to create the world:

> We are incredibly precious creatures. God created us, not because God *needed* us, but wonderfully, exhilaratingly, God created us because God *wanted* us. . . . God was, and is, pulsating love from eternity to eternity. God needed nothing; God needs nothing, outside of God, to be this pleroma; this fullness of love and fullness of being.[16]

---

9. *Ad gentes*, 2, in *Documents of Vatican II*, ed. Austin P. Flannery (Grand Rapids: Eerdmans, 1975), 814.

10. World Council of Churches, *Together Towards Life: Mission and Evangelism in Changing Landscapes* (2013), 1.

11. Ibid.

12. See Kirsteen Kim, *Joining in with the Spirit: Connecting World Church and Local Mission* (London: SCM Press, 2009), 34.

13. Kenneth Ross and Wongsuk Ma, eds., *Mission Spirituality and Authentic Discipleship* (Oxford: Regnum Books, 2013), 225.

14. Kim, *Joining in with the Spirit*, 36.

15. World Council of Churches. *Together Towards Life*, 12-35.

16. Desmond Tutu, *In God's Hands* (London: Bloomsbury, 2014), 74. Italics in original.

The two emphases of this statement—God as eternal pulsating love and human beings as precious creatures wanted by God—are possibly the foundation of all mission. Coupled with the affirmation in Genesis 1:26-27 that God created men and women in God's own image and likeness, it reveals God's gracious yes to humanity and the universe. In a world where many people constantly see, hear, and feel the no of other human beings toward them, the notion of *imago Dei* has rightly been a powerful rallying point for oppressed and excluded women and black people in their struggle to assert their God-given dignity and humanity.

To conclude, the mission performance of a Christian community finds its origin and shape from its participation in the life of the triune God, creator-redeemer-perfector, and source-wellspring-living water.[17]

The life of the church arises from the love of the Triune God. "God is love" (1 John 4:8). . . . Living in that love of God, the church is called to become good news for all. The Triune God's overflowing sharing of love is the source of all mission and evangelism.[18]

THE MISSION OF GOD AS CREATOR:
GOD'S YES! TO THE WORLD

As we have seen, a mission theology starts from affirming God as creator. This implies, first of all, that Christian witnesses who move across boundaries of faith and culture do not venture into "enemy territory" where God has never been to bring God to people for the first time. Without underestimating the depth of human alienation from God or the power of evil, we must affirm that God has been at work in the whole universe (since the Big Bang) and in the lives of all human beings (since the emergence of humanity). Speaking from a South African vantage point, God did not come to Africa by ship with the Portuguese, Dutch, or British traders, settlers, or missionaries. A theology of mission affirms that the living God—as creator-redeemer-perfector—has been present and at work in African communities since time immemorial, instilling in the minds, hearts, and communities of our ancestors a sense of divine transcendence and the values of *ubuntu*.[19] This is the only way that Christians of the global South can banish from their minds the lingering colonial sense that they are stepchildren, rather than genuine children, of the living God. Since missionary traditions brought to Africa negative theological anthropology, which early colonizers used to legitimize colonial exploitation and apartheid, the future credibility of the gospel in South Africa will depend on the extent to which Christians are able to overcome that destructive legacy.

---

17. See David S. Cunningham, *These Three Are One: The Practice of Trinitarian Theology* (Malden, MA: Blackwell Publishers, 1998).

18. World Council of Churches, *Together Towards Life*, 9.

19. African theologians such as Desmond Tutu emphasize the notion of *ubuntu* (e.g., *No Future without Forgiveness* [London: Rider, 1999], 34-36), even though there is a real danger of devaluation by using it to denote everything that is good and nice.

Second, to acknowledge God as creator means to affirm that every human being has a fundamental God-directedness. As Augustine said, "You awaken us to find delight in praising you because you made us to relate to you (*ad te*) and our heart (*cor nostrum*) is restless until it finds rest in you."[20] This is not an imperialist claim that makes all human beings into "anonymous Christians" against their will, but a humble faith affirmation that there is an ontological likeness among all human beings in their directedness toward the God who created them, even if that is not (or not yet) an existential reality in their lives. Augustine did not say, "Our hearts find no peace," but "our heart" (*cor nostrum*), which suggests a communal human solidarity in a restless longing for God. Christians encounter such humble fellow seekers when they cross the boundaries of faith and culture as witnesses of the gospel.

Third, the recognition of God as creator means that Christian fellowship is not a spiritual unity limited to praying, singing, or discussing "holy things." Mission is a mutually transformative encounter through which people become real sisters and brothers "in the flesh," such as Paul sending Onesimus back to Philemon, "As a beloved brother . . . both in the flesh and in the Lord" (Phlm. 16). It is a heretical distortion, as the Belhar Confession affirms, the way in which racist and exclusionist practices were justified theologically in South Africa by emphasizing "invisible" or "spiritual" unity.[21] This earthy creational emphasis is a necessary corrective to the spiritualizing and dichotomizing that passes for the Christian faith today.

Another implication of acknowledging God as creator of the universe is that mission is also concerned about animals, trees, rivers, and the atmosphere. The ecological crisis and global warming should be as much of a priority for mission and missiology as its other concerns, such as evangelism, church planting, reconciliation, addiction, poverty, HIV and AIDS, ethnic strife, war, famine, racism, and human trafficking. Since the creator appointed humans as stewards in God's household, all of these are inescapable priorities of Christian mission. It is particularly important to understand the close connection between the exploitation of the poor and the abuse of the earth.

> We have heard that creation continues to groan, in bondage, waiting for its liberation (Romans 8:22). We are challenged by the cries of the people who suffer and by the woundedness of creation itself. We see a dramatic convergence between the suffering of the people, and the damage done to the rest of creation.[22]

"Earthkeeping" is therefore a nonnegotiable dimension of the church's holistic mission mandate.

---

20. This is my translation of the Latin words *Tu excitas ut laudare te delectet, quia fecisti nos ad te et inquietum est cor nostrum donec requiescat in te.*

21. Uniting Reformed Church in Southern Africa, *The Belhar Confession* (2008), Articles 2 and 3.

22. World Alliance of Reformed Churches, "Covenanting for Justice in the Economy and the Earth," *The Accra Confession* (2004), 4.

A final implication of acknowledging the creator's yes to humanity is a development of the first one mentioned above. If God is actively at work in all human communities before Christians arrived to present the gospel, then a contextual theology will affirm and amplify all cultural values and religious wisdom that resonate with the gospel message. The initiative rests with local Christian believers, who are not just a receiving community, but also an innovating and improvising community. This group does not passively receive external impulses but takes up the impulses that make sense by fitting them into an existing framework of practices, values, and worldview. As we hear God's ongoing yes to the lives of all people, we will begin to notice and celebrate authentic new performances of the gospel that emerge from the redeemed imagination of human communities.

THE MISSION OF GOD AS REDEEMER:
GOD'S NO! TO HUMAN SIN AND SUFFERING

God's intervention in history to save and restore humanity flows from God's creation and preservation of the universe. This is the second perspective that Karl Barth would have us hold in dialectical relation to the first. In the biblical witness, God emerges as a communicating God: God speaks to create the world, yet also to Adam and Eve after their disobedience (Gen. 2:9), and to Cain after murdering his brother (Gen. 4:9). The Bible is a series of stories about how God "seeks the lost" by speaking through prophets, poets, and apostles to call humanity back to its intended purpose as bearers of the image of God. The first dimension of God's saving work in history is therefore to seek and restore those trapped in sin who wandered from God's purpose.

The depth of the human predicament is portrayed in the Bible with images such as slavery (John 8:34; Rom. 6:1-14) and death (Eph. 2:1-5). God saves humanity by raising the dead to life (Rom. 4:17), by becoming incarnate (assuming a human nature) in Jesus Christ to break the power that sin has over human lives. Through the cross of Jesus, the guilt of sin is atoned, and the power of sin over people's lives is broken. In Christ's cross and resurrection, God "entered the nothingness by drawing it into God's own being."[23] To use a more violent metaphor, God entered the realm of death to "blow it up from the inside," thereby saying (and doing) no! to the brokenness of human lives, families, and societies. Through the Holy Spirit, God works within nature, human lives, and communities to give life and create faith, hope, and love.

Complementary to these masculine metaphors of power and victory—which often lose credibility in the face of persistent suffering, resolute resistance to the gospel, or persecution for the name of Christ—we also need to draw on the strong feminine metaphors of God's deliverance found in Scripture. For

---

23. Jürgen Moltmann, *Theology of Hope: On the Grounds and the Implications of a Christian Eschatology* (London: SCM Press, 1965), 198.

example, God as mourner, mother, and midwife.[24] God's Spirit is the midwife of the new creation, sighing with (and within) humanity and nature to foster resilience and perseverance in the struggle of life against brokenness, futility, and despair.[25] L. Juliana M. Claassens movingly explains this metaphor as found in Psalms 22:9-10 and 71:6.

The midwife metaphor is a deeply personal image that portrays a God who acts, a God who is willing and able to change our circumstances. At the height of the pain, in the midst of the anguish, at what seems to be labor without end, we need a God who is not distant but who is present in our pain. We need a God who offers us comfort in our travail and who is willing to reach into the womb and pull the baby out into the light. The metaphor of God as midwife attests to the fact that God is resolutely on the side of life, working hard to allow new life to enter this world.[26]

It is clear that God's saving work is not limited to the conversion of individual sinners from their evil ways. As a caring shepherd looking for lost sheep, God also hears and sees the suffering of God's people, and intervenes in their lives with deep compassion to set them free from the evil that others are doing to them (Exod. 3:7-8). God's mission is to save *sinners*, yet also to have compassion on those *sinned against*, so that justice and peace may prevail. David J. Bosch asserts, "A religion in which compassion occupies so central a position cannot but be a missionary religion."[27]

Gustavo Gutiérrez, the Latin American liberation theologian, has called this God's "preferential option for the poor."[28] In a similar vein, the Belhar Confession affirms:

> We believe that God has revealed Godself as the One who wishes to bring about justice and true peace on earth; that in a world full of injustice and enmity God is in a special way the God of the destitute, the poor and the wronged.[29]

If this is the "nature" of God, it has implications for the performance of the Christian faith:

> [T]he church, belonging to God, should stand where God stands, namely against injustice and with the wronged; that in following Christ the church

---

24. See L. Juliana M. Claassens, *Mourner, Mother, Midwife: Reimagining God's Delivering Presence in the Old Testament* (Louisville, KY: Westminster John Knox Press, 2012).

25. See Kirsteen Kim, *The Holy Spirit in the World: A Global Conversation* (London: SPCK, 2007), 148-50.

26. Claassens, *Mourner, Mother, Midwife*, 78.

27. David J. Bosch, *Witness to the World: The Christian Mission in Theological Perspective* (London: Marshall, Morgan & Scott, 1980), 57.

28. Gustavo Gutiérrez, *A Theology of Liberation: History, Politics, and Salvation*, rev. ed. (Maryknoll, NY: Orbis Books, 1988 [orig., 1973]), for instance. He covers the option for the poor persuasively in many of his writings.

29. Uniting Reformed Church in Southern Africa, *The Belhar Confession*, Article 4.

must witness to all the powerful and privileged who selfishly seek their own interests and thus control and harm others.[30]

Since God has revealed Godself as the one who stands at the right hand of the needy (Ps. 109:31), Christians in mission need to follow God in that stance, as a way of life, regardless of the consequences. God as creator is deeply concerned about the whole of creation, so God's redemptive purpose is encompassing:

> Mission takes place where the Church, in her total involvement with the world and the comprehensiveness of her message, bears her testimony in word and deed in the form of a servant, with reference to unbelief, exploitation, discrimination and violence, but also with reference to salvation, healing, liberation, reconciliation, and righteousness.[31]

The theological basis of such an encompassing mission is grounded in the "nature" of God as creator-redeemer of the universe.

THE MISSION OF GOD AS PERFECTOR: GOD'S GO! AND WAIT! TO CHRISTIAN ACTIVISTS

Implicit in everything said so far is an encompassing narrative or "big picture" stretching from creation to re-creation. I respect the view of postmodern philosophers that the days of oppressive metanarratives are limited since their distortion can easily legitimize oppressive ideologies. Yet, I agree with Ernst M. Conradie, "It may well be impossible to avoid such encompassing narratives," particularly in Christian theology, since religiously informed grand narratives are often simply replaced by "equally pervasive and homogenizing secular worldviews."[32] The big picture of a Christian worldview is often articulated as an overarching narrative of creation-fall-redemption,[33] or, more elaborately, as a five-act drama.[34] Such an encompassing narrative of creation–Israel–Jesus–church–eschaton is essential to any reflection on the nature of God in Christian theology: God is the one who created, sustains, reveals, redeems, reconciles, re-creates, and perfects. This foundational narrative positions Christian mission in the fourth act of an encompassing theo-drama.[35] This is the "in-between"

---

30. Ibid.

31. Bosch, *Witness to the World*, 18.

32. Ernst M. Conradie, *The Earth in God's Economy: Reflections on the Narrative of God's Labour* (Bellville, South Africa: University of the Western Cape, 2007), 10-11.

33. See Albert M. Wolters, *Creation Regained: Biblical Basics for a Reformational Worldview* (Grand Rapids: Eerdmans, 1985).

34. N. T. Wright, *The New Testament and the People of God* (Minneapolis: Fortress Press, 1992), 141-43; N. T. Wright, *Scripture and the Authority of God: How to Read the Bible Today* (London: SPCK, 2011), 122-27; Samuel Wells, *Improvisation: The Drama of Christian Ethics* (London: SPCK, 2004), 45-57.

35. See Hans Urs Von Balthasar, *Theo-Drama: Theological Dramatic Theory*, 5 vols. (San Francisco: Ignatius, 1988–1994).

time of the reign of God, which has already come in the ministry of Christ, is in process through the Holy Spirit, and will receive full consummation at the coming eschaton. Samuel Wells points out that in this penultimate act of the drama, God calls Christians to live out their faithfulness to him by improvising based on the first three acts, and reaching out imaginatively toward the fifth act.

The important contribution of the *regnum gloriae*, Barth's third Tambach perspective, is to mobilize Christian activists for persistent witness and service, while cautioning them against imagining that they can build God's reign with their own hands. It is essential to maintain a clear eschatological "reserve," affirming that the promised future is in God's hands and that Christians, in and through their missionary activism, receive that future as a gift from the hand of God. This eschatological dimension gives Christian mission its orientation. Christian witnesses do not move from the light of those who are "saved" into the darkness of those who are "unsaved." Instead, they keep on turning away from the darkness (including their own) into the light, together with the people whom they invite to wake up and join them on that journey into God's future. It is a transformative gathering of us all into the already-arriving reign of God. Mission ensures the continuing conversion of the church from its residual darkness, as it moves outward (toward people), forward (into the light), and inward (allowing the bright Morning Star to transform its communal life). [36]

CONCLUSION

To conclude this exploration of the impact that faith in the triune creator-redeemer-perfector has on the performance of Christian mission, it is clear that the task of representing the living God and embodying the treasure of God's liberating gospel in today's world can only be done in bold humility, ecumenical partnership, communal prayer, persistent hope, and joyful praise. All of these components are evident in the life and ministry of our friend Charles Van Engen.

---

36. See Darrell Guder, *The Continuing Conversion of the Church* (Grand Rapids: Eerdmans, 2000).

Part 3

Mission Theology in Context

Chapter 7

Carlitos de Las Casas: A Theologian Made in Latin America

Antonio Carlos Barro and Jorge Henrique Barro

We met Charles Edward Van Engen at Fuller Theological Seminary as a professor and mentor in our intercultural studies doctoral program.[1] We became friends, and later worked together for the development of the church in Latin America. Anyone acquainted with Chuck has likely noticed his pseudonym, Carlitos de Las Casas. At first, it may seem strange that he chose to use this penname. However, there is a good explanation for it. Charles, his first name, translates to both Spanish and Portuguese as *Carlos*. *Carlitos* is the diminutive of Carlos, and it is a way to address a person with intimacy and tender care. Yet, why do we call him Carlitos de Las Casas?

We can only understand Chuck's name through consideration of his native state: Chiapas, located in southeast Mexico. There, we find a city called San Cristóbal de Las Casas where he was born to Dutch American missionary parents. Las Casas added to San Cristóbal has to do with a prominent figure in the history of Christianity in Latin America: Bartolomé de Las Casas (1488–1566). Las Casas was a Dominican friar who, in contrast to other conquerors, aligned himself with the indigenous people who suffered under oppressive colonialism. He fought very hard against slavery, cruelty, and ethnic genocide. Eventually Las Casas became the first bishop of Chiapas.

Carlitos grew up in the midst of poor people, most of them peasants, who had to work very hard to make a living. They made a great impression on the young boy. After graduating from Fuller Theological Seminary and marrying Juan (Juanita), Chuck returned to Chiapas to become a missionary and seminary professor. This context of political oppression, social disparity, and religious persecution formed the young theologian. Here, Chuck Van Engen became Carlitos de Las Casas—a new name that is more than symbolic, and truly identifies him with the Latinos.

---

1. Antonio C. Barro graduated in 1993 and Jorge H. Barro in 2001.

This brief account helps us to understand the setting where Van Engen grew up. Carlitos's theology and missiology has the *chiapanesca* mark of storyteller. Carlitos always comes to lectures prepared with stories from Chiapas to illustrate his missiology. He brings the colors, clothes, Mexican hats, coffee beans, *la abuelita* (the grandmother), mountains and roads, climate, food, Indians, poor people, houses, and dogs. He would make us laugh and cry. He would lead us to feel the pain of the poor, and cry for justice against the oppressors. His words were always memorable. Once while slapping his stomach he said, "We cannot do theology only with the brain, but also with the stomach!" There is a noticeable influence of his Latin side in the development of his theology and missiology.

Our purpose in this chapter is to stress some of Van Engen's contributions to missiology in Latin America. Our vision of the *missio Dei* as well as the influence of Carlitos conditioned our choice of topics. He continues to leave an impression on us as we walk together on the roads and crossways of our beloved Latin America. Hence, we decided to interact with one of his books that has helped many Latin Americans—*God's Missionary People: Rethinking the Purpose of the Local Church*. This book, translated into both Portuguese and Spanish, is widely used by pastors and leaders for theological training because the theories are applicable to Latin America. To our surprise, few volumes deal with both the theological and practical issues of the local church. In this work, Van Engen brings this necessary addition, weaving the two together. The local church is not only the major concern of leadership but also a place where the people of God receive refueling to do the mission of God in the world. Van Engen divided his book into three parts, and we will follow the same division in this essay.

LOCAL CHURCHES: GOD'S MISSIONARY PEOPLE

Van Engen affirms that the purpose of the church is more than a location for gathering and fellowship. The congregation is a place that prepares and sends forth its people to be missionaries in the world. He says, "For the first time the Church is large and encompassing enough to be the missionary people of God. The opportunity exists for the one holy, universal, and apostolic community to witness to every tongue, tribe, and nation."[2] Of course, we understand that he is not saying that in the past the church was not a missionary church. It was and has been from the beginning of the Christian movement. What Van Engen is pointing out is that the church now has the means and resources to reach the whole world with the gospel of Jesus Christ. Today's church has the potential to be present in every nation, and to be a concrete sign of the multiform of God's grace.

---

2. Charles E. Van Engen, *God's Missionary People: Rethinking the Purpose of the Local Church* (Grand Rapids: Baker Book House, 1991), 26.

From the beginning of the church, its leaders possessed few resources, and we should realize that the comfortable lifestyle of today's church is incomparable to the primitive church and its experiences. The contemporary church is rich and in most cases powerful. The churches in Europe and in the United State have an abundance of resources to develop any kind of ministry they desire. Despite being poor, many of the churches in locations such as Africa, Asia, and Latin America have potential resources to fulfill the mission of God.

In 1991 when Van Engen published *God's Missionary People*, leaders were challenging the churches in Latin America to become missionary churches. During those days, we heard many Christian ministers saying that the new missionary force would be coming from Latin America, especially Brazil. Unfortunately, that promise did not fully materialize in its complete potential. Nevertheless, that period was extraordinary. Churches became involved in mission, sending large numbers of missionaries. It was like a fever. Hundreds of communities established missions' committees. Prayers for missionaries and countries dominated worship services. The church raised financial resources for Brazilian missionaries, and Christians committed themselves to support missions. Excited with the challenge, we were proud of not only receiving missionaries but sending them as well.

The scenario is now completely different in Brazil. Only a few churches from the 1990s maintain missions' committees, and fewer Brazilians are committing themselves to missions. Those who are departing to do God's mission feel insecure, not knowing what the future will hold. Missionaries are returning home because of a lack of financial and spiritual support. What happened to the cross-cultural momentum of the 1990s?

This is a hard question to answer due to the complexity of the Brazilian evangelical church. Consideration of the rise of Neo-Pentecostalism should be a major element in solving the dilemma. "Neo-Pentecostalism" is defined as a movement whereby people who have had Pentecostal experiences choose to remain in their mainline denominational churches, such as Baptists, Catholics, Lutherans, Methodists, and Nazarenes, instead of joining Pentecostal fellowships. As a Brazilian case study of Neo-Pentecostalism and its affects, we will briefly examine the Universal Church of the Kingdom of God (UCKG).

After this Neo-Pentecostal church of Brazil began in Rio de Janeiro in 1977, a wave of global changes occurred. The UCKG influenced many other Neo-Pentecostal denominations, which historian Alderi de Souza Matos highlights concerning the effect of the movement:

> This impact has been experienced in two ways: first of all, many churches, being Mainliners or Pentecostals, have been losing members to Neo-Pentecostalism. Secondly, these churches, especially Mainliners and Traditional, have been influenced in their theology, liturgy, and organization by the practices of this movement.[3]

---

3. Alderi de Souza Matos, "O desafio do neopentecostalismo e as igrejas reformadas," http://www.mackenzie.br (Centro de Pós-Graduação Andrew Jumper, São Paulo, 2011).

The scope of this article does not allow an in-depth consideration of this movement. We need to mention, however, that the force behind this new wave was the emergence of prosperity theology. There would not be Neo-Pentecostalism without the basic supposition of the prosperity gospel. If in the past the role of the church was outreach, then today it is to remain secluded. Evangelism, as well as worship and discipleship, has taken on a different meaning. The contemporary emphasis is on personal success and receiving the blessing of God. The concept of mission, as we knew it, is a foreign idea for the Neo-Pentecostal movement. As an example of the inward focus, in 2014 the UCKG constructed the Temple of Solomon in the city of São Paulo at a cost of nearly 400 million U.S. dollars, which will house 10,000 people, and occupies an area of over one million square feet.

Along the same line, we may find another problem in the modern Brazilian church. That is, the role of the people of God in society. With the Lausanne Congress, Brazilian churches started to reflect on the role of the church in transforming society. To do so, it is crucial that church members understand their mission outside the church. Van Engen uses the phrase "being for the world." He says, "The Church exists for humanity in that it is the spiritual body of Christ, and—like Jesus—it is sent to be a servant. As the Father sent Jesus, so Jesus sends his disciples into the world for the sake of the world."[4] This aspect is precisely what local churches in Latin America are missing today. People flock to attend worship services geared toward their well-being. When they go to church, they want to feel excitement, experience some kind of spiritual anointing, or have a vision from heaven. Mission is not the priority of the church.

A NEW VISION OF GOD'S MISSIONARY PEOPLE

The purpose of the local church needs to be a crucial theological reflection in Latin America. Typically, when people consider the church they are not reflecting theologically, but they are thinking about a set of buildings. In that sense, the church is a local place where people go to worship God. Consequently, the purpose of the local church becomes very limited to what it does internally—in other words, worship, Sunday school, choir rehearsal, and children's activities. Christians also judge churches based on the development of those undertakings. People evaluate the church based on its activities within the walls of the temple rather than its mission outside the gate.

In his thinking about the purpose of the local church, Van Engen echoes other notable missiologists such as David J. Bosch and Darrell L. Guder. His vision is clear:

> The answer cannot revolve around what we want the Church's purpose to be, or what we think the world desires or needs the Church's purpose to be. Rather, the Church's purpose can be derived authentically only from

---

4. Van Engen, *God's Missionary People*, 26.

the will of Jesus Christ, its Head; from the Spirit who gives it life; from the Father who has adopted it, and from the Trinitarian mission of God.[5]

At the same time that Van Engen published *God's Missionary People*, Bosch spoke along similar lines regarding mission:

Mission was understood as being derived from the very nature of God. It was thus put in the context of the doctrine on the *missio Dei* as God the Father sending the Son, and God the Father and the Son sending the Spirit was expanded to include yet another "movement": Father, Son, and Holy Spirit sending the church into the world. As far as missionary thinking was concerned, this linking with the doctrine of the Trinity constituted an important innovation.[6]

In addition, Guder, Van Engen's friend, claimed a few years later:

This Trinitarian point of entry into our theology of the church necessarily shifts all accents in our ecclesiology. As it leads us to see the church as the instrument of God's mission, it also forces us to recognize the ways in which the Western church has tended to shape and fit the gospel into its cultural context and made the church's institutional extension and survival its priority. As we have used the tools of biblical scholarship carefully, we have begun to learn that the biblical message is more radical, more inclusive, and more transformational than we have allowed it to be. In particular, we have begun to see that the church of Jesus Christ is not the purpose or goal of the gospel, but rather its instrument and witness. God's mission embraces all of creation. "God so loved the world" is the emphasis of the beloved gospel summary in John 3:16. This does not mean that the church is not essential to God's work of salvation—it is. But it is essential, as God's chosen people "who are blessed to be a blessing to the nations" (Gen. 12).[7]

It seems that the church has a mission insofar as it adopts the mission of God. Apart from God, the church becomes a community of people who gather for the sake of socialization and the well-being of individuals.

There is an urgent need to rediscover the real purpose of the church. According to Van Engen, the church derives its power from its nature; the church was born from above and not from human effort. The church was born of God to do God's mission. To act any other way denies its very essence. With this perspective, the fundamentals of evaluating the church are not its size, prestige, or membership, as we have seen in so many cases in Brazil. Latin Americans are prone to glamorize larger churches as a major sign of God's approval. Yet,

---

5. Ibid., 87.

6. David J. Bosch, *Transforming Mission: Paradigm Shifts in Theology of Mission* (Maryknoll, NY: Orbis Books, 1991), 390.

7. Darrell L. Guder, *Missional Church: A Vision for the Sending of the Church in North America* (Grand Rapids: Eerdmans, 1998), 5.

according to what we understand of *missio Dei*, faithfulness to the one who called the church is the real sign of success: "But you are a chosen people, a royal priesthood, a holy nation, God's special possession, that you may declare the praises of him who called you out of darkness into his wonderful light" (1 Pet. 2:9, NIV).

Consequently, for the church to fulfill its mission it needs to develop solid growth in four areas of its life. Concurring with Van Engen, the first area is *koinōnia* (fellowship), which has an internal dimension. Second, *diakonia* (service) has an internal and external direction. As Christians, we should take care of our people, yet not exclusively. As the apostle Paul affirms in Galatians 5, *kerygma* (proclamation) and *martyria* (witness) point toward the world. In the dynamic interaction of these two ministries the church becomes the true church of God in the world. For Van Engen, the church exists for the world. The signs of the true church are evident in the proper administration of the sacraments, preaching, and discipline. Van Engen moves beyond the propositions of the Church Growth Movement, where the major stress is numerical growth.

Orlando E. Costas took a different approach in terms of nomenclatures. For him the church needs to be in the world in four dimensions that help the people of God to fulfill its mission: organic, diaconal, conceptual, and numerical.[8] From the perspective of the *missio Dei*, the church must reflect God's kingdom. Thus, the kingdom of God produces the atmosphere of the church. People do not primarily govern their own community. Instead, Jesus Christ, the king, should govern (see Eph. 5:23).

Furthermore, Van Engen uses an idea of Oscar Cullmann in reference to two concentric circles of Jesus's government. The first inner circle is the rule of Christ in the church, and the outer circle, encompassing the first, is Christ's rule over all things. In other words, the church is the central locus of the rule of the king. Van Engen then adds another circle that surrounds the first two—the rule of Jesus Christ over all unseen spiritual forces (principalities and power). If King Jesus is the ruler of the church, then it is appropriate that the church is the anticipatory sign of the kingdom. For Van Engen, the church is not the kingdom, but anticipates its presence in the way followers of Christ practice the gospel in the world. The church represents the king and his kingdom. Likewise, the church is the bearer and illustration of the message. Finally, the church's mission is to spread the knowledge of the rule of the kingdom. Van Engen is correct when he claims the following:

> The Church cannot create, bring in, or build the Kingdom, but it can and does witness to it. Clearly, this witness happens in word and deed, in miracles, in signs and wonders, in the transformation of the lives of people, in the presence of the Holy Spirit, in the radical recreation of humanity. A local congregation's witness to the rule of the king is itself a part of the

---

8. See Orlando E. Costas, *The Integrity of Mission: The Inner Life and Outreach of the Church* (San Francisco: Harper & Row, 1979).

content of the reign of Christ, which is proclaimed. The kingdom comes as Jesus Christ is made known. So local churches build the Church toward the coming kingdom as they preach, proclaim, and live out their allegiance and obedience to the king. Local congregations participate in the coming of the kingdom as they live out their lives as covenant communities of disciples of the king, as branch offices of the kingdom. As the number increases of those who know and acknowledge the rule of the king, the Church becomes the anticipatory instrument of the already-but-not-yet coming kingdom of God.[9]

Van Engen emphasizes the place of the local church in the world. For him, Jesus Christ is the pattern for the role of the church: "As the Father has sent me, so send I you" (John 20:21).

The Church exercises its commission as the body of Christ by living out the role Jesus assigned to it in the world. A review of the gifts of the Spirit in the Church, for example, would immediately impress us with the fact that these gifts are ministries to be exercised in the world. And as they take shape through the Church in the world, they fulfill a role similar to Jesus Christ's.[10]

LOCAL CHURCHES: BECOMING GOD'S MISSIONARY PEOPLE

The relationship of the local church to the kingdom of God needs careful attention in Latin America. Christians often identify church and the kingdom as the same thing. Each denomination has a tendency to see itself as the kingdom of God, operating as if only its kingdom work is important, and ignoring the rest of the universal church. Often, individual denominations view other church communities as either faulty or unconverted.

In the third chapter of Van Engen's work, he focuses on the kingdom of God. He asserts, "As the missionary people of God, local congregations are the branch offices of the kingdom: the principal instrument, anticipatory sign, and primary locus of the coming of the kingdom."[11] These various kingdom aspects deserve more emphasis. What are the signs of the kingdom; and how do they manifest themselves? Jon Sobrino says,

[that the kingdom has] come on the level of the mediator, and . . . we do not need to await another eschatological mediator. . . . And it has come on the level of signs in the life of Jesus and in subsequent history. It has

---

9. Van Engen, *God's Missionary People*, 111-12.
10. Ibid., 120.
11. Ibid., 101.

not come, however, on the level of the reality of mediation: the world as a whole is not yet conformed to the heart of God, to put it mildly; to a very large extent it is positively contrary to the heart of God."[12]

In other words, the signs of the kingdom are evident in the life of Jesus. This should be the primary understanding of the local church. Even in an age of much confusion, with many battles to establish powerful churches, there is a possibility of identifying the signs of the kingdom within the church. Costas moved in a similar direction by understanding that the signs of the kingdom are primarily in relation to the life and ministry of Jesus Christ. He states, "Jesus not only announced the nearness of the kingdom (Mark 1:15), but also personifies that kingdom (John 1; Luke 7:22-27)."[13]

Accordingly, the mission of the church is to be an instrument of the kingdom in the world. C. René Padilla advances this concept further, and moves toward Van Engen's thesis about the importance of the local church when he states:

> To speak of the kingdom of God is to speak of God's redemptive purpose for the whole creation, and of the historical vocation that the church has with regard to that purpose here and now, "between the times." It is also to speak of an eschatological reality that is both the starting point, and the goal of the church. The mission of the church, therefore, can be understood only in light of the kingdom of God.[14]

For Padilla, the locus of God's mission is the whole of creation. Apart from the world or creation, the church has no purpose for existence. On becoming God's missionary people as agents of the kingdom, Van Engen goes on to say that we need to:

> explore the process by which missionary congregations get a vision of their mission in their various contexts. The Church becomes missionary because of the powerful presence of the Holy Spirit who creates, sustains, directs, and propels. *Emerging* is an adjective, a quality of the Church's missionary nature.[15]

Consequently, the church needs to be careful in defining its goals. It is not a matter of making a strategic plan for the sake of the local church as if this is the purpose of the community. It is a matter of thinking in terms of missional goals in the local church. Missional congregations need well-defined goals and

---

12. Jon Sobrino, *Jesus the Liberator: A Historical-Theological Reading of Jesus of Nazareth* (Maryknoll, NY: Orbis Books, 1993), 109.

13. Orlando E. Costas, *Christ Outside the Gate: Mission beyond Christendom* (Maryknoll, NY: Orbis Books, 1982), 45.

14. C. René Padilla, *Mission Between the Times: Essays on the Kingdom*, 2d rev. ed. (Carlisle, UK: Langham Monographs, 2010; orig., 1985), 199.

15. Van Engen, *God's Missionary People*, 133.

priorities to fill the gap between the act of God and human action in the life of the church:

> When the people of God set goals with vision, by faith, and with serious consideration for achieving those goals, they translate the statements of faith about the Church into statements of purpose, which point toward the Church becoming what it is confessed to be. Goal-setting bridges the gap between the "from below" and "from above" perspectives of the Church, and we begin to express the vision, desire, and purpose of being a missionary church. Goal-setting places us in the middle ground between confession and action, between the uniqueness of the Church as people chosen, gathered, maintained, and sent by God, and the ordinariness of the church as a group of humans who gather in love around a common faith and shared hope.[16]

It is crucial, in building goals, to take into consideration the missionary interaction between the church and its environment—where the community is located. We need to empower local leaders to start where they are, and to illuminate the way to Jesus Christ for the people in the barrio. A few churches with more resources will be able to cross the boundaries of that neighborhood. Holistic mission is done by the sum of the local churches in any given barrio or city, and not by one isolated congregation.

Van Engen contends that one of the greatest barriers of the church in becoming missional is its understanding of place and the people of God. He explains as follows:

> Conversion . . . is the change of those who were "not-a-people" to become the ministering people of God, the active, involved, serving body of Christ (1 Pet. 2:10). This is a conversion out of selfishness, out of self-centeredness, out of serving the rulers of darkness into agape love, discipleship, and serving Jesus Christ. This conversion moves from decision through a process of discipleship, with the disciple seeking to minister in Christ's name as a follower of Jesus. In fact, a case could be made that full and complete conversion in the biblical sense is a three-part process involving (1) conversion to God in Jesus Christ, (2) conversion to the Church, the body of Christ, and (3) conversion to ministry in the world for whom Christ died.[17]

Moreover, Van Engen emphasizes that the church is a missionary church only when every person becomes a missional and kingdom person. It is similar to the Catholic Church in Latin America saying, every baptized person is a missionary. However, the people of God lack this understanding. As a whole, Latino society

---

16. Ibid., 134.
17. Ibid., 152.

cares less for the church, and the church cares less for society. This gap is getting bigger, and one needs to find answers on how to close it. With this in mind, Van Engen examines the missional responsibility of church leadership.

Van Engen understands that "church leadership is very difficult to define with any degree of precision" since much "depends on the personality of the leader; the skills and abilities of the leader; the roles, functions, and power of the leader as perceived by both leader and follower, and the personal perceptions of the followers."[18] He defines leadership from a missiological perspective, which is a unique way to look at this crucial theme of the church:

> Leadership is a corporate event. The people of God move forward in mission in the world as they live out their vision of God's call and will for them, stimulated by a number of leader-catalysts, and mobilized by the Holy Spirit in response to what God is doing in their midst, and in their context of mission in the world.[19]

What is clear is that these leader-catalysts, as he calls them, are more than caregivers, counselors, preachers, managers, organizers, or supervisors. They must be missional leaders! He concludes:

> Merely delegating authority—only telling people what they should do, only devising programs to do it—will not be enough to mobilize the people of God. The people must be shown a model that presses them to want to achieve those intentionally missionary goals of the congregation.[20]

They are leaders not because of their social status or their powerful influence, but because they provide the structure for missional outreach. In turn, the church members provide the hands, feet, and spiritual gifts necessary to carry out the congregation's missional intentions and goals.

One function that Van Engen underscores is the administration of the church. The role of the administrator is to help the local congregation to be a missional church. All resources must run under this vision. He states:

> None of what we have seen thus far is possible unless it is given hands and feet through careful and intentional administration. Administrative structures facilitate the actual doing of congregational mission in the world. Here is the most crucial step in the process of building missionary congregations; the step, which seems to be the most ignored. Time and again as this author speaks with pastors and missionaries they are delighted to hear all that he has said up to this point. But when he begins to speak of administration, they seem to have ears, but cannot hear. So many missionaries and pastors want their churches to grow, and want their

---

18. Ibid., 165.
19. Ibid.
20. Ibid., 165-66.

congregations to reach out in mission, but they are unwilling to pay the price in careful, intentional, disciplined, and visionary administration.[21]

Administration in the local church without the commitment of facilitating the actual doing of congregational mission in the world easily becomes a bureaucratic group of people trying to maintain what they have. Maintenance, the major attention of most in church leadership, explains why many churches are dying around the world, especially in Latin America.

CONCLUSION

When researching the history of the Missional Church Movement, the name of Charles Van Engen appears together with many other authors. In 1991, he published the English version of *God's Missionary People*, however, thereby providing evidence that he was developing his missional thinking many years before the term became a catchword. His book strongly reveals the presuppositions of the original "missional" perspectives, though he does not use that word in his title. We will always be grateful to Carlitos de las Casas in helping us, God's people, to rethink the purpose of the local church. His love of God together with his authentic passion for mission is worthy of imitating and following.

21. Ibid., 179.

Chapter 8

Recovering Reconciliation as God's Mission: Its Implications for North and South Korea

Kyung Lan Suh

My passion is doing mission theology arising out of the ministry context under the guidance of the Holy Spirit. Mission theology seeks to be "multidisciplinary, integrative, biblical, praxeological, definitional, analytical, and truthful."[1] When mission happens, all the various disciplines are occurring simultaneously. Charles E. Van Engen argues, "Mission theologians must study mission not from the point of view of abstracted and separated parts, but from an integrative perspective that attempts to see the whole, while at the same time taking into consideration the unique contribution of each of the four domains."[2] The four domains are word (the primacy of the Bible in all mission theology), church (the primary agent of God's mission in the world), world (the impact of culture, socioeconomics, political realities, and all other arenas of human life in the reality of a given context), and personal pilgrimage (the personal, spiritual, and experiential pilgrimage of the human agents of God's mission). The integrating idea serves as the center through which to approach a rereading of Scripture, an analysis of the church's reflection, an appreciation of the persons as agents of God's mission, and the unique contextual issues affecting God's mission at a particular time and place.

The integrating idea of reconciliation flows out of both my ministry context and my personal experience. My journey toward reconciliation started when I met my mentor, Charles Van Engen. At that time, I was desperately trying to find the answer for the injustice I faced in my ministry context. In the meantime,

---

1. Charles Van Engen, "Mission, Theology of," in *Global Dictionary of Theology*, ed. William Dyrness and Veli-Matti Kärkkäinen (Downers Grove, IL: InterVarsity, 2008), 550-62, 550.

2. Ibid., 553. Over the past three decades, there has been a significant consensus in mission theology of the need to integrate at least three of those domains in a dynamic, interrelated whole. In other words, word (the primacy of the Bible in all mission theology), church (the primary agent of God's mission in the world), and world (the impact of culture, socioeconomics, political realities, and all other arenas of human life in the reality of a given context). Van Engen adds one more arena that is important for constructing a full-orbed theology of mission. That is, the arena of the pilgrimage of people who are the agents of God's mission.

Charles Van Engen recommended Miroslav Volf's book to me. The title of the book, *Exclusion and Embrace*, caught my attention. I was fascinated with the notion of embrace, a metaphor of reconciliation. It reminded me of God's grace and healing. It also led me to realize the need to be reconciled with God, myself, other people, and other creatures. Embrace is immensely powerful as it is the key to healing exclusion and to transforming the excluded.

I started to read the book from a victim's perspective, yet as I progressed, I had to admit that often I was also an offender as well as a victim. Marjorie Suchocki asserts that there is "an intertwining of victim and violator through the very nature of violation."[3] The violence ensnares the psyche of the victim, propels its action in the form of defensive reaction, and robs it of innocence. She continues, "To break the world cleanly into victims and violators ignores the depths of each person's participation in cultural sin. There simply are no innocents."[4] All human beings are living in the community of sinners. Paul writes, "For all have sinned and fall short of the glory of God" (Rom. 3:23).

Because Christianity is not a religion but a relationship, we need to take a relational approach to our broken world. We live in a broken world. The brokenness of our world is a reality that shapes our daily lives. When we start the day reading the newspaper, we come face to face with the sin that separates us from God and builds up walls between people. Although not all of us have experienced the large-scale trauma of war or the violence of brutal racism, we all know brokenness and division at some level through abuse, social injustice, and conflict in our community.

Reconciliation is the heart of the Christian message.[5] The central meaning of reconciliation is the restoration of a right relationship. Reconciliation includes a concept of justice, which restores. We, as God's missionary people, need to restore reconciliation as God's mission. There is a theological bond between reconciliation and mission that anticipates the current contextual need of overcoming violence in the contemporary world. In this chapter, I seek a distinctive vision for reconciliation as God's mission and a journey toward reconciliation of North and South Korea to be God's new creation in Christ. In order to do so, we need to realize that reconciliation is God's gift to the world. We also need to see how Scripture shapes the path of our journey. The journey toward reconciliation entails recognizing that reconciliation as restorative justice requires truth, conversion, and forgiveness. Lastly, the church as an agent of God's mission should participate in the ministry of reconciliation.

RECONCILIATION IS GOD'S GIFT TO THE WORLD

Scripture and Christian tradition employ a range of metaphors, symbols, and words to express God's saving activity in the world. Reconciliation is one of

---

3. Marjorie Suchocki, *The Fall to Violence* (New York: Continuum, 1995), 147.
4. Ibid., 149.
5. John W. De Gruchy, *Reconciliation: Restoring Justice* (Minneapolis: Fortress Press, 2002), 44.

the words used in English to describe this experience. While most translations of the Old Testament omit the word "reconciliation," most New Testament translations contain some fifteen instances of "reconciliation" or "reconcile," which are derived from the Greek *katallagē* and *katallassō*.[6] John W. De Gruchy argues that twelve of these instances appear in the letters of Paul, who deploys reconciliation as his central metaphor for expounding the gospel. In turn, he was pivotal in making reconciliation a central concept for the early church.[7]

It is important to examine the way in which Paul uses the term "reconciliation" to address different issues and needs in varied contexts. In 2 Corinthians, Paul links the gospel of reconciliation to the new creation in Christ, the righteousness of God, and the mission of the church.[8] The background to Paul's teaching is his own rejection by the Christian community in Corinth who questioned his authority and his motives in writing to them. There is an interaction between the divine act of reconciliation in Christ and human appropriation of that act in relating in a new way to each other. The need for and the dynamics of reconciliation between Paul and the Corinthian church become the reason, as well as the basis, for Paul's rhetoric about God's reconciliation.[9]

In his book on reconciliation, Robert J. Schreiter emphasizes that reconciliation is a spirituality more than a strategy. It is not a set of technical, problem-solving skills applied to situations of conflict. It is a response to God's reconciling action in the world. Schreiter proposes, "We experience God's justifying and reconciling activity in our own lives and in our communities, and it is from that experience that we are able to go forth in a ministry of reconciliation."[10]

A Christian vision of reconciliation grows out of the biblical narrative. The story of 2 Corinthians 5 reminds us that reconciliation is not about us. It is about God. It is God's mission in the world. The invitation to be ambassadors of God's reconciliation in the world is clear and urgent when reconciliation connects with God's story and life. We as Christians believe that reconciliation is a gift from God. Healing of the world's deep brokenness does not begin with our actions and us but with God and God's gift of new creation, as we see in 2 Corinthians 5:17-18. We acknowledge that at the center of our interest is not reconciliation but the reconciler in whom God was reconciling the world to himself. Archbishop Oscar Arnulfo Romero of El Salvador said, "The kingdom is not only beyond our efforts, it is even beyond our vision. . . . We are workers, not master builders; ministers, not messiahs. We are prophets of a future not our own."[11]

---

6. Daniel Philpott, *Just and Unjust Peace: An Ethic of Political Reconciliation* (New York: Oxford University Press, 2012), 135.

7. De Gruchy. *Reconciliation*, 44-51.

8. Ralph Martin, *Reconciliation: A Study of Paul's Theology* (Atlanta: John Knox, 1981), 5.

9. De Gruchy, *Reconciliation*, 53.

10. Robert J. Schreiter, *Reconciliation: Mission and Ministry in a Changing Social Order* (Maryknoll, NY: Orbis Books, 1992), 60.

11. See www.intervarsity.org/slj/article/1354.

RECONCILIATION IS A JOURNEY WITH GOD

Reconciliation is a journey with God. Emmanuel Katongole and Chris Rice explain what makes Scripture indispensable to the Christian journey of reconciliation. "When Christians remember well, we are able to explore the story of God's involvement with the world and to draw on that story to locate and understand what is going on at any particular time within that story."[12] Because a Christian vision of reconciliation is rooted in the story of God's people, we can grasp the vision only as we learn to inhabit the story. The story shapes us in the habits of God's missionary people.

Reconciliation is not an event or an achievement but a process or a journey from old to new. In the story, the center of the journey is Jesus: "If anyone is in Christ"; "God who reconciled us to himself in Christ"; "We are therefore Christ's ambassadors" (2 Cor. 5:17-20). What 2 Corinthians confirms is that the gift of reconciliation is given to "anyone in Christ." In addition, an ambassador is an authorized representative or messenger whom authorities send abroad. So are Christ's ambassadors sent on a mission of reconciliation to a world of brokenness. Katongole and Rice add, "God's gift of a call to be Christ's ambassadors of reconciliation intends to unseat other lords—power, nationalism, race or ethnic loyalty as an end in itself—and give birth to deeper allegiances, stories, spaces and communities that are a 'demonstration plot' of the reality of God's new creation in Christ."[13]

The journey of reconciliation begins with a transformation of the human person. "The stories of Scripture point to reconciliation as a costly journey of transformation and hope that includes (but goes far deeper than) firefighting—a quiet revolution that takes shape over time and bursts forth through signs of hope in local places."[14] They continue that, grounded in God's gift of the new creation, a Christian vision insists that reconciliation is ultimately about the transformation of the everyday—a quiet revolution that occurs over time in everyday people, everyday congregations, everyday communities, amid the most broken places on God's earth.[15]

Scripture is central to the journey of reconciliation. As we move deeper into the biblical story, we receive gifts to help us find our way. The Christian ministry of reconciliation is about learning to identify and care for the unique pebbles God provides for us as we confront the Goliaths of this world. The creation story also helps us to see that God invites us to rest in the midst of the chaos and conflict around us since he rested on the seventh day. It is an invitation to imagine that the salvation of the world does not depend on us. To see reconciliation as a journey with God is to let go of control. Sabbath is the time to remember that we are in the hands of God, who rules the universe with love.

---

12. Emmanuel Katongole and Chris Rice, *Reconciling All Things: A Christian Vision for Justice, Peace, and Healing* (Downers Grove, IL: InterVarsity, 2008), 35.
13. Ibid., 41.
14. Ibid., 30.
15. Ibid.

RECONCILIATION AS RESTORATIVE JUSTICE REQUIRES TRUTH, CONVERSION, AND FORGIVENESS

While the criminal justice system defines crime as a violation of the law, restorative justice sees crime as fundamentally relational. De Gruchy emphasizes that restorative justice is not a weak form of justice, nor does it necessarily exclude other forms of justice, such as retribution or the use of punishment.[16] Although the central focus of restorative justice is healing and restoration, it does not exclude different types of punishment. The needs of the victim or survivor and their community drive the process, and hold offenders accountable for harm caused. It is rather an attempt to reach a more complete understanding of justice.[17] The fundamental difference between retributive and restorative justice is that the latter is a process involving those who have a role to play in bringing healing to the offender and the survivor.[18]

While restoration was the ultimate goal of justice in the Bible, God's people were not always open to that possibility. Genesis begins with a recognition that unlimited revenge is a normal response to wrongdoing. For example, "the law of Lamech" calls for a retaliation of "seventy times seven" (Gen. 4:24). It is retribution almost without end. Yet, soon revenge is limited: an eye for an eye only, God tells the Israelites (Exod. 21:22). Rightly understood, God is not commanding vengeance but demanding a limitation on vengeance: "Do this much, but only this much." Following that is another limitation on retaliation: "Do not seek revenge or bear a grudge against one of your people, but love your neighbor as yourself" (Lev. 19:18). Christ continues in this direction. Love not only your neighbor, but also your enemy, he says; do good to those who harm you. Instead of unlimited revenge or even limited revenge, he calls for unlimited love (Matt. 5:38-48), and it is no accident that he graphically calls for forgiveness to seventy times seven (Matt. 18:22).

According to Christopher D. Marshall, justice has to do with the right ordering of the universe, with things being as God intends them to be, and with the restoring of harmony or shalom when things go wrong.[19] Miroslav Volf acknowledges that for Paul, reconciliation with God always implies reconciliation with the other, and therefore it demands justice.[20] He also insists that we not regard the struggle for justice as an end in itself, yet rather as a means to achieve reconciliation, whose ultimate goal is a community of love.[21]

---

16. De Gruchy, *Reconciliation*, 202.

17. Ibid., 202.

18. Zenuella Thumbadoo, "A Restorative Approach to Residential Treatment," *Child and Youth Care* 22, no. 4 (2004): 6-9.

19. Christopher D. Marshall, "Offending, Restoration, and the Law-Abiding Community: Restorative Justice in the New Testament and in the New Zealand Experience," *Journal of the Society of Christian Ethics* 27, no. 2 (2007): 7.

20. Miroslav Volf, *Exclusion and Embrace: A Theological Exploration of Identity, Otherness, and Reconciliation* (Nashville: Abingdon, 1996), 166.

21. Ibid., 163.

In other words, justice is subordinate to reconciliation.[22] Marshall speaks of natural and rough justice, distributive and retributive justice, commutative and remedial justice, poetic and practical justice, each of which is inevitably partial and fallible.[23] He insists that whatever truth there may be in other forms of justice, the Christian tradition is about "restorative" or what he calls "covenant justice," that is, the justice that rebuilds God's intended network of relationships. This is not something in addition to the gospel of God's saving grace or doctrine of atonement. Restorative justice concerns how Paul interprets the gospel.[24] Marshall writes, "Justification by faith is a manifestation of restorative justice."[25] Philpott also argues that restoration of right relationship is equivalent to restoration of justice.[26] In the letters of Paul, he explicitly links restoration and reconciliation.[27]

Reconciliation has become popular in our time, finding its way into the political rhetoric and public policy of many governments. South Africa and its apparently successful Truth and Reconciliation Commission (TRC) have captured the imagination of many postconflict societies. De Gruchy states, "In South Africa, their goal is more than getting at the truth and dealing with the past; it is fostering national reconciliation."[28] What the TRC did was to create space in which victims, perpetrators, and benefactors could encounter one another around the truth for the sake of personal and national healing.[29] De Gruchy suggests four steps in the process of reconciliation: creating space for interfacing, telling the truth, listening to the sound of fury, and forgiveness as wisdom and power.[30]

In the process of reconciliation as restorative justice, it is critical to create space or opportunity for both victims and perpetrators to deal with the past in a constructive way. Reconciliation must be proactive in seeking to create an encounter where people can focus on their relationship and share their perceptions, feelings, and experiences with one another, with the goal of creating new perceptions and a new shared experience. John Paul Lederach suggests that reconciliation deals with three specific paradoxes.[31] First, reconciliation promotes an encounter between the open expression of the painful past and the search for the articulation of a long-term, interdependent future. Second, reconciliation provides a place for truth and mercy to meet. It is also, where we validate and embrace concern for exposing what has happened, as well as letting

---

22. Ibid., 165.

23. Christopher D. Marshall, *Beyond Retribution: A New Testament Vision for Justice, Crime, and Punishment* (Grand Rapids: Eerdmans, 2001), 25.

24. Ibid., 35-95.

25. Ibid., 59.

26. Philpott, *Just and Unjust Peace*, 136.

27. Ibid., 136.

28. De Gruchy, *Reconciliation*, 147.

29. Ibid., 147.

30. Ibid., 148-80.

31. John Paul Lederach, "Truth and Mercy, Justice and Peace," in *Conflict Transformation and Restorative Justice Manual*, ed. Michelle E. Armster and Lorraine Stutzman Amstutz (Akron: Mennonite Central Committee, Office on Justice and Peacebuilding, 2008), 17-18 (18).

go in favor of renewed relationship. Third, it further recognizes the need to give time and place to both justice and peace, where redressing the wrong is held together with the envisioning of a common, connected future. Therefore, the basic paradigm of reconciliation is one that embraces paradox.

We need to learn the anguished cry of lament. Further, the practice of lament grounds the journey of reconciliation.[32] Truth raises images of honesty, revelation, clarity, open accountability, and vulnerability. When faced with truth, the first language of the church in a broken world is not strategy but prayer. Katongole and Rice state,

> Lament is not despair. It is not whining. It is not a cry into a void. Lament is a cry directed to God. It is the cry of those who see the truth of the world's deep wounds and the cost of seeking peace. It is the prayer of those who are deeply disturbed by the way things are.[33]

They also argue, "Lament slows reconciliation down because it sees the challenge of transformation not from the top but from the margins—indeed from the bottom."[34] Lament calls us to engage the past seriously and to take on the challenge of remembering well.

Reconciliation as restorative justice reminds us that Jesus called to repentance not only those who falsely pronounced sinful what was innocent and sinned against their victims but the victims of oppression themselves. Volf talks about the need for victims' repentance:

> To repent means to resist the seductiveness of the sinful values and practices, and to let the new order of God's reign be established in one's heart. For a victim to repent means not to allow the oppressors to determine the terms under which social conflict is carried out, the values around which the conflict is raging, and the means by which it is fought. Repentance thus empowers victims and disempowers the oppressors. It "humanizes" the victims precisely by protecting them from either mimicking or dehumanizing the oppressors. Far from being a sign of acquiescence to the dominant order, repentance creates a haven of God's new world in the midst of the old and so makes the transformation of the old possible.[35]

Reconciliation requires a transformation of desire, habits, and loyalties.[36] This long and costly journey of conversion is impossible without God's forgiveness and grace.

The idea that reconciliation does not happen without a cost is the basis of Christian theology.[37] The nature of reconciliation is expensive. Cheap recon-

---

32. Katongole and Rice, *Reconciling All Things*, 72.
33. Ibid., 72.
34. Ibid., 76.
35. Volf, *Exclusion and Embrace*, 116.
36. Katongole and Rice, *Reconciling All Things*, 161.
37. See Schreiter, *Reconciliation,* and Marshall, *Beyond Retribution.*

ciliation, by analogy to Bonhoeffer's "cheap grace," implies reconciliation without justice. Forgiveness is the means to enlarge community. According to Everett
L. Worthington, "forgiveness happens inside an individual; reconciliation
happens within a relationship."[38]

Forgiveness is the boundary between exclusion and embrace.[39] When we
forgive, we expand our understanding by learning to see the world through the
eyes of the other, our neighbor. We begin to see ourselves as a part of a cycle of
victim and oppressor. We need to learn new skills and competencies of living
safely and with accountability in community.[40] By entering into the process
of forgiveness, we begin to appreciate more fully the meaning of personhood.
As Lewis Smedes stresses, forgiveness is an outrage "against straight-line dues-
paying morality."[41] However, the trouble with revenge is that it enslaves us.
Forgiveness breaks bonds of necessity that yield only alienation, resentment,
and violence. Forgiveness allows for freedom of relationship. Forgiveness brings
good out of evil and offers the hope of healing to the family of the victims and
deliverance from the destructive power of guilt to the offender.

Forgiveness is a part of our corporate worship (Matt. 5:23-24). God calls us
to participate in his forgiveness of us. We confess our sins and receive assurance
of pardon. God urges us to follow Jesus, who in turn asked God to forgive his
offenders. Forgiveness defines the church (John 20:21-23). Forgiveness defines
vocation as it tends toward reconciliation (2 Cor. 5:19).

RECONCILIATION NEEDS THE CHURCH

As God's missionary people, we learn the language of reconciliation from
and through the community called the church. The story of God's new creation
grounds reconciliation. We first learn this story from and through the church
that worships God and reads Scripture to remember God's journey with us. The
church is crucial to the journey of reconciliation because the journey requires a
community to sustain it.

The gospel of reconciliation is the heart of the church's mission to the world.
Signified by the crucifixion, the body of Christ has been created out of a place of
deep humiliation and costly reconciliation (Phil. 3:4-9; Eph. 2:14).[42] The church

---

38. Everett L. Worthington, "The Pyramid Model of Forgiveness: Some Interdisciplinary
Speculations about Unforgiveness and the Promotion of Forgiveness," in *Dimensions of
Forgiveness: Psychological Research and Theological Perspectives*, ed. Everett L. Worthington
(Philadelphia: Templeton Foundation, 1998), 107-38, 129.

39. Volf, *Exclusion and Embrace*, 125.

40. See Olga Botcharova, "Implementation of Track Two Diplomacy: Developing a Model
of Forgiveness," in *Forgiveness and Reconciliation: Religion, Public Policy, and Conflict
Transformation*, ed. Rodney L. Petersen and Raymond G. Helmick (Philadelphia: Templeton
Foundation, 2001), 279-304, 291-98.

41. Lewis Smedes, *Forgive and Forget: Healing the Hurts We Don't Deserve* (San Francisco:
Harper & Row, 1984), 124.

42. J. Andrew Kirk, *What Is Mission?: Theological Explorations* (Minneapolis: Fortress, 2000),
79.

has the twofold function of being a community of reconciliation who witnesses to the world not only in the proclamation of the gospel in word but also in its constructive engagement in the political, social, and cultural life. The church should be both a sign and an agent of God's reconciling love in the fragmented world of the twenty-first century.

An emphasis on a right relationship with God is crucial to a Christian vision of reconciliation. There is a Christian movement that views the biblical call to reconciliation as only about reconciling God and humanity, without reference to social realities. Preaching, teaching, church life, and mission are solely about a personal relationship between God and his people. Christian mission focuses on winning converts, planting and growing churches, and evangelistic efforts. The gospel of prosperity is so popular in many parts of the world. This false gospel promises either an afterlife of eternal blessings or individual well-being, which does not connect to the transformation of social realities. To be a sign and agent of reconciliation, the church must embody the gospel of reconciliation in this broken world. God places the church at the very heart of his purpose. Katongole and Rice argue,

> Unless the church is able to be the space where people who share different cultures and histories can receive their common gift and invitation to the same journey, then the church herself becomes just one more actor in the history of division and conflict. Instead of healing the tensions and brokenness of the world, the church can become an epicenter that radiates and intensifies these divisions.[43]

IMPLICATIONS OF RECONCILIATION THEOLOGY FOR NORTH AND SOUTH KOREA

For too long, political risk taking, the wall of ideology, and the scourge of militarism have divided and caused suffering to the Korean people. The Korean government has tried to instill anti-communism as an important ideology. Everyone desires and talks about change in South Korea. Korean church leaders have the responsibility to lend their voice to the issues of corruption, injustice, impunity, and other ills in the land. Keeping quiet communicates support for unethical activities of politicians. It is the responsibility of the Korean church to proclaim reconciliation as restorative justice in the land.

Christ is our peace. As our Lord Jesus Christ broke down the walls of hostility that divide God's people, we too are called to the ministry of reconciliation and peacemaking (Eph. 2:14-16). Understanding the gospel as a message of reconciliation and peace is crucially pertinent to Korean churches for participating in national reunification as an important part of mission.[44]

---

43. Katongole and Rice, *Reconciling All Things*, 113-14.
44. Eunsik Cho, "Christian Mission toward Reunification of Korea," *Asia Journal of Theology* 14, no. 2 (2000): 376.

Since the 1980s, a small part of the Korean church has actively engaged in the reunification movement. However, the general sentiment among Korean churches settles for a strong anti-communist position, which has kept them from engaging reunification issues from a biblically informed perspective of reconciliation and from moving beyond their evangelistic interest and humanitarian concern toward undertaking peacemaking initiatives.[45] It is crucial for the Korean church to construct a theology of reconciliation based on the peace message of the gospel, for without forgiveness of the history between the North and the South, genuine reunification is not likely.[46]

The different mediating roles the Korean church implements flow out of the theology of reconciliation in relation to North and South Korea. The Korean church needs to remember the three brief disclaimers that Volf offers in the efforts toward reconciliation.[47] First, the final reconciliation is not a work of human beings but of the triune God. Second, it is not an apocalyptic end of the world but the eschatological new beginning of this world. Third, the final reconciliation is not a self-enclosed "totality" because it rests on a God who is nothing but perfect love. The hope for such "nontotalitarian" final reconciliation is the backdrop against which Christians engage in the struggle for peace under the conditions of enmity and oppression.

In light of the theological grounding of reconciliation as restorative justice, God summons the Korean church to challenge those who benefited from past injustices to make restoration for past moral, economic, and political injustices. Restorative justice does not only restore the survivor, but also the offender and the community. The Korean church needs to take up the challenge to create a safe space where offenders and survivors can meet and proceed together on their journey toward reconciliation between North and South Korea. By doing this, Korean churches, as well as all involved parties, will truly take responsibility for the healing process. The Korean church needs to know, however, the limits of applying restorative justice in the context of North and South Korea because it is impossible to break the world cleanly into victims and violators.

Since it is crucial to create opportunities for both North and South Koreans to meet and build a relationship, the Korean church seeks to provide a place for truth and mercy to meet. Green Doctors, an NGO founded in Busan in January 2004, provides a good example. It received official government permission to open a hospital in 2005 in the region of Kaesong industrial park. Run by a South Korean committee, it has a 50-year lease, which began in 2004. Since then, it has provided medical treatment to the workers at Kaesong. The doctors who work there receive no salary. It has earned the trust of the North Korean workers and medical team, and it wishes to become a catalyst for a closer relationship between the two Koreas. Jungyong Kim, the director of the Green Doctors

---

45. See Glen H. Stassen, ed., *Just Peacemaking: The New Paradigms for the Ethics of Peace and War* (Cleveland: Pilgrim Press, 2008).

46. Joon-Sik Park, "Korean Protestant Christianity: A Missiological Reflection," *International Bulletin of Missionary Research* 36, no. 2 (2012): 62.

47. Volf, *Exclusion and Embrace*, 110.

Kaesong Hospital, describes the work thus: "The good Samaritan told us long ago who our real neighbors are. . . . It is honor and joy for me to live in the land of Kaesong where the Korean people from North and South work and live together. This land is the yard of unification, the hill of hope, and the starting point to become one."[48]

CONCLUSION

Reconciliation is at the heart of God's mission to the world. As God's gift to the world, reconciliation is a long and difficult journey with God. The Korean church, as God's missionary people, should recover reconciliation as the Lord's mission, and participate in the ministry of understanding as restorative justice, which requires truth, conversion, and forgiveness to reconcile North and South Korea. It is time to create space for the divided nation, and to learn how to lament together in the journey of reconciliation.

48. Jungyong Kim, "Real Joy for Them," Green Doctors.org.

Chapter 9

Redeeming Mission Theology in Africa: A Congolese Perspective toward Resolving Ethnic Conflict

Mossai T. Sanguma

Charles E. Van Engen encouraged his doctoral students, while doing missions-in-context, to draw four circles representing the world, church, Bible, and personal experience. Those four circles became his special trademark. As Chuck's disciple, I embraced this approach and used his master diagram. As Van Engen lectured, we amused ourselves by counting down one circle at a time. When he would say the word "church," we would draw one circle; the world, one more circle; the Bible became a third circle; and when he talked about his childhood missionary experiences, we drew the fourth circle. The game was that each student drew these circles so that they connected with each other to prove we understood the integrated parts. Even though it seemed as if we were teasing our teacher, his method became a meaningful way of learning the four dimensions of mission-in-context. We discovered that the four components were connected, and could bring light to the application of God's mission in our context. This chapter will focus on the topic of redeeming mission theology within a Congolese context by reflecting on Van Engen's four dimensions with the intention of describing factors that make Africa unique.

METHODOLOGICAL APPROACH

The paper will attempt this task by using two contextual methods: the anthropological and transcendental models.[1] The anthropological model takes integrative themes according to the study of humankind. This model asks, what has touched people's hearts enough to communicate to the deepest concerns of their suffering souls? Deep level themes are a part of a people's culture; they seek the best way of getting rid of the pain. The second model is the transcendental model. This model finds the truth lying within the subject, particularly the

---

1. Dean Gilliland,"Contextualization," in *Evangelical Dictionary of World Mission,* ed. A. Scott Moreau, Harold Netland, and Charles Van Engen (Grand Rapids: Baker Books), 225-28, 227.

members of the subject's community. Does this truth match God's truth, or does it state only the world's truth? In each case, how do we deal with such truths as they become theological and missiological issues? Therefore, the method of our studies will enable us to culturally explore and gain understanding of those themes to raise missiological and theological questions. In studying the mission theology of Africa, one has to relate to the question of what makes Africa different from other continents. What are the missiological concerns, and/or what is God's response to his people of that continent?

REDEEMING MISSION THEOLOGY

A theology of redemption is important. I chose to use an active verb as a two-way process. Redeeming mission theology is both descriptive and prescriptive since the process needs to continue. It challenges and changes all who get involved in the process. For most of time, African theologians have directed their theology toward redemptive theology, which is an end in itself: expressing the redemptive action of God. Yet, I would prefer to use the term "redeeming" mission theology for this study to highlight the continuous redeeming action of the mission we all need to embrace in dealing with mission in Africa. Colonization and slavery have directed theologians into a redeeming theology of mission. Theologians have published so many books on the "theology of liberation" expressing great hope of affecting theology in pressured areas such as apartheid, slavery, economic domination, third-world stereotypes, and Western domination. In this arena, culture combines with the biblical commentaries to advance personal ambitions and desires.

While still on earth, Jesus gave to his disciples power to heal the sick and raise the dead (Matt. 10:8). He came to set citizens and slaves free, to heal the blind and fulfill his purpose—to redeem those who suffered under a heavy burden of human domination. This is why I intentionally use the expression "redeeming mission theology in Africa." Jesus brought food to five thousand people when they were hungry. Jesus healed people who sought healing at the Sea of Galilee. Jesus asked sinners to sin no more. Now, the theological and missiological question is, do we act in the way of Jesus as he calls us to missions in Africa? Are we redeemers or enslavers? Are we liberators or imprisoners? Africa has become a paradoxical continent because of a lack of redeeming mission theology. We have accomplished little in our efforts to eradicate poverty in Africa, while some countries, with no apparent potential for wealth, have become superpowers. Africa still has great economic crises, political instability, and ethnic divisions.

GOD'S SOCIAL CONCERN
IN CROSS-CULTURAL MISSION THEOLOGY

The other aspect of mission theology we need to reflect on is cross-cultural mission theology. We often ignore the fact that Africa is a cross-cultural and multi-ethnic continent. Too often, theologians group the continent into a single culture. Theologians and missiologists who failed to realize the African continent is multifaceted only encouraged past explorers to divide Africa into northern and southern regions. In addition, because of this stereotype, the West called southern Africa Black Africa, or Dark Africa. The fact is, Africa is multi-ethnic, and all are in God's image. Interconnectedness through cultural diversity raises a missiological question and appreciation. How can we relate to one another while we are so different? How can we proclaim the gospel to people who do not look like us, and how can we relate to one another to bring the Good News to unreached people? We will now consider the issue of a redeeming mission theology of difference from an African outlook.

Living in harmony with one another is living with differences according to God's purpose in the world. A redeeming mission theology of difference begs reflection on why it is so difficult to embrace unity in most parts of the world. Why is division so common among God's people, and why cannot they live in harmony? What is God's purpose regarding differences? Why does not God create people to look, act, and behave alike, instead of creating individuals with their own unique fingerprints and behaviors?

In his incarnated Son, Jesus Christ, God accomplished his intention for the diverse people of the earth. Jesus demonstrated this sense of unity in diversity to the public as he was eating, sitting, dialoguing, and drinking with sinners and tax collectors. He spoke to a Samaritan woman, and allowed a prostitute to wash and kiss his feet (1 Cor. 12:12-31; Eph. 4:11-16; John 4:7; Mark 14:4-9; Luke 19:5). Can these texts speak to us in a special way to understand God's concern for everybody? Jesus teaches we must not attempt to restrict people from being part of the church. Christians often incorporate predispositions based on erroneous religious beliefs, and have a tendency to disregard unity. This cannot be! In the Pauline writings, we learn about the unity of the followers of Christ. To be one in Christ does not mean being dependent on oneself. Rather, it is being mutually interdependent. Paul's wonderful symbol of the physical body provides a good image for the necessity of unity (1 Cor. 12:12).

Oneness in Christ should be a prominent concept in searching for ethnic identity that could otherwise cause disunity among God's people. This theory should help us connect with others despite our differences. John D'Arcy May writes, "One of the greatest challenges faced by any culture is the degree of difference it is prepared to tolerate, the limits it sets on the dialectic of sameness and otherness, both in its own internal development and in its encounters with others."[2]

DEGREE OF DIFFERENCE

The "degree of difference" May discusses is what happened among Jewish people while integrating Gentiles within their first-century communities. Their level of tolerance stopped at circumcision. To prevent obstacles that would hinder

---

2. John D'Arcy May, "The Quest for Christian Unity, Peace, and Purity," in *Thomas Campbell's Declaration and Address: Text and Studies,* ed. Thomas H. Olbricht and Hans Rollman (Lanham, MD: Scarecrow Press, 2000), 223.

relationships, we need to search for common elements of societal worldview that are the foundations of the differences. It can be language, color, circumcision, status (cast), ethnic group, age, or any kind of specific interest group. When I lived in California, for example, 85 percent of my friends, particularly the Westerners, upon our first meeting immediately asked me, "Where are you from?" How should I answer them? When I answer that I am from Pasadena it is not what they expect. Should I respond with the questions: "Why? Do I look different?" I am black, yet there are many other blacks in the United States as well. At the time, I assumed they thought I was different because of my English accent. An African, on the other hand, would have been able to tell the difference between accents and resisted the questions to avoid offense. Now I realize their question probably had as much to do with my skin as my accent.

The central issue concerns why people are sensitive to differences. Is this because they want to learn from those differences, or because they are careful in dealing with someone different? Unity of differences is always a big problem in most societies. I believe, "For all Africans, unity is that ideal state (not to share their beliefs with outsiders) in which they wish to live but they remain open to cooperation."[3] In a discussion of a holistic approach to the ministry of healing, I affirmed that healing among Africans involved the necessary tools of love, faith, and reconciliation to build unity.[4] As seen through biblical history, we know God has blessed diversity, and the harmonious combination of differences is what God blesses.

In Ephesians 4:1-6, Paul exemplifies how difficult it is to live in harmony with one another; but it is not impossible. In the church, he called for congenial relationships, and demonstrated to the congregation how to live and work together in unity as they also grew together. This ideal is possible only if there is a harmonious combination of differences. We cannot ask God for his blessings while we are seeking to exclude others. People must work to resolve differences. Tribal, racial, or ethnic connectedness within itself is not enough for unity of diversity. There is another way of unity, however, as shown in Genesis 11, where God dealt with the citizens of Babel. The question is not the existence of those groups, but the way they treated other groups outside their circle.

GOD'S BLESSING IN DIVERSITY

Along these lines, J. Andrew Kirk argues, "Belonging to a particular group of people is a gift of creation."[5] The author implies that human diversity is a blessing of God. The loss of this diversity can lead people, within that particular group, into a serious "selfhood and disorder." Kirk raises the issue of the "right of being different." If people have the right to be different, and can still fit into a

---

3. Mossai T. Sanguma, *Health Care in Africa: Traditional and Missionary* (Chicago: North Park Theological Seminary, 1990), 128.

4. Ibid., 140.

5. J. Andrew Kirk, *What Is Mission? Theological Explorations* (Minneapolis: Fortress Press, 2000), 78.

group, diversity is richer. Moreover, when diversity correlates well, then we can discover God's blessing on this group. People who have difficulty cooperating with others should ask themselves, do these people have a right to be different? Are they people created in God's image, or am I alone created in God's image?

There is no way we can escape differences. People find differences everywhere and anywhere. Our task is to bring those differences into the harmony of Christ. When we understand how blessed we are living with our differences, then we will be able to encourage others to live in harmony with one another and not allow those differences to be the cause of disorder and conflict in our society. This is what redeeming mission theology is all about.

AFRICAN REDEEMING MISSION THEOLOGY

We need to consider three aspects as we come to understand the complexity of God's mission in the world and his intentions for his people. Mission theology in Africa should be relational, differential, and sacrificial. God's initiative to seek the fallen creature long ago and his willingness to go after the lost people in the garden of Eden sufficiently prove his desire to see his people being socialized with him. His expectation is to see his people come to know him and serve him obediently. Throughout the Old Testament, people who failed to obey his will faced discipline.

The world in God's eyes ought to be a dwelling place of redeemed people—a place of salvation where people seek God's kingdom and righteousness. All that opposes the kingdom of God is the work of Satan. Redeeming mission theology must address all the worldly behaviors that do not allow God's kingdom people to rejoice in this inheritance. In Africa, God is concerned with the issues of poverty, political instability due to injustice, and ethnic strife, which are the bases of ethnic divisions and inequality, especially among God's people. As God seeks to have a relationship with humanity, the people of God should live in harmony with one another. For all of the above confirmation about God's purpose in the world, African redeeming mission theology must be relational by placing God at the center of our relationships and sensitive to ethnic differences.

THE VALUE OF RELATIONSHIPS IN AFRICAN SOCIETY

African people enjoy their traditional way of living in community. Relationships are the most important components of their society. Breaking relationships in Africa is extremely rude. In the context of Africa, redeeming mission must be relational. Relationships in Africa are above the law, which means that someone can break the law because of his or her broken relationship with another. The reason that breaking the relationship of marriage (divorce) is infrequent in Africa is because of the fear of brokenness between husband and wife. For this reason, the concept of polygamy provides a substitute. An African man may not love his first wife anymore, yet because he does not want to break this relation forever, he may decide to keep his first wife and add another wife.

Africans do not talk about polygamy because they value their society and want to highlight the good of their culture.

This chapter is not advocating polygamy as an ideal Christian practice. Yet, it does become the means of avoiding breaking connections. Since the love is no longer as strong as it used to be, the easiest way to move forward is to add more wives. If we understand that relationships are the most valuable thing in the African community, then redeeming mission in this context must be relational. We need to maintain relationships within our society, the church, and with our God.

Redeeming mission theology in Africa should be relational and sensitive to ethnic differences. While doing mission in the African context we need to consider the theory of difference as affirmed by God when he promoted diversity in Genesis at the time of the tower of Babel. The oneness in diverse culture, language, and race is a blessing and not a threat to humanity. Africa by itself has so many tribal groups. My own country of the Democratic Republic of Congo alone has 450 tribal groups with several cultural backgrounds. Those diversities are a means of harmony rather than a means of taking advantage, dominating, or looking down someone else's back.

Redeeming mission theology in Africa should be sensitive to differences and work toward the oneness of the diversified cultures. People who practice exclusiveness according to cultural boundaries or racial benefits or intellectual categories should reflect on the purpose of God in making people different, and seek to harmonize their differences so that in place of exclusiveness, connectedness should gain a place in Africa. Robert J. Schreiter said that humanity could survive only if we accept the concept of peaceful coexistence.[6] We need one another for real mission work in Africa.

SACRIFICIAL AND REDEEMABLE: REDEEMING MISSION THEOLOGY IN AFRICA

Considering all the damage colonial history has done to Africa, mission to Africa should be redeemable. What do we need to do to redeem Africa from its history, poverty, political instability, and ethnic strife? Redeeming mission theology should be at stake as it fits into God's will for all the nations. This *missio Dei* concept makes mission relevant in Africa. The approach of most mission focuses on making disciples of all the nations (Matt. 28:16-18), yet we neglect to emphasize the redemptive action of freeing God's people. Mission theology in Africa must take into consideration the redeeming aspect of releasing Africans from their colonial damage. Talking about the redeeming mission theology of Africa means talking about redeeming Africans from the colonial sting, apartheid, ethnic strife, and many more issues that are the work of the devil.

---

6. Robert J. Schreiter, "Peacemaking and Reconciliation," in *Global Dictionary of Theology*, ed. William A. Dyrness and Veli-Matti Kärkkäinen (Downers Grove, IL: InterVarsity Press, 2008), 637-41, 641.

Mission theology in Africa should be sacrificial. The death of Christ on the cross enables his followers to love and make a difference in the lives of others, to take up their cross and follow Jesus. Taking up the cross means also to bear the marks of the sacrificial act of salvation. Someone shows the greatest love when one lays down his or her life for others. This refers to sacrificial acts with great love to make all efforts to bring someone out of his or her trouble and suffering. What are we doing to make the lives of others better? Does capitalism and individualism help, or are they systems that enable some to be greedy and others to suffer ceaselessly? Jesus took his own initiative to redeem and restore relations with humanity. What can we do as Christians in response? Is it not sacrificial work that could save somebody? Though we understand that worship, prayer, and offerings are means to present our bodies as living sacrifices to God, we must also live that sacrificial social action for the sake of saving others physically and spiritually.

THE PRACTICE OF REDEEMING MISSION THEOLOGY

The practice of redeeming mission theology cements true and harmonious relationships, as expected by Christ. This is a call to renew all human relations that have been broken due to past failures or past history and the day-to-day sending of someone to contribute to retaliation. Redeeming mission theology will be real if and only if we put into practice our relationships with one another and exercise mission in a real redeeming way in Africa. It is good to share some of our personal experiences as we discuss the issue related to ethnic conflict reconciliation. When I was president of the Evangelical Covenant Church of Congo, tribal conflict was a serious challenge as Christians complained about what each of their individual regions needed. With the main idea of solving the ethnic conflict within the church, we were able to organize a ministry of reconciliation. We established peace-building people in forty-two church districts to help victims of ethnic division, and to resolve the tension among people of the Ubangi, located in the northwestern region of the Democratic Republic of Congo. This was to help church members to be reconciled with one another because the tribal tension was so evident.

In 2005, the program brought people to oneness for the kingdom of God. The initiative interested the whole denomination, and we decided that the first Sunday of January each year would be set aside to celebrate reconciliation. Since the beginning of the initiative, politicians have asked for forgiveness from the population, parents from their children, and husbands from their wives. The most important testimony one could confess to the congregation was that he or she was doing something wrong. A politician, for instance, spoke to the congregation in January 2014 apologizing for the actions of the government and of politicians that were harmful to the general population. Her public apology encouraged the members of the church. Forgiveness can restore relationships.

HOPEFUL EXPECTATIONS: THE RELATIONSHIP OF
FORGIVENESS TO RECONCILIATION

Anything that deals with tensions or conflict must consider forgiveness as a pathway to resolution. Forgiveness is one of God's characteristics, as well as that of his unique Son, Jesus Christ. God is a unified, integrated being whose personality is a harmonious whole.[7] A forgiving being and full of compassion, God knows how difficult it is for us to live in harmony with one another. Here is the question: Who has asked God to be born from one family and not from another family, whether African or American or Asian or European? This tribal identity has nothing to do with our own will. God decides who is assigned to a very special ethnic identity. The blessing of diversity is crucial in God's will. When we are diverse then we are powerful and blessed. Being wholly reconciled to carry on the Good News of redeeming mission means being able to relate to someone who is different, and act as brothers and sisters, while serving the Lord.

CONCLUSION

The redeeming mission theology in Africa is a critical reflection of God's attribute of care for his creatures. This theological reflection aims to develop an understanding that will enable us to have compassion toward others who do not look like us. It emphasizes the continuous action of setting people free. This action is mutual and deals with the one who redeems as well as the one redeemed, as illustrated by the reconciliation ministry in the Ubangi area in the Democratic Republic of Congo.

Jesus Christ, the redeemer of humanity, has demonstrated a redeeming mission for all called to this noble ministry, enabling God's missionary people to be active in social awareness and merciful to all, especially to those who suffer, and even to those whom we consider enemies (Jon. 4:10-11). Thus, redeemed people humble themselves to observe God's will so that they can give thanks with gratitude to the redeemer in mission.

Mission to Africa should be a redeeming mission full of forgiveness, reconciliation, and freedom because our God is a merciful God, the God of the universe, and a God of those who love their enemies. Redeeming mission theology in Africa must be directed toward the needy, the helpless, suffering and oppressed people. The redeemed missionary people should be those with a tenderhearted call for mission that emphasizes a critically missiological attitude. Colonialists, paternalists, and imperialists confused those in mission during the colonial era; they could not express their tender hearts to people on the mission field. Nationalistic conduct reinforced their colonial and ethnocentric propensities. However, mission to Africa should be a redeeming mission full of forgiveness, reconciliation, and freedom because our God is a merciful God, the God of the universe, and a God of those who love their enemies.

---

7. Milliard J. Ericksen, *Christian Theology* (Grand Rapids: Baker Books, 1998), 323-24.

Part 4

Mission Theology and the Church

Chapter 10

Matthew's Experience of Discipleship and the Great Commission

Paul Hertig

The calling of Matthew provides an important backdrop to the Great Commission and signals key missiological themes in the Gospel of Matthew (9:9-13). Initially, Jesus said, "Follow me" (9:9), and Matthew did. Yet, in an interesting turn, the succeeding verse states that Jesus enters into Matthew's context, the home of tax collectors and sinners. Just as Matthew enters into the unknown and unpredictable world of discipleship, so "Rabbi" Jesus enters the strange and unfamiliar world of tax collectors and sinners. To paraphrase: "Follow me, yet I will participate in your community as well" represents a radical shift in Judaism in which outsiders become insiders, and dining with sinners does not defile the Righteous One, but heals the sinner!

Notice, Jesus defends himself to the Pharisees, explaining that he comes not to call the righteous but sinners (9:13).[1] Traditionally, such a meal would render him impure. Jesus states a proverb, however, that it is not the healthy but the sick that need a doctor, and that he desires mercy, not sacrifice. Jesus is quoting Hosea 6:1-6, in which God describes Israel as sick and in need of divine healing, and invites sinners to repent and turn to God in covenant mercifulness. Tax collectors are prime examples of unhealthy people, sold out to the Roman Empire, collecting taxes in excess for their own gain. Jesus, a doctor and disciple maker, a healer and caller, focuses on mercy (covenant faithfulness); the Pharisees, however, focus on sacrifice (the law). Mercy involves treating the sick with compassion and hospitality. Christ restores the sick to wholeness and calls his followers to discipleship. Jesus changes the rules of the game. His assertive presence with sinners restores them to covenant purity and God's faithful love, thus imparting a mission to go and do the same. The disciples too will be "fishers of people" (Matt. 4:19).

---

1. The Pharisees' very name means "those who separate themselves," and Pharisaic law overtly excludes tax collectors from table fellowship. See Jacob Neusner, *Politics to Piety: The Emergence of Pharisaic Judaism* (KTAV Publishing House, 1973), 73.

Two people who normally mix like oil and water, a tax collector and a rabbi, enter into each other's communities. This reciprocal process of missional engagement provides an important backdrop to the Great Commission. We now turn to the Great Commission text in which Jesus gathers his disciples on a mountain in Galilee and decrees a mission to "make disciples [main verb] of all nations" (28:19).

EXPERIENTIAL FAITH AND UNBELIEF

Stunning in this Great Commission text is the phrase "but some doubted" (28:17). Whether the doubting related to Jesus's resurrection or disbelief that Jesus was really the one present, the mixed response of the disciples serves as a helpful reminder that faith requires struggle. After all, belief is the constant conquest of unbelief.[2] Jesus's disciples are always on a journey, always in process, having never fully arrived.

We should commend even the doubters. They did show up to the appointment Jesus had set: with reminders (26:32; 28:7, 10, 16)! It has been said that every man, woman, and child is a religious enthusiast. These religious enthusiasts turned up to see if Jesus would make good on his promise. Yet, even enthusiasts doubt. The doubting disciples serve as a reminder that success in mission is dependent on the mission giver. Therefore, "the disciples' carrying out of the charge will not at all be determined by the excellency and strength of their own will and work; nor will it be jeopardized by their deficiencies."[3]

A disciple (literally, "pupil") is a learner who always struggles with human limitations, fear, and doubt. However, God's mission occurs in the midst of our doubts. Mission is not a triumphant enterprise. It occurs in weakness and humility. Yes, the *resurrected* Jesus speaks authoritatively from a mountain in Galilee, yet only after stumbling along the road to Golgotha, carrying his cross, helped by an advocate (27:32), then dying an agonizing and publicly humiliating death (27:35-44). Vulnerability and suffering are genuine marks of mission, and core reasons why Jesus closes the Great Commission with the comforting words, "I am with you always." Jesus chooses to encourage rather than condemn the doubting disciples. When we are weak, then we are strong, because in our weakness the genuine power of God becomes a genuine possibility.

The doubters remind us, "Mission never takes place in self-confidence but in the knowledge of our own weakness, at a point of crisis where danger and opportunity come together."[4] For this reason, Jesus envelops the text with his abiding assurances.

---

2. Karl Barth, "An Exegetical Study of Mathew 28:16-20," in *Landmark Essays in Mission and World Christianity,* ed. Robert L. Gallagher and Paul Hertig (Maryknoll, NY: Orbis Books, 2009), 17-30 (21).

3. Ibid., 22.

4. David J. Bosch, *Transforming Mission: Paradigm Shifts in Theology of Mission* (Maryknoll, NY: Orbis Books, 1991), 76.

Jesus's words began with a declaration of his authority in heaven and earth; they end with the statement "I am with you always." These were words of comfort given in the midst of doubts. Jesus did not separate the worshipers from the doubters like sheep from the goats. No one was condemned; none omitted from the mission mandate.

In this call for experiential learning, Jesus sent out ambassadors still filled with doubts. "Go therefore and make disciples of all nations." As they went, God strengthened their faith and dispelled doubts. Someone once told John Wesley, "Preach faith until you have it." In a similar vein, Jesus told his disciples to go forth in the midst of your doubts, and you will gain faith along the way. In this mandate for experiential mission, Jesus calls the disciples to step out into unfamiliar territory, to cross social, cultural, ethnic, religious, and geographic boundaries. A cynic once stated that a person who wants to find Christ should go not to the churches but to the slums.[5]

Certainly, Jesus beckons disciples to a personal journey with God, yet in the final mandate he emphasized a journey into the world. When one journeys into new regions, one must do so first as a learner. Even tourists do this. They learn about current events and the history of the host country as well as phrases in the language. How much more rigorously should missionaries be learners? Lila Watson, an aboriginal woman from Australia, stated, "If you come to help me, you can go home again. But if you see my struggle as part of your own survival, then perhaps we can work together."[6] The invitation to experiential learning is a call to humility. In the midst of our mission, we discover limitations and our need to learn from those to whom we minister. Furthermore, authentic mission integrates spiritual, intellectual, and experiential dimensions.

Jiddu Krishnamurti stated that the uneducated person is not the ignorant person, but the educated person is foolish when dependent *solely* "on books, on knowledge and on authority" to gain understanding because such a person does not know oneself.[7] The journey of mission is a discovery of new worlds and cultures, but also a journey of self-discovery. This includes discovery of our limitations and acknowledgment of doubts, which reveal areas for growth and thrust us into deeper dependence on Immanuel. The mission propels us into community with people who challenge us, and in turn whom we challenge. Through boundary crossing and communal living, the missionary becomes vulnerable and gains self-awareness along the road to truth.

Long-standing Western tradition considers truth to be an objective concept that individuals understand and analyze apart from community. In reality, the

---

5. Jürgen Moltmann, *The Crucified God: The Cross of Christ as the Foundation and Criticism of Christian Theology*, trans. R. A. Wilson and John Bowden (Minneapolis: Fortress Press, 1993), 12.

6. Glory Dharmaraj and Jacob Dharmaraj, *Mutuality in Mission: A Theological Principle for the 21st Century* (New York: General Board of Global Ministries, United Methodist Church, 2001), 43.

7. Jiddu Krishnamurti, *Education and the Significance of Life* (New York: Harper & Row, 1953), 17.

derivation of the word "truth" comes from "troth" and refers to a personal and intimate relationship. Truth is a courtship with another person, an intimate encounter. We should not merely *present* truth but also *represent* it to others. In our participation in the Great Commission, we do not merely recount the truth to others so that they may be aware of it; we relate the truth to others so that it might captivate them.[8] This is what discipleship is all about. We spend time with people building relationships, enjoying one another, laughing, socializing, discovering, committing, and reciprocating.

BODY, SOUL, AND COMMUNITY

Included in the Great Commission is the phrase "teaching them to obey everything that I have commanded you" (Matt. 28:20). Preeminent in that "everything" are the commandments to love God and love one's neighbor (Matt. 22:37-40). Love demands respect for people and their culture as foundational in the process of disciple making. Thus, the Great Commission does not supersede the great commandment. We go forth loving the whole person and the person's community. Our neighbor "is neither a bodiless soul" that we should love only our neighbor's soul "nor a soulless body that we should care for its welfare alone, nor even a body-soul isolated from society."[9]

The mandate of Jesus, then, is holistic and without ulterior motive. Mission is not a proclamation sundae that we top with social responsibility; neither is it a socially responsible sundae topped with proclamation. Once we regard mission as the combination of separate components, then each component has a life of its own. It then becomes possible "to have evangelism without a social dimension, and Christian social involvement without an evangelistic dimension."[10] Furthermore, when one component becomes primary and another secondary, it implies that "one is essential, the other optional."[11] Historically, people often viewed Christianity's amazing initiatives toward the poor, sick, orphans, and suffering people, as well as educational and agricultural agendas, as second-rate services rather than legitimate aspects of the mission of God. As a result, the church historically has often focused on the spiritual without engaging in the social, economic, and political realities of people's lives. The phrase "teaching them to obey everything," however, is a safeguard that Jesus built into the mandate that protects the disciples through the ages of narrowing the mission of God to dogmatic agendas. Like every Christian endeavor, mission hinges on the motives of love and authenticity. The sum total of the Great Commission coupled with the implicit great commandment is "love in action."

---

8. Robert J. Banks, *Re-envisioning Theological Education: Exploring a Missional Alternative to Current Models* (Grand Rapids: Eerdmans, 1999), 174.

9. John R. W. Stott, *Christian Mission in the Modern World* (Downers Grove, IL: InterVarsity Press, 1975), 29-30.

10. Bosch, *Transforming Mission*, 405.

11. Ibid.

Yet we often find ourselves comfortable in disengaged lifestyles through social distancing. Traveling internationally with a group of North American mission educators, I found that our conversation often centered on mosquitoes, malaria pills, repellent, the possible danger of ice cubes, and bottled water. These obsessions caused us to set ourselves apart rather than fully engage with people of the culture. Phobic precautions easily lead to obsessions with fear. When strolling around in public, as if more righteous than others, we publicly condemn ourselves and dehumanize others. "Holier-than-thou" social distancing changes the I–Thou category of relationships into the I–it category due to a lack of self-awareness:

> Unable to engage our interior lives, we are incapable of engaging the interior lives of other people. Not knowing ourselves, we are unable to reveal who we are before the face of another person. And we are unable to receive them in their personhood since we are out of touch with our own.[12]

Experiential learning begins from within. Once we understand ourselves, with all of our personal and cultural limitations and baggage, then we can begin to encounter others authentically. Bryan P. Stone has observed that the Christian church has become middle class and dangerously distant from the poor, often sending its missionaries "to convert the poor of the inner city to its own private brand of suburban holiness."[13] A paradigm shift is underway in mission that includes comprehensive and long-range partnerships and reciprocal initiatives in urban communities.[14] We need "others" as much as "others" need us.

RECIPROCAL RELATIONSHIPS

One of my Global Studies students at Azusa Pacific University, Azusa, California, shows the importance of reciprocity in intercultural relationships. Having returned from her "Global Learning Term" in Guatemala, she expressed her surprising reciprocal learning experience in the following poem:

> Dear Guatemala,
>
> You were nothing I expected
> and everything
> I needed

---

12. John Kavanaugh, *Still Following Christ in a Consumer Society* (Maryknoll, NY: Orbis Books, 1991), 8.

13. Bryan P. Stone, *Compassionate Ministry: Theological Foundations* (Maryknoll, NY: Orbis Books, 1996), 90-91.

14. See, for example, Steve Corbett and Brian Fikkert, *When Helping Hurts: How to Alleviate Poverty without Hurting the Poor—and Yourself* (Chicago: Moody Publishers, 2009).

I thought
you would reveal to me the
                    POVERTY
of the world.

Instead,
you showed me the
                    poverty
                    of my soul
                    . . . and awakened it.

With the *movement of dance,* the *aliveness* of the music, the *embrace
of community*, the utter humility of utter dependence.

You were supposed to
                    bolster my intellectualism
(give me a reason to feel proud in a scholarly environment).

                    INSTEAD
You made me feel sheepish as I learned to
                                        speak all over again.
Like a child, not yet two years old, at the mercy of those in the know.

Your
          VIVID COLORS
                    STARTLING SOUNDS
                              CELEBRATION OF LIFE
                                        SLOW PACED DAY
replaced the perfectionism, the drive, the insecurity.

You replaced busyness and hurry with
slowness
friendship.
                    You never gave me a sense of
                    accomplishment
                    RATHER
eternal friendships. Memories to make my heart burst with emotion.
Children's hugs. Homestay cooking. Language learning (frustration).
Toothless smiles. Oppressed, yet incredible women's courage and love.

This is what you gave me.

You refuse to be captured on paper.
                    But you will always remain captive in my heart.[15]

---

15. These are portions of a poem written by Jessica Sully, a Global Studies student at Azusa Pacific University. Written in 2004, the poem was an assignment for my course "Christian Mission in the 21st Century," and is used here with her permission.

Having described her semester in Guatemala as a desire to learn about poverty and bolster herself intellectually, the student instead discovered the poverty of her soul and the need for authentic relationships.

Surely, mission motivated by self-confidence and self-affirmation will fail. In fact, "the Christian faith, which once 'conquered the world,' must also learn to conquer its own forms when they have become worldly."[16] Jesus's resurrection mandate is rooted in the suffering at the cross. Therefore, a disengaged form of mission is unbiblical and unthinkable. It creates,

> a conscience-soothing Jesus, with an unscandalous cross, an otherworldly kingdom, a private, inwardly limited spirit, a pocket God, a spiritualized Bible, and an escapist church. Its goal is a happy, comfortable, and successful life, obtainable through the forgiveness of an abstract sinfulness by faith in an unhistorical Christ.[17]

This comfortable and successful model of Christianity interprets to "make disciples" as adding new church members into a congregation or filling up church pews in a sanctuary. However, "Biblically speaking, the preeminent activity of the church is in the public arena, *not* in the sanctuary."[18] Matthew's presentation of discipleship is a costly journey into the world, fully participating in the kingdom of God and challenging the kingdoms of this world. Matthew urges the disciples both to understand Jesus's words and to apply them without compromise. The goal of making disciples refers to the experiential process of God transforming us into the likeness of Jesus, as demonstrated by Jesus's example of making disciples. Disciple making is more than listening to sermons, attending services, or joining a church; it demands nothing less than total submission to God's reign in public life (28:18).

Mission in weakness and submission restores the person and community to genuine faith and dependence on God. When Christianity assimilates to mainstream society or institutionalism, however, it tends to abandon the vulnerability required of faith and mission.

VULNERABILITY AND DEPENDENCE

Jesus has a way of reengaging us in reality, as found in his final words, "And surely I am with you always, to the very end of the age." Matthew appropriately closes his gospel with the promise of Jesus's presence. The theme of Immanuel runs throughout the book of Matthew, from beginning to end, with a literary inclusion (Matt. 1:23; 28:20). Jesus is blanketing the final mission mandate with

---

16. Moltmann, *The Crucified God*, 36.

17. Orlando E. Costas, *Christ Outside the Gate* (Maryknoll, NY: Orbis Books, 1982), 80.

18. Dennis A. Jacobsen, *Doing Justice: Congregations and Community Organizing* (Minneapolis: Fortress Press, 2001), 14.

the idea that "I am your major resource."[19] The last verse of Matthew might be paraphrased, "Pay attention disciples! I am right beside you at every stage of your journey."

The promise of *Immanu-el* (with us-God) Isaiah announces in 7:14 during a time of desperation when the hearts of the people were shaken by the fear of ruthless aggression by the enemy. The God-with-us theme is utilized in the context of danger (cf. Isa. 8:8; Exod. 3:14). Indeed, the disciples, as they prepared to venture forth, had to deal with the fear of danger as well as with doubts. For this reason, in the record of Acts, the early disciples prayed for boldness (Acts 4:31). The boldness that God granted gave them the courage to move forward and overcome their doubts and failures. Only after one passes the mountain peak of failure does one arrive at the village of success.

In 1957 in Montgomery, Alabama, early in the civil rights movement, African Americans boycotted buses because of segregation. In the midst of setbacks, there were bombings in the city, and officials ordered all buses off the streets; successes appeared to turn into failures. At this low point, the key leader of the movement, Martin Luther King, Jr., broke down in public. Gripped with emotion he declared, "Lord, I hope no one will have to die as a result of our struggle for freedom in Montgomery. Certainly, I don't want to die. But if anyone has to die, let it be me."[20] In the depth of despair came the courage to press on toward the victory that would ultimately prevail. King explained that during the civil rights movement, the power brokers were unaware that they were dealing with African Americans freed from fear. As a result, every move made by the opposition proved to be a mistake.[21]

FEAR AND FAITH

Although it had happened many times before, one night a phone call in which his life was threatened awakened King. Unable to sleep, he heated up a pot of coffee and thought of a way to "move out of the picture without appearing a coward." He bowed over the kitchen table and prayed, "Lord, I'm down here trying to do what's right. I think I'm right. I am here taking a stand for what I believe is right. But Lord, I must confess that I'm weak now, I'm faltering. I'm losing my courage. . . . The people are looking to me for leadership, and if I stand before them without strength and courage, they too will falter. I am at the end of my powers. I have nothing left. I've come to the point where I can't face it alone."[22] Suddenly, King felt a calm assurance and an inner voice saying, "Martin Luther, stand up for righteousness. Stand up for justice. Stand up for truth. And lo, I will be with you. Even until the end of the world."[23] At this

19. Frederick Dale Bruner, *Matthew, A Commentary*, vol. 2 (Dallas: Word Publishing, 1990), 1105.

20. Martin Luther King, Jr., *The Autobiography of Martin Luther King, Jr.*, ed. Clayborne Carson (New York: Warner Brothers 1998), 102.

21. Ibid., 88.

22. Ibid., 77.

23. Ibid., 77-78.

point he heard the final words of the Great Commission, "And lo, I will be with you," and knew that Jesus was saying to press on in faith. His fears melted. Uncertainty disappeared. He was now ready to face any challenge. The very presence of Jesus gripped King in the midst of his faltering faith. God enters into the midst of our most fearful moments.

The promise of Jesus to be present "always, to the very end of the age" indicates that his presence and mission extend to the end of human history. The disciples who first heard this mandate have all passed on, yet the age has not ended. Therefore, the contemporary reader now interconnects in space and time. The Great Commission is an eschatological mandate given in a period between the resurrection and the end of human history (cf. Matt. 24:14). Since the reader lies between these two points in time, Dorothy Jean Weaver concludes,

> It is now clear that the boundaries between the story world of the text and the real world of the implied reader have disappeared. The world into which "the eleven" will go out to "make disciples of all the nations" is also the world of the implied reader, located between the Resurrection and the *Parousia*.[24]

The implied reader connects to the eleven recipients of the experiential mission mandate and, therefore, in fact, shares in that very mission. The present and future have merged into one in the new eschatological age of mission. The implied reader is an active participant in the mandate of Jesus and "an actor in the ongoing 'afterlife' of the story itself."[25] The Gospel of Matthew, then, is a story without an ending. We enter the story in the reading of the text, and participate in the unfinished mandate as we draw nearer to the end of the age (28:20). Jesus tirelessly devoted his life to the ongoing task of building relationships and leading others nearer to God—in his words, making disciples. Every Christian shares in this mandate.

ENTERING THE UNFINISHED STORY

Jesus's final mandate is a challenge to cross over the social, cultural, ethnic, racial, spiritual, geographical, and political boundaries of the world, to enter new contexts and engage in experiential mission through discipleship. Our starting point begins where Matthew concluded. We enter the unfinished story that "affects all people in all aspects of their existence" and that "embraces both the church and the world."[26]

Jesus does not say "good-bye" in the final mandate. Rather, he says, "I am with you always. . . ." Furthermore, "Jesus does not lay heavy burdens on

---

24. Dorothy Jean Weaver, *Matthew's Missionary Discourse* (Sheffield: JSOT Press, 1990), 152.
25. Ibid., 153.
26. Bosch, *Transforming Mission*, 391.

disciples and then fail to lift a finger to help them."[27] In contrast to the typical leaders of his day, Jesus empowered others (23:4). He challenged his followers to cross over every boundary and engage in the world experientially.

A church that is not engaged in mission is not the true church of Jesus Christ. It is time to cease dialogue about the church *and* mission, and to begin dialogue about the mission *of* the church.[28] Such dialogue must ultimately lead to a mission practice that engages in the concrete issues of people and their contexts. The moment he began calling his disciples, in Matthew 4:19, Jesus declared, "Follow me, and I will make you fish for people." Fishing for people is not the same as fishing for fish. The verbs in the Great Commission clarify that mission is incompatible with getting people to swallow a message hook, line, and sinker:

> All three of the main responsibility verbs in this commission—disciple, baptize, teach—are three slow or earthly ways of circling the same object, saying the same thing: *disciple*—take your time with people, work carefully with them, bring them along gently. First, we disciple by living among people and talking with the inquiring; then we disciple by teaching the baptized an ever-increasing loyalty to Jesus' commands.[29]

It takes great time and effort to make disciples. It involves entering into unfamiliar settings and relating to people in their unique social and political communities. In this process, the church dies to itself, engages in God's mission, is renewed, energized, and gains a sense of purpose and identity. The mission that Jesus modeled and proclaimed was rooted in conversation, presence, and community. In interacting with doubters, sinners, and tax collectors, Jesus's experiential approach was both relational and reciprocal. Immanuel: God with us.

---

27. Bruner, *Matthew*, 1105-6.
28. Bosch, *Transforming Mission*, 391, 392.
29. Bruner, *Matthew,* 1102.

Chapter 11

Missionary Churches in Acts: A Model of Intercultural Engagement with the Nations

vanThanh Nguyen, S.V.D.

Diversity in the church is not only a contemporary experience. The church has been diverse since the very beginning of its existence and in its early years wisely recognized diversity not as a threat to unity but a gift and a blessing. Motivated by the belief that salvation was available for everyone, the early followers of Jesus Christ risked everything, even their very lives, to share the Good News of redemption. As a missionary and New Testament scholar, I find great inspiration in the early church's missionary spirit and zeal. Thus, in this article I wish to retrace the missiological agenda found in the Acts of the Apostles to show that the church's intercultural engagement with the nations is the primary reason for its rapid expansion and success in the proclamation of the Good News. I will then conclude by suggesting several marks of an ideal missionary church for the twenty-first century. I hope that by examining the missionary churches in Acts, committed Christians today will find inspiration in the earliest witnesses to continue in the missionary enterprise of the church.

MISSION IN ACTS

A Universal Mission of Salvation

New Testament scholars widely recognize that the author of the Gospel of Luke and the Acts of the Apostles develops a single theological vision. Acts fulfills the Gospel's prediction as the apostles imitate what Jesus did. The author therefore intended these two volumes, also known as Luke–Acts, as one continuous work for the reader. Interestingly, the division of Luke–Acts forms the basic movement of a single story with a double three-part geographical structure. Acts 1:1-2 points back to the geographical structure of the gospel ("All that Jesus did and taught until he was taken up," NAB):

- in Galilee   Luke 1:1–9:50
- on the way to Jerusalem   Luke 9:51–19:44
- in Jerusalem   Luke 19:45–24:53

Acts 1:8 looks ahead to the missionary expansion of the church ("You will be my witnesses"):

- in Jerusalem   Acts 1:1–6:7
- in Judea and Samaria   Acts 6:8–12:25
- to the ends of the earth   Acts 13:1–28:31

Since Jerusalem and its temple have special geographical and theological significance, Jesus's ministry and mission are naturally centripetal, or a movement *toward* its center (Jerusalem), while in Acts, the disciples' activities are centrifugal, or a movement *away* from its center (Jerusalem) to the ends of the earth. Both the structure and content of Luke–Acts emphasize the universal mission of salvation.[1]

Guided by the Holy Spirit

From beginning to end, Luke shows that the Holy Spirit directs and guides the work of salvation every step of the way. The Spirit is an essential prerequisite for witness and mission. The Holy Spirit inaugurated the missionary church.[2] The disciples dared not to begin without the Spirit; they must wait (Acts 1:4) and pray (1:14; 2:1) for him. However, once the gift of the Holy Spirit was poured out at Pentecost (2:1-4), fulfilling the promise made by Jesus (Luke 24:44-49; Acts 1:5, 8), the universal mission of salvation began with a force that could not be stopped or hindered (Acts 4:31; 5:42; 12:24; 16:5; 28:31). Any attempt to interfere with the progress of the Word was futile for it was "fighting against God" (5:39).[3]

Just as Jesus's whole life was "filled with the Holy Spirit" in the gospel (Luke 1:35; 3:22; 4:14, 18; 23:46), Luke demonstrates in Acts that it was the same Spirit that gave birth to the church (Acts 2:1-4), inspired a community of believers to "share all things in common" (2:44), and united them in "one heart and mind" (4:32). Furthermore, it is through the empowerment of the Spirit that the apostles, as well as other women and men, were able to boldly witness to the risen Christ as the Messiah (Acts 2:14-41; 3:11-26; 4:8-12; 7:2-53; 10:34-43; 13:16-41; 17:22-31). More importantly, Luke takes special interest to show

---

1. This section is adapted from a previously published article. See vanThanh Nguyen, "Mission in Acts: An Inspiration for the Pilgrim Church," *The Bible Today* 52, no. 3 (2014): 133-39.

2. Arthur F. Glasser, with Charles E. Van Engen, Dean S. Gilliland, and Shawn B. Redford, eds., *Announcing the Kingdom: The Story of God's Mission in the Bible* (Grand Rapids: Baker Academic, 2003), 259-68.

3. Unless otherwise stated, all scriptural quotations are from the New Revised Standard Version.

that the Holy Spirit directly initiated and guided the mission to the Gentiles. It was through the action of the Spirit that Philip left Jerusalem to initiate the Samaritan mission (8:5), which Peter and John verified (8:14-15). The same Spirit guided Philip to a southern desert road of Gaza to encounter and convert the Ethiopian eunuch who probably brought the message of Jesus Christ to the southernmost end of the earth (8:26-39).

It was through Peter (a leading pillar of the Jerusalem church), however, that the Gentile mission was officially recognized. Luke masterfully shows that the Spirit carefully guided Peter to go to the house of the Gentile Cornelius to preach, baptize, and have table fellowship. This watershed conversion, which was also known as the "Gentile Pentecost" because the Holy Spirit was poured out on the Gentiles in a way similar to that of the Jewish disciples in the upper room, helped validate the legitimacy of the Gentile mission at the Jerusalem Council (15:7-11; see also 11:1-18). Thus, the stage was set for Paul to carry the message of salvation to the ends of the earth. Acts shows that the Spirit intervenes directly in the life of Paul and the mission of the church. The Spirit sent Paul and his companions on missionary journeys (13:4; 16:9), caused decisions to be taken (15:28; 19:21), disrupted plans (16:6, 7), testified before kings and rulers (22:21; 23:11; 24:10-21; 27:23-24), and even appointed leaders (20:28).

The age of the church is the age of the Holy Spirit, and the Spirit is "the primary agent of mission."[4] There are approximately seventy references to the Holy Spirit in Acts, which are more than are found in Mark, Matthew, and John combined. Luke's mission theology in Acts is unmistakably that of the Spirit. The Spirit is both the catalyst and the guiding force of the church's missionary enterprise. The Spirit sometimes acted like a leading character, constantly abiding, inaugurating, speaking, ordering, forbidding, redirecting, inciting actions, and comforting. It is not without cause that John Chrysostom (fourth century CE) called the book of Acts "the Gospel of the Holy Spirit."

INTERCULTURAL ENGAGEMENTS

Empowered by the Holy Spirit and motivated by the belief that salvation is available for everyone, the early followers of Jesus Christ brought the Good News of salvation from "Jerusalem, throughout Judea and Samaria, and to the ends of the earth" (1:8, NLT). As a missionary, I have always wondered how they coped with so many difficult situations and managed to achieve the task of spreading the Good News in such a short time. We can find the answer embedded in their intercultural engagements and exchanges.

Concisely, interculturality is a mutual multidirectional exchange and enrichment.[5] It might be helpful to note that interculturality differs significantly from cross-cultural encounter. Interculturality is a multidirectional exchange whereby

---

4. Glasser, *Announcing the Kingdom*, 263.
5. See Roger P. Schroeder, "Interculturality and Prophetic Dialogue," *Verbum SVD* 54, no. 1 (2013): 8-20.

the encounter enriches both parties; cross-cultural encounter, however, is one-directional communication that does not necessarily involve mutual exchange and enrichment. Consequently, both of these terms—intercultural and cross-cultural—are not synonymous. What follows is an examination of two examples of intercultural engagements; one each by Peter and by Paul.

Peter, an Intercultural Jew

Peter was born and brought up in a specific culture. He was a Jew who spoke a Palestinian Aramaic, and grew up in a context of Semitic ways of speaking and thinking. One must realize that Peter dressed like a Jew, prayed like a Jew, and taught and argued like any Jew of first-century Palestine. Yet, after the Pentecost experience, Peter demonstrated cross-cultural sensitivity in his teaching and preaching. As the apostle to the Jews and the pillar of the church in Jerusalem, Peter dominates the first half of Acts (chaps. 1–12). Representing the Twelve, Peter is the primary witness to Jesus as Messiah and Lord in Jerusalem, Judea, and Samaria. Bearing witness is an important theme in the book of Acts.[6] Having received the gift of the Holy Spirit, Peter boldly delivered the powerful mission sermon at Pentecost (2:14-41) and other evangelical speeches (3:12-26; 10:34-43), performed miraculous deeds (3:1-10; 5:12-16; 9:32-43), fearlessly confronted hostile opposition (4:18-20; 5:29-32), and endured flogging and imprisonment (5:18, 40-41; 12:3).[7]

Peter definitely engages in many missionary activities in Acts: in several Samaritan towns and villages (8:25); throughout Judea (9:32); in Lydda (9:32-35); and in Joppa (9:36-43). In Acts 10:1–11:18, Peter is a missionary whom God summons to journey to a Gentile territory, namely, Caesarea (10:5, 22, 29; 11:13). Furthermore, Peter entered into Cornelius's house, which was the home of a Roman soldier, to preach the Good News of salvation to him, his household, and friends; and then unconventionally partook in table fellowship with the uncircumcised. As one who had been filled with the Spirit (Acts 2:4) and commanded by the Lord to preach to the people (Acts 10:42), Peter courageously crossed over into unchartered territory and dismantled all sorts of cultural barriers—namely, language, ethnicity, and traditions—to include the Gentiles in the mission of the church. Peter's acts of testimony and intercultural sensitivity are hallmarks of one sent (*apostolos*) on a mission in the name of the risen Christ. As an intercultural missionary, Peter faithfully gives witness to Jesus without ethnic or racial distinctions (Acts 10:34-35).

Prior to Acts 10, Peter, filled with the Spirit, frequently offered testimony to Jesus as the resurrected Messiah: to Jews in Jerusalem (2:14-41); to the Israelites at Solomon's portico (3:12-26); to the religious leaders in Jerusalem (4:8-12); and to the Sanhedrin council (5:29-32). Then in Acts 10:1–11:18, Peter claimed that he had been chosen by God to be a witness of Jesus Christ as the "Lord of

---

6. See Peter G. Bolt, "Mission and Witness," in *Witness to the Gospel: The Theology of Acts*, ed. I. Howard Marshall and David Peterson (Grand Rapids: Eerdmans, 1998), 191-214.

7. Peter gives many significant speeches in the first half of Acts. Prior to Acts 10:1–11:18, Peter delivers five important speeches (Acts 1:15-22; 2:14-40; 3:12-26; 4:8-12; 5:29-32).

all" (10:36) to anyone who fears God—without showing partiality and racial distinction. Consequently, I portray Peter as a model for Christians to imitate even if it means crossing and dismantling social barriers based on geography, ethnicity, and language.[8]

Paul, a Culturally Sensitive Theologian and Missionary

Once the Gentile mission had been fully endorsed and authorized by the Jerusalem church (Acts 11:1-18; 15:1-35), Paul—the apostle to the Gentiles—took the central stage of Acts (chaps. 13–28) as the primary instrument for carrying the message of repentance and salvation to Galatia, Asia Minor, Greece, and finally to the heart of the Roman Empire—Rome. To fulfill the missionary mandate of the risen Christ, however, the great apostle had to endure many trials and sufferings for the sake of Christ and the gospel. As one imbued with the fire of the Holy Spirit (9:17; 13:2-3), Paul ventured into uncharted terrains, establishing Christian communities in many towns and cities. Luke recounts that nothing could weaken Paul's missionary zeal and spirit—not stoning (14:19), imprisonments (16:23; 28:30-31), physical torture and beatings (16:22-23; 22:22-30), constantly being chased away or pursued (13:50; 23:12-22), shipwreck (27:1-44), nor interrogations (24:23-35; 26:1-32), just to name a few incidents. See 2 Corinthians 11:21-28 for a longer list of Paul's own testimony of sufferings. As Acts presents, Paul's relentless determination to share the Good News of the risen Christ altered the landscape of the Mediterranean basin within a short period.

Paul is surely the most influential early Christian writer and missionary. He was a diaspora Jew who was born in Tarsus (Acts 21:39), a city well known for its intellectual environment. He eventually moved to Jerusalem to be "at the feet of Gamaliel," a leading Jewish scholar of the time (Acts 22:3). Paul personally admitted that he was fully a Jew—"circumcised on the eighth day, of the race of Israel, of the tribe of Benjamin, a Hebrew of Hebrew parentage, in observance of the law a Pharisee" (Phil. 3:5); so much so that he persecuted the early disciples of Jesus and was determined to extinguish the Christian movement (Acts 9:1-2; Phil. 3:6). Nevertheless, that was prior to his encounter with Christ on the road from Jerusalem to Damascus.

Paul's revelatory (*apocalypsis*) experience dramatically changed the course of his life. He was commissioned by the risen Lord to be an apostle to the Gentiles (Gal. 1:12). Filled with zeal, he embarked on various missionary endeavors, which the book of Acts arranges into three journeys, and founded many Christian communities or *ekklēsia*. Through his missionary activity and writings, Paul eventually altered the landscape and transformed the religious character around the Mediterranean basin. Many Gentiles gradually embraced monotheism, and, more importantly, believed in Jesus Christ as their Lord and Savior.

No one doubts that Paul was instrumental in the expansion of early Christianity. Yet, the question is, "How was Paul able to influence and convince

---

8. See vanThanh Nguyen, "Dismantling Cultural Boundaries: Missiological Implications of Acts 10:1–11:18," *Missiology: An International Review* 11, no. 4 (2012): 455-64.

Gentile communities that had a different set of beliefs and customs to adhere to the Christian faith and way of life?" I believe that Paul was able to plant the gospel of Jesus Christ in ways that made sense and intersected with the concrete aspects of the lives and cultures of his listeners. As a contextual theologian and missionary, he applied an "audience-sensitive approach"[9] in his evangelism. In other words, Paul contextualized the gospel within the cultural setting of his audience. This method required flexibility, creativity, and humility. To intellectual Greeks, he used sophisticated rhetoric for effective persuasion (1 Cor. 1:17-31). To conservative and observant Jews, he appealed to the Hebrew Scriptures and applied Hebraic midrash to explain the Torah (Gal. 2:19). To those who were familiar with sports and tools of warfare, Paul used athletic (1 Cor. 9:24; 2 Tim. 4:7) and military (Eph. 6:11-14) images and metaphors to get his message across. For ordinary folks, he used images of body parts (Rom. 12:4; 1 Cor. 12:12-17; Eph. 4:11-16), or everyday tools (e.g., mirror in 1 Cor. 13:12 and earthen vessels in 2 Cor. 4:7) that everyone could understand. Although a Jew, Paul understood the paganistic world in which he lived. Dean Flemming correctly notices that Paul was "audience-sensitive without being audience-driven,"[10] because he had the right attitude toward culture, namely, affirming as well as confronting culture. Because of this attitude, Paul was able to be "a Jew to the Jews and as a Greek to the Greeks" (1 Cor. 9:19-23). Flemming further states, "[Paul's] 'at-homeness' within overlapping Jewish, Greek, and Roman environments put him in a singular position to contextualize the gospel for both Jews and Gentiles, not as a foreigner, but as a cultural insider."[11]

Paul's Areopagus speech to the Athenians (Acts 17:22-34) clearly demonstrates his cultural sensitivity and "at-homeness" with his audience, and therefore serves as a compelling example of ideal cross-cultural exchange. While this comes from the book of Acts, Luke nevertheless depicts the genuine character of the historical Paul.[12] In this missionary sermon, Paul demonstrates a willingness to interact with the worldview, belief, and practices of his audience. He begins the speech, "You Athenians, I see that in every respect you are very religious. For as I walked around looking carefully at your shrines, I even discovered an altar inscribed, 'To an Unknown God'" (17:22b-23). Paul is fully aware of the Athenian culture, religious beliefs, and practices. Also, he shows a remarkable familiarity with the Athenians' philosophical traditions by quoting well-known sayings from their philosophers and poets. The saying "In him we live and move and have our being" (17:28a) is based on an earlier saying of Epimenides of Knossos from the six century BCE. As for the saying "For we too are his offspring" (17:28b), it is a quote from Aratus of Soli, a third-century BCE poet from Cilicia. Flemming summarizes Paul's Athenian speech this way: "[Paul] uses this

---

9. Dean Flemming, *Contextualization in the New Testament: Patterns for Theology and Mission* (Downers Grove, IL: InterVarsity Press, 2005), 92.

10. Ibid., 116.

11. Ibid., 150.

12. See Charles E. Van Engen, *Mission on the Way: Issues in Mission Theology* (Grand Rapids: Baker Books, 1996), 105-14, for a careful study of Ephesians from the perspective of a dynamic ecclesiology that reveals Paul's view of the missionary nature of the local congregation.

insight to respectfully engage their worldview, drawing upon indigenous language, images, and concepts to communicate the gospel in culturally relevant forms."[13] While Paul takes a respectful and conciliatory approach by beginning where the audience resides, he does not simply conform to their worldview and beliefs; rather he seeks also to confront, correct, and transform their understanding of God. Despite Paul's painstaking effort to contextualize the gospel for his audience, the message proved too much for many to accept. Yet, it was not all a failure, for some were convinced and believed; for example, "Dionysius, a member of the Court of the Areopagus, a woman named Damaris, and others with them" (17:34). Paul's Areopagus sermon is an outstanding example of cross-cultural evangelistic witness since it reveals Paul's cultural sensitivity in preaching to people from other backgrounds.[14] While Paul is flexible and conciliatory in his approach, he remains firm in his interaction seeking for transformation without compromising the truth of the gospel message.

MARKS OF A MISSIONARY CHURCH

Unity amid Diversity

Diversity is not a new phenomenon. The church has been diverse since the very beginning of its existence.[15] It is true that the earliest followers of Jesus Christ were all Palestinian Jews, yet soon after Pentecost, Hellenistic Jews also became followers. The list of people who were present at Pentecost indicates that people came from all over the Roman Empire. There were "Parthians, Medes, and Elamites, inhabitants of Mesopotamia, Judea and Cappadocia, Pontus and Asia, Phrygia and Pamphylia, Egypt and the districts of Libya near Cyrene, as well as travelers from Rome, both Jews and converts to Judaism, Cretans and Arabs" (Acts 2:9-11). The book of Acts also records that the Hellenist believers became numerous, resulting in tension within the community. Thus, the apostles had to choose seven deacons to attend to the various ethnic groups (6:5-7). Eventually, other Gentiles also joined the mix.

Through the success of the preaching of Paul and Barnabas, many Gentiles turned to the Lord Jesus. While Paul and Barnabas readily received the Gentile believers into the church without many restrictions, some Jewish believers forced the new converts to follow the Mosaic Law, especially the circumcision ritual. In other words, Gentiles had to become proselytized, or fully Jewish, to be Christians. This obligation prohibited Paul, Barnabas, and other early missionaries from associating or having table fellowship with Gentiles. Such a restriction would surely interfere with the missionary work of the church.

---

13. Flemming, *Contextualization in the New Testament*, 82.

14. See Lynn Allan Losie, "Paul's Speech on the Areopagus: A Model of Cross-cultural Evangelism—Acts 17:16-34," in *Mission in Acts: Ancient Narratives in Contemporary Context*, ed. Robert L. Gallagher and Paul Hertig (Maryknoll, NY: Orbis Books, 2004), 221-38.

15. See Van Engen. *Mission on the Way*, 115-24. Van Engen's four attributes of the church, namely, unity, holiness, catholicity, and apostolicity, fully capture the fundamental missional actions of the church.

This issue concerning the inclusion of the Gentiles, particularly enforcing circumcision, was no small matter for it could have divided or even destroyed the church (see Gal. 2:11-14 and Acts 15:1-2). The crucial debate led to the convening of the Jerusalem Council, the first council of the church. Through the guidance of the Holy Spirit and the testimonies of Paul, Barnabas, and Peter, the church imposed only minor conditions on Gentile converts (see Acts 15:1-29). The decision was monumental for the church's growth and development!

Since its very beginning, the church wisely recognized that diversity was neither a cause of separation nor of uniformity, yet rather that there could be diversity in unity. The church did not view diversity as a threat to unity, but a gift and blessing, fostering it for the enrichment of the church. The early Christians accepted that there were two different ways of spreading the gospel: one to the circumcised, entrusted to Peter, and the other to the uncircumcised, entrusted to Paul (Gal. 2:7-9). Nevertheless, it is faith in Jesus Christ that kept the church tied together as one body. Paul often used the image of the body and its members to confront the various factions in the churches (see Rom. 12 and 1 Cor. 12). He recognized that diversity is indispensable, such as a body with many parts (1 Cor. 12:12-13). Paul accepted the differences between the members as an enrichment of the body, and since each one was unique, the Spirit distributed his gifts to each person as he chose, and in an orderly fashion (1 Cor. 12:4-7). God, Jesus Christ, and the Holy Spirit guarantee unity through faith and love. The apostle Paul saw a deep bond of unity between particular churches. The preaching of a common gospel united all the believers. Furthermore, baptism and the Eucharist also created and fostered communion among Christians. The words of the institution of the Lord's Supper, found both in Paul's letter (1 Cor. 11:23-26) and in the gospels (Matt. 26:26-28; Mark 14:22-24; Luke 21:17-20), infer that the Eucharist was fundamentally the same in Corinth, Antioch, or Rome.

Then, as well as now, the church is a communion, a community modeled on the love among Father, Son, and Holy Spirit. It seeks to imitate that communion found in the oneness of the Trinity. Moreover, the church is catholic! In its universality, it welcomes and gathers all people without exception—"from every tribe and tongue, people, and nation" (Rev. 5:9). It is a communion in diversity, not in uniformity. Hence, an essential mark of a missionary church in today's world is the promotion of unity in the midst of diversity.[16]

Partnership in Mission

The second mark of a missionary church is collaboration in mission. Peter and Paul did not and could not complete the mission by themselves. They relied on other apostles, co-workers, companions, friends, and associates. Noticeably, John often accompanied Peter (Acts 3:1, 11; 4:13, 19; 8:14). There were also seven Hellenist (Jews who spoke Greek) deacons who were appointed by the

---

16. See Cathy Ross, "Introduction: *Taonga*," in *Mission in the 21st Century: Exploring the Five Marks of Global Mission*, ed. Andrew F. Walls and Cathy Ross (Maryknoll, NY: Orbis Books, 2008), xii-xvi, for Ross's five marks of mission.

apostles to serve at tables (6:5). However, two of them gave outstanding witness to Christ in Jerusalem and Samaria: Stephen (6:8-7:60) and Philip (8:4-40). Likewise, those scattered because of the persecution of Acts 8 brought the message beyond Judea (11:19-20).

Paul too depended on a network of friends and co-workers. The most notable ones were Barnabas (Acts 13:2), John Mark (12:25), Silas (15:22), Judas (15:22), Timothy (16:1), Apollos (18:24), and Luke (16:11). There were also women who worked alongside Paul and assisted him in his ministry. Lydia, the first European convert, was a dealer in purple cloth who migrated to Philippi from the city of Thyatira in western Asia Minor. After her conversion, Paul and his traveling companions frequented her home and found great encouragement in her generosity (16:15, 40).

Another outstanding couple worth highlighting was Priscilla and Aquila.[17] While in Corinth, Paul connected with this migrant couple, whom Rome exiled after the Edict of Claudius in 49 CE, and he resided in their house. The three worked together as tentmakers and as collaborators in developing the church in Corinth (Acts 18:1-3). Having spent eighteen months working side by side in Corinth (18:11), they accompanied Paul on a 250-mile journey across the Aegean Sea to Ephesus. Luke records that Paul left them at Ephesus as soon as they arrived, which indicates that the missionary couple must have founded the church in Ephesus, and subsequently prepared the stage for Paul when he rejoined them on his third missionary journey. This immigrant couple was constantly on the move for the cause of the gospel. Even though they relocated both their home and their trade to three different sites (Rome, Corinth, and Ephesus), they never faltered in their commitment to preach the gospel of Jesus Christ, risking everything because of their faith. Not surprisingly, Paul mentioned this couple in several letters, giving them the highest accolades by regarding them as "co-workers" and faithful friends who risked "their necks" for his life (Rom. 16:3-5; 1 Cor. 16:19; 2 Tim. 4:19). Paul had many other co-workers and associates that Luke did not mention in Acts. Hence, the farewell address in Romans 16 is testimony to the women and men he relied on in his missionary endeavors. The Spirit animated all sorts of women and men in the early church, and rallied them for the universal mission of salvation.

Mission by Everyone and in All Places

The third authentic mark of a missionary church is its recognition that mission is everywhere and a privileged task for everyone. Pope Francis's apostolic exhortation *Evangelii gaudium,* or *The Joy of the Gospel,* has been the focus of much discussion and attention since its promulgation in 2013. His description of the church as a "missionary disciple" particularly inspires me. Pope Francis writes:

---

17. See vanThanh Nguyen, "Migrants as Missionaries: The Case of Priscilla and Aquila," *Mission Studies* 30, no. 2 (2013): 194-207.

In virtue of their baptism, all the members of the People of God have become missionary disciples (cf. Matt. 28:19). All the baptized, whatever their position in the Church or their level of instruction in the faith, are agents of evangelization, and it would be insufficient to envisage a plan of evangelization to be carried out by professionals while the rest of the faithful would simply be passive recipients. The new evangelization calls for personal involvement on the part of each of the baptized. . . . Every Christian is a missionary to the extent that he or she has encountered the love of God in Christ Jesus: we no longer say that we are "disciples" and "missionaries," but rather that we are always "missionary disciples."[18]

Pope Francis also stresses that a missionary disciple must do more than just simply evangelize. Rather, he or she must radiate and demonstrate the joy of one's faith, which is a sign of an authentic follower, or disciple of Jesus. Francis says, they, as evangelizers or missionary disciples, "must never look like someone who has just come back from a funeral" or "whose lives seem like Lent without Easter."[19]

Since every Christian is a missionary disciple, mission therefore involves everyone and can be anywhere. Stephen B. Bevans has already accentuated this important point saying, "Today, it is probably more important to think not where is mission, but who is mission. Mission is about people—youth, young adults, men, women—outside the boundaries of the church and the parish."[20] Bevans further states, "Being a community in mission—a missionary parish—is much more a state of mind than anything else. It is being really present to the world in which we live."[21] When everyone engages mission and it takes place everywhere, then the missionary community actually moves from a "service station or spiritual gas station"[22] that is concerned more about maintenance, to one that is truly missionary.[23]

CONCLUSION

The book of Acts is a theological masterpiece that recounts the origins and development of the Christian mission from Jerusalem to Rome—the heart of the Roman Empire. At every turn of events, giving witness to the gospel of Jesus Christ takes the central stage of the narrative. Driven by the belief that salvation is available for everyone, the early followers of Jesus Christ risked everything, even their very lives, to share the Good News of redemption to

---

18. Pope Francis, *Evangelii gaudium*, 120.

19. Ibid., 10, 6.

20. Stephen B. Bevans, "A Missionary Parish: Beyond the Spiritual Service Station," *New Theology Review* 24, no. 2 (2011): 14.

21. Ibid.

22. Ibid., 7.

23. See Robert S. Rivers, *From Maintenance to Mission: Evangelization and the Revitalization of the Parish* (Mahwah, NJ: Paulist Press, 2005).

all people everywhere. As a community that was mission driven, they entered into intercultural engagements, and the process enriched them. I believe that their sensitive and respectful engagement with the nations was the main reason for the church's rapid expansion and success in the proclamation of the Good News. Consequently, the examination of the missionary churches in Acts as a model of intercultural engagement with the nations should encourage every baptized Christian to participate in the mission of the church since the church is "missionary by her very nature."[24]

---

24. Pope Paul VI, *Ad gentes*, 2.

Chapter 12

Group Identities and Boundaries during the Pauline Mission

Adam D. Ayers

As a pastor, I rely upon the Bible when leading our community. This naturally drew me first into biblical studies, and later into missiological hermeneutics at the urging of Charles Van Engen. For decades, Chuck has sounded a clarion call to employ the concerns of mission as keys to unlocking Scripture, urging missiologists to bring all of their interdisciplinary tools to the task. I believe that he has been prophetic on this point. Even though missiological interpretation is young, it is a discipline with amazing promise, and Chuck deserves many thanks for being its champion. I remain grateful to him always for introducing me to it.

Chuck often highlights missiology's capacity to bring multiple disciplines into play during interpretation. In this chapter, I bring anthropological perspectives into interaction with literary and sociorhetorical agenda, under the umbrella of missiological hermeneutics. The chapter explores Acts' descriptions of Paul's early mission(s), the conflicts at Syrian Antioch and Pisidian Antioch, and Paul's encounter with the disciples at Ephesus, observing group boundaries and identifiers. I then apply those insights to current issues in mission theology and interpretation.

MISSIOLOGICAL THEORY ABOUT GROUP BOUNDARIES AND IDENTIFYING CENTERS

"What makes someone a Christian?" Although it may appear simple, this is a deeply complex question, one that often divides mission workers. Without attempting a final resolution, I want to propose that we can take a step toward articulating an answer by recognizing that there are varied ways to create social identity. This is where anthropology, biblical studies, and mission can cross-pollinate.

In my alternate vocation as a professor of anthropology, a semester cannot pass without mentioning the works of Kenneth L. Pike and Paul G. Hiebert.

146

Pike is well known for developing the linguistic categories of *emic* and *etic*, which describe viewpoints from inside (*emic*) or outside (*etic*) of specific social locations.[1] Mission scholars often use Pike's distinction to negotiate issues concerning relevance, contextualization, translation, and culture-based meaning.

After Pike's work, anthropologist and missiologist Hiebert published an essay on conversion that explored the concept of a "centered set," which he juxtaposed against a traditional "bounded set."[2] Hiebert argued that mission often approaches conversion in bounded ways, which see individuals as either "in" or "out," but that it could be fruitful to identify people relative to an identifying "center," such as the person of Jesus. He also noted that boundaries sometimes are not clear to our view but "fuzzy."[3]

Taken together, Pike and Hiebert show that groups can have both boundaries and centers, which work in different ways to establish their members' identities, and that a group boundary can become "fuzzy" at certain points. If we can imagine a tent's center pole and fabric edge, we can visualize how a "center and boundary" model might look, especially if the edge frayed at certain points.

However, we should keep in mind that groups usually do not have solitary identifying centers. Definitions of group membership can vary, and subgroups often compete for the right to identify the traits of a "real" constituent. With religious groups, it is quite common to find sects under a common religious rubric disagreeing about what makes someone a "real" believer, and, while one subgroup may consider a particular individual to be "in" the overarching community, another subsect may consider that same person to be "out." These competing centers coexist unevenly within the broader group's definition. They may overlap at points or extend beyond the limits of other centers at other points. This would be like combining a number of tents, with each tent's center pole competing to be the tallest or most central.

BOUNDARIES AND CENTERS IN EMERGING CHRISTIAN IDENTITY

If we keep boundary and center dynamics in mind, an interesting picture of the early Christian movement emerges, in which different ways of identifying with Jesus appear. We can see these through the varying words that we use for

---

1. Karl Franklin, "K. L. Pike on Etic vs. Emic: A Review and Interview," Summer Institute of Linguistics (November 27, 1996), http://www-01.sil.org.

2. Paul Hiebert, "The Category 'Christian' in the Mission Task," *International Review of Mission* 72, no. 287 (1983): 421-27. Hiebert distinguished between "centered," "bounded," and "fuzzy" identification strategies. He favored "centered" identification, but recognized the reality of "fuzzy" horizons.

3. In Hiebert's words, "On the other hand, we must recognize that from the human point of view we often see 'through a glass darkly.' God, who sees the hearts, knows who are his. However, we, who must depend upon verbal statements and behavioral changes, often see the boundary as fuzzy. There are those who are clearly followers of Jesus, and those who reject him. But there are many in the church whose commitment is not all that clear. It may be for this reason that we are cautioned about passing judgments (Matt. 7:1; 1 Cor. 4:5)," ibid., 427.

Christians. Conceptually, these differing terms reveal varied identifying "centers" with distinctive domains and boundaries.

Initially, Jesus was a rabbi who had students (John 1:38; 3:2, 26; 6:25). This was a typical arrangement, since Judaism at the time had many schools and movements, which people identified with particular teachers.[4] Jesus's students were disciples" (*mathētai* [pl.]), which signals a social-status relationship between a teacher and a "follower" (Matt: 8:19). However, in Jesus's case, an identifying center that emphasized confessional belief about or in Jesus complicated the familiar Jewish rabbi–pupil status relationship. This distinction acknowledged Jesus as the Messiah (Christ), the "Son of the Living God."[5] Thus, Jesus's adherents were "believers" (*pisteuontes* [pl.], Acts 5:14; cf. John 4:42; 6:29, 64; 8:24; 9:35-36; 11:26-27) as well as "disciples," even if they were not formally his students. Jesus also called for repentance and baptism for the forgiveness of sins (cf. Matt. 3:2, 8 and Matt. 4:17; 9:13; also Mark 1:4-5, 14-15). This emphasized "conversion" (Matt. 18:3; Mark 4:2; Luke 22:32), evidenced by ritual and change of conduct.[6]

After Jesus's ministry, Acts calls Jesus-adherents "disciples" (1:15), along with a select subgroup of "apostles" (1:26). At Pentecost, this combined group received the "gift of the Holy Spirit" (2:38), which changed the community's limits. Suddenly, a hard, clear boundary appeared between those who manifested the gift and those who did not. Unlike the preceding centers that identified via belief, conversion, or following, this charismatic identifier was not prevalent in existing Judaism.

While Pentecost opened a door of engagement with many nations, it was not a one-way street. Pentecost also consolidated a loosely defined movement into a recognizable social community by clarifying the "fuzzy" boundaries that had existed between Jesus followers per se and devout proselytes or ethnic Jews.[7] This boundary made it possible to convert others "in" to a clearly identified group.

Acts calls this group "the church" (*ekklēsia*, Acts 2:47; 5:11; 8:1-3; and, notably, 9:31). As a social group, persons could be "added" to the church through social inclusion, which Acts refers to as "them" (Acts 2:41; 4:33-34, 5:13). This formed a new fictive fraternity of "brothers and sisters,"[8] which had a different domain of meaning than the ethnic family of Israel. A further signal

---

4. Martin Hengel, *Judaism and Hellenism: Studies in Their Encounter in Palestine during the Early Hellenistic Period*, ed. and trans. John Bowden, 2 vols. (Philadelphia: Fortress Press, 1981), 247-54; John Drane, *Early Christians: Life in the First Years of the Church* (San Francisco: Harper & Row, 1982), 12-34.

5. Matt. 16:13-20; John 1:35-40, 49-50 complement the two aspects of Jesus as (1) Messiah and (2) Son of the Living God.

6. Matt. 3:8; John 3:22-30; these ground identity using different "sacralized" dimensions of life. See Howard Clark Kee, *Miracle in the Early Christian World: A Study in Sociohistorical Method* (New Haven: Yale University Press, 1983), 54-60.

7. Adam D. Ayers, "In Search of the Contours of a Missiological Hermeneutic" (PhD diss., Fuller Theological Seminary, 2011), 271-301. Note Peter's use of "we" and "you" throughout his Pentecost sermon.

8. *Adelphōi* (brothers [pl.]), e.g., Acts 1:16; 6:3 (diverse ethnicity). "Brothers" is frequently gender inclusive. It is used often in Acts, but rarely in the gospels.

trait was that these had "received" "life" or "forgiveness."[9] These terms identify group members by a quality, so adherents were labeled "saved" (Acts 2:47; 10:1-48), "forgiven," or "alive." Thus, someone could be associated with Jesus as a "disciple" by following, as a "believer" by faith, as "saved" by repentance, or as "one of them" through demonstrating the Spirit or through welcome into the church. Each of these ways of distinguishing Jesus adherents carried a special nuance as an identifying center, establishing what it meant to be a Christian. Each designation also carried unique horizons relative to other Christian identifiers and to other religious and social groups.

EXPANDING BOUNDARIES DURING PAUL'S MISSION

It then should come as little surprise that contentions would arise about who should be deemed "inside" or "outside" of the Jesus community and over which identifiers served as watersheds. There is also small wonder that Acts places Paul at the center of those contentions.[10]

Paul's Base at Antioch

In the Acts accounts, Paul initially focuses mission toward Jewish audiences, which follows a pattern established earlier at Syrian Antioch (Acts 11:19-21). At Antioch, "scattered" Jesus adherents founded the community, "spreading the word only among Jews" (11:19).[11] Although their original mission was for Jews alone, that goal was adjusted by the addition of "Greeks" after "some of them" "spoke to the Greeks also" (11:21).[12]

While it remains unclear if the "men of Cyrene and Cyprus" (11:21) were ethnic Jews, this subgroup of evangelists at Antioch abandoned the precedent of Jewish exclusivity and proclaimed to Greeks. The "Lord's hand" favored this move, and the Greeks "believed" in such numbers that Barnabas was sent to them from Jerusalem. Barnabas in turn sought out Saul, their founders' former persecutor (Acts 8:1-3), and brought him to Antioch, where they taught together for a year (11:25-26).

In this complex social context, we find the first distinct naming identifier for Jesus adherents: "The disciples were called Christians first at Antioch" (11:26). This broad christocentric label covered those who "believed" (11:21), who "turned to the Lord" (11:21), who were "brought to the Lord" (11:24), and who were "disciples" (11:26). Antioch's umbrella term reveals an emerging transethnic

---

9. For "receiving" see Acts 10:43; 17:11; and 1:8; 2:38; for "life," Acts 5:20; 11:18; 13:46-48; for "forgiveness," Acts 10:43; 13:38; 26:18.

10. Although biblical scholars do not agree about the historicity of Acts, it remains valid for analyzing the social and discursive worlds of the early church.

11. All scriptural quotations come from the New International Version.

12. Paul Hertig, "Dynamics in Hellenism and the Immigrant Congregation," in *Mission in Acts: Ancient Narratives in Contemporary Context,* ed. Robert L. Gallagher and Paul Hertig (Maryknoll, NY: Orbis Books, 2004), 74-75.

identifying center for the community. While the domain of "Christian" could overlap with "Jew" or "Greek," the term's nonethnic centering allowed the community to shift its self-identification away from those preceding ethnic distinctions. This transethnic, "Christian" community became the base that sent Paul and Barnabas out to engage Cyprus and Asia Minor.

PAUL'S "FIRST" MISSIONARY JOURNEY

While on mission, Paul and Barnabas follow precedent from Antioch by preaching first to Jews (Acts 13:1, 14; 14:1), yet the outcome is different at Pisidian Antioch. Acts portrays Paul's kerygmatic language there as ethnically divided, but the centering of his identifiers remains "fuzzy." His sermon distinguishes between Jews as "fellow Israelites," "people of Israel," and "fellow children of Abraham," and non-Jews as "you God-fearing Gentiles"[13] (13:16, 26). He also speaks of "the God of the people of Israel," "our ancestors" (13:17), and "us, their children" (13:33). However, he mitigates these ethnic identifiers by using the distancing pronoun "them" to speak of historic Jews and Jerusalemites (13:17-19, 21, 23, 27-29). Also, while Paul's message focuses on God's promise to the fathers (13:32-33), it highlights "salvation" (13:26), "forgiveness of sins" (13:38), and "justification" (13:39). Further, Paul locates the community boundary at "everyone who believes," centering on faith and contrasting that faith against the demands of Mosaic Law (13:38-39).

Some respond by "follow[ing]" (13:43), while the message appeals to city dwellers who are not associated with the synagogue. A division results, and Paul relocates God's promise to non-Jews (13:46-47), while the resistant "Jews" are cast as outsiders, opposers (13:45, 50) who are not "worthy of eternal life" (13:46). The "Gentiles" respond, overwhelming the original Jewish audience. This group identifies with Jesus as the one who brings "salvation to the ends of the earth" (13:47). Acts depicts this as a success, emphasizing, "All who were appointed for eternal life believed" (13:48). It calls the final group "disciples [who] were filled with joy and with the Holy Spirit" (13:52).

Conflict at Syrian Antioch and the Jerusalem Debate

When Paul and Barnabas return home, they find "certain people" from Jerusalem asserting that the Antiochene "Christians" need to be circumcised according to Mosaic custom in order for them to be "saved" (Acts 15:1). This claim places Jesus-adherent identity within the boundaries of Jewish identity, championing ethnic heritage and tradition. Their proposal arouses Paul's virulent opposition, with significant implications for Christian identity and boundaries.

Acts records the Antiochene story using language that carries ethnic distinctions. Yet, it also laces the account with identifiers that blunt ethnic identification. This serves to undermine the ethnic character of the conflict.

---

13. While the NIV translation reads, "God-fearing Gentiles," there is no mention of "Gentiles" in the Greek text; only "God-fearers."

In 15:1-3, the visitors are identified by place ("Judea") and the Antiochenes by filial relation. The church sends Paul's delegation, and their report of Gentile conversions gives joy to filial kin in Phoenicia and Samaria. Regardless of whether these kin are Jews in residence or Samaritans and Phoenicians, talk of the "converted" "Gentiles" implies that they recognize ethnic distinctions. More importantly, the report that the Gentiles have been "converted" openly contradicts the Jerusalemites' assertion that without Jewish inclusion the Gentiles cannot in fact be "saved."

At Jerusalem, the church welcomed the delegation (15:4), which identifies itself by social organization, yet circumcision advocates identify themselves primarily by sect (15:5). While Peter's speech uses the social-status term "disciples" for the Antiochenes (15:10),[14] James goes further. Initially, he contrasts "brothers" with "Gentiles" (15:13), but he shifts to an inclusive position by modifying Amos 9:11-12.[15]

In the letter that follows, the Jerusalem leaders use the relational term "brothers" equally to refer to those in Jerusalem and the mixed group in Antioch (15:23). They marginalize the ones insisting on circumcision (15:25), and reaffirm consensus, having "all agreed" (15:25). They seal their decision as divinely authoritative, that "it seemed good to the Holy Spirit and to us" (15:28) to call for abstinence from food offered to idols, blood, strangled things, and sexual immorality.

Significance of the Jerusalem Decision

The Jerusalem decision marks a crucial shift in the foundations upon which identity boundaries are set. It abandons key signals of ethnic identity and replaces them with terms of fictive kinship, using boundaries of conduct that are not distinctly Jewish,[16] which deemphasizes ethnically bounded covenant. Even though identifying terms such as "believers," "disciples," and "followers" are available, we make the choice to identify through fictive filiality and religious conduct. After the Jerusalem decision, the concept of fictive kinship dominates. While various terms still occur in the story of Paul's first mission, adherents at Antioch are not called "Jews," "Gentiles," "saved," "believers," or "disciples"; only kinship terms occur for the remainder of the account.[17]

Paul and the Disciples at Ephesus

Later in Paul's journeys the tables turn. Paul "found some disciples" at Ephesus (Acts 19:1) who were unfamiliar with Jesus. Paul asks of their experience

---

14. Peter's use of "us and them" complicates his assertion that God "made no distinction between us and them," as does "neither our fathers nor we" (15:10), and "we" and "they" (15:11).

15. See the discussion by David Strong, "The Jerusalem Council: Some Implications for Contextualization," in *Mission in Acts: Ancient Narratives in Contemporary Context,* ed. Robert L. Gallagher and Paul Hertig (Maryknoll, NY: Orbis Books, 2004), 202.

16. Mosaic custom, circumcision, and Sabbath-keeping would be distinctly Jewish markers.

17. Acts 15:23, 32, 33, 36, and 40; v. 30 appears to be a "gathering" of the "brothers and sisters."

with the Holy Spirit and then backtracks through an introduction to Jesus when he finds that they only know John's baptism (19:1-5). Paul distinguishes first between the baptisms of John (for repentance) and Jesus (of belief) (19:4). He then baptizes the disciples in the name of Jesus (19:5) before introducing them to the Holy Spirit by the laying on of hands, accompanied by the identifying behavior of speaking in tongues (19:6).

In Acts, "disciples" is used to indicate valid members of the true faith community; the term is not used for members of other sects.[18] Yet, at Ephesus, these "disciples" are not "believers," who are identified via faith in Jesus. Neither are they "brothers," who are identified through association. They are "disciples," a term that identifies them by one's status as a learner. This is appropriate to the story, for they are in the process of coming to full knowledge. However, even though these are in process, Paul treats them as fellows from the outset, and legitimate adherents who only need to walk through the lacking identifying centers of belief, filial association, and spiritual experience.

Significance of the Pauline Accounts

As it portrays the groups, events, and speeches in Paul's ministry, Acts demonstrates that the identifying centers and boundaries of the Christian community are not fixed but subject to definition by authoritative decision[19] and based upon varied criteria. The disciples at Ephesus do not have to know about Jesus or have the Spirit within them before the church acknowledges them. They are part of the community, although they need polemic instruction, formal inclusion, and manifestation of the Holy Spirit. At Syrian Antioch, the Christians have right teaching and the activity of the Holy Spirit, but they need apostolic welcome into fictive kinship and a code of identifying conduct. At Pisidian Antioch, Paul's declaration redraws community boundaries, even kerygmatic boundaries, in response to a moment of social strife, deliberately excluding ethnicity as a criterion.

In each account, ecclesial authority establishes the emic/etic boundary between what is "we" and "not-we." The apostles do this by affirming or denying some type of criterion, some "identifying center," which also creates a boundary. Yet, the criteria that the apostles choose to recognize vary from situation to situation, and the terms for adherents vary. Whether the key identifier is belief, confession, ritual inclusion, social inclusion, conduct,[20] spiritual manifestation, or ritual appears to depend on the situation, the group, and the discretion of the leader(s) establishing the boundary. This indicates that early Christianity did not have a monolithic identifying center. Alternate identifiers coexisted, and the apostles chose which criteria to acknowledge at specific points.

---

18. Paul's warning (Acts 20:30) refers to the apostasy of believers.

19. Note the decisions at Jerusalem and at Pisidian Antioch.

20. In Acts and the Pauline letters, the conduct standards that signal Christian identity appear to vary by context. Mosaic observance is endorsed at Jerusalem (Acts 21:15-26), but not at Syrian Antioch (Gal. 2:11-14). Paul modifies the Antiochene rules of food abstinence for Corinthians (1 Cor. 8:1-13).

IMPLICATIONS FOR MISSION STUDIES: THEOLOGY AND HERMENEUTICS

Theology of Mission

Accounts of Paul's mission in Acts demonstrate that as missionaries engage the nations, people come to Christ in different ways and people qualify as Christ adherents by varied criteria. Some qualify through belief, others through association with the community of faith. Some qualify by submitting to clear behavioral codes and others via charismatic experience. Some must negotiate a "hard" boundary in conversion; others develop within the faith community or within cognate movements and must encounter Christ in new ways later. The church inducts some through clear rituals, while others migrate slowly toward Christ across "fuzzy" frontiers that do not fully distinguish between "disciples" who are unaware of Jesus and "believers" who have more developed theologies.

These accounts also show different ways for representatives of Christ to engage audiences. In some cases, Christians can target exclusive, ethnic communities for proclamation. In other situations, we need to abandon ethnic distinctions. Some contexts call for Christ's agents to suspend traditional expectations about the behaviors of new communities. Other moments call for new communities to ask for guidance from older traditions and to accept the advice of established leaders as coming from the Holy Spirit.

The Pauline stories also show that Christ's representatives sometimes need to make judgment calls and that they can exercise discretionary authority[21] in order to establish or redefine identities and boundaries. Sometimes, mission situations call for expansion or suspension of doctrinal boundaries in light of others' encounters with the Holy Spirit or in consideration of their status as God-learners. In such cases, it appears from Paul's ministry that the church may acknowledge certain others as legitimate fellows and may declare them to be "disciples" or kin before all criteria are met.

Considering Paul's instructions to Corinth in light of conduct codes at Antioch and Jerusalem, it also appears that some latitude prevails about the behaviors that demonstrate Christian commitment. In certain contexts, strict adherence to a long list of behaviors may signal that one is a Christian, while elsewhere the canon of conduct may reduce to a handful of signal actions. These are issues that theologians of mission may wish to examine in greater depth with an eye to the biblical witness.

Missiological Hermeneutics: "They" and "We," "Then" and "Now"

The boundary dynamics that we see during Paul's ministry also reveal truths about the natures of *groups* and *events*. From a missiological perspective, these

---

21. For instance, James states, "It is my judgment, therefore, that we should not make it difficult for the Gentiles who are turning to God," and in the Jerusalem letter, "it seemed good to the Holy Spirit and to us" (Acts 15:19, 28).

truths may offer a solution to the problem of the so-called historical gap, which has troubled many biblical interpreters.

For many years, biblical scholars have been careful to grant priority of meaning to the situation of the text's composition. In this scheme, the primary meaning for the text is the meaning that most resembles what a "first reader" (or reading community) might have understood, which is related to what the author may have intended. Thus, contemporary interpreters attempt to negotiate a historical gap between what the text "meant" then and what the text "means" now,[22] and scholars caution them to check their readings against "original" understanding for validity.[23] However, some interpreters reject the primacy of early readers or authors, asserting the priority of contemporary readers who read from their own contexts.[24] Many missiological readers have used this approach, interpreting texts as they appear "here and now," which has led to complaints that mission interpreters have been haphazard in their readings.[25]

Both hermeneutic approaches proceed on the notion that there is an insurmountable, real divide between "they, then" and "we, now." But, what if that did not have to be the case? What if those who read "now" could join those who read "then"? Is this possible without a time machine? Perhaps so, if we apply boundary and identity strategies similar to those exercised in Acts. However, in order to do so, we will need to apprehend the ways in which members of the community of faith can exercise the capacity to determine who constitutes "we," "them," "then," and "now."

"Hooked in": Enduring and Expanding Group Events

Charles Van Engen makes a telling observation that sheds light on the nature of groups:

> My local congregation is now hooked in *spiritually, organically, temporally, and spatially to all those who everywhere have believed* in Jesus Christ . . . a local congregation . . . *is* the whole in which it participates. The whole church is there in that local congregation, and that local congregation exists precisely because it is part of the whole. (emphasis added)[26]

22. Ayers, "Contours of a Missiological Hermeneutic," 178-80, 217-36. Also Johannes Nissen, *New Testament and Mission: Historical and Hermeneutical Perspectives* (Frankfurt am Main: Peter Lang, 2004), 15-16; and David J. Bosch, *Transforming Mission: Paradigm Shifts in Theology of Mission*, American Society of Missiology Series (Maryknoll, NY: Orbis Books, 1991), 20-24.

23. Some missiological interpreters (e.g., Bosch and Nissen) follow in this tradition.

24. This description encompasses diverse theorists (e.g., Wimsatt and Beardsley, Derrida, de Man, and Searle) who champion the "autonomy" of the text. It is also common among liberation theologians, contextual theologians, and postcolonial readers (e.g., West, Sugirtharajah, Segovia, Tolbert).

25. Michael Barram, "The Bible, Mission, and Social Location: Toward a Missional Hermeneutic," *Interpretation* 61, no. 1 (2007): 45-46; and Charles R. Taber, "Missiology and the Bible," *Missiology* 11, no. 2 (1983): 229-30.

26. Charles Van Engen, "The Glocal Church: Locality and Catholicity in a Globalizing World," in *Globalizing Theology: Belief and Practice in an Era of World Christianity*, ed. Craig Ott and Harold Netland (Grand Rapids: Baker, 2006), 163.

Van Engen notes that group events can endure in time beyond particular constituencies and that group boundaries can be dialectically universal and local. Although certain constituents may join or leave, a group may continue, as may the event of its existence. The church today remains the institution that arose at Pentecost; it is simply older. The synagogue at Pisidian Antioch could be "Israel" and claim promises made to "our fathers," even though the population and location of Jews had changed. Van Engen calls this being "hooked in spiritually, organically, temporally, and spatially."

Adding members or "churches" during Paul's mission did not cut Jerusalem off. Rather, the movement that began at Jerusalem *expanded* its boundaries *socially* and *extended* its event *temporally*. As new churches emerged, Paul's mission agency served to stretch the group event in time and social space, multiplying its centers.

Missiological Reading: Kingdom as Group and Mission as Event

In missiological perspective, newcomers who join the expanding *group* of Christ's kingdom followers also join the expanding *event* of Christ's mission. Christ's kingdom endures from before us; his mission started before us, even though we participate in his kingdom and mission today. Christ's gospel also does not emerge *in vacuo*; it diffuses from where it has already been. As it did at Antioch and Ephesus, this diffusion creates links of continuity and solidarity, expanding and extending the (kingdom) group (mission) event.

When we consider the kingdom as an ever-expanding group with mission as its ever-expanding event, the problem of the historical gap in biblical interpretation vanishes. It is not necessary to relate "we" who read "now" to "they" who read "then." "We" may be one expanding group that has been reading the Bible continuously, and "now" may be the ongoing event of our reading, since "we" began. "We" can include current readers along with those who began the group event. Under this approach, we are all the "first" group of readers, participating together in an extended "first" reading. We "first readers" simply have not yet concluded our "first reading" event. Approaching the text in solidarity with the (so-called) "first" readers, via kingdom and mission, using the variable boundaries found in the Pauline mission, is a uniquely missiological angle of approach to the text, a missiological hermeneutic. We do not interpret "them." Instead, we all participate together in reading the text, since "they" are not "them"; "they" are "we."

We can approach the Bible this way because group boundaries are not intrinsic; they are subject to definition. Paul and the Jerusalem authorities could define persons at Antioch or Ephesus as being "in" as they saw fit. They could reject criteria that separated, decide upon new criteria that included, and set boundaries as the situation demanded. By the same strategy, we may define contemporary readers as "within" the first reader group and identify ourselves as participants in the first reading event.

Reading at Centers and Margins

This does not require existing readings to dominate newcomers, nor does it imply that only one conversation is in progress. As Acts shows, many group centers may coexist dialectically, and their domains may overlap or extend into different regions. Thus, readers may choose to read as members of the overarching "we" and also choose to read as local readers. Readers may elect to read as "here, in this place, from this outlook," or according to broader definitions of inclusion. In other words, we may read "linked in" and centered by the whole as "we, since then, who all are 'in' here" *and* we may read in distinct ways, at the margins of the whole, as "we, right now, 'out' here." Either way, the reading is always from "here," but the location of "here" changes socially and temporally.

CONCLUSION

Our missiological reading of Paul's mission revealed that the early church had variable group boundaries and multiple identifying centers. These expanded, contracted, and became redefined under complex influences. Initially, precedent ethno-religious boundaries held sway, but the apostles endorsed new boundaries and identifiers, emphasizing the brotherhood and salvation of "Christian" believers, evidenced through conduct, charismata, and baptism.

These observations correlate with Paul Hiebert's and Kenneth Pike's proposals about group identity, which open new avenues in mission practice, mission theology, and missiological hermeneutics. In mission practice and theology, the uses of boundaries and identifying centers during Paul's mission call for greater consideration of how group definitions may integrate others as "we," using selective and context-specific criteria. In missiological hermeneutics, the same observations offer an alternative to the historical-gap scheme for defining reading groups and events.

Finally, I believe the events that we see during Paul's mission offer a response to the question that I mentioned at the beginning of this chapter. "What makes someone a Christian?" The Acts accounts offer a response: "Do you wish to be one? Christ has provided many avenues. Let us bring you in!"

Part 5

Mission Theology and Church History

Chapter 13

Historical Perspectives on Catholic Mission Theology

Mary Motte, F.M.M.

Catholic mission is rooted in the beginning of Christianity as recounted in the Acts of the Apostles, a beginning all Christians share.[1] Dynamic energy seeps out from the words of Acts, sharing the energizing experience of a personal encounter with Jesus. There is tangible grace transformative for everyone entering this accompaniment. Here lies the source of mission, the purpose of which is the reign of God.

The point of the church is to point beyond itself to be a community that preaches, serves, and witnesses to the reign of God. So completely does the church live for God's reign that when it finally is fully established, the church will be subsumed into its all-encountering reality. It is this understanding of the church that the Second Vatican Council expresses when it describes the pilgrim church as missionary by its very nature (*Evangelii nuntiandi* 8).[2]

In the history of Christian mission, there is a visible progression in the early Christian community's insights concerning God's presence. Particular contexts mark the church's growing understandings of mission throughout history, including the divisions that arose in the early church. As Pope Francis has noted frequently, sinfulness, error, grace, and suffering have been present in all the families of Christian belief. The core message of missionary proclamation, however, remains essentially constant amid challenges marked by shifts in theological, political, and ecclesial understandings. I will focus on the impact of the Second Vatican Council on mission in the Roman Catholic community, and especially the major insights and developments that carry forward its convictions. Four responses in particular illustrate this development:

---

1. Cf. Stephen B. Bevans and Roger P. Schroeder, *Constants in Context: A Theology of Mission for Today* (Maryknoll, NY: Orbis Books, 2004).

2. Ibid., 7.

1. missionary orders of women and men in the Catholic Church, especially in their collaboration through SEDOS[3]
2. growth of the continental expressions of the church, closely related to the synodal movement since Vatican II
3. rapid development of lay mission groups after the Council
4. ecumenical developments.

MISSIONARY ORDERS OF WOMEN AND MEN AND THEIR COLLABORATION THROUGH SEDOS

Prior to Vatican II, missionary orders of women and men almost exclusively carried out mission in the Catholic Church. In the Conciliar decree on religious life, *Perfectae caritatis,* the Council asked all religious orders of men and women, including those specifically founded for mission, to examine the purpose of their foundation in the writings and practice of their foundress or founder; and to update their Constitutions accordingly. Within my congregation, the Franciscan Missionaries of Mary (F.M.M.), these efforts extended over a number of years, from 1966 to the present, involving our total membership of several thousand women throughout the world. The results have led to a radical renewal of our purpose, a deepening of our commitment to seek God, and solidarity with the poor. Mary of the Passion, our foundress, envisioned mission as including both the Christian/Catholic world and the non-Christian world.[4] This understanding of mission is in contrast to the Catholic Church's, which did not generally consider Europe, and largely North and Latin America, places to send missionaries prior to Vatican II.

Our community, on the other hand, considered all continents places of mission. Mary of the Passion was a woman imbued with the thinking of her time, viewing the world from a colonial perspective. The originality embedded in her theology is her understanding of every member of the community as a missionary, by virtue of their church membership, and an openness to be sent out as a witness to God's love. Being a missionary did not depend on the location of one's ministry. For Mary of the Passion, universal mission, a significant expression of the community's identity, meant *the everywhere of God's love.*[5]

The retrieval of the founding intuitions and practices led to changes rooted in the foundation of a congregation and adapted to current situations. For the F.M.M. today, examples of these insights nourished by the founding intuition of Mary of the Passion are the following: the total gift of oneself in the living

---

3. SEDOS is an acronym for *Service of Documentation and Study of Global Mission,* which is located in Rome, Italy. The superiors general at Vatican II founded the organization.

4. Marie-Thérèse de Maleissye, *A Short Life of Mary of the Passion* (Mumbai, India: St. Paul's, 2002), 79-80; Marcel Launay, *Hélène de Chappotin and the Franciscan Missionaries of Mary* (Paris: Cerf, 2001), 123-29.

5. Anne-Marie Foujols, F.M.M., "Mary of the Passion's Perception of Universal Mission," *Universal Mission Series,* no. 2 (Rome: Franciscan Missionaries of Mary, 1995).

and proclaiming of the gospel message; the grace of sending (i.e., being sent to a people, and with them, to become part of the continuing incarnation of the Word of God); and identification with the poor. These were lived differently in the context of early F.M.M. history, yet draw from the same vision. Other missionary congregations mirror a similar trajectory such as the Maryknoll Fathers and Brothers, Maryknoll Sisters of St. Dominic, the Medical Mission Sisters, the Missionaries of Africa, the Marist Missionary Sisters, and the Sisters of Notre Dame de Namur, among many others. For all of the above, the alterations are the fruit of intensive research, prayer, and life experiences over the last fifty years resulting in directives, which the congregations study and renew regularly in these rapidly changing times.

Originating during Vatican II, SEDOS continues to meet with an increasing number of member religious congregations. This expansion reflects a major shift in the developing understanding of mission. Namely, missionary proclamation is not determined geographically, yet relates to the deepening insight into the mystery of God, the Incarnation in contemporary society related to the situations of the poor, questions of justice, peace, and mercy, and the reality of so many profound experiences of the Holy. Since the time of its founding, SEDOS has held periodic mission seminars that have provoked deeper understanding of the emerging trends in mission. The first of these, held in the late 1960s, considered the important question of a future for mission. This question of missionary identity surfaced particularly in relation to Vatican II's decrees on the missionary activity of the church, religious freedom, and the dignity of the human person.

The Roman Catholic Church founded many missionary congregations based on the need to reach those who had never heard the word of God, and very often formed them for work on a particular continent or situation in the world. Their purpose of missionary proclamation remained valid after the Council, yet their understanding of mission was challenged by the end of colonialism, growth of new independent states, and an improved psychosocial understanding of the person. The first seminar focused on the clarification of the missionary call within the Roman Catholic Church, and Orbis Books published the results in 1969 with the title *Foundations of Mission Theology*. There were two questions especially sensitive to the missionary institute: (1) salvation through non-Christian religions, and (2) mission work and development.

While it is not possible to detail the findings of this symposium, it is interesting to note some points indicative of the direction of mission understanding since 1969. Henri de Lubac, S.J., noted in a closing seminar:

Obviously, everything true and good comes from God. One may challenge the terminology, but it is after all, traditional. What we must maintain is the radical distinction between the natural manifestation of God in nature, through the creation order, and the supernatural manifestation of God in the Old and New Testament, which culminates with Christ. The former is ordered to the latter, but we must not confuse the two. And we must of course understand that both are gratuitous, that they represent God's challenging summons to man.[6]

Concerning the importance of witness, Jean Frisque and George Delcuve remarked:

I think the only essential element of mission work is witness that speaks of Christ; this is more than a simple intention. The goal of missionary work is to lead men to Christ, by revealing his presence through the missionary. It involves the very life of the one who is bearing witness. Now is this witness first and foremost a tool for conversion? No. The fact that I, through my commitment, hope to lead men [sic] explicitly to Christ does not prevent me from respecting human autonomy and the freedom of the one I am helping.[7]

Commenting on the role of the church in development, Charles Henry Buttimer, F.S.C., stated:

We have spoken a lot about priests and lay people, but thousands of brothers and nuns are in development work. It is even the essential part of missionary work: e.g., educational formation, intellectual training, medical work, etc. They would ask the same question as priests, even more insistently because it involves their distinctive work. Is their work truly missionary? I would simply like to remind the theologians that these people are engaged in missionary work, and that they have problems too.[8]

A Filipino Jesuit, C. G. Arevalo, S.J., remarked on the importance of community:

We must stress the role of the Church as a community. Development should be conceived as the establishment of a harmonious human community, that is, a community living in peace, justice, and ultimately charity. Christian communities should be visible signs of Christ's grace. The role of the local church is to present a model vision of a community living in charity, totally at one with Christ, and fully integrated into the life of the nation.[9]

The rapid changes that marked the late twentieth century became particularly evident when in the late 1970s the SEDOS membership launched another major mission research seminar. By this time, the globalized reality of the church had become evident, with contributing participants from Asia, Africa,

---

6. SEDOS, ed., *Foundations of Mission Theology,* trans. John Drury; Maryknoll Documentation Series (Maryknoll, NY: Orbis Books, 1969), 151.

7. Ibid., 156.

8. Ibid., 157.

9. Ibid., 158.

Latin America, North America, and Europe. Women, as part of the SEDOS membership, participated in this meeting from beginning to end. The subjects covered in the papers presented for study and reflection at the seminar indicate how rapidly changes were affecting mission understandings. These topics were:

- the missionary dimensions of the local church, with studies from Haiti, India, Indonesia, Lesotho, Mexico, and Japan
- the mission of the local church in secular society, with studies from Sri Lanka, Peru, Nigeria, and the Latin American church
- Christian mission and ecumenical relations in the context of the local church, with studies from the Pacific, East Africa, and Australia, and from the experiences of evangelization among Catholic, Evangelical, and Reformed Christians
- the mission of the local church and the missionary institutes, with studies from the United States, Australia, the Philippines, and Black Africa, and analyses of the experiences of integrating mission societies into the local church, the role of missionary institutes, and consideration of the implications of a new age in mission
- mission in the local church in relation to other religious traditions, with studies from Zaire (now Democratic Republic of Congo), Trinidad, Melanesia, and India, with analyses of the universality of salvation, the diversity of religious aims, and the non-Semitic religions of Asia
- religious freedom and the local church's responsibility for mission, with studies from the situation in Poland, the Philippines, North America, and Brazil
- the mission of the local church and the enculturation of the gospel, with studies from Denmark, the Aymara people, India, and Ghana, and an analysis of a framework for a discussion of enculturation
- the liberation and justice dimension of the mission of the local church, with studies from New Zealand, United States, Africa, Australia, and the Philippines, and an analysis of the task of the church in the liberation for freedom.[10]

After about two weeks of intensive work and study, the seminar proposed four major directions of mission: proclamation, dialogue, enculturation, and liberation of the poor.[11]

An annual gathering of SEDOS members continues to study new emerging themes in the theory and practice of mission. In 1990, SEDOS looked again at the emerging trends in mission. Contributions affirmed and showed the development in a number of the trends identified in earlier gatherings. In particular, underlying this development were the great commonalities experienced in renewal by the member congregations, both female and male.

---

10. Mary Motte and Joseph Lang, *Mission in Dialogue: The SEDOS Research Seminar on the Future of Mission* (Maryknoll, NY: Orbis Books, 1982).

11. Ibid., 634.

SYNODS, LOCAL CHURCHES, AND
CONTRIBUTIONS TO MISSION UNDERSTANDING

The synod of bishops took on importance after the Council. An early initiative of Pope Francis was the further development of the synod as an expression of collegiality among the bishops of the world. The pope initiated sending a preparatory questionnaire to all members of the church for the synod in 2014 and 2015. The concerns raised through these consultations have been included in the working documents.

Episcopal conferences throughout the world have increasingly assumed an important role in the work of evangelization. In preparation for the third millennium, John Paul II convoked a synod of bishops for each continent beginning with Africa in 1995, and concluding with that of Europe in 2003. He issued an apostolic exhortation following each of these continental synods, examining the need of evangelization and related challenges. This example illustrates the development in understanding mission. The synodal structure is rooted in the importance of the local church as recognized by the Council. The collegiality of the bishops of the world together with the bishop of Rome is in need of further development as Pope Francis indicated. The pope has already taken significant steps to move this process forward.

GROWTH IN THE LAY MISSIONARY MOVEMENT

The colonial perspective in the first half of the century framed missionary concerns within the expansion of Christianity throughout the world. As the century progressed, the right of every person to hear the gospel, as well as the missionary responsibility of every baptized person, triggered motivations for change. The Western-dominated church gave way to a global church with local leadership on every continent. New approaches in evangelization and mission began to appear. World church contributions are gradually developing mission theology and praxis with new insights, enriched by multiple cultural perspectives.

In 1962, Pope John XXIII, carrying forward an idea of John R. Considine, M.M., called for religious congregations to send 10 percent of their personnel to the church in Latin America.[12] This proposal included Canada, the United States, and, eventually, Europe. A generous response came from the newly founded Missionary Society of St. James the Apostle, Maryknoll, and international congregations who eventually wrote a memorable chapter in the history of both missiology and inter-American relations.[13] A deepening awareness of the significance of the Incarnation accompanied collaborations with Latin

---

12. Robert Hurteau, *A Worldwide Heart: The Life of Maryknoll Father John J. Considine* (Maryknoll, NY: Orbis Books, 2013), 180-82. This call also contributed to the changing understanding of what constitutes a missionary congregation, since many congregations not generally recognized as missionary sent members to the churches in Latin America, and transformation occurred by the experience.

13. Tom Quigley, "The Great North–South Embrace," *America* 201, no. 18 (2009): 20.

American counterparts. Faith strengthened these partnerships—a faith stretched by experiences among the poor, the painful realization of underlying injustices, and theological reflection. The gift of a developing liberation theology in the Latin American church became evident in these instances. Missionaries and their partners began to see in new ways. Many institutions experienced profound restructuring through theological visioning embedded in the Incarnation. A new era of martyrdom emerged in the world. Pope Francis, referring to this fact, speaks of the *ecumenism of blood*, which unites Christians.[14]

A rush of missiological chaos erupted in the aftermath of Vatican II. In addition to raising serious theological questions, the Council affirmed the missionary nature of the church and the missionary responsibility of every baptized person. The Council provided the immediate context of this chaos, yet there was a contributing factor in the emerging postcolonial world as recently independent countries sought confirmation for ancient cultural identities often drained of dynamism by colonialism. Recognizing the missionary responsibility of all the baptized, a number of clerical or religious missionary societies initiated lay mission groups. In 1968, the Latin American Bishops Conferences (CELAM) met in Medellín, Colombia. During their gathering, insights from liberation theology challenged mission theology typical at the time. Common mission theology perceived the proclamation of the gospel as integrally bound to actual concerns about poverty, injustice, identity of the people, and just relationships. A few years later, in 1971, the synod of bishops indicated that action on behalf of justice is constitutive of evangelization.[15]

Evangelii nuntiandi, the apostolic exhortation of Paul VI (1975), examined various situations in modern society as challenges to evangelization. John Paul II (1978–2005) frequently called for a new evangelization. In *Redemptoris missio* (1990), he reiterated the right of all to hear the gospel, and introduced the idea of the *areopagus* as a challenge to evangelization (*RM*, 37 and 56). In other words, the pope asked for the church to be in dialogue with areas of public life and develop a theology of God's presence through Word and Spirit. Missionary practices expressing this understanding had already surfaced in various parts of the world. Through John Paul II's missionary travel to so many parts of the world, along with the particular attention he gave to ordinary people, the young, and the poor, he incorporated the missionary fiber of a global church. While missionary societies of women and men continued as important contributors to this thinking and action, very meaningful inputs were coming from lay groups and episcopal conferences throughout the world. A number of missionary congregations organized lay groups either as missionaries or as associates. These groups shared in the founding inspiration of the community, and collaborated with its mission in various ways. The Society of African Missions, Comboniani, Maryknoll, Missionaries of Africa, Colombans, and Scarboro Missions,

---

14. John L. Allen Jr., "Francis Calls Anti-Christian Violence 'Ecumenism of Blood,'" *National Catholic Reporter*, December 15, 2013, http://ncronline.org.

15. Bill Ryan, S.J., "Justice in the World," *Jesuit Forum for Social Faith and Justice* 4, no. 2 (2012), www.jesuitforum.ca.

together with several other groups, first organized lay missionaries. There are also episcopal conferences and dioceses on each of the continents that have lay missionary groups.[16]

Another continuing question centers on long-term or short-term missionaries. Formation of lay missionaries or associates by missionary congregations partly answered this question. The changing shape of mission, however, owes a great deal to new lay groups of missionaries, independent of the missionary congregations that have grown exponentially since Vatican II. These groups are concerned about evangelization, or proclamation of the Good News. They are very often international in membership and living in the place of their ministry. Their membership includes single persons and married couples. Among the groups, there are both long-term and short-term commitments. Such lay mission groups give us understanding for a much fuller and more developed meaning of mission.

New missiological insights continue to emerge. Contemporary groups of laity witness to recent surges of energy and commitment in the proclamation of the gospel. Several shared elements have arisen:

- lay persons predominate even though some include religious men and women among their members
- activities present a wide variety through which members are committed to live and communicate the gospel
- their dedication illustrates how fidelity to the gospel leads them into new *areopagi* and/or how these challenge them to discover new expressions of faithfulness to the gospel (*RM*, 37c)
- just relationships across boundaries take on a new importance in globalization, including collaboration with a network of partners
- incarnational theology has taken a greater hold of Christian consciousness, and increasingly provides insights regarding how to approach those still unreached by the gospel
- they are generally international.[17]

The Vatican refers to lay ecclesial movements as International Associations of the Faithful. They share the "newness which baptismal grace brings to life," allowing for a renewed missionary zeal that reaches out to the men and women of our era in the concrete situations where they find themselves, and turns its loving attention to the dignity, needs, and destiny of each individual.[18] Benedict XVI described their purpose:

to proclaim the joy of believing in Jesus Christ, and to renew the commitment to be faithful disciples in our time.[19]

---

16. Cf. Mary Motte, "Catholic Missionary Movements of the Twentieth Century," in *A Century of Catholic Mission,* ed. Stephen B. Bevans (Oxford: Regnum Book International, 2013), 75-82.

17. Motte, "Catholic Missionary Movements," 78-79.

18. Message of Pope John Paul II for the World Congress of Ecclesial Movements and New Communities, May 27, 1998, www.vatican.va.

19. Homily, Benedict XVI, June 3, 2006, www.vatican.va.

They are one of the most important innovations inspired by the Holy Spirit in the Church for the implementation of the Second Vatican Council.[20]

These groups embrace missionary incentives that "announce the power of God's love, which in overcoming divisions and barriers of every kind, renews the face of the earth to build the civilization of love."[21]

ECUMENICAL MISSION COLLABORATION AMONG CHRISTIANS

Another important moment in Catholic mission occurred through increased ecumenical collaboration because of the vision developed in Vatican II. Prior to the Council, Catholics had very limited ecumenical experience. Early in the Council, members sent Roman Catholics to participate as consultants in the World Mission Conference held in Mexico in 1963.[22] It is not possible to indicate here all the ecumenical undertakings since Vatican II, specifically the influence of the Council's decree concerning Christian unity. I will include, however, collaborations between the Catholic Church and Orthodox, Anglican, and Protestant Christians at all levels.[23] A number of these examples involve bilateral dialogue between a specific group within these confessions, and a comparable group in the Vatican Pontifical Council for Christian unity or at the diocesan level. Many other forms of collaboration concern peace, immigration, and other social justice issues.

Development of common Christian witness and the principle that we should not do separately what we can do together continue to bear fruit. Participation through prayer, Bible study, and collaboration enables a friendship built on truth and charity to grow, leading to common witness. The common witness theme was the focus of the Joint Working Group made up of members from the World Council of Churches/Commission on World Mission and Evangelism (WCC/CWME) and the Pontifical Council for Promoting Christian Unity. Examples of Christians praying or working together became a part of the published work of the common witness committee.[24]

---

20. "Address of His Holiness Benedict XVI to the Bishops of Hong Kong and Macao on Their 'Ad Limina' Visit," June 27, 2008, www.vatican.va.

21. John Paul II, "Come, Holy Spirit!" (*Veni, Sancte Spiritus!*), Homily on Pentecost, May 31, 1998.

22. Prepared and carried out by the Commission on World Mission and Evangelism of the World Council of Churches.

23. John A. Radano and Cardinal Walter Kasper, *Celebrating a Century of Ecumenism: Exploring the Achievements of International Dialogue* (Grand Rapids: Eerdmans, 2012); Stephen B. Bevans and Jeffrey Gros, *Evangelization and Religious Freedom:* Ad Gentes, Dignitatis Humanae: *Rediscovering Vatican II* (Mahwah, NJ: Paulist Press, 2009).

24. World Council of Churches, "Toward Common Witness," *World Council of Churches/Commission on World Evangelism*, September 19, 1997, www.oikoumene.org.

While there are numerous instances of ecumenical collaboration within the World Council of Churches, I will focus on the Commission on World Mission and Evangelism. After Vatican II, Catholic consultants in cooperation with the Pontifical Council for Christian Unity worked on a daily basis with the CWME. In 1985, Sister Joan Delaney, a Maryknoll sister who had worked in Hong Kong and later as the executive director of SEDOS in Rome, became the first permanent Catholic consultant. Other sisters and laywomen have subsequently served in this position. Since Vatican II, Catholics have participated fully in the developing work and vision of the CWME.

Orthodox Christians are also actively involved in the CWME gatherings and activities. The participation in the CWME brings together many of the different traditions in Christianity. Evangelical Christians, conciliar Christians, and Roman Catholics have found common lines in Christian mission through their ideas expressed in documents on mission and evangelism. Vatican II, although not solely responsible for growing ecumenism, opened the way for Catholic participation with other Christians. The search to discern the church's mission more fully requires deeper levels of understanding through the Holy Spirit.

Participation in the Association of Professors of Mission and the American Society of Missiology expresses ecumenical collaboration in the United States. Both of these groups have a tripartite concept of leadership, involving the ecumenical representation of evangelical Protestants, conciliar Protestants, and Roman Catholics in their perspectives on mission theology. Another ecumenical undertaking that addressed the interaction between gospel and culture in the United States was the Gospel and Our Culture Network. The International Association for Mission Studies is also made up of members from the above three strains of Christianity. Several of the Catholic members have contributed leadership in the group, among them Michael Amaladoss, S.J., and Joan Chatfield, M.M.

In addition to insightful publications, reflections on how to become effective missionary disciples, and how to identify the contemporary cry of the poor, many wonderful friendships have contributed to unique ways of recognizing the grace and love of God in our midst. A missionary perspective has emerged with renewed appreciation of the roots of the faith that has shaped each one and each religious movement. Shared welcome of the Word of God has led to conversations, research, and exploration of challenges faced by all Christian traditions.

CONCLUSION

The Second Vatican Council, through its representation with participants from a global church, still contributes insights into the gospel and its call to missional living. Together with all Christians, Catholics are more deeply aware of their call to seek a deeper relationship with God, and this realization provokes all of us to see in a new way. The process is not finished, yet we already perceive more deeply the mystery of God present among us. Our journey together enables us to recognize how we hold the working out of challenges in our hands. Such experiences call us forward to explore more deeply our shared life and mission rooted in the gospel of Jesus. As Pope Francis said in his meeting with the delegation from the Eastern Church on June 28, 2015:

> We know very well that this unity is a gift of God, a gift that even now the Most High grants us the grace to attain whenever, by the power of the Holy Spirit, we choose to look at one another with the eyes of faith, and to see ourselves as we truly are in God's plan, according to the designs of his eternal will, and not what we have become as a result of the historical consequences of our sins.[25]

The Second Vatican Council has opened a new moment of history. Through its decrees we experience God's call into the future, *Behold I make all things new* (Rev. 21:5). Our ecumenical common witness dares us to take different approaches rooted in the Word of God. Catholic scholars continue to seek how we are to relate with sisters and brothers of other faith traditions.[26] Increasingly our lived experiences of solidarity with the poor allow us to look at the world from below and discover relationships that reach beyond faith, culture, language, and economy. Building genuine trust in relationships through reconciliation that does not ignore painful, violent acts creates new spaces for being sisters and brothers.[27] As the synod of bishops enters more actively into reflections starting from experiences and the gospel, a new dynamism will open up. This dynamism of God's work in creation is turning toward ecumenicism.

Many writers have pointed to the need of contemplation regarding God's action in creation. Today scientists point to an emerging universe—one in which creation continues. John F. Haught, Ilia Delio, and Denis Edwards, among others, are exploring what might be before us in the future.[28] The past has certainly taught us that this call for creation care is to all people who follow the gospel of Jesus the Christ, as well as to all the people of the earth whom God does not leave without the experience of God's love. We can move into the future only by being together ecumenically and learning how to look at one another with the eyes of faith, appreciating the insights of each one's contemplative prayer.

---

25. "Pope Francis Meets Delegation of Ecumenical Patriarchate," *Vatican Radio,* June 28, 2015, http://en.radiovaticana.va/news.

26. Karl Josef Becker and Ilaria Morali, eds., *Catholic Engagement with World Religions* (Maryknoll, NY: Orbis Books, 2010).

27. Cf. the work of Desmond Tutu, John Paul Lederach, and Robert Schreiter.

28. Denis Edwards, *Partaking of God: Trinity, Evolution and Ecology* (Collegeville, MN: Liturgical Press, 2014); John F. Haught, *Christianity and Science: Towards a Theology of Nature* (Maryknoll, NY: Orbis Books, 2007); Ilia Delio, ed., *From Teilhard to Omega: Co-creating an Unfinished Universe* (Maryknoll, NY: Orbis Books, 2014).

Chapter 14

Historical Perspectives on Protestant Mission Theology: Striving toward a New Model for a Postmodern Context

Pablo A. Deiros

Protestant mission theology began to appear in theological academia more than a century ago. The history of this field of study is well known through an abundance of literature.[1] In this essay, my purpose is to summarize the basic two models of Protestant mission theology that in my understanding have developed in the past and in recent times. These two models represent the theological understanding of Christian mission: (1) Protestants through the era of modern missions, and (2) the contemporary era of globalized missions. The reflections done at the International Missionary Conference held at Edinburgh in 1910, and the prevailing mission theology of the majority world today, illustrate these two approaches.

Each one of these different approaches to mission theology is the result of a rich variety of diverse contributions to the field. The most substantial difference lies in the conceptual model that each one of them represents. It is possible to mark the differences starting with the application of the theory of scientific models to the development of the Christian mission with each one expressed

---

1. See Rodger Bassham, *Mission Theology, 1948–1975: Years of Worldwide Creative Tensions Ecumenical, Evangelical, and Roman Catholic* (Pasadena, CA: William Carey Library, 1979); David J. Bosch, *Witness to the World: The Christian Mission in Theological Perspective* (Atlanta: John Knox Press, 1980); David J. Bosch, *Transforming Mission: Paradigm Shifts in Theology of Mission* (Maryknoll, NY: Orbis Books, 1991); Joel A. Carpenter and Wilbert R. Shenk, eds., *Earthen Vessels* (Grand Rapids: Eerdmans, 1990); Orlando E. Costas, *Christ Outside the Gate: Mission Beyond Christendom* (Maryknoll, NY: Orbis Books, 1984); William Jenkinson and Helene O'Sullivan, eds., *Trends in Mission: Toward the Third Millennium* (Maryknoll, NY: Orbis Books, 1991); James A. Scherer, *Gospel, Church and Kingdom: Comparative Studies in World Mission Theology* (Minneapolis: Augsburg Press, 1987); Wilbert R. Shenk, ed., *The Transfiguration of Mission: Biblical, Theological, and Historical Foundations* (Scottdale, PA: Herald Press, 1993); and Charles E. Van Engen, *Mission on the Way: Issues in Mission Theology* (Grand Rapids: Baker Books, 1996).

in diverse missionary ways. To that end, we will first consider what a scientific model is and then later describe both models: the one represented at Edinburgh and the other that is in process today in most of the majority world. We will then draw conclusions, and open the debate of the present pluralistic and globalized model.

WHAT IS A SCIENTIFIC MODEL?

There are various ways to define a scientific model. In the hard or pure sciences, and above all in applied sciences, a model is the result of the process of generating an abstract, conceptual, graphic or visual, physical, or mathematical representation of the phenomena, systems or processes, to the end of analyzing, describing, explaining, or simulating. This practice explores, controls, and predicts in general those phenomena or processes. The creation of a model is an essential part of any scientific activity and critical analysis of reality. This approach is valid also for missiology, and more specifically for mission theology as a science, or the study and reflection on the Christian mission in the more ample field of theology. It is appropriate to consider the remarks of A. Scott Moreau, Gary R. Corwin, and Gary B. McGee on the scientific character of missiology and Gerald H. Anderson's definition of mission theology.[2] Charles E. Van Engen states that "mission theology is a difficult enterprise because its object of reflection is the entire field of missiology, which itself is a multi- and inter-disciplinary enterprise."[3]

In spite of the fact that there is scarce generalized theory about the use of models, modern science offers a growing collection of methods, techniques, and theories about diverse kinds of models. This is especially true about the philosophy of science, general systems theory, and the relatively new field of scientific visualization. To my knowledge, in the field of missiology, no scholar has yet applied the theory of models. What I am presenting in this essay, therefore, is a preliminary contribution in this direction.

The development of a model requires the presentation of a series of hypotheses to ensure that an idealization or abstraction sufficiently expresses an idea. What is usually being looked for, however, is for the elaborated model to be simple enough so as to be capable of being manipulated, studied, used, and transformed to win a deeper understanding of the reality under investigation.

A model is a comparable idea, created in the human mind, that exposes an aspect of what happens in nature or in a given human phenomenon. In this essay, I will develop and discuss two models of mission theology using three categories of modeling adequate for our missiological analysis: the mental, semantic, and

---

2. A. Scott Moreau, Gary R. Corwin, and Gary B. McGee, *Introducing World Missions: A Biblical, Historical, and Practical Survey* (Grand Rapids: Baker Academic, 2004), 17; and Gerald H. Anderson, John Goodwin, and Stephen Neill, eds., *Concise Dictionary of the Christian World Mission* (Nashville: Abingdon Press, 1971), 594.

3. Van Engen, *Mission on the Way*, 18.

analogical models. Mental representations of traits, structures, and processes constitute *conceptual or mental models*. The linguistic formalization of a mental model gives room for the elaboration of *semantic models*. *Analogical models* occur when structures elaborated with materials or forms are very different from the ones of the object or process under analysis. The model offers us a description capable of predicting what will happen in many similar situations.

WHAT IS THE VALUE OF A SCIENTIFIC MODEL?

A model can help explain the behavior of a part of the universe or reality, reducing it to the most basic of fundamental facts. At the same time, it serves to make predictions of the behavior of a certain system of the universe or reality, and to test these predictions in diverse circumstances. Models are elaborated when the creativity and perspicacity of a scientist is combined with data and observations of many similar conditions. Scientists try to identify and generalize patterns of such observations. The value of a model is that we can trust in its predictions with similar situations, even if we do not know each one of them. In all branches of science, including missiology, we employ models to represent our ideas as to how a determined part of reality functions. This also applies to mission theology. That representation can be conceptual (for example, an equation), or it can be material (for example, a map or a diagram). Throughout our education systems, we use a great variety of conceptual and material models.

A good model should be capable of explaining apparently different phenomena. Yet, on the other hand, models change. Never has there been an absolute or complete scientific model. Something has to change when accepted observations of a new situation come into conflict with the predictions of a model. In other words, either the data collected or the model itself is incorrect. No one model is capable of explaining every detail of a phenomenon.

Two basic mission frameworks have helped describe the practice of Protestant mission theology through the centuries. Neither of the two exhausts reality. Despite their limitations, however, they may help us understand the different ways history has shaped mission theology. These two models differ not only in their dimension, but also in the value of each one to help our understanding of contemporary mission theology.

THE BIDIMENSIONAL MODEL OF MISSION THEOLOGY

The bidimensional model describes the performance of modern missions from the days of William Carey (1792) to the present. The nineteenth century and most of the twentieth century was the golden age of Western missionary activity around the world. In fact, Kenneth S. Latourette dedicates four out of his seven volumes of *A History of the Expansion of Christianity* to this period, which he calls the "Great Century of Modern Missions."[4] During this period the strength of the missionary activity, though, created a series of problems, among which competition, duplication of efforts, lack of coordination, and divisionism were not minor evils but a true denial of the Christian faith.[5] As a result of these controversies and scandals, different national organizations emerged, and international meetings were held to bring together many of the missionary agencies of the Northern Hemisphere to discuss the issues of their global activity. Gatherings in New York and London (1854), Liverpool (1860), London (1878 and 1888), and again in New York (1900), revealed the urgency and commitment with which people were engaging in missionary activity. Nevertheless, the model in mission theology behind these agreements, strategies, and plans was the bidimensional type. According to this model of mission theology, the Christian nations of the Northern Hemisphere were responsible for carrying the gospel to all the other nations of the world. This bidimensional model represented a mission theology that did not change significantly under the Christendom paradigm, particularly in its manifestation through modern missions. According to Wilhelm Pauck's general historical observation,

> It is a remarkable fact that the missionary enterprise does not engender theological creativity. With the possible exception of the early Church where the missionary spirit decisively shaped theology, no part of Christendom has produced major theological responsibility and creativeness in connection with evangelistic endeavors. This is strange because one should expect that precisely that encounter with other religious claims would cause the missionary to justify and explicate the grounds and reasons for his own faith by means of theological thinking.[6]

This bidimensional model of mission theology reached its maximum expression at the World Missionary Conference in Edinburgh, Scotland (June 1910). This conference represented the end of the first stage of missionary conferences and the beginning of a new era in modern missions, the era of the International Missionary Council, and, eventually, of the broader ecumenical movement. Latourette wrote, "Edinburg 1910 was the outgrowth and climax of the earlier gatherings through which Protestants had been drawing together in their purpose to give the Gospel to the world." He continues, "Edinburgh 1910 summed up and focused much of the previous century's movement for

---

4. Kenneth S. Latourette, *A History of the Expansion of Christianity*, 7 vols. (Grand Rapids: Zondervan, 1970), vols. 4, 5, 6, and 7. See Latourette, *The Great Century: Europe and the United States*, vol. 4 of *A History of the Expansion of Christianity*, 1-3.

5. Kenneth S. Latourette, "Ecumenical Bearings of the Missionary Movement and the International Missionary Council," in *A History of the Ecumenical Movement*, vol. 1, ed. Ruth Rouse and Stephen Neill (Geneva: World Council of Churches, 1986), 354.

6. Wilhelm Pauck, "Theology in the Life of Contemporary American Protestantism," in *Religion and Culture*, ed. Walter Leibrecht (New York: Harper & Brothers, 1959), 278.

uniting Christians in giving the Gospel to the world."[7] Moreau et al. underline the following:

> Although Christianity by now had become the first religious faith to become a world religion, the center of gravity remained in the northern hemisphere. Missionaries traveled on a one-way street from Europe and America to the non-Christian world, and paternalism (the practice of controlling others by acting like a parent without giving them responsibility for themselves) too frequently marked their posture toward indigenous church leaders. The Edinburgh conference, a landmark in many ways, including its recognition of the growing maturity of the "younger churches," still fenced Christendom off from the non-Christian world.[8]

This model is bidimensional for various essential characteristics in its way of understanding mission theology and the missionary task. It interprets mission as integrated by only two factors, considered as essentials in the missionary process: the emitting agent of the message and the receptor agent of it. The model considers mission unidirectional, and goes from a determined point to another determined point (A → B). In this sense, we speak of sending countries and receiving countries, of a Christian world and a non-Christian or pagan world. The Edinburgh 1910 conference affirmed this unidirectional polarization. Erasmo Braga, an outstanding leader of the emerging Latin American Protestant community, expressed it thus:

> The particularity of the Edinburgh Conference was that the representation was restricted to the missions, which were operating in non-Christian lands. This excluded the missions established in countries in which the predominant religion was any of the historical forms of Christianity. The major missionary territory in such lands was Latin America. This exclusion brought the issue of the legitimacy of the Evangelical churches to continue the support to the missions in this continent except among the tribes of the pagan Indians.[9]

This model of mission theology understands mission in a unilateral way in terms of a dynamic agent that proclaims the gospel and another passive agent that hears and accepts it. The missionary is somebody who actively goes to do missions, as the pagan or non-Christian is somebody who passively receives the message. The church or mission agency is the sending institution that sends in mission, while the pagan peoples outside Christendom are those who receive the mission. The first are the subject of the process while the second are its object. It is not strange, then, that this model has ended up as diverse expressions of paternalism. In 1912, Roland Allen who served as missionary in northern China lamented on the legacy of paternalism, "We have simply transplanted abroad

---

7. Latourette. "Ecumenical Bearings," 355.

8. Moreau et al., *Introducing World Missions*, 136, 137.

9. Erasmo Braga, *Pan-Americanismo: Aspecto Religioso*, trans. Eduardo Monteverde (New York: Sociedad para la Educación Misionera en Estados Unidos y Canadá, 1917), 82.

the [church] organization with which we are familiar at home." He added, "We have maintained it by supplying a large number of European officials who can carry it on." Allen argued that when national leaders finally are ready to take charge, "The system will proceed precisely as it did before, natives simply doing exactly what we are now doing."[10]

We can represent this bidimensional model by tracing an arrow on a plane that unites the point of emission of the message with the point of reception.

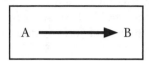

Usually this plane is a map. The agent or subject of missions considers himself/herself as having the right to decide where to go and what to do. This is the fundamental reason why in Edinburgh, Latin America was not considered as a legitimate field for missions.[11] As Latourette comments,

> Not all missionary societies were invited. Only those were included which were operating among non-Christian peoples. Efforts to win Christians from one form of the Faith to another—as by some American denominations on the continent of Europe, or among the ancient Churches of the Near East, or among the Roman Catholics of Latin America— were not to be in the purview of the gathering. Missions whose purpose it was to hold to the Faith emigrants from Europe to other lands were not included.[12]

This decision taken at Edinburgh provoked the strong reaction of evangelical leaders and churches in Latin America. The General Conference of the Episcopal Methodist Church in South America was the one group that most earnestly rejected this notion, especially in their Annual Conference of 1911. The official magazine of this church in the River Plate, *El Estandarte Evangélico*, was outspoken.

> The *Estandarte [Evangélico]* was the first periodical in a Latino language to give the voice of alert, and almost the only one to criticize that behavior; in that campaign, it requested the cooperation of its Spanish-speaking colleagues, but its request only found an echo—to our knowledge—in our Methodist colleague from Mexico *El Abogado Cristiano*. The others were silent or spoke with ambiguity.[13]

---

10. Roland Allen, *Missionary Methods: St. Paul's or Ours?* (Grand Rapids: Eerdmans, [1912] 1962), 135-36.

11. Latourette, "Ecumenical Bearings," 396. The only Latin America missionary society invited to participate in the Edinburgh Conference was the Anglican South American Missionary Society.

12. Ibid., 356.

13. "Nuestra Conferencia General desaprueba la conducta de la Conferencia de Edimburgo," *El Estandarte Evangélico* 29, no. 27 (1912): 417.

Those who criticized the absence of Latin America as a mission field in the 1910 Conference of Edinburgh regrettably also followed this bidimensional model of missions. Missionary societies and agencies, especially the North American ones that were operating in Latin America in those first few decades of the twentieth century, also had a bidimensional understanding of missions and mission theology. In 1912, Robert E. Speer wrote a pamphlet in which he dealt with the questions and doubts that Edinburgh had created in the North American missionary setting. Using eight arguments, he expressed his opinion in favor of the legitimacy and need of missions in Latin America, yet he did this in unidirectional and unilateral terms, which were characteristic of the discussions at Edinburgh.

1. The moral condition of the South American countries warrants and demands the presence of those forms of evangelical religion that will war against sin and bring men the power of righteous life.
2. The Protestant missionary enterprise with its stimulus to education and its appeal to the rational nature of man is required by the intellectual needs of South America.
3. Protestant missions are justified in South America in order to give the Bible to the people.
4. Protestant missions are justified and demanded in South America by the character of the Roman Catholic priesthood.
5. Protestant missions in South America are justified because the Roman Catholic Church has not given the people Christianity.
6. Protestant missions are justified in South America because the Roman Catholic Church is at the same time so strong and so weak there.
7. The Roman Catholic Church in Latin America needs the Protestant missionary movement.
8. Evangelical Christianity is warranted in going to South America because it alone can meet the needs of the Latin American natives.[14]

In the same manner, North American missionary agencies justified the sending of missionaries from the North to the South using the same bidimensional argument typical of the Christendom paradigm supported by Edinburgh 1910. In essence, this argument was that Latin America is a pagan continent because the Roman Catholic Church has failed in evangelizing it with the true gospel. This was also the argument presented by Hubert W. Brown in five conferences on the subject under the title "The Religious Development and Need of Latin America," presented at Princeton Theological Seminary some ten years before Edinburgh. Brown stated:

There is corruption in morals that will not bear recital, gross ignorance, superstition, and practical idolatry. The intelligent reject the system, and

---

14. Robert E. Speer, *The Case for Missions in Latin America* (New York: Board of Foreign Missions of the Presbyterian Church in the United States, 1912), 1, 2, 4, 5, 7, 9, 10.

become infidel, or at least indifferent to all religion. . . . Millions of souls . . . are in as urgent need of the gospel as are the pagans of China, India, or Africa; and . . . are in an extraordinary degree prepared to receive it; yea, more, are urgently beseeching that it be sent to them. The united voices of all the Protestant workers in Latin America echo these statements and urge this appeal. . . . It is the universal testimony of all such that the Romanism of Latin America has failed as a religious guide and educator. There is need for a reformation similar to that which awakened Europe in the days of the great religious reformers. It is both our duty and our privilege, to oppose truth to error, and win the victory for the pure gospel against Romish idolatry.[15]

The bidimensional model of missions and mission theology corresponded to the Christendom paradigm, which was predominant since the days of the Roman emperor Constantine, at the beginning of the fourth century. This paradigm, however, seems to be dying. In the past, it produced models of mission and mission theology (theological presuppositions) that still influence our way of understanding mission. The bidimensional model is no longer useful today to help us in this purpose. To examine mission in a post-Christendom and a postmodern setting implies taking a fresh look at the task of reflecting on mission. In this new historical perspective, we need to consider the interpretations proper to the Christendom paradigm. Beyond the contradictions of history, it is necessary to look for a new light and provide a new model of mission theology more adequate to the complex and global ways in which people understand and do mission today around the world.

THE POLYHEDRAL MODEL OF MISSION THEOLOGY

A polyhedron is a geometrical solid or structure formed or limited by plane faces or polygons, that has a determined number of faces defined by a number of edges that are the straight lines or sides on which the faces are cut, and its vertices are the points where three or more faces concur. I have in mind an image of the icosahedron or a polyhedron. An icosahedron consists of twenty faces, twelve vertices, and thirty edges or sides with equilateral triangles integrating this structure. A polyhedron, however, can have a larger number of faces, and as a consequence, a larger number of vertices and edges. This geometric image is not bidimensional but tridimensional, offering a model to understand contemporary missiological facts, mission theology, and their multiple concatenation. Application of this same idea is necessary to our way of understanding Christian mission and mission theology today.

Traditionally, we have followed bidimensional patterns when reflecting on the Christian faith and in defining the mission of the church. Yet today, we need a tridimensional model for understanding Christian mission in the world and mission theology. In other words, if we want a missiology that will be more

---

15. Hubert W. Brown, *Latin America* (New York: Fleming H. Revell, 1901), 117, 118, 121.

contextualized to the postmodern times in which we live, then we need models that will be less lineal and planes, and more organic and integral. No longer do we speak about mission in terms of who sends and who receives missionaries. This is outdated. Today we need to talk about a mission in which *all* send and *all* receive at the same time. It is not a linear process such as an action, which connects opposite points by way of a succession of intermediate dots, which make up a bridging segment in between the extremes. We do not identify a country that *sends* and another that *receives*. Until recently, this was typical of our bidimensional, unidirectional model. Nowadays, mission resembles a more tridimensional model, and for this very reason, it is more organic.

A tridimensional or polyhedral understanding of the reality of mission will be better adjusted to a more globalized and postmodern image of reality. A polyhedral network of multiple relationships and connections has already succeeded the bidimensional, unidirectional, and lineal understanding of "sending countries" and "receiving countries" as a missiological model. In this pluridirectional model, everybody sends the message of the gospel to everybody, and all receive the message from all. It is in this sense that the church evangelizes, and people evangelize the church. In the polyhedral model of mission and mission theology, the Christian mission is multidirectional. It expands in all directions at the same time. All the vertices touch all others in the structure through their interconnection. Therefore, the model is also hyperdynamic and plurifunctional.

In this way, there is a new variety of possible contacts and relationships at the service of the Christian mission. Not only is it that the evangelist is evangelized, and the dynamics of evangelization go around the whole of reality (the world), but also every nation (*panta ta ethnē*) or people remains linked or enters into relationship with all the other nations through the vertices and edges that unite them. This globalization of the "mission field" makes possible the globalization of the missionary task, which in this way reaches "all nations . . . to the ends of the earth."

The polyhedral model has the added advantage of being an organic structure without a defined beginning or end. Some members of the universal body of Christ will contribute missionary personnel, financial resources, prayers and experience, and/or sending structures, while others will provide logistic and technical support. We can all work dynamically with everybody else in the world to *missionize* wherever the gospel needs communication. This model also allows us to predict the contribution of every *ethnē* to the evangelizing process, an aspect that current scholars have not sufficiently studied in the missiological field. All Christians in the world can dynamically operate with all other Christians and even non-Christians, to do missions. In the Constantinian or Christendom model (bidimensional mission theology) consecrated by the World Missionary Conference at Edinburgh in 1910, missionary agencies and societies had the goal of taking Christ to the nations. In the polyhedral model, the objective is to take the nations to Christ. This is what I am seeing in the development of Christian testimony around the world today. In addition, this phenomenon is increasing rapidly.

In the bidimensional model, there is no room to place Jesus Christ as the fundamental agent and mentor of the Christian mission. In the polyhedral model, Christ occupies the very center of the structure, and from there he is in equidistant contact with all the vertices, edges, and faces of the structure. In this way, it is possible to create an imaginary point at the center of the figure that is equally distant to all its vertices. In our missiological and mission theology model, we see this central point as Christ himself. Churches, missionaries, nations, and reached and unreached peoples are fully connected. He is truly the Lord of all. He is in touch with all the nations, and he draws them all to himself. From this central position, Christ maintains and gives meaning to the whole structure. Its geometric perfection—as well as the evenness of all of its faces, and the perfect spacing between the vertices—depends on the perfect centrality of this imaginary central point—Jesus Christ. Let us now explore the tridimensional polyhedral model further.

The *missio Dei* consists in placing Christ at the center of all things. I believe that this is what Paul refers to when he skillfully speaks about the preeminence of Christ in Colossians 1:15-23. The goal of our participation in God's mission, under the lordship of Christ as the head of the church, is to build a network of relationships that are centered in him and that are united to/in him until Christ himself "is over all and through all and in all" (Eph. 4:6). In other words, this model of Christian mission proclaims, "Christ is all, and is in all" (Col. 3:11).

Missiologically, each point or vertex closely connected advances along with all the others. At the same time, the central point connects all vertices, which gives stability and meaning to the whole structure. In tectonic terms, beyond the force that each vertex exerts on all its contacts, the structure finds its equilibrium in the strength (or force) of each radius linking the central point to each vertex. This central point, although invisible, keeps the polyhedral structure together, integrated, and stable. That this is true can be verified by the fact that if the distance between the vertices is changed—that is, if the intersections were unequal—the whole structure would collapse. The same would happen if the edges or the radii were not equal. The structure would lose its tectonic equilibrium and would collapse since it would have lost its basic form. In the ideal polyhedron, however, the symmetry is dynamically perfect, and the structure maintains itself in place and form.

I think this polyhedral model can help us better represent the theological-missiological network that is in the process of being developed all over the world today and the globalized way in which we should attempt the missionary commitment. This will also help us to enrich our mission theology, making it more contextualized to a globalized and postmodern understanding of the Christian mission. As we advance into the twenty-first century, we need a new model to help us in our reflection and action on the mission entrusted to us by the Lord Jesus. The centrality and strength of the central point in this model might be an adequate representation of the centrality and power of Christ in the whole process.

Chapter 15

Historical Perspectives on Pentecostal Mission Theology

DeLonn L. Rance

My missionary story began when my parents dedicated me to the Lord Jesus in a small rural Assemblies of God church in Egeland, North Dakota, one of the first organized Pentecostal churches in the state.[1] During that dedication, a prophetic word announced that I would become a missionary. A few years later, when I was eight years old, having just recently experienced the "baptism in the Holy Spirit" during a midweek missionary service, I responded to an altar call expressing to Christ my willingness "to go where you want me to go." When I got up from the altar, I knew God had called me to be a missionary. Pentecostal theologies of mission emerge from the narratives of people such as the above. These stories find meaning in their connection to the divine narrative and the empowering presence of the third person of the Trinity. "The story of God's dealings with humankind is not finished. In a profound sense the missionary acts of the Holy Spirit through the church to the world are still going on—until Jesus comes again."[2]

Thirty years later, having served as an Assemblies of God missionary among the people of El Salvador for fourteen years, I entered Charles E. Van Engen's office to explore how doctoral studies might facilitate my call and engagement in missions' mobilization and missionary training in Latin America. As the research drilled down into a Pentecostal missions theology, a mission "of, in, and on the Way" surfaced, grounded in the activity of the Holy Spirit in calling and empowering God's missionary/apostolic people. God's apostolic/missionary people are fundamentally able to hear the voice of the Spirit, and obey by yielding to the Spirit's empowerment through both natural and supernatural means. The Lord "builds" his house, which is his missionary people.

---

1. Darrin J. Rodgers, *Northern Harvest: Pentecostalism in North Dakota* (Bismarck: North Dakota District Council of the Assemblies of God, 2003), 131-32.

2. Charles Van Engen, "Introduction: Mission of, in, and on the Way," in *Footprints of God: A Narrative Theology of Mission*, ed. Charles E. Van Engen, Nancy Thomas, and Robert L. Gallagher (Monrovia, CA: MARC, 1999), xxv.

The purpose of this chapter is not to write a Pentecostal theology of mission or a history of Pentecostal missions.[3] Rather, from a Pentecostal narrative, to identify theological truths, and principles of the indigenous church that point to how one group of Pentecostals (Assemblies of God World Missions, USA) have engaged in what Van Engen describes as that "multidisciplinary field that reads the Bible with missiological eyes, and based on that reading, continually reexamines, reevaluates, and redirects the church's participation in God's mission in God's world."[4] This chapter reviews the historical context that birthed the missiology of the indigenous church, narrates the emergence of the indigenous church in early Assemblies of God missions, seeks to redefine the principles of the indigenous church for the twenty-first century, and identifies indigenous church core values.

THE BEGINNINGS OF INDIGENOUS CHURCH MISSIOLOGY

The principles of the indigenous church emerged as a prophetic voice in a historic era of missionary expansion, the great century of missions. "Civilization" and colonial dominance accompanied the gospel message resulting in a "Christianization" of many nations. Small choices, seemingly good choices, resulted in a "missionary compound" that isolated the believing community both literally and culturally from the people they intended to reach. These foreign-controlled missions' stations rarely exhibited the vitality of the New Testament church. Rather, these anemic "missions" depended on the missionary with very little indigenous outreach or growth.

Over time, supporters, administrators, and a few missionaries began to see the ineffectiveness of the paradigm. Missions administrators like Rufus Anderson and Henry Venn called for an indigenous church that could care for itself, recognizing that the sending churches could not support all the missions stations required to reach the world. John Livingstone Nevius made practical recommendations, and Roland Allen called the church back to the "methods" of the biblical text.[5] For the most part, their prophetic words fell on ears deafened by the seduction of power.

The point here is not to analyze the "great century" of missions but to note that missional ineffectiveness does not usually occur because those involved in missions are selfish power mongers who desire to have the nations of the world under their control. Rather, with access to resources, motivated by compassion, guided by reason, and a desire for excellence, missions' leaders made decisions based on available assets and empowered by human resources, rather than by Spirit direction and empowerment. That is, they did not intend to build a dependent church, yet missiological drift took them there. However,

---

3. Praxis, field, and context-driven Pentecostal missions theology remains largely unwritten with the notable exception of the writings of Melvin Hodges.

4. Van Engen, "Introduction," xvii.

5. Roland Allen, *Missionary Methods: St. Paul's or Ours?* (Grand Rapids: Eerdmans, 1962).

Whenever in any period of the Church's history a little company has sprung up so surrendered to the Spirit and so filled with His presence as to furnish the pliant instruments of His will, then a new Pentecost has dawned in Christendom, and as a consequence the Great Commission has been republished; and following a fresh tarrying in Jerusalem for the endowment of power has been a fresh witnessing for Christ from Jerusalem to the uttermost parts of the earth.[6]

Pentecost is the Trinity's answer to the "how" of the Great Commission—not what men and women can do, but what the Spirit of Christ does through them. Jesus declared, "I will build my church; and the gates of hell shall not prevail against it" (Matt. 16:18b). Pentecostal missions emerge from the fire of the Spirit and, when guided by the principles of the indigenous church, result in communities of faith that bear the DNA of the New Testament church, a church directed and empowered by the Spirit, giving witness of the resurrected Christ to peoples of the world with signs and wonders following.

THE INDIGENOUS CHURCH IN EARLY ASSEMBLIES OF GOD MISSIONS

Early Assemblies of God missionaries did not automatically embrace the principles of the indigenous church when experiencing Holy Spirit baptism. The power of culture and tradition continued to dominate the missionary enterprise. Many Pentecostal missionaries impelled by the Spirit traveled to distant lands without adequate support. They asked themselves, "Is it possible to do missions without resources?" As the following narrative illustrates, these missionaries found a resounding "yes!" in the missiological writings of Roland Allen, and more importantly in the biblical text, for it is "'not by might, nor by power, but by my Spirit,' says the Lord Almighty" (Zech. 4:6).

In response to the call of God and the invitation of several small independent congregations that had experienced a new Pentecost, missionary Ralph Darby Williams and his young family entered the city of Santa Ana, El Salvador, on Christmas Eve 1929. Immediately, he began visiting the various congregations and surveying the country in order to develop a strategy to reach the entire nation. He detailed his plan in a letter to his supervisor, Noel Perkin, requesting five additional missionary couples in order to complete the task. Perkin replied that even support for the Williams's was uncertain. Instead of being discouraged, Williams found himself saying, "Our missionaries are already on the field. They are here; I see them every day for they are many. The Lord will use them and the devil cannot stop them. . . . It was a revival carried forward by the inspiration of the Holy Spirit. "[7]

Although familiar with the writings of Roland Allen, the New Testament provided Williams with the model for missionary work. He identifies "three

---

6. A. J. Gordon, *The Holy Spirit in Missions* (London: Hodder & Stoughton, 1893), 52-53.
7. Lois Williams, *Hands That Dug the Well* (Springfield, MO: RDM, 1997), 41-42.

Holy Spirit principles" in which "The Lord carried this work forward by the Holy Spirit in perfect, practical harmony with the three principles of self-propagation, self-government, and self-support."[8] Williams discovered God's model for missions that affirmed the need for contextualization in terms of forms and strategy yet simultaneously was Spirit-directed and Spirit-dependent. Even in a context of extreme poverty with little or no outside resources,[9] the church could be planted and grow, members could be equipped for ministry, and the gospel could be communicated in word and deed with signs and wonders to those who had never heard.

Some argue that these "Holy Spirit principles" no longer apply or would be ineffective in another context. Along with his missionary colleague, Melvin L. Hodges, Williams heard these same arguments when advocating for a Spirit-driven missiology and praxis in the last century. What the church knows today—evidenced by the spectacular growth of the Pentecostal movement around the world, particularly in the Assemblies of God—is that an indigenous church can be planted. Paul and the apostles did it in the New Testament. Williams and Hodges did it in El Salvador and throughout Latin America. Other missionaries did it in Africa and areas of Asia. As Hodges, the missionary statesperson and pioneer Assemblies of God missiologist, so clearly articulates, an indigenous church patterned after the New Testament church is "possible because the Gospel has not changed. We serve the same God and his Holy Spirit is with us as he was with the church in the New Testament times."[10] Hodges contended that converts empowered by the Spirit could carry on the work of the church. The key was that the missionary "must have faith in the power of the gospel to do for others what it has done for us."[11]

The missiology of the indigenous church has been the standard for the Assemblies of God almost from the beginning. Alice E. Luce, Ralph William's mentor, first outlined this philosophy in a series of articles in the *Pentecostal Evangel* in 1921.[12] Donald Gee spelled it out for the Assemblies of God of Great Britain and Ireland in 1937 in a booklet entitled *The Indigenous Principle: An Explanation of a Great Missionary Policy*.[13] Official Assemblies of God documents and popular publications advance the principles of indigenous church missiology. Yet what does it look like in the twenty-first century?

---

8. Ibid., 61.

9. Ibid., 176. God birthed the Assemblies of God in El Salvador during the Great Depression. Rather than the national church borrowing from the missionary, Williams observes, "Many times I borrowed from a national brother to meet unavoidable household needs."

10. Melvin L. Hodges, *The Indigenous Church* (Springfield, MO: Gospel Publishing House, 1953), 14.

11. Ibid., 14, 21.

12. Alice E. Luce, "Paul's Missionary Methods," *Pentecostal Evangel* (January 8, 1921): 6-7; Alice E. Luce, "Paul's Missionary Methods," *Pentecostal Evangel* (January 22, 1921): 6-7; Alice E. Luce, "Paul's Missionary Methods," *Pentecostal Evangel* (February 5, 1921): 6-7.

13. Donald Gee, *The Indigenous Principle: An Explanation of a Great Missionary Policy* (London: Redemption Tidings, 1937).

REDEFINING THE INDIGENOUS CHURCH
IN THE TWENTY-FIRST CENTURY

Hodges articulates a seminal definition of the indigenous church in his classic and world-impacting work *The Indigenous Church*, which he penned in 1953:

> The New Testament church then was first, self-propagating; that is, it had within it sufficient vitality so that it could extend throughout the region and neighboring regions by its own efforts. It produced its own workers and the work was spread abroad by the effort of the Christians themselves. Second, it was self-governing; that is, it was governed by [people] who were raised up by the Holy Spirit from among the converts in the locality. Third, it was self-supporting; it did not depend on foreign money in order to meet the expenses of the work.[14]

Gary B. McGee notes, "The book came at a time when leaders discerned that Assemblies of God missions stood at a crossroads: either to follow New Testament methods and realize more conversions through evangelistic activities of indigenous churches or to see needed funds continue flowing to charitable institutions resulting in fewer conversions."[15] A key issue for Hodges was what would remain if for any reason the missionary had to leave the field or if financial support from the mission was cut off.

According to Hodges, the New Testament church planted in Acts characteristically proclaimed the gospel to the lost, gathered new believers for worship and instruction, and chose leadership from among them in order that they could equip the membership for ministry and witness. Stated in the language of Anderson, Venn, Nevius, Allen, Luce, and Gee, the characteristics of the New Testament church are those of an indigenous church—a contextual self-propagating, self-governing, and self-supporting church.[16]

We can define an indigenous church for the twenty-first century as a community of believers birthed in a specific context that is Spirit-driven (Spirit-led and Spirit-empowered) to accomplish God's purposes for and through that community. As the various churches described in the New Testament, particularly in Acts, these local and national communities of faith are to be *Spirit-governed*, *Spirit-supported,* and *Spirit-propagated*. God, by his Spirit, calls and equips local leaders to disciple and mobilize believers in the faith and guides them in discerning and fulfilling the will of God for their community–Spirit-governed. As a responsible community, the indigenous church turns to the unlimited resources of the Spirit for its sustenance so as not to depend on the missionary, institutions, ministries, or agencies–Spirit-supported. As a community of faith,

---

14. Hodges, *The Indigenous Church*, 12.

15. Gary B. McGee, *Miracles, Missions, and American Pentecostalism* (Maryknoll, NY: Orbis Books, 2010), 172.

16. See Alan Tippett, *Verdict Theology in Missionary Theory* (Pasadena, CA: William Carey Library, 1973).

indigenous church members are impassioned and empowered by the Spirit to reach their neighbors, their nation, and their world with the gospel–Spirit-propagated.

Indigenous church proponents of the Three-Self formula never intended it to create a "self"ish church, as critics contend.[17] Rather, it marked the fact that churches, properly planted on the mission field, should be independent of the missions that planted them and the missions' stations that sought to control and fashion them in the image of the mission culture. Allen, Gee, and Hodges alike affirmed the central role of the Holy Spirit to empower the church and never separated method from Spirit-direction and empowerment. Methods can inhibit the work of the Spirit, yet they can never produce fruit by themselves. The missionary must seek methods through which the Spirit can flow and then trust the Spirit for the results. Gee states:

> Paul's methods succeeded simply and solely because they were directed and empowered by the Holy Spirit. . . . The establishing of indigenous churches that conform to the pattern of the New Testament will remain a practical impossibility without that Pentecostal dynamic which can alone account for the existence of the true church anywhere.[18]

CORE VALUES OF THE INDIGENOUS CHURCH

The principles and values of the indigenous church emerge from a biblical theology of missions forming a philosophy of missional praxis that guides missionary attitudes, decision making, and actions. The brief Williams's narrative above reveals the following core values of a Spirit-driven missions' theology.

A Spirit-Empowered Church

The Lord Jesus fulfills mission through his church by the direction and power of the Holy Spirit. The apostolic mandate requires the communication of the gospel of the kingdom in word and deed by the church to the world. The church is central to the plan of God in mission. The greatest act of social justice in a broken world is to plant a local church. In love, the community of God, the church, continues Christ's ministry in the world in the power of the Spirit, giving witness to the nations, in holiness and service, that Jesus rose from the grave (Acts 1:8).

A false dichotomy exists between kingdom and church, between incarnational ministry and representational ministry, between the missiology of Jesus and the missiology of Paul.[19] Based on his study of the Gospels, Scot McKnight asserts:

---

17. Robert Reese, "The Surprising Relevance of the Three-Self Formula," *Mission Frontiers* (July–August 2007): 25-27. Reese provides a concise response to critics of the three-self formula.

18. Gee, *The Indigenous Principle*, 15.

19. David J. Hesselgrave, *Paradigms in Conflict: 10 Key Questions in Christian Missions Today* (Grand Rapids: Kregel Publications, 2005), 141-65, 315-56.

There is no kingdom without faith and attachment to Jesus Christ, and there is no kingdom without attachment to Jesus' followers. In other words, Jesus' kingdom vision is not that far from Paul's church vision. . . . According to the New Testament, the kingdom vision of Jesus is, it seems, only implemented through the church.[20]

The church is not the kingdom, yet when believers yield to Spirit-direction and empowerment, both individually and corporately, the king manifests his rule on the earth. The apostolic community, birthed at Pentecost, is to be a signpost of the kingdom of God. The purpose of the apostolic people of God is expressed in community (*koinōnia*: "love one another"), in proclamation (*kerygma*: "Jesus is Lord"), in service (*diakonia*: "the least of these my brethren"), and in testimony (*martyria*: "you shall be my witnesses; be reconciled to God").[21] Pentecostals resolve the tension between *missio Dei*, the mission of God, and *missiones ecclesiarum*, the missions of the church, by recognizing and affirming that the activity of the church in missions proceeds out of the mission of God as directed and empowered by the Holy Spirit. The Spirit communicates the Good News of the kingdom of God through the agency of the church.

Hodges framed it by stating, "The Goal of Missions—a New Testament Church."[22] This does not signify that we should mire the church in the first century; rather, the characteristics—the signs that identify the church—should be the same: revelation and reconciliation. The gospel remains unchanged, yet we communicate it uniquely according to context. The church is one church, the body of Christ, but each local congregation is unique. The seed remains the same, but the distinct soils produce diverse expressions within the broader community of faith. "The gospel has been designed by God himself, so it fills the need of the African, the Chinese, or the Indian. As a result, there is no place on earth where, if the gospel seed be properly planted, it will not produce an indigenous church."[23]

A Spirit-Propagated Church

All members of the church carry the responsibility for the apostolic mandate to reach all peoples with the Good News of the kingdom. Every believer and every local congregation needs to assume responsibility for the apostolic mandate. By definition, the church serves as the apostolic people of God. Even as missional praxis is not optional to the church, neither is it possible outside

---

20. Scot McKnight, "McLaren Emerging," *Christianity Today* 52, no. 9 (September 26, 2008): 59.

21. Charles Van Engen, *God's Missionary People: Rethinking the Purpose of the Local Church* (Grand Rapids: Baker Book House, 1991), 87-99.

22. Hodges, *The Indigenous Church*, 9.

23. Ibid., 14. Hodges added the critical element of contextualization to the principles of the indigenous church. Appendix B in *The Indigenous Church* is the "Standard of Faith and Fellowship," a contextual catechism for converts in El Salvador that defined what it meant to be a member of the church in that "soil."

of the church. The objective of all missionary activity focuses on planting and nurturing the church. Local and national churches are essential in missions, for they serve as tangible expressions of God's community of the redeemed and his redeeming community.

The primary task of the missionary is discipleship[24]—not to produce seed or shape the church to the trellis of the sending church, but rather to prepare the soil, remove the rocks, plant the seed, nurture the church, and foment the development of leadership.[25] Missionaries must competently discern divine direction and walk in obedience through the power of the Spirit modeling and facilitating surrender to the Spirit. The missionary's role focuses on pioneer ministries such as planting the church among an unreached people or initiating innovative ministries in response to the needs of the national church. This requires incarnational ministry in which the missionary commits to a lifetime of service, while willingly following divine direction to another people or task at a moment's notice. "His [or her] work is to make Christ the permanent factor, and . . . pass on to other pioneer tasks as quickly as he [or she] can. . . . The true measure of success is not that which the missionary accomplishes while on the field, but the work that still stands after he [or she] has gone."[26]

A Spirit-Governed Church

Leadership equips the church in contextually appropriate ways by creating space for supernatural encounters held to the standard of the Word. The principles of the indigenous church require missional leadership (missionaries, leaders of the sending church, and leaders of the receiving church or church plant) to steward control/power as modeled in the New Testament (servant leadership under the authority of Christ). Allen argued that many missionaries desire growth, but growth they could control.[27] "Such missionaries pray for the wind of the Spirit but not for a rushing mighty wind. I am writing because I believe in a rushing mighty wind, and desire its presence at all costs to our restrictions."[28]

When the Spirit fills followers of Christ in any land or context, they are empowered to give witness. Hodges observes,

> On the mission field, the emphasis, which Pentecostal people place on the necessity of each individual believer receiving a personal infilling of the Holy Spirit, has produced believers and workers of unusual zeal and power. . . . The faith which Pentecostal people have in the ability of the Holy Spirit to give spiritual gifts and supernatural abilities to the common people . . . has raised up a host of lay preachers and leaders of unusual

---

24. Hodges often used the term "soul winner" to refer to discipleship.
25. Leadership development serves as a key dynamic in both the writings of Allen and Hodges.
26. Hodges, *The Indigenous Church*, 18.
27. Roland Allen, *The Spontaneous Expansion of the Church* (Grand Rapids: Eerdmans, 1962), 5.
28. Ibid., 12.

spiritual ability—not unlike the rugged fishermen who first followed the Lord.[29]

An indigenous church is Spirit-governed where leadership development and discipleship occur in culturally appropriate ways, thus producing its own theology, missiology, and missional praxis.

A Spirit-Supported Church

Effective missional praxis requires the church to exert great effort while relying fully on the power of the Spirit. A practical manifestation of Spirit-dependence and a constant challenge to a Spirit-driven missiology and the implementation of indigenous principles relate to the use of finances and other material resources. A dual temptation exists: those who seek material gain without effort rather than depending on the Spirit; and those who have access to resources (e.g., the sending church, the missionaries, and funded national leaders) who depend on the power of those resources rather than the power of the Spirit, thus undermining their spiritual authority.

Hodges observes, "Self-support is not necessarily the most important aspect of the indigenous church, but it is undoubtedly the most discussed."[30] Gee concurs: "One of the most delicate and crucial points in the practical application of the Indigenous Principle affects the financial support of native workers."[31] Gee argues that converts from any land experience richer spiritual blessings when taught "to give to the support of the work of the ministry in their midst from the very outset."[32] An indigenous church from its inception must be a generous, Spirit-dependent, Spirit-supported church. To plant an indigenous church the missionary must be able to trust the Holy Spirit to do what the Holy Spirit has done in the life and ministry of the missionary in the lives of the people with whom the missionary labors.

A Spirit-Praying Church

Reliance on the Spirit requires a commitment to prayer. According to Paul, the authentic source for ministry is Christ's resurrection power (Eph. 1:17-23). Paul prays that the church might be strengthened with power through his Spirit, rooted and established in love (Eph. 3:14-19). "Now to him who is able to do immeasurably more than all we ask or imagine, according to his power that is at work within us, to him be glory in the church and in Christ Jesus throughout all generations, for ever and ever! Amen" (Eph. 3:20-21).

God can and does use human ingenuity and effort if placed on the altar of surrender to his will. He utilizes gifts, personalities, cultures, resources, and strategies in missions, but only when yielded to his rule. Historically, Assemblies

---

29. Hodges, *The Indigenous Church*, 132.
30. Ibid., 74.
31. Gee, *The Indigenous Principle*, 9.
32. Ibid.

of God missions' leadership affirmed that planning and spirituality could work in harmony when directed by the Holy Spirit, but that one without the other could jeopardize missionary work.[33] Hodges concludes in his classic work:

> A great revival can die out or become ineffective if it is not channeled in a scriptural course toward New Testament goals. Furthermore, even the best methods will produce nothing unless accompanied by the work of the Holy Spirit. What gasoline and spark are to the mechanism of a well-tuned motor, spiritual power is to indigenous church methods, for two essential factors combine to make the church a going concern. The mechanics of a successful church on the mission field are the New Testament methods: the dynamics are the power and ministries of the Holy Spirit. Either factor alone is incomplete and inadequate.[34]

The New Testament church was a dependent church—dependent on the direction and empowerment of the Holy Spirit. The relationship between the churches in Antioch, Jerusalem, and Rome was not one of dependence on one another or independence, but one of mutual dependence on the Spirit. Likewise today, the relationship between the missionary and the indigenous church should not be dependent or interdependent, but mutually dependent on the Spirit. As the Spirit leads, the members of the body meet one another's needs and fulfill the task of engaging the nations.

A Spirit-driven missiology begins by creating space for encounters with God in prayer. In prayer, the people of God discern God's direction as he reminds them that he can, and they cannot. The power to fulfill mission must come from above. God's answer to the challenge of the harvest is clear: Pray (Luke 10:2). When God's people pray, they surrender to the Spirit and yield to apostolic power. The church becomes in reality what it is already by faith—the apostolic/missionary people of God, fulfilling the apostolic mandate in apostolic power.

CONCLUSION

The history of Pentecostal missions' theology calls the church, the apostolic/missionary people of God, to a Spirit-driven missiology that recognizes the need of dependence on the Spirit for direction, empowerment, and fruit in the missionary enterprise. Identified and defined as the principles of the indigenous church for the twenty-first century, this Spirit-driven missiology's core values include that the Lord Jesus fulfills mission by the direction and power of the Holy Spirit through his church. In other words, the goal of missional praxis is making disciples of all nations through the planting of local and national churches with New Testament DNA. In addition, that all members of the body of Christ carry

---

33. Gary B. McGee, *This Gospel Shall Be Preached: A History and Theology of the Assemblies of God Foreign Missions since 1959*, vol. 2 (Springfield, MO: Gospel Publishing House, 1989), 106.
34. Hodges, *The Indigenous Church*, 131.

the responsibility of the apostolic mandate to reach all peoples with the Good News of the kingdom (*a Spirit-propagated church*); that leadership equips the church in contextually appropriate ways by creating space for supernatural encounters held to the standard of the Word (*a Spirit-governed church*); that effective missional praxis requires the church to paradoxically exert great effort while relying fully on the power of the Spirit (*a Spirit-supported, responsible church*); and that reliance on the Spirit requires a commitment to prayer.

God's promise of apostolic power is the basis of Pentecostal optimism in fulfilling the apostolic mandate. Gee concludes,

> And so, at the heart of it all, the success of our missionary endeavour to plant scriptural Assemblies of God in other lands by means of following the Indigenous Principle finally depends upon our whole Fellowship keeping filled with the Spirit and possessing the sacred Fire ever burning upon the altar of its heart.[35]

Believing they were a part of God's cosmic eschatological design, Assemblies of God pioneers committed themselves to the seemingly impossible task of global evangelization, believing the impossible possible in the power of Pentecost. Every member of the body of Christ was responsible for the task, for every member was a temple of the Spirit of the living God. They adhered to the New Testament narrative patterns based on the conviction that biblical patterns were Spirit-empowered patterns, missiological truth was to be biblical truth, and the New Testament narrative was to be a contemporary narrative.[36] Charles Van Engen proposes that the community of faith continues to participate in missions because God's story and the story of humankind have yet to finish. The acts of the Holy Spirit through the church in witness to the world will continue until the return of Christ.[37]

A Spirit-driven, indigenous New Testament church does not just emerge. God births it by believers intentionally following the way of the Cross, in the power of the Spirit. In the twenty-first century, the apostolic/missionary people of God must be a people of prayer, exerting great effort to create space for the actions of the God of the impossible. The greatest miracle of all is a sinner saved by God's amazing grace. May this be the generation of the apostolic/missionary people of God who surrender to a Spirit-driven missiology and praxis, and experience the fulfillment of the apostolic mandate in apostolic power.

---

35. Gee, *The Indigenous Principle*, 16.
36. DeLonn L. Rance, *The Empowered Call: The Activity of the Holy Spirit in Salvadoran Assemblies of God Missionaries* (Ann Arbor, MI: ProQuest Information and Learning Company, 2004), 81.
37. Van Engen, "Introduction," xxv.

Part 6

Mission Theology and Religious Pluralism

Chapter 16

Good News for All People: Engaging Luke's Narrative Soteriology of the Nations

Robert L. Gallagher

In August 1976, Barry Silverback, an Australian missionary, macheted five days through Papua New Guinean jungles to the remote village of Kurereda in the Oro Province, and proclaimed the Good News of Christ for all people. On the night of his arrival, in the glow of a kerosene lamp, he witnessed to the living God, whose love of the nations brings salvation through his Son. He stopped in the midst of his preaching, and announced that God desired to heal a woman's eyes. Following this declaration, four women left the gathering, and ten minutes later returned carrying a blind woman. Upon praying in the name of Jesus, the woman immediately received her sight. The next day the missionary baptized over one hundred and forty people, and sixty villagers received the infilling of the Holy Spirit, as the village moved its allegiance from animism to the Lord Jesus. This power encounter with Christ caused a radical transformation of the village that resulted in a church of more than four hundred people, and an evangelistic overflow that affected the nations of Oceania in an ensuing Holy Spirit revival that continues today.[1] The woman of that eventful night received forgiveness of sins, cleansing from community shame, deliverance from a fourteen-year satanic curse, physical healing of her blindness, and the fullness of the Holy Spirit with an accompanying prayer language. Yet, few in Western Christianity embrace Christ's salvation with such holistic perspective. Often the global North restricts God's salvation to the sinner's prayer, an altar call, or sprinkling of baptismal waters. In the biblical perspective, however, could the experience of the Melanesian woman and her village be more representative of Christ's salvation of the nations?

---

1. The author obtained this story from a private conversation with Barry Silverback in Port Moresby, Papua New Guinea (August 1997). See Sarita D. Gallagher, *Abrahamic Blessing: A Missiological Narrative of Revival in Papua New Guinea*, American Society of Missiology Monograph Series 21 (Eugene, OR: Pickwick Publications, 2014), 137-53.

This chapter explores Christ's salvation in the narratives of Luke's Gospel, and examines the author's understanding of God's engagement of the nations. In this hermeneutical journey, the essay affirms the oral tradition behind the Gospel of Luke as being uncorrupted, reliable, and authentic, as well as contributing to a mission theology that has relevance to any global context.[2] After a brief overview of salvation in the gospels and Acts, the paper considers Luke's use of the Greek word *sōzō* and its derivatives in his gospel stories. Having completed the investigation, I will analyze Luke's understanding of Christ's mission theology with the hope that this study of the Savior's connection with the nations will assist God's people today.

SALVATION IN THE GOSPELS AND ACTS

The following is a summary of God's salvation in the gospels and Acts. Luke's concept of "salvation"—mentioned ten times in Luke–Acts (Luke 1:69, 77; 2:30; 3:6; 19:9; Acts 4:12; 13:26, 47; 16:17; 28:28), and only once in the other three gospels (John 4:22)—asserts that only God has the power "to save."[3] This was indicated fifteen times in Luke (6:9; 7:50; 8:12; 9:24 [two times], 56; 13:23; 17:33; 18:26, 42; 19:10; 23:35 [two times], 37, 39) and eleven times in Acts (2:21, 40, 47; 4:12; 11:14; 15:1, 11; 16:30, 31; 27:20, 31), compared to Matthew (thirteen times), Mark (ten times), and John (five times). The way of God's salvation is only via his Son, Jesus the "Savior" (Luke 1:47; 2:11; Acts 5:31; 13:23)—with one other reference in the gospels (John 4:42). Not all will be saved (Luke 8:12; 16:8; cf. Luke 12:29-30, 51-53), however, only those who embrace the responsibility to repent (Luke 12:13-21; 17:26-37; Acts 17:30-31). To summarize Luke's argument, he underscores that self-salvation is not even a remote biblical possibility. Salvation belongs to Jesus the Messiah, our God. The essay now moves from a comprehensive early church perspective to a focused Lukan understanding of salvation through his narrative case studies, and his application of the primitive Greek root *sōzō* and its derivations.

Christ the Savior (Sōtēr) Is Born

At the beginning of Luke's Gospel, the birth narratives of Jesus the Messiah declare God as Savior (*sōtēr*, the deliverer) on two occasions. First, in Luke 1:47, Mary speaks of her spirit rejoicing in God her Savior at the confirmation of Elizabeth concerning the pronouncement of the birth of the Son of God. The God of the Hebrew people was the personal Savior of a peasant girl discovering grace within her shaming community. To whom was Mary referring when she rejoiced in "God my Savior (*Sōtēr*)"? Was it the God of the First Testament, or the

---

2. See Robert L. Gallagher, "Missionary Methods: St. Paul's, St. Roland's, or Ours?" in *Missionary Methods: Research, Reflections, and Realities*, ed. Craig Ott and J. D. Payne, Evangelical Missiological Society Series 21 (Pasadena, CA: William Carey Library, 2013), 6-9, for this paper's biblical methodology of interpretation.

3. All scriptural quotations are from the New International Version.

God-baby in her womb? It was the latter since Spirit-filled Elizabeth had already pronounced that Mary was "the mother of my Lord" (1:43). The teenager was pregnant with the God-Savior, the blessed fruit of her womb (1:42). In joyous response, Mary's Magnificat resounds with repeated declarations highlighting God's provision of deliverance. God has "raised up a horn of salvation" for his people—that will "give his people the knowledge of salvation through the forgiveness of their sins" (Luke 1:69, 71, 77). Finally, Israel, God's people, was to receive their *sōtēr*.

Second, in Luke 2:11, the angel of the Lord, encircled by God's glory, brought to disregarded shepherds near Bethlehem "good news of great joy which will be for all the people." The news was that in the city of David, the long-awaited Savior was born. Again, the God Savior, Jesus the Messiah, was personal to relegated farm laborers, yet available to all nations. "There has been born for you [frightened shepherds] a Savior (*sōtēr*), who is Christ (Messiah) the Lord" (2:11), and the gospel is for all people (2:10). In reaction to this broadcast, a multitude of the celestial hosts joined the angel of the Lord singing praises, "Glory to God in the highest, and on earth peace among men [humanity] with whom he is well pleased" (2:14). In the song of the heavenly choir, there is a repetition of the theme of salvation for all nations. After visiting the child, the shepherds returned to their flocks "glorifying and praising God for all that they had heard and seen, just as had been told them" (2:20).

A compilation of these two *sōtēr* scriptures declares that God is the Savior. There is no other Savior. There is no other path to salvation. God sent his Son in the form of a human being to be God the Savior on earth. The Lukan message is clear. There is only one Savior: the Messiah, Jesus.

A midwestern Christian center for spiritual formation has its core values founded "in Christian history, influenced by the mystics, and rooted in the person of Jesus with insight from Trinitarian understanding, Incarnational grace, and the gift of the Holy Spirit."[4] In regards to how to love your enemy, a blogger on its website states, "How could Jesus give us such an impossible mandate without a user's handbook on how to actually love those who make our lives difficult? For me, I found the answer in Thich Nhat Hahn's writings."[5] Interestingly, the blogger does not recognize the guidance of Jesus through the Holy Spirit, Luke's focus, in showing how to do the impossible, such as love, but instead goes to a Buddhist monk to find the answer. What is ironic is that this Buddhist monk, Thich Nhat Hahn himself, said this:

> The Holy Spirit descended on Jesus like a dove, penetrated him deeply, and he revealed the manifestation of the Holy Spirit. Jesus healed whatever he touched. With the Holy Spirit in him, his power as a healer transformed many people. All schools of Christianity agree on this . . . all of us have

---

4. Retrieved from the Christos website: www.christoscenter.org.
5. See Thich Nhat Hahn, "An Adapted Buddhist Lovingkindness Meditation for Christians, Part 1," www.christoscenter.org.

the seed of the Holy Spirit in us, the capacity of healing, transforming, and loving.[6]

The Buddhist monk, as stated above, understood the important role of the Holy Spirit of Jesus providing "the *capacity* of healing, transforming, and *loving*." The Buddhist monk brings the blogger right back to Jesus and the Holy Spirit, even though the blogger assumed that the monk himself provided the answer. This demonstrates the universal influence of Jesus and the Holy Spirit on the nations and religions, and that we do not need to assume that the answers lie outside of Scripture.

Luke declares that Jesus is the Savior who offers all nations salvific deliverance. The "good news of great joy, which will be for all the people" was not only for the powerful, but also for the powerless: shepherds of the Bethlehem hills, and a provincial girl of Nazareth. The Messiah's delivering salvation is inclusive of young and old, men and women, rich and poor: it is for all "with whom he is pleased," regardless of age, gender, title, or religious affiliation (cf. Acts 2:17-18; 13:38-39). How then do we receive God's good pleasure of salvation? Luke's answer is unfolded with his consideration of *sōtērion*, which portrays God as the defender.

Light of Christ's Salvation (Sōtērion)

This portion of the essay considers two narratives in which the author of the Gospel of Luke uses the Greek word *sōtērion*.[7] First, the words of Luke 2:30, "My eyes have seen your [God's] salvation (*sōtērion*)," were spoken from the lips of Simeon of Jerusalem, who was "looking for the consolation of Israel." In other words, this righteous and devout man was expecting the coming of the Lord's Messiah as a defender of his people; Luke records that the Spirit of God was upon Simeon, revealing to him that he would not die until he saw God's Messiah, and led him into the Temple to behold the messianic Jesus. In a death blessing, the old sage prophesied that the child was God's salvation: "My eyes have seen your salvation."

Yet, who would receive God's salvation? Simeon continues, "Your salvation, which you have prepared in the sight of all nations, a light of revelation to the Gentiles, and the glory of your people Israel." The prophet uses synonymous parallelism in this statement regarding the Lord's salvation. God's salvation, by the human–divine Jesus Messiah, is for all peoples. Simeon repeats this idea using different terms, whereby God's salvation is a light to the non-Jews and the glory of God's nation. In simpler terms, the Gentiles and Israel combine together to account for all peoples. What is more, Simeon was quoting from a passage in the book of Isaiah.

---

6. Thich Nhat Hanh, *Living Buddha, Living Christ* (New York: Riverhead Books, 1995), 15.

7. This essay will not deal with the Lukan narrative of Jesus's encounter with Zacchaeus, the chief tax collector of Jericho, because of its limited scope. "Jesus said to him [Zacchaeus], 'Today salvation (*sōtērion*) has come to this house, because this man, too, is a son of Abraham'" (Luke 19:9).

Isaiah, whose name means, "Yahweh is salvation," was the prophet of salvation in ancient Israel. He announced that God's salvation was for the nations as well as for the ethnic family of Abraham. In underscoring this point of God engaging the nations with his salvation, the gospel writer quotes Isaiah 49:6 (see Acts 13:47). Using poetic synonymous parallelism, the Hebrew prophet says of the Messiah, the Servant of God, "I will make you a light of the nations so that my salvation may reach to the end of the earth." Analogous to Simeon, the Isaianic metaphor of light describes the Lord's salvation that was available and continuous to all the nations.

Turning to Luke 3:6, the gospel writer again uses *sōtērion*. Luke begins chapter 3 with an impressive list of dignitaries during the fifteenth year of the reign of Tiberius Caesar: the Roman politicians—Pontius Pilate, Herod, Philip (Herod's brother), and Lysanias—and the religious clerics, Annas and Caiaphas. Yet, even though these people had secular authority, "The word of God came to John . . . in the wilderness." To substantiate the divine consultancy of the son of Zacharias, Luke once more draws on the prophecy of Isaiah. Both Luke 3:5-6 and Isaiah 40:3-4 speak poetically of the roads, highways, and valleys becoming straight and smooth for God the King (see Luke 7:24-30; esp. v. 27). The last verse in each passage, nevertheless, is different.

Following the accomplishment of this envisioned engineering feat, Isaiah has King Messiah arriving with purpose: "Then the glory of the LORD (Yahweh) will be revealed, and all flesh will see *it* together; for the mouth of the LORD has spoken." In comparison, Luke's Isaianic quote simply says, "And all flesh will see the salvation (*sōtērion*) of God" (cf. Acts 2:21). Upon correlating the two verses, it becomes evident that "the glory of the LORD" in Isaiah matches the gospel's "salvation of God." Accordingly, the salvation offered through Jesus of Nazareth is the glory of God, which throughout Scripture represents the presence and power of the LORD. Again, Luke interprets that the clearing of the way for the LORD in Isaiah 40:3 is for none other than Jesus Messiah (cf. Luke 3:4, 15-17; 7:18-28, esp. 7:27; and Joel 2:32 with Acts 2:21). That is, Jesus is God.

The ushering in of the kingdom of God through the coming of King Jesus brings salvation to all humankind, which manifests itself as the LORD's glory, or the presence and blessing of God. At the beginning of Luke's Gospel, he establishes that the king and his kingdom permit salvation for all the nations. The entrance of Jesus the Christ enables God to engage the nations. This offer of God's salvation allows humanity to experience his presence as before the high treason of our first parents in Genesis that brought expulsion. God's desire throughout the Bible is to bring faithful humans into his presence to bless them (cf. Gen. 1:22, 28; 2:3 with Gen. 3:24). "Meanwhile, the Church, the believing and active community of Christ, is raised up by God among all nations to share in the salvation and suffering service of the Kingdom."[8]

---

8. Johannes Verkuyl, "The Biblical Notion of Kingdom: Test of Validity for Theology of Religion," in *The Good News of the Kingdom: Mission Theology for the Third Millennium*, ed. Charles Van Engen, Dean S. Gilliland, and Paul Pierson (Maryknoll, NY: Orbis Books, 1993), 73.

Luke's Salvation So Far

Up to now, our study of Luke's soteriology from his gospel narratives reveals the following. With the commencement of the Messiah's invasion of the earth, Luke festoons the birth stories with the focal adornment of his visit: salvation belongs to our God. The Savior (*sōtēr*) is God himself: Jesus Christ, the LORD. There is no other Savior (Luke 2:30). Additionally, the Gentile writer establishes a universal paradigm in Luke 3:6, "And all flesh will see the salvation of God." Christ's salvation (*sōtērion*) is available for all people no matter their age, gender, rank, or ethnicity. Luke's contention is that King Jesus, in bringing his kingdom to this world, desires that all peoples receive his deliverance or salvation. The presence of God is to dwell with humanity, as at the beginning of creation, and thus allow believers to experience the blessings of God through his Holy Spirit. Luke understands that salvation belongs only to our God, available for all peoples, yet only through Jesus Christ the Savior. God's salvation is both broad and narrow.[9]

Jesus's Lukan ministry was not exclusive to the Jewish people of Judea since he taught and performed miracles through multicultural Galilee (4:14-15, 40-44; 6:17; 8:40), in Samaria (4:38-39), among the Gadarenes (8:26), in Chorazin (10:12), and Bethsaida (9:10).[10] Yet, the gospel writer did not compromise in declaring Jesus is the Lord of all humanity, and the only Savior.[11] The next section of this chapter continues the examination of Luke's narratives and his concepts of salvation by studying *sōzō*, the Greek root word of "save." In doing so, the study not only reinforces the singular importance of Christ as the source of God's salvation for all nations, but also God's all-inclusive provision of deliverance from sin, disease, and Satan.

Your Faith Has Saved (Sōzō) You

Luke's Gospel records nineteen occasions in which the author uses the word *sōzō* (meaning safe, save, deliver, or protect).[12] The focus of our study,

---

9. Charles E. Van Engen expands this concept: "The particularity of Jesus Christ's incarnation, ministry, death, and resurrection in history continues to stand in dialectical tension with the universality of Jesus Christ's claims to be the Savior of the world. In the midst of this universal-particularism, the disciples of Jesus confess that 'Jesus Christ is Lord.'" See Van Engen, "The Uniqueness of Christ in Mission Theology," in *Landmark Essays in Mission and World Christianity*, ed. Robert L. Gallagher and Paul Hertig, American Society of Missiology Series 43 (Maryknoll, NY: Orbis Books, 2009), 171.

10. See Paul Hertig, "The Multi-Ethnic Journeys of Jesus in Matthew: Margin-Center Dynamics," *Missiology: An International Review* 26, no. 1 (1998): 23-35.

11. Charles E. Van Engen, *God's Missionary People: Rethinking the Purpose of the Local Church* (Grand Rapids: Baker Book House, 1991), 93-94. Compare Sarita D. Gallagher, "Building Bridges of Peace in the Midst of Religious Diversity," *Occasional Bulletin*, Evangelical Missiological Society (January 2016): 12-13.

12. The Greek word *sōzō* occurs thirty-two times in Luke–Acts (Luke 6:9; 7:50; 8:12, 36, 48, 50; 9:24 [twice], 56; 13:23; 17:19 ["made well"], 33; 18:26, 42; 19:10; 23:35 [twice], 37, 39; and Acts 2:21, 40, 47; 4:9 ["made well"], 12; 11:14; 14:9 ["made well"]; 15:1, 11; 16:30, 31; 27:20, 31).

however, will consider five narrative episodes.[13] First, in response to a theological trap, Jesus questioned the scribes and Pharisees about what was lawful on the Sabbath: "To do good or to do harm on the Sabbath, to save (*sōzō*) a life or to destroy it?" (Luke 6:9). Jesus then commanded a man in the synagogue to stretch out his withered right hand. The man obeyed the word of Jesus, and his hand received God's restoration. Jesus demonstrated goodness, and a life received *sōzō* through divine healing. Indeed, this action confirms the rescuing power of Jesus's salvation, as he taught in Luke 9:10 and 9:24, respectively. "For the Son of Man came to seek and to save (*sōzō*) the lost." Further, "For whoever wants to save (*sōzō*) their life will lose it, but whoever loses their life for me will save (*sōzō*) it." The healing of the man with the withered hand displays the saving of a lost soul as he humbly loses his life by obeying the command of Jesus.

Second, Luke 7:50 records the words of Jesus to "a woman in the city who was a sinner." At a luncheon of Simon the Pharisee, the host rejected Jesus as a prophet for allowing the sinner to touch him. Kissing Jesus's feet, the party crasher anoints them with her tears and expensive perfume, mopping up the shame with her hair. Her many sins forgiven, the audience responds indignantly, "Who is this who even forgives sins?" The rhetorical answer is God! Jesus then said to the woman, "Your faith has saved (*sōzō*) you; go in peace" (7:50). Through the behavior of the woman, Jesus recognizes faith, and she receives salvation or deliverance of her sins, and the peace of God, during the exclusive all-male luncheon.

Then, in Luke chapter 8, the gospel author uses *sōzō* not only to speak of Jesus's salvation in terms of deliverance from physical suffering and sin but also to propagate the thought of hindering Satan from undermining a belief in God's word (Luke 8:12), the challenge of entering the kingdom of God (Luke 13:23; 18:26), and freedom from demonic forces (Luke 8:26-39). The latter concerns the narrative of Legion, the Gentile demoniac of Gerasa, a town and surrounding region on the eastern shore of the Sea of Galilee. The concept of a legion refers to five thousand soldiers, which indicates that a demonic stronghold on the man and region was through a person controlled by thousands of unholy spirits affiliated with a city of the non-Jewish and Hellenistic Decapolis. Luke structurally places this episode as an example of the personification of the parabolic lesson of Luke 8:12, and to demonstrate that the spiritual authority of Jesus Messiah was not limited to Jewish geographic territory, unlike that of the surrounding regional polytheistic gods. Legion, possessed with demons who enabled him to have insights into the spirit world, recognized "Jesus, Son of the Most High God." Even in his tortured soul, he knew that this "One is indeed the Savior of the world" (John 4:42).

Jesus confronted this confederation of spirits as "the demons came out of the man and entered the swine" (8:33). The non-Jewish inhabitants of Gerasa witnessed the power encounter and saw "the man who was demon-possessed

---

13. This essay will not observe the Lukan narratives of Jesus healing ten lepers (17:19), and of a blind beggar (18:42) because of its limited scope. In both instances, the Lord recognized that the person's faith had healed [*sōzō*] them and made them whole.

made well (*sōzō*)" (8:36). What was the result of Legion's receiving Christ's salvation (*sōzō*)? He sat at Jesus's feet, clothed, with a healed mind, and begging the Savior that he could accompany him. In response, Jesus sent him back home to testify to the great things God has done for him; and Legion, the saved, became an evangelist among his own people and the other nations around Gerasa (cf. John 4:28-30, 39-42). What an astounding example of Jesus Christ engaging the nations with the salvation of God![14]

Lastly, toward the end of chapter 8 in Luke's Gospel, the author inserts two episodes of Jesus's salvation via physical healing: the woman hemorrhaging for twelve years, and the failing daughter of Jairus, the official of the Capernaum synagogue. Jesus responded to the healed woman, "Daughter, your faith has made you well (*sōzō*); go in peace" (8:48; cf. Luke 18:42). This repeats the statement that the Lord Jesus made to the woman with the alabaster vial of perfume, "Your faith has saved (*sōzō*) you; go in peace" (7:50). Both women expressed faith without a word spoken by Jesus. The two women exercised faith by means of their behavior: one in loving worship as she received forgiveness; the other touching Jesus and releasing the healing power of God. Inserted within the narrative of the dying child was the story of the hemorrhaging woman. Luke then returns to the father of the young girl. On hearing of the daughter's death Jesus says to him, "Do not be afraid; only believe, and she will be made well (*sōzō*)" (8:50). Moreover, the girl received wholeness (8:55). Here are two instances of marginalized females obtaining salvation by physical healing where believing played a role in receiving the *sōzō* of the Lord Jesus.

In summarizing Luke's use of *sōzō* within these five selected narratives, there was a concentration of Christ's salvation in chapters 7 and 8. This falls within the Lukan structure of the actions or miracles of Jesus (see Acts 1:1-2), which underscores the deeds more than the teachings of the Messiah. For the Gentile author, the salvation of God incorporates forgiveness of sins (7:50), demonic deliverance (8:36), and healing (8:48, 50), which is a more experiential approach than in many evangelical churches with their objective salvific beliefs associated with altar calls, confessions, sinner's prayers, and public testimonies.

INTERRELIGIOUS DIALOGUE TODAY

This chapter has explored Luke's understanding of salvation in his gospel by concentrating on the narratives in which the writer uses *sōzō* (or one of its derivatives) to observe the salvific relationship between God and the nations. In dialoguing with persons of other religions, could these insights of the Gentile author guide followers of Christ? In this quest, I must not assume that salvation is understood in the same way among Catholics, Orthodox, or Protestants,

---

14. Compare Paul Hertig, "The Magical Mystery Tour: Philip Encounters Magic and Materialism in Samaria (Acts 8:4-25)," in *Mission in Acts: Ancient Narratives in Contemporary Contexts*, ed. Robert L. Gallagher and Paul Hertig, American Society of Missiology Series 34 (Maryknoll, NY: Orbis Books, 2004), 103-13.

let alone evangelicals; and that issues related to the theology and practice of interfaith dialogue are a secondary matter of God's purposes. Following Luke's example, this chapter prayerfully seeks a scriptural approach in relating to other religions that is faithful to Christ and the Bible.[15]

For Luke, salvation flows from God, which should be central within inter-religious dialogue. Every religion has central tenets, and we should not compromise those for authentic dialogue to occur. Luke does not state that religion saves; only that God does. Indeed, the gospel writer decorates his perception of salvation around the birth narratives of Jesus by streaming the idea of salvation seven times in his first three chapters: Luke 1:47, 69, 71, 77; 2:11, 30; 3:6.[16] This essay shows that Luke supports his argument by referring in particular to the word "Savior" being exclusively used for God and Jesus, even though the word was in common use throughout the first-century Greco-Roman world.

In the Gospel of Luke, the Gentile author was communicating predominantly to non-Jewish Christians, declaring Jesus of Nazareth as the road to God's salvation. In God's concern for all people (Luke 2:14), the writer specifically included Gentiles (Luke 2:30-32; 4:25-26; 4:27; 7:2-10; 13:29; 24:47) and the marginalized (those whom traditional Judaism placed beyond the boundaries) in God's panorama of salvation, especially highlighting the Samaritans (Luke 9:51-55; 10:30-37; 17:15-19). All these people were encountering Jesus through interreligious dialogue. Yet, the Lukan message was consistent.

CONCLUSION

Five key points emerge from this study of the Lukan view of the biblical theology of salvation in the narratives of his gospel. First, that only God is the Savior through Jesus Christ the Lord. Second, the Savior, Jesus Messiah, offers salvation to all nations and peoples who believe, no matter what their gender, rank, position, or spiritual orientation in the community. God's kingdom of salvation is for all. Third, it is through believing that salvation comes to the nations; and this salvation brings forgiveness, freedom from all kinds of bondage, including bondage to the Law of Moses, and the presence and blessing of the Holy Spirit. Fourth, the individual case studies of *sōzō* and its variations demonstrate that Luke's concept of salvation holistically incorporates forgiveness of sin, healing, and demonic deliverance. Lastly, Luke adopts the Isaianic mantle of engaging the nations in salvation and places it upon the church. As a result, the Lord Jesus commands each generation to realize that he sends them "as a light for the Gentiles" to bring salvation to the nations of the world.

---

15. See Robert L. Gallagher, "The Holy Spirit in the World: In Non-Christians, Creation, and Other Religions," *Asian Journal of Pentecostal Studies* 9, no. 1 (2006): 17-33.

16. See Robert L. Gallagher, "Salvation: Narrow Way but Broad Mission. A Response to Christopher J. H. Wright's *Salvation Belongs to Our God*," *Evangelical Interfaith Dialogue* 1, no. 4 (2010): 10-11.

Why was there such a strong emphasis by the non-Jewish Luke to his largely Gentile audience concerning God's only way of "salvation," by Jesus the "Savior," who "saves," compared to the other three gospels? Luke provided part of the answer to this question in his narrative of salvation being a celebrated experience, especially his emphasis on the important role of the Scriptures. Luke recorded the story of the teachings, miracles, death, burial, resurrection, ascension, and ongoing Spirit mission of Jesus the Messiah—the testimony of these events by those who experienced them firsthand (Luke 24:49-53; Acts 4:33)—so that coming generations might also embrace for themselves the salvation of God through Jesus Christ. By knowing the narrative, people assimilate it, and trust the God of the testimony. Woven together within the Scriptures is the story of biblical salvation, which then becomes a biblically informed experience.

A further perspective of this salvific idea is to acknowledge that every person has a religious journey. In other words, within that narrative framework, whether animist, atheist, or agnostic, God in the creative dynamics of his communication skills could reveal himself through a multitude of ways—nature, vision, dream, or cross-cultural worker—regardless of the non-Christian's religion, still all pointing to God's eternal creator Son.[17] Even the First Testament has the story that explains the promised Messiah, Jesus of Nazareth, and his mission to all the nations (Luke 24:44-49; Acts 26:22-23).[18]

Another solution to Luke's highlighting the idea of salvation considers God's bigger purpose in light of the outcome of mission. God through the church is reaching across barriers of culture, language, geography, ideology, and ethnicity to bring people to the kingdom of Christ by announcing the gospel in speech and social action. Luke's major purpose was to write a missional-theological history of the ministry of Jesus and the early church (Luke–Acts) to encourage the people of the Way to follow these two historic examples to give hope and courage to their fear-filled future that would be full of persecution in the midst of a pluralistic world. This was consistent with the preaching record of Acts that pronounced that the salvation of Yahweh and Jesus was identical (2:38; 5:31; 13:38) and the outcome of the Jerusalem Council: "We believe it is through the grace of our Lord Jesus Christ that we [Jews] are saved (*sōzō*), just as they [Gentiles] are" (Acts 15:11). Finally, if Jesus was proclaiming the kingdom of God surrounded by many cultures and peoples of other faiths, then we also need to participate in being gospel influencers. In Van Engen's words, "Let's learn to be bold evangelists: faith particularist, culturally pluralist, and ecclesiologically inclusivist."[19]

---

17. See Van Engen, "Mission of, in, and on the Way," in *Footprints of God: A Narrative Theology of Mission*, ed. Charles Van Engen, Nancy Thomas, and Robert L. Gallagher (Eugene, OR: Wipf & Stock, [1999], 2011), xvii-xxviii.

18. See Robert L. Gallagher, "Coming to Gath: Migration as Mission among the Philistines," in *God's People on the Move: Biblical and Global Perspectives on Migration and Mission*, ed. vanThanh Nguyen and John M. Prior (Eugene, OR: Pickwick Publications, 2014), 42-45, for God's mission to the nations.

19. Van Engen, "The Uniqueness of Christ," 175.

Chapter 17

Interfaith Education and the Missio Dei: *A Case Study in the Pacific Northwest*

Sarita D. Gallagher

My first introduction to interfaith dialogue took place during my graduate studies at Fuller Theological Seminary. I was in the midst of my doctoral program when the seminary invited me to attend a Latter Day Saint–Evangelical Christian Interfaith Conference in Salt Lake City, Utah. Up until this point, my exposure to the Church of Jesus Christ of Latter Day Saints (LDS) was limited to occasional encounters with LDS missionaries and often-unflattering depictions of the LDS Church by the national media. After a crash course on the history of the Church of Latter Day Saints, I believed I was fully prepared to engage in meaningful interreligious conversation. Yet, as I found myself standing in the conference foyer, I realized that I knew so little about the LDS faith and practices.

A personal turning point took place during a plenary presentation by a professor from Brigham Young University. In her presentation, the professor narrated her spiritual journey, which in turn led to an increased emphasis on Jesus Christ as she spoke about all her Bible classes. After the plenary session, my evangelical friends quickly huddled together with the unspoken question, "What was that?" hanging tangibly in the air. Tentative explanations of what we had just witnessed soon jettisoned back and forth. Questions such as "What does it mean to be a follower of Christ?" and "Can people be true followers of Christ outside the boundaries of the historical Christian church?" were raised and discussed at length. Questions that were often restricted to theoretical classroom discussions became instantly relevant to our Christian faith with a force that was unanticipated just an hour before.

North American Christians no longer find themselves in a silo of religious isolation. The demographic transformation of the United States increasingly reflects the sociocultural, political, and religious diversity of the world.[1] While

---

1. The Pew Research Center's *2014 Religious Landscape Study* indicates an uptrend since 2007 in the number of U.S. adults that identify with religions other than Christianity. See "The Changing

sharing the gospel of Christ remains central to Christian witness, loving our neighbors in the midst of religious diversity and theological difference is at the heart of Christ's imperative. Unfortunately, there has been less movement toward understanding the religious belief systems of non-Christian neighbors. How can we truly love our multireligious neighbors if we do not know them? In this chapter, I present a case example where I examine the missiological outcomes of a christocentric model of interfaith engagement in an academic setting. In particular, I highlight how interfaith education can positively affect the spiritual development of students, as well as their understanding of the broader multireligious community, and the kingdom of God. The case study is based on an analysis of my undergraduate World Religions course at George Fox University from 2011 to 2015. Participant-observer analysis is the basis of the missiological suppositions highlighted in this essay, with over 370 students' reflections articulated in written essays, class discussions, and personal conversations.

INTERFAITH ENGAGEMENT IN THE CLASSROOM

"Islam is a religion of violence and terrorism. The Qur'an is the only religious text that supports violence." As soon as the undergraduate student in my World Religions course uttered these words, the atmosphere in the classroom immediately shifted. In a matter of seconds, tension and anticipation immersed the room. Thirty-five sets of eyes focused on me with piercing intensity as hands shot up around the classroom. The thoughtful conversation that followed reflected the class's recent experiences visiting the local Islamic community. As an educator, I have found creating a space for authentic dialogue and community engagement has led to transformative experiences that positively challenge students' cultural worldview. Through these encounters with otherness, students have grown in their personal faith, developed a greater appreciation for religious diversity, and gained a deeper understanding of God's love for the nations.

Educational Context

The World Religions course at George Fox University is a three-unit course that serves as a requirement for International Studies and Christian Ministries-Missions majors, and an elective course within the general education package. The course goals are as follows: students will (1) gain an understanding of basic tenets of several major world religions, (2) engage with religious beliefs and rituals, (3) explore personal faith in light of religious traditions, and (4) gain a foundation for effective and sensitive Christian witness to persons adhering to other faiths.[2] In this survey course, students learn about the belief systems and

---

Religious Composition of the U.S.," *2014 Religious Landscape Study*, 28. Pew Research Center, May 12, 2015, www.pewsocialtrends.org.

2. Ron Stansell, Professor Emeritus of Religious Studies at George Fox University, Newberg, Oregon, originally created the World Religions course outcomes.

rituals of Judaism, Islam, Hinduism, and Buddhism, as well as other prominent religious traditions such as Shintoism, Confucianism, Sikhism, and Jainism. Additional topics discussed include interfaith dialogue, insider movements, exclusivism, inclusivism, pluralism, and faith integration.

The average class size of each course section is approximately thirty-five students, which includes students representing the entire spectrum of majors offered at the institution. The majority of the students are traditional undergraduate students between the ages of eighteen and twenty-two years of age. Although affiliated with the Quaker denomination, the university's undergraduate students represent a wide range of Protestant denominations, with a growing number of students outside the Christian faith. The majority of students enrolled in the course indicate little to no exposure to religious traditions outside of Christianity before taking the course.

In light of the postmodern orientation of the learners, the methodological approach of this course is narrative, experiential, and discussion based. Student engagement is multifaceted and includes in-class simulations, film, lecture, group discussions, case studies, guest speakers, and field experiences. As a part of the course assignments, students are required to attend three religious services that are not Christian. At the services, students are encouraged to observe religious rituals and practices, asking questions for understanding and clarification, and connecting informally with the religious community. In particular, interreligious dialogue plays a significant role in classroom discussions and field activities.

There are several distinct approaches to interfaith dialogue. In its classic definition, "Dialogue . . . means a sustained conversation between parties who are not saying the same thing, and who recognize and respect the differences, the contradictions, and the mutual exclusions between their various ways of thinking."[3] Whether engaged in informal or structured interreligious conversation, interfaith dialogue adopts a variety of objectives. Of these goals, the most common include the establishment of mutual understanding, appreciation of other traditions, evangelism, reflection, and spiritual growth. In the World Religions course, the objectives of interfaith engagement are twofold: (1) the development of mutual understanding, and (2) personal spiritual growth.

While engaging in interfaith conversations, students are encouraged not to disregard their own religious convictions. Interreligious dialogue for Christian believers should affirm "both the understanding and communication aspects of dialogue without surrendering biblical absolutes."[4] As confirmed by the Uppsala report of the World Council of Churches,

> A Christian's dialogue with another implies neither a denial of the unique-
> ness of Christ, nor any loss of his own commitment to Christ, but rather
> that a genuinely Christian approach to others must be human, personal,

---

3. John V. Taylor, "The Theological Basis of Interfaith Dialogue," *International Review of Mission* 68, no. 272 (1979): 373.

4. Steven J. Pierson, "Dialogue," in *Evangelical Dictionary of World Missions*, ed. A. Scott Moreau, Harold A. Netland, and Charles E. Van Engen (Grand Rapids: Baker, 2000), 274.

relevant, and humble. In dialogue, we share our common humanity, its dignity and fallenness, and express our common concern for that humanity.[5]

This approach upholds that "through interpersonal dialogue, one listens and learns as well as shares scriptural truth."[6] Additionally, it insists that true biblical interchange reflects authenticity, humility, integrity, and sensitivity—all without relinquishing essential biblical mandates of salvation. It is this desire to recognize our religious neighbors as ones loved by Christ that should be at the heart of interfaith discourse.

CULTURAL CONTEXT

To understand the importance of interfaith engagement in Christian higher education, we must examine the theological and eschatological questions of the current generation. Surrounded by the increasingly secular environment of the Pacific Northwest, students often examine their Christian faith with increasing concern, unanswered questions, and at times, growing doubt. According to the Pew Research Center's *2014 Religious Landscape Study*, this theological shift is not a regional development but a national trend. In the United States, the number of religiously unaffiliated individuals has grown exponentially since 2007. "The share of self-identified atheists has nearly doubled in size since 2007, from 1.6% to 3.1%. Agnostics have grown from 2.4% to 4.0%. And those who describe their religion as 'nothing in particular' have swelled from 12.1% to 15.8% of the adult population since 2007."[7] In addition, "the religious 'nones' have grown from 16.1% to 22.8% of the population in the past seven years."[8] This shift in the United States away from a majority Christian culture has led to the questioning of basic Christian beliefs and doctrine. Within the context of higher education, questions accumulate as students attempt to reconcile the voices of secularism with the spiritual teaching of religious communities.

Caught between the intersection of postmodernity and modernity these questions are especially significant for millennial students.[9] While considering the physical world of science and technology to be concrete, exact, accurate, and real, millennials understand religious truth and the spiritual world to be unknowable, imprecise, vague, and subjective.[10] This perspective mirrors

---

5. Norman Goodall, ed., *The Uppsala Report 1968: Official Report of the Fourth Assembly of the World Council of Churches*, Uppsala July 4-20, 1968 (Geneva: WCC Publications, 1968), report 2, para. 6.

6. Pierson, "Dialogue," 274.

7. "Changing Religious Composition," 30.

8. Ibid., 30.

9. Demographers Neil Howe and William Strauss first coined the term "millennial" to describe the generation of North Americans born between 1982 and 2000.

10. Lesslie Newbigin identified this cultural shift toward secularism as the "powerful current . . . that would sweep away such a claim [of Christ's uniqueness], and insist that the story of those events is simply one among the vast variety of 'religious experience.' . . . The current is

classic secularism, which "maintains that the only real world is that of sensory experience, and regards the universe as a closed system in which humankind operates without recourse to any real or imagined powers outside of itself."[11] According to the *2007 U.S. Religious Landscape Survey*, in contrast to previous generations, millennials are less certain about the existence of God (64%), and evangelicals are less likely to view the Bible as the literal word of God (47%).[12] For many, this increasingly secular worldview eventually causes a crisis of faith as the continuous advances of physical science seemingly invalidate the possibility of spiritual realities.

This religious struggle is particularly evident among evangelical college students. In a recent study researchers found that while there are "rising levels of struggle across all institutional types," the greatest increase of religious uncertainty was among students attending evangelical colleges: "From seven percent reporting high levels [of religious struggle] as freshmen to seventeen percent reporting high levels as juniors."[13] In assessing this data, the researchers suggested, "For many evangelical college students, being in college may . . . represent their first sustained experience in critical thinking, where ideas, regardless of their source, are subjected to investigation, discussion, argument, and debate."[14]

While prior generations of educators addressed students' theological concerns through analysis of the historicity of Jesus Christ and the testimony of Scripture, today's generation find these explanations increasingly unconvincing. Most millennials are not looking for historical data or theological discourse alone. Instead, there is a longing to understand the Christian faith within the wider religious context. How does Christianity compare, for instance, with Buddhism or Islam? As students perceive the complexity of the global context, they seek to understand how the Christian faith is more valid than other religious belief systems.

Similarly, students desire to understand the relationship between Christianity and the physical and social sciences. Historically, the institutional church has supported scientific and sociopolitical claims, yet often the assertions suffered challenge and falsehood. For example, the statements that the earth was flat; the practice of slavery was a God-ordained social construct; and global warming is irrelevant. As the United States moves toward a predominantly post-Christian culture, social and national media continually project skepticism regarding the Christian worldview. In a series of surveys conducted by the Barna Group from

---

strong because it is part of the drift of contemporary Western culture . . . away from belief in the possibility of knowing truth and toward subjectivity." See Newbigin, "The Gospel and the Religions," in *Landmark Essays in Mission and World Christianity*, ed. Robert L. Gallagher and Paul Hertig (Maryknoll, NY: Orbis Books, 2009), 150.

11. Eddie Gibbs, "Secularization," in *Evangelical Dictionary of World Missions*, ed. A. Scott Moreau, Harold A. Netland, and Charles E. Van Engen (Grand Rapids: Baker, 2000), 865.

12. "Millennials: A Portrait of Generation Next," Pew Research Center, 96, February 2010.

13. Alexander W. Astin, Helen S. Astin, and Jennifer A. Lindholm, *Cultivating the Spirit: How College Can Enhance Students' Inner Lives* (San Francisco: Jossey-Bass, 2011), 103.

14. Ibid., 104.

January 2008 to January 2014, the findings show the following: "The three primary components that lead to a disbelief in God's existence were (1) rejection of the Bible, (2) lack of trust in the local church, and (3) cultural reinforcement of a secular worldview."[15] This third component, the formation of a secular worldview, has in many ways jaded the millennial generation. The national media portrays Christianity for what it stands against rather than for what it supports.[16] It bombards students with the mounting argument that if the church has been incorrect about the realities of the physical world, it is possible that Christianity is wrong about everything.

MISSIONAL OUTCOMES OF INTERFAITH EDUCATION

The classroom is a unique space where students can explore Christianity within the wider global context. In the midst of educational experiences, students' interest in academic knowledge often transforms into a desire for spiritual truth. While teaching the World Religions course, I often observe three missiological outcomes in students: (1) a spiritual growth, (2) an increased respect for other religions, and (3) an increased understanding of the mission of God.

Spiritual Development

When I originally began teaching the World Religions course, my primary goal was academic. That is, students would listen and learn from religious practitioners outside the church. I was surprised when I first heard that my students also received a strengthening of their faith in Christ while taking the course. At first, I dismissed their comments of spiritual renewal as the Christian equivalent of the mission-trip commentary: "I'm so glad that I was born in the United States." Unintentionally, the World Religions course provided students with a space to freely question, explore, and analyze Christianity. It is within this act of reexamination that students' religious convictions were frequently refined and consolidated.

In the course, the lectures weave theological questions throughout, and small group assignments encourage students to reflect on their religious beliefs. In using the Socratic method to stimulate ideas and discussion, the teaching does not automatically provide the answers. Instead, significant theological questions such as, "Is Allah the same god as Yahweh?" and "Is the Hindu concept of the *trimurti* similar to or different from the Christian concept of the Trinity?" are open to group discussion and analysis. As students visit non-Christian religious services and talk with practitioners of other faiths, questions begin to surface such as, "Does God hear and answer the prayers of Muslims?" "How could God send people of other faiths to hell?" "How do I know that Christianity is the only true faith?" "Is Christian mission work a form of ethnocentric paternalism?"

---

15. "2015 State of Atheism in America," Barna Group, March 24, 2015, www.barna.org.
16. David Kinnaman and Gabe Lyons, *Unchristian: What a New Generation Really Thinks about Christianity, and Why It Matters* (Grand Rapids: Baker, 2007), 26.

While often creating disequilibrium, these questions enable students to define and articulate personal religious convictions. Kelly, a sophomore student, ponders: "Taking this class has forced me to examine my own faith. I have not questioned what I believe so much as how I articulate what I believe. I was inspired by how well members of other faiths could answer my questions about their religions."[17] Another student, Jaynani, a junior in the same course, notes:

> I've got the opportunity to gain the facts on different religious traditions and beliefs, but I've also got to experience what those people are like and be reminded by God that they are His children whom He loves just as much as me. . . . I think all of these shifts have occurred because God has been poking and challenging my beliefs in order to give them better shape. My belief to love all others has grown monumentally from this class because I've got to experience different faiths.

This clarification of personal beliefs and shift in worldview are common themes in students' personal reflections within the course. As students analyze their religious beliefs and interact with people of other faiths, a deeper understanding of their own belief system develops.

Academic presentations by guest speakers from other religions also encourage students to investigate the foundations of their faith. For example, in one class session when a Muslim guest stated that Jesus Christ did not die on the cross, yet continued his ministry in India, students were compelled to examine the historicity of Jesus's death on the cross. On another occasion, the class revisited Jesus's unique role as the only Son of God when an LDS speaker noted that Jesus of Nazareth was the first of many sons and daughters of God. Additionally, when a Buddhist Tibetan monk expounded the various eschatological beliefs of the Mahayana, Theravada, and Vajrayana schools of thought, the reality of God the Creator gained renewed importance. In these formal and informal interactions, students dust off and reconsider afresh core tenets of Christian doctrine.

This process of analysis encourages the development of spiritual authenticity and ownership of faith for pupils. By embracing the questions that interfaith engagement generates, students participate in the universal search of truth. Some people come to the course with a subconscious perception of avoiding religious questions since they are potentially dangerous. Thomas Merton, in speaking of the relationship between contemplation and doubt, addresses the true place of doubt in the Christian faith:

> You cannot be a man of faith unless you know how to doubt. You cannot believe in God unless you are capable of questioning the authority of prejudice, even though that prejudice may seem to be religious. Faith is not a blind conformity to a prejudice—a "pre-judgment." It is a decision,

---

17. The students' quotes are from an in-class written assignment in two spring 2015 sections of the World Religions course. All quotes and names in the chapter are included with the students' permission.

a judgment that is fully and deliberately taken in the light of a truth that cannot be proven. It is not merely the acceptance of a decision that has been made by somebody else.[18]

In accepting Christ, believers do not leave behind their God-given ability to ponder, question, and analyze. Instead, followers of Christ, in embracing the message of the gospel through the power of the Holy Spirit, do so as whole beings, with their minds, hearts, and souls, and subsequently experience spiritual development. Following this missiological outcome of spiritual growth, students may also experience an increased respect for other religions.

Bridges of Communication and Respect

On the first day of each World Religions course, I ask the students to indicate what they are most looking forward to, and what makes them most apprehensive. The answer is uniform: the students are simultaneously excited and nervous about visiting non-Christian religious services, and talking with religious practitioners outside of Christianity. Although the media display a variety of religious traditions, in most areas of the United States, not only socio-economic and racial backgrounds segregate our communities but also religious. The North American cultural mantra that broadcasts never to discuss politics, sex, or religion in public still holds precedence. The classroom gives students permission to put aside these cultural taboos and to engage in interreligious conversations with their family and friends and communities of different faiths. This interfaith engagement in turn leads to the development of mutually respectful relationships.

As students listen to the faith stories of religious practitioners, their perception of the individual and his or her religious tradition often undergoes significant transformation. In reflecting on her course experience, Mary Beth, a sophomore, writes:

> This semester my mind has been blown at least a hundred times. My perception of other religions has become so much more open and understanding. After visiting the mosque, and the synagogue, and places of worship, I feel as though I am more capable of interacting with people of those faiths. . . . Through learning about these other faiths, I have had mine tested for the first time, and it was an incredible experience. Where I used to have fear or misunderstanding of these people and cultures, I feel as though I now have love.

Daniel, another sophomore, states of his own transformation:

> My worldview initially was that other religions weren't valuable; either they detract from the story of the True God or they just outright contradict it. . . . This class helped to give another dimension to my pretty flat view of

---

18. Thomas Merton, *New Seeds of Contemplation* (New York: New Directions, 1961), 105.

other religions. . . . The reminder that we are equals—children of God—
with the same capacity to understand, deteriorates my attitude that I've
got it all figured out . . . and inspires me in my Christian walk.

While the changes in students' perceptions varied, the majority of students
indicated that a positive renovation had occurred in their understanding of
other religions since the commencement of the course.

In the Christian life, the crossing of sociocultural, racial, and religious
barriers is crucial in developing bridges of communication and respect with
non-Christian neighbors. One basic requirement of mutual understanding and
open dialogue is civility. In speaking of Christian civility, Richard J. Mouw
identifies the need of both inner and outer civility. He explains, "Civility is public
politeness. It means that we display tact, moderation, refinement, and good
manners toward people who are different from us. It is not enough, though, to
make an outward show of politeness. Being civil has an 'inner' side as well."[19]
Mouw explains that inner civility requires "genuine care" for "the larger society
. . . [and] a heartfelt commitment to your fellow citizens. It [is] a willingness to
promote the well-being of people who [are] very different, including people who
seriously [disagree] with you on important matters."[20]

Building relationships of respect and compassion is one way to emulate
Christ's love of all people. At the core of authentic interaction is an attitude of
humility, trust, and love. In a culture of constant media noise, active listening has
become an act of love and respect. In speaking of the importance of listening in
interfaith conversations, Harold A. Netland explains,

> A genuine willingness to listen to others, and to learn from them, can be a
> mark of humility and common courtesy. If we expect a Muslim or Hindu,
> for example, to listen carefully to our proclamation of Jesus Christ as
> Savior and Lord, surely we owe them the same courtesy and respect we
> expect from them. How can we expect a Buddhist to take Christian claims
> seriously if there is no evidence of willingness on the Christian's part to
> carefully consider the claims of the Buddhist?[21]

We should not underestimate the power of listening as a means through which
Christians can demonstrate the love of Christ to individuals and communities.
In listening to people's personal narratives and beliefs, we acknowledge the
inherent value of that individual as a human being created by God in his image.
As John V. Taylor notes, respectfully listening to "an opinion that conflicts with
one's own" is an act of love. He continues, "There will generally have to be a

---

19. Richard J. Mouw, *Uncommon Decency: Christian Civility in an Uncivil World* (Downers
Grove, IL: InterVarsity Press, 2010), 14.
   20. Ibid.
   21. Harold A. Netland, "Application: Mission in a Pluralistic World," in *Christianity and the
Religions: A Biblical Theology of World Religions*, Evangelical Missiological Society Series 2, ed.
Edward Rommen and Harold Netland (Pasadena, CA: William Carey Library, 1995), 266.

great deal of that kind of loving before we can expect any genuine reconciliation of ideas and beliefs."[22]

Missional Encounters

A final missiological outcome I have observed in students participating in my World Religions course is an increased understanding of the mission of God. While learning about other people's religious beliefs, occasions may arise for Christian witness. Speaking of the missional potential of informal interfaith dialogue, J. Samuel Escobar writes,

> To the degree to which missionaries are ready to listen to local people (in the same way in which Jesus did), and willing to follow the promptings of the Holy Spirit, their understanding of their own faith will grow and deepen as they find new, creative ways of responding to those questions, in word and deed.[23]

Through listening and learning about the beliefs and traditions of other religious practitioners, a thoughtful and contextualized expression of the Christian gospel can emerge. While this witness often develops out of sustained and genuine relationships, opportunities can arise for students to share their own beliefs in the context of the course with family, friends, and neighbors.

Although some scholars criticize Christian evangelism in interfaith dialogue, followers of Christ should not exclude sharing the gospel through interreligious relationships.[24] As mutual conversations take place, the exchange of religious beliefs may be appropriate and reflective of an authentic reciprocal association. Lesslie Newbigin comments on the essential role of Christian witness in inter-religious fellowship. While "it is the Holy Spirit of God who can so touch the hearts and consciences of the others that they are brought to accept the story as true and put their trust in Jesus," it is the contribution of Christians to tell the story of Jesus.[25] Newbigin adds, "The Christian must tell [the story], not because she lacks respect for the many excellences of her companions . . . [yet] as one chosen and called by God. . . . She will indeed—out of love for them—long that they may come to share the joy that she knows, and prays that they may indeed do so."[26]

In addition to providing opportunities of Christian witness outside the classroom, the World Religions course can also be a vehicle for students to

---

22. Taylor, "Interfaith Dialogue," 373.

23. J. Samuel Escobar, "'Good Missiology' and Interfaith Dialogue," *Evangelical Interfaith Dialogue Journal* 4, no. 2 (2014): 3.

24. John Hick holds that the position of Christian exclusivism is destructive and ethnocentric. Instead, he asserts, "God is at work wherever there is a costly commitment to the struggle for human justice." See Hick "The Non-Absoluteness of Christianity," in *The Myth of Christian Uniqueness: Toward a Pluralistic Theology of Religions*, ed. John Hick and Paul F. Knitter (Maryknoll, NY: Orbis Books, 1988), 33.

25. Lesslie Newbigin. *The Gospel in a Pluralist Society* (Grand Rapids: Eerdmans, 1989), 182.

26. Ibid.

encounter Christ. John is an example of one student who became a follower of Christ in the midst of his religious journey.[27] At the beginning of the semester, he confided that although he was attending the Christian university he was not a believer, but an agnostic. John explained that he chose to align himself with Christianity because he did not know what other religious path to choose. Following each religious service, visit, or speaker, John mentioned how compelling he found each tradition, stating that he now wanted to become Jewish, Muslim, Hindu, or Ba'hai. Although I sometimes feel led by the Holy Spirit to connect with students in the processing of their beliefs, in this case I felt repeatedly that I should not intervene. Instead, I listened and waited for those fateful words, "I took the World Religions course, and became a Buddhist." However, that did not happen. It was during the final weeks of the semester that John met with me, and shared that he had decided to become a Christian. He explained that during our visit to the Buddhist temple he clearly saw the emptiness of all the other religions he had encountered. Without the God of Abraham, Isaac, and Jacob nothing made sense or had any meaning. Joy and conviction radiated from John's face as he explained that this experience had pointed him toward following Jesus Christ.

CONCLUSION

As North America becomes increasingly multireligious, there is a growing need to teach students how to interact with their religious neighbors in a respectful and thoughtful manner. This knowledge is not intuitive. Instead, religious education and the development of mutual interfaith relationships need to contest the religious bias and stereotypes that permeate American culture through family systems, education, and media. Educational platforms such as the World Religions course at George Fox University create opportunities for students to explore the essential convictions of their faith with fresh eyes. Participation in interfaith conversation challenges and strengthens theological understanding. This process in turn creates opportunities for students to participate in the universal mission of God. By thoughtfully engaging with their religious neighbors, students embody God's enduring call to love their neighbors through communicating the Good News of Christ via word and deed.

---

27. The author changed the student's name to protect his or her privacy.

Chapter 18

Interreligious Dialogue and Convivence:[1]
Missional Challenge and Charge for Today

Jerald D. Gort

To look at the [other] is . . . to look within ourselves in order to purify all that makes us closed to what is new and true; . . . to accept being questioned by him about our faith and to be ready to give an account of it; . . . to be available to work with all persons of good will for the common good.[2]

In this essay, I will first touch briefly on historical and contemporary attitudes of Christianity toward other religions. I will follow this explanation by a discussion of those aspects of the concept of contextualization and certain insights of postmodernism that are germane to my construal of dialogue. Then, against this background, I will sketch out what in my view are the four constitutive modes of interreligious dialogue. Yet, before going into these matters, it might be well to begin with one or two general remarks about religion.

RELIGION[3]

Though some, particularly Western neo-atheist enthusiasts, assert that religion is passé, objective observation reveals that religion continues to be vitally important to the vast majority of people on earth. According to the late Dutch missiologist J. H. Bavinck, all humans have a "religious consciousness." This consciousness entails a deep awareness of a number of fundamental enigmas:

---

1. Convivence: "to live together."

2. Cardinal Jean-Louis Tauran, president of the Pontifical Council for Interreligious Dialogue, at the Global Forum sponsored by the King Abdullah Bin Abdulaziz International Centre for Interreligious and Intercultural Dialogue (KAICIID), Vienna, November 19, 2013.

3. The first two sections of this essay are radically abridged and amended and the final one on dialogue is an extensively revised adaptation of parts of an earlier article that appeared in University of Pretoria's *Verbum et Ecclesia: Journal of the Faculty of Theology* 29, no. 3 (2008): 744-63. Used with the knowledge and kind leave of its editor.

the puzzle of all-embracing cosmic cohesion, the mystery of the ambiguity of human life, the awareness that things are not the way they ought to be, giving rise to the universal longing for redemption.[4] In the end, all such riddles coalesce into one profoundly religious question: "Who am I, small mortal man, in the midst of all these powerful realities with which my life is most intimately related?"[5]

Following in the vein of Bavinck, an op-ed article in the Dutch Daily News states:

> Philosophers and theologians knew this long since, but now it has also been demonstrated scientifically: humans are religious by nature. Of course, no one comes into the world with a developed faith. . . . But a fast growing amount of research shows convincingly the extent to which religiosity is ingrained in our system. People are naturally inclined to see meaning in seemingly meaningless matters.[6]

Corollary to this basal "religious consciousness," humans everywhere engage in one or another form of worship or religious observance. Thus, not only radical religiosity but also religious beliefs and their expression are in the very fabric of human nature and life.

From the outset of the Enlightenment, religion has been recurrently subject to harsh criticism.[7] Indeed, religions have often slid into betrayal of their central teachings by colluding with injurious forces: "as a social phenomenon religion was, is, and will be a contributory factor to conflict."[8] Notwithstanding this potential for degeneration, however, it is clear that most people cannot get along without religion as a means of coping with existential disquietude and as a medium of faith and hope.[9]

CHRISTIANITY AND THE OTHER RELIGIONS

We now turn to a brief examination of historical Christian attitudes toward other traditions, followed by a concise review of the shifting stance of Christians vis-à-vis people of other faiths and their creeds and practices.

---

4. Cf. J. H. Bavinck, *The Church between the Temple and Mosque* (Grand Rapids: Eerdmans, 1966), 107-11.

5. Ibid., 113. See further on Bavinck's concept of religious consciousness in *Religieus besef en christelijk geloof* (Kampen: Kok, 1989 [orig., 1949]), 12-75.

6. Rik Peels and Stefan Paas, "Religiositeit is nu lang genoeg de kop ingedrukt," *De Volkskrant* (2013) (translation mine).

7. Today neo-atheists such as Richard Dawkins, Sam Harris, and Christopher Hitchens view religion as not only backward but evil and thus the foremost source of human cruelty.

8. John O'Grady and Peter Scherle, "Ecumenics in the 21st Century: Plumbing the Relationships of Theology, Inter- religious Dialogue and Peace Studies," in *Ecumenics from the Rim: Explorations in Honour of John D'Arcy May,* ed. J. O'Grady and P. Scherle (Berlin: LIT Verlag, 2007), 17.

9. On the ambiguity of religion, see Jerald D. Gort and Hendrik M. Vroom, "Religion, Conflict, and Reconciliation," in *Religion, Conflict, and Reconciliation: Multifaith Ideals and Realities*, ed. Jerald D. Gort, Henry Jansen, and Hendrik M. Vroom (Amsterdam: Rodopi, 2002), 3-10.

Historical Attitudes

For most of its history, Christianity regarded other religious traditions in overwhelmingly negative terms. During its earliest period, however, thinkers such as Justin Martyr (c. 100–c. 165) and Clement of Alexandria (c. 150–c. 215) evinced an altogether different spirit. They argued that the religious and philosophical traditions of humankind all owe their existence to God's revelatory initiative. Thereby these practices could function as *praeparationes evangelica* (preparations for the gospel), and as *paedagogoi* (instructors) capable of making people receptive to the fullness of the truth revealed by God in Christ.

Unfortunately, this generosity of mind was not long lived. From about the middle of the third century the affirmative openness that had informed much of early patristic theology gradually gave way to increasingly negative feelings on the part of the church toward the exterior world, which found concise expression in the watchword *extra ecclesiam nulla salus* (outside the church no salvation). Originally pastoral in intent, this early-third-century axiom soon took on an exclusionist bent. "He cannot have God for his Father," Cyprian of Carthage (d. 258) wrote, "Who does not have the Church for his mother."[10] In addition, the gradual establishment of Christianity as the official religion of the Roman Empire from around 350 CE led to a further hardening of this segregationist attitude. The "outside world" came to be qualified as "non-Christian" and disqualified as "heathen," as the "kingdom of darkness," whose redemption rested solely in assumption into the enlightened *corpus Christianum*. For the next fifteen hundred years or more, the overall picture shows that Western Christian thinking (in respect of other religions and the external world in general) was deeply shaded by unconstrained feelings of superiority, and almost wholly governed by an ethos of exclusion.

Pursuant to the Anglo-American missionary conferences of 1888 (London) and 1900 (New York), and the advent of the modern cooperative missionary and ecumenical movements after 1910, however, this prevailing ecclesiastical-theological mind-set began to undergo an adjustment, which gained ever-greater momentum through the years, primarily during the past six decades.

New Understandings and Shifting Stance

After World War II and particularly since the late 1950s and early 1960s, an awareness began growing that this world is the *theatrum Dei*, the arena of the activity of the triune God, Father, Son, and Holy Spirit. As attested by the sixteenth-century reformers, all of nature, the entire universe, the whole of the cosmos discloses God: *finitum capax infiniti* (the finite carries within it the infinite). The entire world, being the product of God's creative action, is the permanent object of God's inexhaustible love and universal salvific concern. God exists nowhere without witness.

---

10. J. N. D. Kelly, *Early Christian Doctrines* (London: Adam & Charles Black, 1965), 206.

God knows every human being. Buddha would never have meditated on the Way of Deliverance if God had not touched him. Mohammed would never have delivered his prophetic witness if God had not been working with him. Every religion contains within it the quiet, secret work of God in one form or another.[11]

Furthermore, the very nature of God's work as creator bears significant implications for the matter of stance vis-à-vis the religiously and culturally other. Genesis 1 and 2 reveal that:

God's original design included patterns of distinction and union, and distinction-within-union that would give creation strength and beauty. . . . God . . . orders things into place by sorting and separating them. . . . At the same time, God binds things together: he binds humans to the rest of creation as stewards and caretakers of it, to himself as bearers of his image, and to each other as perfect complements.[12]

This pattern of creation shows, in the words of Paul Ricoeur, that "the selfhood of oneself implies otherness to such an intimate degree that one cannot be thought of without the other."[13]

Even so, the way, life, teaching, and work of Jesus Christ most fully, clearly, and powerfully discloses God the creator-redeemer: herein is found what in the most final of salvific terms can be known about God. Yet God's revelation through Christ is within the framework of the "universality of the God . . . who as the Holy Spirit is ever anew present and active at the very heart of every religion."[14] If God, through the Spirit, is thus directly involved with the whole of humanity, people of other faiths must have encountered God and bear witness to this by way of the faith, hope, and love it has engendered in their lives and communities.

New theological insights such as these generated movement in the direction of greater openness toward and acceptance of the religious "other," further fueled by the articulation of the concept of contextualization within ecumenical Christian thought.

CONTEXTUALIZATION

In Christian parlance, "contextualization" refers to the process of bringing the gospel of Jesus Christ into rapport with the whole experience of people

---

11. Bavinck, *The Church between the Temple and Mosque*, 200.

12. Cornelius Plantinga, Jr., *Not the Way It's Supposed to Be: A Breviary of Sin* (Grand Rapids: Eerdmans, 1995), 29.

13. Paul Ricoeur, *Oneself as Another* (Chicago: University of Chicago Press, 1990), 3.

14. "Universalität Gottes heißt, daß der Gott . . . der sich als Heiliger Geist neu und neu präsent macht, in dem Grundereignis aller Religion wirksam ist." See C. H. Ratschow, "Theologie der Religionen," in *Lexikon missionstheologischer Grundbegriffe*, ed. Karl Müller and Theo Sundermeier (Berlin: Dietrich Reimer Verlag, 1987), 502.

living their everyday lives. This missional approach of relating the message of salvation to people where they stand is not of recent origin, but initiated by Jesus himself, most acutely when he asked his disciples, "But what about you, who do you say that I am?" (Matt. 16:15).[15] New Testament writers carried it on in their interaction with contemporary Jewish, Hellenistic, and Roman cultures; the church also contextualized the message of salvation to a greater or lesser degree during the period of the gradual evangelization of Europe. Once Europe became "Christianized," there was little further effort in the direction of contextualization of the gospel. This resulted in the gradual emergence of a frozen *kultur-Evangelium* (gospel-culture), during most of which the West and Christianity were virtually interchangeable entities, ostensibly superior to all other cultures and religions. This notion remained largely intact throughout the North Atlantic imperial and colonial era.

After World War I, Christians began to question this congealed gospel-culture link, particularly in the face of the sweeping social-cultural transformations following the Second World War, including the rise of scores of newly independent nations in Asia and Africa, whose people were becoming keenly aware of the legitimacy and value of their cultural and religious heritages. Misgivings about this Western cultural captivity of the gospel intensified to the point where it became necessary to look for a new reading of the relationship between gospel and culture.

Shoki Coe introduced the concept of contextualization at a World Council of Churches consultation in 1972.[16] Though not inherently wrong, earlier models such as that of indigenization and adaptation did not suffice, Coe argued, in that they lay emphasis on traditional cultures, most of which no longer even existed. These new conditions called for a more dynamic approach that was open to change and more oriented toward the future.[17] Coe described the method of contextualization as continuous back-and-forth movement between Scripture and ever-changing situational realities.[18]

Contextualization includes a sense of both inculturation and liberation. This means that its concerns are as broad as earthly life, including not only matters of religion and spirituality but also those of power and powerlessness, privilege and oppression, wealth and poverty, gender and communal relations, race and ethnicity, environment and earth care. In short, contextualization seeks to operate within the totality of people's *Sitz im Leben* (setting in life). Old Chinese words of wisdom aptly reflect this approach:

---

15. Biblical citations in this paper are from the NIV Study Bible, New International Version, ed. Kenneth Barker et al. (Grand Rapids: Zondervan Bible Publishers, 1985).

16. Born in Taiwan in 1914, Shoki Coe, grandson of a Taoist priest who converted to Christianity, was general secretary of the WCC Theological Education Fund, a position he held from 1965 to 1979.

17. Cf. Gerald H. Anderson and Thomas Stransky, eds., *Mission Trends No. 3* (New York: Paulist Press/Grand Rapids: Eerdmans, 1976), 20ff.

18. Cf. Ray Wheeler, "The Legacy of Shoki Coe," *International Bulletin of Missionary Research* 26, no. 2 (2002): 78.

Go to the people.
Live among them.
Learn from them.
Love them.
Start with what they know.
Build on what they have.[19]

Contextualization has now become part of theological-missiological discourse. Anthropologically trained missiologists such as Charles H. Kraft fortified the perception that God works in and through all human cultures, which accordingly contain compelling elements of grace, beauty, and truth.[20] As the Fifth Assembly of the WCC in Nairobi put it, "No culture stands any closer to Christ than any other culture."[21] Nowadays there seems a consensus among ecumenicals and most evangelicals that Christians are called, by virtue of their own core faith, to cultivate and engage in open, positive encounter with people from different cultural settings and religious traditions. The appearance of postmodernism, to which we now turn, ran concurrently with this gradually developing posture.

POSTMODERNISM: AMBIGUITIES AND AUTHENTICITY

The paradigm shift from modernism to postmodernism established new ways of thinking about questions of truth and human and natural existence. In sharp contrast to the individualistic mind-set of late modernity, the postmodern focus lies on shared life. In addition, postmodernists are wary of "propositional and methodologically secured objectivity."[22] They "look beyond reason to nonrational ways of knowing, conferring heightened status on the emotions and intuition,"[23] and hence are open to spirituality. Indeed, postmodernists "affirm that personal existence may transpire within the context of a divine reality."[24] Further, in rejecting notions such as neutral objectivity and supra-local universality postmodernism creates room for hermeneutical relativity and plurality. This implies, among other things, that there is not one collectively valid religious spirituality.[25]

---

19. George G. Hunter, III, *The Celtic Way of Evangelism, Tenth Anniversary Edition: How Christianity Can Reach the West Again* (Nashville: Abingdon Press, 2000), 120.

20. Cf. Charles H. Kraft, "The Development of Contextualization Theory in Euroamerican Missiology," in *Appropriate Christianity*, ed. Charles H. Kraft (Pasadena, CA: William Carey Library, 2005), 15-34.

21. D. M. Paton, ed., *Breaking Barriers: The Official Report of the Fifth Assembly of the WCC, Nairobi, November 23–December 10, 1975* (Grand Rapids: Eerdmans, 1976), 79.

22. James De Jong, "Review of *Not Sure: A Pastor's Journey from Faith to Doubt* by John Suk," *Calvin Theological Journal* 48, no. 2 (2013): 357.

23. Stanley J. Grenz, *A Primer on Postmodernism* (Grand Rapids: Eerdmans, 1996), 14-15.

24. Ibid., 14.

25. Cf. Christopher J. H. Wright, "Hermeneutiek, postmodernisme en de waarheid," *Soteria: Kwartaalblad voor evangelische theologische Bezinning* 18, no. 1 (2000): 9.

But the relativism and pluralism espoused by postmodernists, if radically elaborated, also bear detrimental outcomes for theology, religion, religious belief, and both intra- and interreligious dialogue. Christian thinkers who follow a strict postmodern approach would be unwilling to accept a characterization of theology as reflection "on God talking within human God-talk," which "seeks to offer, as it were, a vertical dimension that keeps the horizontal true."[26] Rigorist postmodern theologians maintain that theology cannot speak about a self-disclosing God because such a God does not exist. According to a recent critic, this standpoint means:

> All our talk about "God" and the holy has to do with our existence here and now, this also includes talk about heaven, the afterlife, and primal beginnings. Talk about the holy is a way to speak about existence itself, about one's heart, being, soul, about our self and society and about the awareness that all sorts of things happen to us, go beyond us, speak to us, and create us.[27]

According to pure postmodernism, any God-talk grounded on the belief that there is a God who makes himself known is nothing more than a fairy tale. This belief-based truth claim is an immanentist dictatorship of the horizontal. From this radical horizontalism and rejection of vertical transcendence, it is an easy step to the position that there is no universal truth, but only my truth and yours.

The postmodernist position that "beliefs are ultimately a matter of social context," along with the attendant conclusion that "what is right for us might not be right for you,'"[28] plainly rules out submissions of claims to categorical truth for consideration by others, especially by one's religious interlocution partners. As we shall see below, however, believers need not and should by no means keep silent in dialogical encounter about their commitment to truth that they hold to be of universal validity.

DIALOGUE

A question confronting Christians and other religious believers ever more urgently today is how to foster harmonious interreligious convivence and establish networks of exchange with the aim of healing divisions of hatred and suspicion. How can religious groups replace existing walls of religious separation with neighboring open verandas? The pursuit and practice of interreligious dialogue, while not a magic formula for bringing about a world of perfect peace and harmony, are not unrealistic, useless activities, but persuasively promising means of attenuating interreligious conflict and bringing about reconciliation.

---

26. O'Grady and Scherle, "Ecumenics in the 21st Century," 6.
27. Rik Peels, "Theologie als makelaar in levenswijsheid? Waarom elke vorm van theologie zonder waarheidsaanspraak gedoemd is tot inconsistentie en intolerantie," *Soteria: Kwartaalblad voor evangelische theologische Bezinning* 30, no. 4 (2013): 72.
28. Grenz, *A Primer on Postmodernism*, 15.

Dialogue assumes that despite real differences between cultures and religions, there is a basic stratum of shared human experience that makes it possible for people to connect with those belonging to traditions other than their own. Contrary to postmodern thinking—which takes what I term "communal or social atomization" as its starting point—it is manifestly evident to me that there are many questions, fears, sorrows, and joys that people everywhere share. Humans also all generally hold some perception of "wrong" and troubled by dearth of "right." Without this ontological and epistemological concurrence, intercultural and interreligious communication could not exist. The very possibility of dialogue, thus, presupposes the existence of an anthropological floor of human commonalities.

Preconditions for Dialogue

We best understand the missional vocation of dialogue as an expression of the imitation of Christ—the constitution of whose life and work was utterly dialogical—and thus, by virtue of its very nature, this involves vulnerability. Love and genuine openness and honesty toward the other involve risk. Accordingly, dialogue takes careful mental, psychological, and spiritual preparation to engage confidently and meaningfully in interreligious converse.

Further, Christians should engage dialogically with people of other faiths in humility, shedding any vestige of the supercilious disdain that often typifies Christianity's stance vis-à-vis other religions—the kind of arrogance expressed by Empedocles in Matthew Arnold's dramaturgic poem "Empedocles on Etna":

> But we—as some rude guest
> Would change, where're he roam,
> The manners there profess'd
> To those he brings from home—
> We mark not the world's course,
> but would have *it* take *ours*.[29] (original italics)

What is more, Christians should approach the other religions in a spirit of open expectance, in the full realization that we humans are finite beings holding only a quantum of truth perception and hence are incapable of seeing anything wholly or perfectly. "To the extent that we articulate what is real to us, we . . . [see] it from our own partial point of view, thus filtering the infinite or indeterminate through the lenses of our own finite experience."[30] As Empedocles has it:

> The out-spread world to span
> A cord the Gods first slung,
> And then the soul of man

---

29. Act 1, scene 2, line 230, in Matthew Arnold, *Arnold: Poems*, selected by Kenneth Allott (Harmondsworth: Penguin Books, 1985), 31.

30. William Franke, "Language and Transcendence in Dante's *Paradiso*," in *The Poetics of Transcendence* ed. Elisa Heinämäki, P. M. Mehtonen, and Antti Salminen (Amsterdam: Rodopi, 2014), 119.

There, like a mirror, hung. . . .
Hither and thither spins
The wind-borne, mirroring soul,
A thousand glimpses wins,
And never sees a whole. . . .[31]

The following counsel of St. Augustine, though penned with fellow Christians in mind, could serve as a kind of charter or guide for interreligious dialogue as well:

Let the reader, where we are equally confident, stride on with me; where we are equally puzzled, pause to investigate with me; where he finds himself in error, come to my side; where he finds me erring, call me to his side. So we may keep to the path of love, as we fare on toward Him "Whose face is ever to be sought."[32]

In sum: adequate preparation, love, openness, honesty, readiness to assume risk liberally seasoned with confidence, humility, and expectant openness, are *sine qua non* prerequisites for healthy, salutary interreligious dialogue, which, in my view, consists ideally of a complex whole comprising four interdependent equal components.

THE FOUR PARTS OF DIALOGUE

The *first segment* of interreligious colloquy is what may be termed the dialogue of histories. This dialogue begins with a serious analysis of past relations between or among the religions involved. What stance have they assumed with respect to one another? More importantly, what is the position they occupied vis-à-vis one another on the political, social, and economic planes? It is at this level of dialogue that questions of justice and injustice, power and domination, wealth and poverty come to the fore. Interreligious conflict, division, and hatred are very often occasioned by exploitation and oppression via forces and structures with which a certain religion is or has been either rightly or wrongly identified in local, national, or global contexts. At this stage of interlocutory exchange, dialoguers will forthrightly discuss the matter of interreligious histories, tending to the reconciliation of the sinner and sinned-against parties.

A *second facet* of discussion among religions is the dialogue of theologies, whose purpose is to remove interreligious nescience and misunderstanding and to foster respect among people of differing faiths. Each participant in this kind of dialogue recognizes the right of the other interlocutors "to speak their own mind."[33] This level of dialogue offers a means of gaining a sense of the meaning

---

31. Act 1, scene 2, lines 80, 85; Arnold, *Poems,* 27.
32. Augustine, *De trinitate* 1.5, in *Saint Augustine,* trans. Garry Wills (London: Phoenix-Orion Books, 2000), xiii-xiv.
33. Jacques Maritain, *On the Use of Philosophy: Three Essays* (New York: Atheneum, 1965), 29.

and intention of one another's religious tenets. Moreover, if the parties involved open themselves truly and fully to the divinely inspired truth that enlightens all people of faith, this type of dialogue might yield a new interreligious hermeneutics, an auxiliary tool that we could employ to arrive at a fuller comprehension of the sense and significance of life and the world.

Participation in a dialogue of theologies by no means requires a stance of uncritical relativism or an attitude of detachment with respect to one's own religion. People of faith are duty bound to open themselves and attend to the other's theological-philosophical views in an unfeigned, fair, and tolerant manner. Yet, this kind of open-minded approach to the other is possible only when one "is firmly and absolutely convinced of a truth, or of what he holds to be a truth."[34] Put in another way, a dual-polarity stance is crucial to the success of any dialogical meeting: "The dialogue partners should preserve *who and what they are* without *closing* themselves off from those of other faiths" (original italics).[35] Interfaith understanding is attainable only if the partners in dialogue communicate with each other as committed believers.

A *third constituent* of interreligious dialogue is the exchange of spiritualities. In the Christian ecumenical view, religious faith itself—basic trust in acceptance by God[36]—is an exceptionally important key to the realization of interhuman reconciliation. "God is 'for us' and therefore we can and must be 'with one another' and not 'against one another.'"[37] This trust in divine acceptance makes it possible to be freely and fully open to the spiritual beliefs of the "other." From the Christian perspective, thus, genuine interreligious colloquy in no way precludes bearing witness to the truth as one receives, perceives, experiences, and believes it. Moreover, the truth claims of the various religions, based on the authority of their Holy Scriptures and living traditions, would appear strongly to imply an obligation to interfaith witness.

On this plane of dialogical converse, the partners would speak frankly about their deepest fears and highest hopes, desiring both "to understand" and "to be understood."[38] Their aim would be to affect a respectful exchange of religious experiential feelings and beliefs regarding the elemental questions of human existence. They would share spiritualities of redemption and reconciliation. For Christian partners this would surely mean voicing the conviction of Jesus as the human face of God and explaining why the words and deeds and the cross and resurrection of Jesus as Christ are central to the Christian faith.

---

34. Ibid.

35. Marianne Moyaert, *Fragile Identities: Towards a Theology of Interreligious Hospitality* (Amsterdam: Rodopi, 2011), 1.

36. Cf. Jürgen Moltmann, *Mensch: Christliche Anthropologie in den Konflikten der Gegenwart* (Stuttgart: Kreuz-Verlag, 1971), 165.

37. Jürgen Moltmann, *Die Sprache der Befreiung: Predigten und Besinnungen* (Munich: Chr. Kaiser Verlag, 1972), 48. "Gott ist 'für uns,' darum können en sollen wir 'miteinander' und 'nicht gegeneinander' sein."

38. Frans Wijsen, *Seeds of Conflict in a Haven of Peace: From Religious Studies to Interreligious Studies in Africa* (Amsterdam: Rodopi, 2007), 171.

Discoveries about one another's faith convictions, it may be expected, will lead the partners in the dialogue of spiritualties to a broader, more inclusive understanding of the *consortium vitae divinae* (partnership in divine life). Moreover, the convictions that they themselves hold can take on sharper contours, more deeply understood and nourished in and through such exchanges of faith beliefs with those who adhere to other faith traditions or world and life views.

Mindful of the fact that they are participants in joint pursuit of a Truth that remains always just beyond them, religious believers would talk together at this level of dialogue in the spirit of Saint Augustine's encouraging direction to fellow Christians:

> Press on where you can. When we reach our final destination, you will not have to question me, nor I you. We are presently seeking in faith what we shall then share joyfully in vision.[39]

The *fourth seam* of interreligious encounter, the dialogue of life, concerns existential human experience. Dialogical endeavor "cannot confine itself to the problem of pluralism" but must also take full account of the matter of "power and domination" and the "problem of poverty."[40] In this dialogue, religious believers, rising above narrow ideological, national, or ethnic considerations, will work together as a diaconal ensemble, share energies, bend their best efforts to the development of a united front against the evils that cause the poverty and injustice found throughout our world. In addition, to boost up this collaborative undertaking they will engage with synergy with civil governments, together with other secular institutions, visionary movements, and moral agencies that seek to effect transformation of nonideal situations. Here, in the dialogue of life, the wider ecumenism of the first three parts of dialogue becomes wider *liberative* ecumenism, in which Christians, distinctly called to the vocation of doing good,[41] should certainly take keen part.

Beyond mutuality of concern with injustice and poverty, we note pragmatic grounds for joint interreligious action. Separate religions can do only so much to confront and combat the old and new demonic powers that give rise to poverty and oppression. Moreover, besides being a much more effective means of addressing the urgent needs of the victims of social and economic exclusion, broad interreligious solidarity with people in distress could also serve as a substantial fillip to efforts aimed at bringing about a greater degree of structural justice and socioeconomic equity at both the global and local level.

However, concerned first with life situations of marginalization and exclusion, sustained wider ecumenism of this kind may expect to yield as an added benefit the discovery of imbrications at the levels of theology, spirituality, and

---

39. Augustine, *Sermones* 261.3, trans. Wills, xiv.

40. Wijsen, *Seeds of Conflict*, 188.

41. Cf. James 1:22 and 2:14-16: "Faith by itself, if it is not accompanied by action, is dead" (NIV Study Bible).

religious experience. Multireligious "liberative praxis has a special capacity for bringing areas of interreligious overlap to light,"[42] which, in turn, would likely move people of faith to engage in even greater joint effort on behalf of the poor and oppressed.

COLLECTIVE OBLIGATION

The quest for open, peaceful, and cooperative interreligious coexistence constitutes an ongoing challenge and charge for all religions and religious people. This calling and obligation require contextual articulation and shaping, with full account of existing local or, as the case might be, worldwide realities. In the context of the present globalized world, so fraught with seemingly epidemic conflict, rife destitution, and rampant dislocations of people, the need to build and maintain convivial relations among people of religious faith takes on special urgency. Today, the practice of dialogue in all four of the modes described above at local, national, and world levels are categorical necessities for securing the well-being of humanity.

---

42. Jerald D. Gort, "Liberative Ecumenism: Gateway to the Sharing of Religious Experience Today," in *On Sharing Religious Experience: Possibilities of Interfaith Mutuality*, ed. Jerald D. Gort, Hendrik M. Vroom, Rein Fernhout, and Anton Wessels (Amsterdam: Rodopi, 1992), 103.

Part 7

*Modernity and Postmodernity
in Mission Theology*

Chapter 19

Mission Theology and Stewardship of the Earth

Young Lee Hertig

As our ecosystem radically changes, we witness a dramatic human toll due to extreme floods, droughts, and massive oil spills. Meanwhile, politicians remain stuck in endless ideological debates; some continue to oppose the science behind global climate change, in effect denying our dire environmental situation. Modernity disconnected humanity from the rest of God's creation, and the evangelical Christian faith upholds and furthers this position.

As a result, too many of us stand idle as we witness the poisoning and squandering of our most basic resources: the air we breathe and the water we drink. Daily reports come in of catastrophic air pollution, scarce access to clean water, rising ocean levels that fuel hurricanes, record snow in the northeastern United States, and severe droughts on the west coast. California farmers lack water to produce their crops while its residents insist on watering decorative lawns. The *Los Angeles Times* runs headlines such as, "Antarctic glaciers said to be 'past point of no return'" (May 13, 2014). Do droves of disaster reports numb us while we experience the groaning of all creation (Rom. 8:22)?

My journey toward ecological living began in 1992 with the study and understanding of the Asian cosmology of Taoism. Impacted by internalized syncretism, I could not embrace Taoism as a theological paradigm, yet found permission from Fritjof Capra's seminal book, *The Tao of Physics*. As Taoism provided an answer to Capra in explaining a *both–and* phenomenon in quantum physics, it also provided an alternative paradigm to my dissonant reductionist Cartesian paradigm in the educational curriculum. Emboldened by the connection between quantum physics and Taoism, I coined the term *Yinist* in 1993 as a comprehensive and holistic paradigm. The term also provided me with an intrinsic category of belonging beyond the existing feminist discourses and amid emerging womanist and *mujerista* approaches. Compelled by the missing link of Asian Americans in the conversation, the *Yinist* concept filled the void.

Unfortunately, I have found the presentation of the *Yinist* paradigm a lonely journey. Fellow Christians too often receive the idea as (1) too foreign to the dominant discourse and (2) too fearful of syncretism, if not marginalization, of the minority.

THE FEAR OF SYNCRETISM

Despite Christianity's long-standing history of transformations into Judaization, Hellenization, Westernization, and others, the term "syncretism" is a stumbling block in approaching Christianity from cultural lenses. As Adolf Harnack puts it, regarding Christianity, "From the very outset it had been syncretistic upon pagan soil; it made its appearance, not as a gospel pure and simple, but equipped with all that Judaism had already acquired during the course of its long history."[1] Lamin Sanneh states, "Pluralism was rooted for Paul in the Gentile experience, which in turn justified intercultural openness in mission. . . . As the absolute gift of a loving, gracious God, faith is the leveling, transcendent force in culture."[2]

Most Asian Americans educated in the United States have little exposure to innate Asian concepts such as Taoism. Yet Taoism speaks into all areas of life, from ecology to diet. Its ancient, comprehensive cosmology is as relevant today as ever, especially as Mother Earth moans and groans with seven billion inhabitants.

This essay first explores the origins of the Protestant disconnect between humanity and God on the one hand and the rest of God's creation on the other. Second, I will interact with convergent theologies—*Yinist* cosmology with ecotheology and planetary theology. These three systems share similar concerns and strive to retrieve the lost concept of ecological stewardship and humanity's responsibility as caretakers, not conquerors, of God's creation.

A great resource in attempting to answer the role of religion and ecology, Girardot, Miller, and Liu's *Daoism and Ecology* addresses pertinent questions:

- Have issues of personal salvation superseded all others?
- Have divine/human relations been primary?
- Have anthropocentric ethics been all consuming?
- Has the material world of nature been devalued by religion?
- Does the search for otherworldly rewards override commitment to this world?
- Did the religions simply surrender their natural theologies and concerns with exploring purpose in nature to positivistic scientific cosmologies?[3]

---

1. Adolf von Harnack, *The Mission and Expansion of Christianity in the First Three Centuries,* vol. 1 (New York: Putnam, 1908), 314, quoted in Lamin Sanneh, *Translating the Message: The Missionary Impact on Culture*, 2d ed., American Society of Missiology Series 42 (Maryknoll, NY: Orbis Books, 2009), 49.

2. Ibid., 54.

3. N. J. Girardot, James Miller, and Liu Xiaogan, eds., *Daoism and Ecology: Ways within a Cosmic Landscape* (Cambridge: Center for the Study of World Religions, 2001), xvii.

The answer to these questions continues to be "yes," pushing for an investigation of the historical roots for this regrettable divorce.

THE HISTORICAL ROOTS OF THE
DESACRALIZATION OF NATURE

The key architects of modernity elevated humanity while reducing nature to a subjugated and utilitarian role, departing from medieval values of seeing nature as sacred and mystical. Thomas Hobbes "audaciously desacralized and demystified the medieval view of nature."[4] René Descartes took Hobbes's view further and saw humans as "lords and possessors of nature."[5] Furthermore, Bertrand Russell posited, "God might have made the world, but that is no reason why we should not make it over."[6]

Francis Bacon ushered in the reductionistic and mechanistic worldviews of modernity, promulgating the subjugation of nature. In an effort to relegate the dominant Renaissance worldview of magic and alchemy, Bacon focused on the practical pursuit of scientific knowledge and technological innovation, relating it to biblical and religious ideas more congenial to Protestant England.[7] Hence, Bacon's view began the era of early modern scientific enterprise that ignited the manipulation of nature for human interest. Departing from the patristic and medieval reverence toward nature, this seventeenth-century scientific paradigm became a dominant force, utilizing Greek philosophy in the subjugation of nature, deeming these ideas as "biblical."[8] The theology of dominion then bolstered this secularized view of nature, rooted in the literal interpretation of the Genesis texts.

Bacon promulgated the idea of human capacity to reshape the world at will with a central goal to implement God-given human dominion over nature, impaired during the Fall, based on Genesis 1:28. Therefore, he envisioned its recovery through "the technological exploitation of nature for human benefit."[9]

Today, this seventeenth-century worldview continues to dictate contemporary theological disconnection with nature. Considering the history of the philosophical underpinnings could offer clarification and possible solutions, Lynn White traces "the modern pillage of planet earth" to the Hebraic-Christian religion rooted in Greek philosophical tradition that bifurcates the sacred as

---

4. Douglas J. Hall, "Stewardship as Key to a Theology of Nature," in *Environmental Stewardship: Critical Perspectives—Past and Present,* ed. R. J. Berry (London: T & T Clark International, 2006), 132-33.

5. Nicols Fox, *Against the Machine: The Hidden Luddite Tradition in Literature, Art and Individual Lives* (Washington, DC: A Shearwater Book, Island Press, 2002), 298.

6. Bertrand Russell, *The Scientific Outlook* (New York: Routledge, 2009), 108.

7. Richard Bauckman, "Modern Domination of Nature: Historical Origins and Biblical Critique," in *Environmental Stewardship: Critical Perspectives—Past and Present,* ed. R. J. Berry (London: T & T Clark International, 2006), 39-40.

8. Ibid., 33.

9. Ibid., 37.

otherworldly and the profane as worldly. A polemic worldview literally justifies the biblical concept of dominion in Genesis 1:28. *Kabash* (subdue) comes from a Hebrew root meaning "to tread down," conveying the image of a heavy-footed man.[10] The connotation of *radah* (dominion) also conveys "treading" or "trampling" and suggests the image of a conqueror.[11] The table below lists the contrast between the Hebrew and Greek worldviews. Concerned scholars lament the misuse and justification of Genesis 1:28 with little sense of responsibility for stewardship of God's creation.[12]

THE HEBREW AND GREEK WORLDVIEWS

Core shapers of Christianity stem from Hebrew and Hellenic cultures.

Hebrew Worldview	Greek Worldview
Importance to history: God reveals Godself mainly in history	Little significance to history Viewed history with distrust
Nature played a secondary role in this revelation	Nature was viewed as a source of security
Book of Revelation: "cosmological prophecy"	Cosmology was a major concern of the Greek philosophers
Rising above history: marks the beginning of a new approach to human relationship with nature	Saw God present and operating in and through its laws of cyclical movement and natural reproduction

As shown in the chart above,[13] the Hebrews invested in history at the expense of cosmology. Meanwhile, the Greeks showed suspicion of history and instead regarded nature as the source of security. Hence, for the Greeks, cosmology was a major concern, and they saw God's presence in the cyclical movement of nature.[14] This view is similar to the Taoist worldview.

The introduction of Gnosticism, however, instigated a polemic view of the material world and the otherworld. First, this view tied together salvation and the otherworld, and therefore cosmology subsided. Second, with the belief that the *imago Dei* connected with human consciousness and introspection, the superiority of humanity over nature dominated. The early church assumed the negative attitudes of Gnosticism, despite opposition from key leaders such as Irenaeus, the bishop of Lyons. For St. Augustine, nature had no place in his

---

10. Douglas J. Hall, "Stewardship as Key," 131-32.

11. Loren Wilkinson, "Global Housekeeping: Lords or Servants?" *Christianity Today*, July 24, 1980, 27.

12. Ross Kinsler and Gloria Kinsler, *The Biblical Jubilee and the Struggle for Life: An Invitation to Personal, Ecclesial, and Social Transformation* (Maryknoll, NY: Orbis Books, 1999), 25.

13. John Zizioulas, "Priest of Creation," in *Environmental Stewardship: Critical Perspectives—Past and Present,* ed. R. J. Berry (London: T & T Clark International, 2006), 275-76.

14. Ibid., 275.

theology. Instead, the eternal soul was his main concern. Nature disappeared from sacramental theology in the West.

Scholasticism and the Reformation also associated the *imago Dei* with human reason, widening the gap between humanity and nature. The Enlightenment further widened the gap until only the rational being mattered. Furthermore, Romanticism solidified the dichotomy between the thinking, conscious subject and nonthinking, nonconscious nature. Pietism, mysticism, and other traditions also separated their theologies from nature. Puritanism and mainstream Calvinism justified the absence of nature in theology through Genesis verses which said "to multiply and to dominate the earth" and which gave "rise to capitalism and eventually to the technology" that today dominates Western civilization.[15] Max Weber posited that the Protestant ethic, disconnected from nature, fostered the spirit of capitalism and vice versa. Calvinists, more than any other sect, took profit and material success as signs of God's favor. The confluence of capitalism and Calvinism unleashed the spirit of modern capitalism, which then took on a life of its own.[16]

In summary, the lineage of the polemic worldview continued from Gnosticism, scholasticism, Darwinism, the Reformation, the Enlightenment, Romanticism, pietism, mysticism, puritanism, Calvinism, and the technological revolution. These all led to the dominance of a Western civilization focused on a human-centered and reason-dominated worldview. In this chapter, I will now consider the modern theological worldview.

THE MODERN THEOLOGICAL WORLDVIEW

The rise of modernity and Protestantism accompanied the desacralization of nature and thus shifted the worldview of the theocentric community of creation to an anthropocentric hierarchy. In fact, the anthropocentric view claims humanity's duty and right to rule over the rest of God's creation despite the fact that the Genesis creation narrative is theocentric, not anthropocentric. In his critique, Douglas J. Hall raises pertinent questions for mission theology today:

> How can we reconcile (or can we?) the apparent contradictions of a religion that on the one hand clearly makes the world—God's good creation— the very object of the divine *agape*, and on the other hand seems to give to greedy *anthropos* all the justification needed for turning the beautiful place God made into a pigsty?[17]

With all of the conveniences modernity offers, the limitless valuing of *the bigger the better* finally confronts us with a dire flipside—the risk of destroying

---

15. Ibid., 276-78.

16. Max Weber, *The Protestant Ethics and the Spirit of Capitalism* (New York: Routledge, 2009).

17. Hall, "Stewardship as Key," 132.

all of creation. Mother Nature is striking back with severe drought, tsunamis, and floods, which endanger the very sustainability of her inhabitants.

The anthropocentric domination of nature has become the towering force of our time, sanctioned by modernity and its theology, combined with ubiquitous *marketdom*. Jacques Ellul warned of the dangers society faces when we replace humanity with the machine. Ellul differentiates the external machine from the internalized technique. This technique, "the totality of methods rationally arrived at, and having absolute efficiency (for a given stage of development) involves *every* field of human activity."[18] Ellul's warning against the inevitable absorption of humanity by autonomous technique is becoming a reality today as robots increasingly replace humans in the workforce.

Framing the world solely as a resource for economic development accompanies the downward spiral of ecological degradation, social alienation, and violence. Ellul's seven characteristics of the technological society merit our attention today: (1) rationality, (2) artificiality, (3) automatism of technical choice, (4) self-augmentation, (5) monism, (6) technical universalism, and (7) autonomy. For Ellul, the dilemma that all living organisms confront under modern civilization is the convergent forces of the "science-technology-commodity complex" that shapes and conditions humanity. The fusion of technology with capital demands endless technological innovation directed at the global market.[19] It also requires an insatiable demand for growth and profit.

In contrast, the medieval theology of stewardship viewed the earth as sacred and thus placed limits on how much to take from her. The loss of these previous traditions robbed humanity of restraint in the excessive use of the earth's resources. Anthropocentrism filled this vacuum, defining nature as godless and conveniently desacralizing nature for maximum human benefit and exploitation. The disconnection between God and humanity from the rest of God's creation therefore shifted a theology of stewardship to a theology of domination. Surely, humanity's unfettered industrial and technological advances, despite certain human benefit, also damaged the quality of life on this planet.

COUNTERSTREAM TO MODERNITY

As Enlightenment logocentrism and humanism championed the anthropocentric worldview, key Romantics critiqued Cartesian reductionism: Giambattista Vico, Johann Gottfried Herder, Joseph De Maistre, and Johann Georg Hamann.[20] In speaking out against the reduction of irreducible realities, I resonate with the counter-Enlightenment critique of the "Cartesian fallacy." The Romantic critics foresaw an end where compartmentalized and

---

18. Jacques Ellul, *The Technological Society* (New York: Vantage Books, 1964), xxv.

19. José Luís Garcia, Helena Mateus Jerómino, and Carl Mitcham, eds., *Jacques Ellul and the Technological Society in the 21st Century* (New York: Springer, 2013), 4.

20. Isaiah Berlin, *Three Critics of the Enlightenment: Vico, Hamann, Herder,* ed. Henry Hardy (Princeton, NJ: Princeton University Press, 2000).

fragmented realities would lead to the loss of meaning. Along with this sense of meaninglessness would come depression, anxiety, and violence against humanity and nature. An earlier countervoice from the West is the fourth-century moralist Pelagius, whose theology is expansively inclusive of all God's creation. Contrary to his opponents, he emphasized the goodness of God's unifying creation as a reflection of God rather than separate from God's creation.[21]

It is important to note that modernity is not entirely negative. On the contrary, developments in technology and science have improved human life enormously. However, all good things taken to their extremes result in imbalances. Managerial ecclesiology and numerically driven successology weaken the church's prophetic witness in the public sector.

The following section depicts my theological imagination—an attempt to construct a cosmocentric theology that departs from the anthropocentric approach to the Bible, God, and the world.

THEOLOGY OF THE EARTH

The human-centered scientific worldview and the literal interpretation of Genesis texts contribute to the exploitation of land, sea, and sky. Howard Snyder refers to this disconnect as "the great divorce of heaven and earth in Christian theology":

> The disease of sin brought alienation, a divorce between people, and their maker, and between people and their world, their habitat, which is planet earth. . . . Divorce is an apt metaphor for the whole problem of the relationship between God, humans, and the earth.[22]

In bridging this "great divorce," Snyder emphasizes creation stewardship. Meanwhile Jürgen Moltmann emphasizes trinitarian theology as foundational for stewardship. For Moltmann, trinitarian theology extends God's presence in God's creation through the unity of Father, Son, and Holy Spirit. This calls for a shift from a modern paradigm of domination to an alternative paradigm that links God, humanity, and earth. In the mid-1980s, Moltmann's Gifford Lectures at Edinburgh described the "ecological crisis" as a crisis of human domination over nature and of our understanding of God. Moltmann warned against seeing the world as godless and the sanctioning of humanity's destructive domination and exploitation of nature.[23] This theological disconnect bears substantial responsibility for our current ecological crisis. How can we shift our warped worldview and overcome the *anthropos* that results in ecological crisis?

---

21. J. Phillip Newell, *Listening for the Heartbeat of God: A Celtic Spirituality* (New York: Paulist Press, 1977), 13.

22. Howard Snyder, with Joel Scandrett, *Salvation Means Creation Healed: The Ecology of Sin and Grace, Overcoming the Divorce between Earth and Heaven* (Eugene, OR: Cascade Books, 2011), 3.

23. Jürgen Moltmann, "Creation and the Spirit of God," *Gifford Lectures at Edinburgh on Ecological Crisis (1984–85).*

Often the answers to problems reside in the problems themselves. If the bulk of the ecological crisis resides in a fragmented theological belief, then a reconnecting of the missing links in theological constructs offers an alternative paradigm. If the confluence of capitalism and Protestantism wreak havoc on the ecosystem, then recovering the abandoned theology of stewardship may curtail the excessively anthropocentric view of God's creation. Einstein already broke through the modern paradigm and began the postmodern paradigm of the unity between the observer and the observed. Through quantum physics, the modern paradigm that separates subject from object caused its reign to wane. Hence, postmodern holism emerged as a countervoice that sees reality as interrelated.

A *YINIST* STEWARDSHIP

I now propose a *Yinist* epistemology, which partially parallels planetary theology and ecotheology. The *Yinist* concept highlights yin, the Taoist feminine energy, over our current state of excessively dominant masculine yang energy. Together, yin–yang is an inclusively interwoven *both–and* concept rather than an *either–or* concept. Overarching problems ensue with an imbalance of these two energies. Chinese medicine describes this imbalance of disease in people as well as in ecosystems. As a philosophical paradigm, Taoism promotes a balanced and holistic practice of simple living and responsible stewardship.

Placing yin explicitly in the foreground, the overburdened yang energy oscillates into the background. Rather than asserting and competing, the yin energy embraces and balances, encompassing gender, ecology, nature, health, and God. Yin is holistic, synthesizing, and complementary. *Yinist* feminism, therefore, diffuses false dichotomies derived from dualistic paradigms: male versus female, humanity versus nature, God apart from humanity, this world apart from the other world.[24]

According to Jung Young Lee, the yin–yang concept offers a "cosmocentric anthropology" that comprehensively covers gender, nature, and food, among other things. Hence, according to Taoism, human beings and nature are inseparable. Lee's work greatly furthered the development of theology based on Asian paradigms. Using a Taoist lens, Lee critiqued reductionistic Western theology:

While the West is interested in an anthropocentric approach to cosmology, East Asia is more interested in a cosmocentric approach to anthropology. In East Asia, anthropology is a part of cosmology; a human being is regarded as a microcosm of the cosmos. The inseparable relationship between humanity and the world is a distinctive characteristic of East Asian philosophy.[25]

---

24. Young Lee Hertig, "The Asian American Alternative to Feminism: A Yinist Paradigm," *Missiology: Mission and Marginalization* 26, no. 1 (1998): 15-22.

25. Jung Young Lee, *The Trinity in Asian Perspective* (Nashville: Abingdon Press, 1996), 18.

Tao is translated into English as "path" or "way," the source of all living creatures.[26] *Tao Te Ching*, referring to the immanence and transcendence of formlessness and namelessness, was translated into Latin in the sixteenth century by Jesuit missionaries in China, which James Legge presented to the British Royal Society. The translators commented that the *Tao Te Ching* showed that "the Mysteries of the Most Holy Trinity and of the Incarnate God were anciently known to the Chinese nation."[27] In earlier research, I noted the confluent worldviews of Taoism and Celtic druids, which suggests the interchange of the two cultures. The list below documents the similarities.

Daoism	*Celtic*
The nameless eternal Dao	Belief in ultimate reality
Interweaving of yin/yang	Interweaving of heaven and earth
Paradox	Paradox
Triad as the ultimate reality	Triad as the ultimate reality
Respect for women	Respect for women
Divine in nature	Divine in natural revelation
Analogies	Analogies
Monastery	Monastery
Aesthetic	Aesthetic
Mythic	Mythic
Wisdom	Wisdom
Communal	Communal
Tao Te Ching (embodied truth)	Embodied truth
Art	Art
Inner landscape	Inner landscape
Imagination	Imagination
Poetry	Poetry[28]

In contrast to the yang-dominated Newtonian and Cartesian worldviews, Taoist and Celtic worldviews reflect both yin and yang traits. The beauty of Taoism is its comprehensive approach to gender, ecology, nature, health, and food. Humanity and nature are inseparable in Taoism from the life-giving energy of *ch'i* extending to all creation. *Ch'i* keeps yin–yang from collapsing into dichotomy.[29]

---

26. Paul S. Chung, "The Mystery of God and Tao in Jewish-Christian-Taoist Context," in *Asian Contextual Theology for the Third Millennium: Theology of Minjung in Fourth-Eye Formation*, ed. Paul S. Chung, Veli-Matti Kärkkäinen, and Kim Kyoung-Jae (Eugene, OR: Wipf & Stock, 2007), 245.

27. James Legge, *The Texts of Taoism*, vol. 1 (New York: Dover, 1962), xiii.

28. Young Lee Hertig, "Why Asian American Evangelical Theologies?" *Journal of Asian and Asian American Theology* 7 (2005–2006): 11-12.

29. Chung, "The Mystery of God," 265.

RUACH AND CH'I

Overlaps between Taoist and Celtic spirituality correspond to overlaps between the Hebrew concept of *ruach* and the ancient Chinese cosmology of *ch'i*. Many Asian American theologians have researched the parallel concepts of *ruach* and *ch'i*. Renewed interest in a pneumatological approach to theology, unlike the Christological perspective, may steer discourses in a unifying manner among world religions with "the ubiquity of the cosmic Spirit."[30]

Among theologians, Jürgen Moltmann from Germany and Stanley Samartha from India bridge Western and Eastern theology through the ubiquitous Spirit of *ruach*. Moltmann's pneumatologies and Taoists' *chi* connect the sacred Holy Spirit (the primordial *ch'i*) and the human spirit (substantial *ch'i*).[31]

Ch'i is the life force that interpenetrates all entities, animate and inanimate. Likewise, *ruach* is described by Yun as "a storm or force in both body and soul" that is found in everything, keeping all things in being and in life, similar to *ch'i*.[32] I concur with Yun's critique of Barthian theology that disconnects God's Spirit from human spirit, whereas Moltmann argues for the continuity of the Spirit in both God's creation and the church. Because of the fear of syncretism embedded in many non-Western Christians, Moltmann's voice offers permission for Asian/Asian American theologians to bridge pneumatology and Taoism. They may offer a paradigmatic shift in our views of humanity, nature, God, and the Bible toward a more sustainable world.

(*YINIST*) THEOLOGY OF THE HEART

In Romans, the apostle Paul emphasizes, "God's love has been poured into our hearts through the Holy Spirit that has been given to us" (Rom. 5:5).[33] Luke states, "The good is produced by the good treasure of the heart" (Luke 6:45). A pioneer of Asian theology, Choan-Seng Song, echoes Scripture stating, "To know one's heart is to know one's whole being."[34] Quoting prophets in the Hebrew Bible and the apostle Paul in the New Testament, Song highlights the importance of the integrated heart in a Western, reason-based theology and notes that the prophets Jeremiah and Ezekiel "highlight the conversion of the heart as most fundamental in our life."[35] The prophet Ezekiel speaks to the condition of a new heart: "I will give you a new heart and put a new spirit in

---

30. Koo D. Yun, "Pneumatological Perspectives on World Religions: The Cosmic Spirit and *Ch'i*," in *Asian Contextual Theology for the Third Millennium: Theology of Minjung in Fourth-Eye formation*, ed. Paul S. Chung, Veli-Matti Kärkkäinen, and Kim Kyoung-Jae (Eugene, OR: Wipf & Stock, 2007), 165.

31. Ibid.

32. Ibid., 168.

33. All scriptural quotations come from the New International Version.

34. Choan-Seng Song, *Third-Eye Theology: Theology in Formation in Asian Settings* (Maryknoll, NY: Orbis Books, 1979), 71-72.

35. Ibid., 72.

you; I will remove from you your *heart of stone* and give you a *heart of flesh*" (Ezek. 36:26, italics added). Song interprets the two contrasting hearts: the former representing the heart in "revolt against God" and the latter, "the person who has been transformed by the redeeming love of God." Furthermore, the heart is not only "the seat of mental and spiritual power and capacities" but also the root of "religious and moral conduct."[36]

The core theory in the school of Neo-Confucianism (see Wang Yang Ming) is "the heart principle," which emphasizes cultivating the nature of the heart. These core Confucian spiritual exercises integrate human experience with immanent transcendence. Neo-Confucianism synthesized Buddhism and Taoism with its core principle of the heart.[37] Therefore, in seeking a holistic theological construction, these concepts emphasize the fact that the heart embodies the whole person in relationship to God. A theology of heart cultivates human hearts, creating a bridge to the reductionistic Cartesian theology of the West. Song's critique of Western reductionistic theology merits our attention today:

> When emotion takes leave of the heart as the seat of human spirit, our theology becomes an emotional theology. . . . On the other hand, when reason is separated from the heart, there emerges a cold theology that tries to penetrate the mystery of God with a cold logic.[38]

Song sees the heart as transrational and beyond the worldviews that "intuit the mystery of Being" and that neither reason nor emotion alone can grasp. We perceive and encounter this Being, *agapē,* at the crossroad of creation and redemption.[39]

A theology of heart, therefore, offers ample missiological implications in overcoming what Paul G. Hiebert addressed as the two-tiered Neo-Platonic theology of religion and science that creates an excluded middle. In the West, the middle level offers guidance to the unknown future, the crises of present life, and the unknown past. This middle level began disappearing during the seventeenth and eighteenth centuries with the rise of Cartesian dualism in science and religion.[40] The consequence of the polemic worldview includes secularization on the one hand and the rise of the charismatic movement on the other.

In constructing a holistic and inclusive middle theology, I therefore argue for a theology of heart that also extends to the outer contexts of ecology and the planet. Sallie McFague's planetary theology helpfully bridges the missing link of theology and extends the concept of stewardship to time, resource, talents,

---

36. Ibid.

37. Kyoung-Jae Kim, "Christianity and Culture: A Hermeneutic of Mission Theology in an East Asian Context," in *Asian Contextual Theology for the Third Millennium: Theology of Minjung in Fourth-Eye formation*, ed. Paul S. Chung, Veli-Matti Kärkkäinen, and Kim Kyoung-Jae (Eugene, OR: Wipf & Stock, 2007), 159.

38. Song, *Third-Eye Theology*, 56-57.

39. Ibid., 72-73.

40. Paul G. Hiebert, *Anthropological Reflections on Missiological Issues* (Grand Rapids: Baker Books, 1994), 196-97.

and nature. In *Life Abundant*, McFague refers to humanity's alienation from nature and self. This alienation leads to "apartheid thinking"—"belief that our lives and our economy exist apart from nature."[41] It is impossible to see how individuals or the human community can prosper apart from a sustainable planet. In contrast to the atomic values, God's ecosystem is synergistic and interdependent for all creation. McFague warned a decade ago that neoliberal economic policy would ravage God's earth. Therefore, an alternative economic paradigm of the household economy, *oikos*, maximizes the optimal functioning of the planet's gifts and services for all.[42] In the face of global homogenization of human culture around "maximum profit," our world begs for paradigmatic change, not merely a programmatic change.

CONCLUSION

I first addressed the origin of the theological disconnect between humanity and nature, and, second, offered the *Yinist* theology of heart as a holistic theological construct that contributes to overcoming the binary theology that results in anthropocentrism and the desacralization of nature. Ironically, history repeats itself. Taoism emerged during the time of Confucian domination and its corruption in ancient China. China today has become a global economic force and consequently is among the leading climate polluters, which demands a retrieval of ancient Chinese cosmology. It is my belief that this cosmology of the Tao applies also to the realm of theology. For some time now, theological education has stood at the crossroad between the practical application of theology and its academic study. This tension has unfortunately led to an emphasis on the intellectual over the experiential, the yang over the yin. It is my hope that a holistic epistemology that brings a *yinist* balance may offer an integrative theological construct that honors all of God's creation for many generations to come.

---

41. Sallie McFague, *Life Abundant: Rethinking Theology and Economy for a Planet in Peril* (Minneapolis: Fortress Press, 2001), 118.

42. Ibid., 100.

Chapter 20

Korean Women Missionaries: Agents of God's Mission

Bokyoung Park

In the last three decades, the missionary zeal of the Korean church became one of the most obvious phenomena in modern Korean Christianity. In this movement, women advanced the Good News of Jesus Christ, all the while encountering gender discrimination. Although Korean society seems modernized and democratic on the surface, patriarchy is still the norm not only in Korean churches but also in Korean missionary communities. Men expect female members of the missionary communities to take an assisting role in ministry and administration. The women themselves tend to assume secondary roles as well, and it is difficult to deviate from such expectations.

In spite of the discouraging social norms, women's contributions in missions have not only increased in the past three decades but also challenged the missionary community by raising feminist consciousness. Married women missionaries especially were not satisfied on the sidelines. The women started their own independent projects and formed women's missionary gatherings to support one another. As a result, their activities significantly raised feminist consciousness even as they were perhaps unaware of their long reaching contributions.

This essay takes a narrative approach, because stories not only give us deeper insights but also open up new possibilities for creative integration as they meet with other stories. My purpose is to explore how Korean women missionaries have contributed to the *missio Dei* within the context of Korean mission history. The first person discussed in this essay is Kim Soon-Ho, the first Korean single female missionary to China, and the most notable role model of Korean female missionaries today. Brief life-sketches of three contemporary women missionaries of the Presbyterian Church of Korea (PCK) follow. Their lives and ministries resonate with that of Kim Soon-Ho, each of them continuing her legacy and wielding her ministerial authority for her specific missionary context.

THE FIRST STORY: KIM SOON-HO

Kim Soon-Ho, born on May 15, 1902, in a Christian family living in Jaeryeong in Hwanghae Province, completed her secondary education in a Christian school, then entered an all-female seminary for theological training and became an evangelist at a local church. While she was working at the local church, the Presbyterian Women's National Association selected her to be the first female missionary to China.[1]

Sent to Shandong, China, in 1931, after three years of language training, she became very fluent in Mandarin. Rev. Bang Ji-Il, her senior missionary, hosted her for over six months when she first arrived at the Shandong region.[2] He remembers her as a talented and brilliant woman, but also a relatively introverted and prudent person.

After completing her initial language learning, she traveled throughout various villages and rural areas to preach the gospel to the women in Shandong Province. According to Bang Ji-Il, Chinese women especially welcomed and favored Soon-Ho because of her fluent language skills. Her preaching was inspirational and moving. As Rev. Bang recalled, whenever he visited these villages, Chinese women often asked for Kim *cu-nyang* (an informal way of addressing a young woman).

Kim Soon-Ho's grandnephew, Dr. Jung Ahn-Deuk, residing in Beijing, witnessed the fruit of his great aunt's missionary work:

> In 1990, when Dr. Jung was visiting a region in which Kim *cu-nyang* had worked, Mrs. In-Ok, the elderly host, shared how during the Cultural Revolution she kept her faith while many Christians departed from their faith in the face of persecution. The lady shared how she first became a believer by attending a revival meeting. When she went to church for the first time, she heard a message preached by a young lady. This preacher was so confident and her preaching so moving, she said, that she could not but believe in Jesus. Out of curiosity, Dr. Jung asked this elderly lady, "Can you tell us the name of that young female preacher?" And the name of the preacher was Kim *cu-nyang*.[3]

This is one of countless accounts of Chinese women's lives transformed through the faith and ministry of Kim Soon-Ho, a woman missionary who against all expectations spread the gospel.

---

1. Bokyoung Park, *Sun Gyo Wa Yeo Sung* [Mission and Women] (Seoul: Presbyterian University and Theological Seminary, 2008), 220.

2. Rev. Bang Ji-Il is one of the earliest missionaries sent to Shandong, China, and currently the oldest living pastor in the PCK denomination. Information regarding Kim Soon-Ho was obtained through an interview conducted on February 16, 2007, for the publishing of *PUTS Women Alumni Association Half-Centennial History*, ed. Bokyoung Park et al. (Seoul: PUTS Alumni Association Publication Committee, 2009).

3. The writer reconstructed the story of Dr. Jung's personal account through an email on May 15, 2014.

After six years of work, she returned to Korea for furlough. During this time, she traveled to various cities in Korea and visited many churches to preach and mobilize women for missions. Unfortunately, after her furlough, she was not able to go back to the mission field due to the Sino-Japanese War. In October 1938, the official missionary work in Shandong ended. In 1939, the PCK relocated her mission to Manchuria. She ministered to many Chinese women there until the year 1942, when the denomination decided to withdraw her from mission work.

After she came back to Korea, Kim Soon-Ho continued to inspire Korean Christian women. She worked as a professor and a housemother in the women's dormitory at Pyeongyang Seminary. Her life became the symbol of women's leadership in the seminary. Chu Sun-Ae, who was a student of Kim Soon-Ho, recalls her as "a loving shepherd with an inspirational and powerful message."[4] According to Chu, Kim Soon-Ho was considerate, keen, and observant, with a sharp intellect.[5] Another student, the late Rev. Lee Dong-Sun,[6] had the following recollection:

> Professor Kim Soon-Ho seemed strict at first glance. She was someone who had great influence, and had a thorough and disciplined lifestyle, but her eyes were always wet with tears from her constant fervent prayers. She was always concerned with the students' academic and living conditions, guiding us to keep walking with God, and caring for us like a mother.[7]

Once the Communists occupied North Korea, Christians in the north fled to the south. Kim Soon-Ho's students in Pyeongyang Seminary also went to the south. When they urged her to join them, she refused, saying, "I will stay and protect the church." Communists martyred her after bursting into the church while she was leading a dawn prayer meeting. She was only fifty-one years old.

THE STORY CONTINUES: MODERN KOREAN WOMEN IN MISSIONARY MOVEMENT

Kim Soon-Ho's life and ministry reverberate throughout recent history in the lives of many. These stories become more noticeable particularly in the 1980s. As the number of female missionaries increased, their roles diversified and their contributions expanded. They participated in church planting, discipleship training, education, as well as in various Christian NGOs.

---

4. Chu Sun-Ae, "The First Woman Missionary Kim Soon-Ho," in *Jin Cuyang of Sandong, China,* ed. Jung An-Deuk, unpublished material, 7-8. Chu Sun-Ae, the first female professor of Presbyterian University and Theological Seminary, retired as an honorary professor and is currently living in Seoul.

5. Chu Sun-Ae, "The First Woman Missionary," 7-8.

6. This interview was conducted on February 10, 2007; Park et al., eds., *PUTS Women Alumni Association Half-Centennial History,* 96-100.

7. Ibid., 97.

In sketching out how modern-day Korean women missionaries are continuing the legacy of Kim Soon-Ho, I interviewed three missionaries commissioned by the PCK. I initially contacted the three women for my previous research on current statistics of female missionaries in the PCK. I selected five female missionaries with approximately twenty years of missionary experience for interviews, and three persons actively and graciously responded. Through email interviews, these three missionaries described their missionary activities.

Pioneer Spirit in Mission

Song Kwang-Ok, the youngest child in a typical non-Christian family, visited churches with her sisters occasionally, yet more often visited Buddhist temples and Korean Shamans to go pray with her mother.[8] When she turned sixteen, she left her traditional religions and became more committed to Christianity.

However, after graduating from high school, she followed her dream to become a soldier and entered the military. In the army, her faith grew stronger as she attended the dawn prayer meetings, Bible studies, and various other prayer gatherings. She wanted to learn more about the Christian faith during those years, and such longing naturally led her to knock on the door of a Christian university.

In her third year attending the university, she became involved in outreach work, mainly at a very remote region near Jirisan, a mountain in Jeolla Province. Every Friday, she took the train for seven hours to reach Jirisan. When she arrived in the Sanchung region, she went deeper into still more remote rural villages where there were no churches. Deciding that this was her mission field, she visited house to house to share the gospel. Her tireless visits eventually saw fruit in several church plantings. During her second year in her Masters of Divinity (M.Div.) program, she served as the pastor in one of these new churches. Her zeal for pioneer outreach work was exceptional, considering the Korean social climate of the 1980s, where Christians typically viewed such ministry in a remote region as suitable for males, and women were not ordained but expected to serve in a more supporting role.

After graduating from the M.Div. program, in 1990, the PCK finally commissioned her to Indonesia as a missionary. Following the initial three years of language learning, she began her ministry as a professor of missiology at Sekolah Tinggi Theologia Injili Arastamar (SETIA)[9] Seminary in Jakarta, the largest seminary in Indonesia.

In this period, her pioneer spirit began to flame again. In 2000, she spearheaded the opening of a new extension of SETIA in Ngabang, at the western part of

---

8. The writer conducted Song Kwang-Ok's interview by email on May 18, 2014, and May 30, 2014. More information on Kwang-Ok's story can be found in Jeong-Soon Lee, *Sae Ge Sun Gyo Wa Han Guk Yeo Sung Sun Gyo Sa Deul* [World Mission and Korean Women Missionaries] (Seoul: CLC Publisher, 2009), 131-35.

9. It literally means Sekolah Tinggi (university), Theologia (theology), Injili (gospel), Aras (palm tree), and Tamar (cedar).

Kalimantan. It was a bold attempt, and by no means easy, with her regular teaching schedule at SETIA Jakarta. Nevertheless, she was up for the challenge, and now this school has grown to be the largest seminary in West Kalimantan in terms of the size and facilities. Among the twelve extensions of SETIA Seminary in Indonesia, SETIA Ngabang became the best-established school.

The mission of SETIA Ngabang shares the mission of all SETIA seminaries: equipping church planters with evangelical theology. The school especially seeks to equip church planters and evangelists for the remote regions of Kalimantan. The unique feature of this school is its practical curriculum. During their third year, students must go to remote villages and either plant a church or do evangelistic ministry. The program always exposes students to endemic diseases, and some might even lose their lives. When they enroll in the program, however, they sign a commitment to follow through the training fully aware of the possible dangers. After one year of extremely hard practicum training, the students take two more years of academic study, amounting to five years total. Only after these rigorous experiences are they eligible for graduation. Yet, before they can receive their graduation certificates, they must serve three more years planting a church, ministering a new church plant, or teaching in a small school. These three years of service in the extremely remote villages instill in the students the Christ-like spirit of service. Those who complete all these steps become well-equipped Christian workers to serve the Lord and their communities. Many graduates with a Christian education degree become public school teachers while working as evangelists in their local church.

Such a rigorous training program echoes from Kwang-Ok's own ministry experience at Jiri Mountain when she was in Korea. After her own experiences with church planting and evangelism in the very remote regions of the Jiri Mountain, she became a mentor for students who are sent off for similar work. According to Kwang-Ok, more than two hundred churches were planted, and the Christian population in the region increased in number, thanks in part to the teams of evangelists whom SETIA consistently sends to remote regions to do evangelistic outreach and church planting work.

As the founder and the dean of the seminary, Kwang-Ok is a role model especially for female students in the seminary. Currently, female students make up 60 percent of the student body. The most notable student is Pastor Asnat, who planted twenty-three churches in the Kuala Behe region. Kwang-Ok spiritually and financially supported Asnat's church-planting ministry, which expanded to the political arena in the local community. She campaigned to elect Pastor Markus, a graduate of the same seminary and the current assistant dean. Since the area population is predominantly Muslim, it is very uncommon for the people to elect Christians to public office. However, thanks to the efforts of Pastor Asnat, the populace elected Pastor Markus three times as a municipal member, and this year, they elected him as a provincial member.

Kwang-Ok's pioneer spirit extended to planting a Korean church. In 1997, she boldly started a congregation named Korean All Nations Church near Jakarta airport, where a Chinese Indonesian community resides. The church has become fully organized and operational with two elders, three deacons, and twelve *kwonsa* (female elderly deaconesses) nominated as the lay leaders of the church. Considering that women rarely assume the senior pastor role in the Korean church, Kwang-Ok's church planting and organization signify an amazing accomplishment. Moreover, in 1999, she opened a kindergarten for underprivileged children. With five teachers and forty-five children, Grace Kindergarten earned a reputation among the locals as an outstanding Christian kindergarten.

Kwang-Ok continues to live out her pioneer spirit in shaping the missionary community. Working alongside other Korean missionaries for twenty-five years, she often observed an initial reluctance on the part of women to take up leadership in the missionary community. She realized that believers could not foster female leadership when each woman had to fend for herself. Believing in the need for intentional support of the general missionary community, each woman must also cooperate to minimize unnecessary competition and foster a spirit of sisterhood. To fulfill this need, she organized the women's missionary gathering within the PCK missionary community. The first conference occurred in 2007, and in this conference, attendees elected her as the first president of the women's gathering. She has held the presidential seat until today.

FROM MISSIONARY WIFE TO INDEPENDENT MISSIONARY

Kim Jeong-Im has been working with her husband in the Batam Island of Indonesia for twenty-three years.[10] When her family first arrived in the island, the remote town of Batam was underdeveloped. Although commissioned by the PCK as a missionary in her own right, Jeong-Im's initial priority was raising her three children and being a good homemaker. A willing helper for her husband, she stayed mainly on the sidelines.

She remembers the first several years of language learning as the most difficult period. She had the burden of raising three children with little help from her husband. Jeong-Im considered quitting her language class, but her husband always encouraged her to continue. Sometimes he would even warn her by saying, "If you cannot acquire the language now, you will never learn it later." The stinging advice was quite painful at times, but in the end, thanks to such constant advice, she was able to learn the Indonesian language.

Jeong-Im's husband often encouraged her in ministry. He constantly reassured her to be a more active partner, although she was content with child-rearing and housework. Thus, early in her missionary life, she became an active participant in various ministries. When her husband started a Korean congregation in Batam, she also was in charge of the Sunday School program, employing her Christian education undergraduate major from Presbyterian University and Theological Seminary (PUTS). At the same time, she was also in charge of Hangul School (Korean Language School) that they ran in church.

---

10. The author obtained the story of Kim Jeong-Im from an email interview on May 23, 2014.

Due to the rapid urbanization of the local community, Korean workers started migrating into town. For the children of the Korean families who did not have the chance to learn the Korean language, Hangul School was the only place where they could learn it. As Hangul School developed, Jeong-Im's role became more crucial.

After Jeong-Im sent her children to a boarding school, she dedicated more time to ministry. With the urbanization of Batam, people from nearby villages were flooding in for better education and job opportunities. As the population burgeoned, troubles also followed. The children and teenagers often experienced neglect and exposure to violence. To keep them off the streets, she started a mission center at a small and shabby apartment. This mission center held various cultural activities, such as taekwondo, soccer, keyboard, guitar, and drum lessons. The young people had never been to a church before, were uneducated, and at the poverty level. Many came from unfortunate circumstances, with no family to rely on. This mission center was their only safe space. At this mission center, Jeong-Im took care of these children and teenagers as if they were her own children. She encouraged them, gave them a vision, and embraced them with love and care. Numerous windows were broken during indoor soccer games held inside such a small place. Jeong-Im did not scold them but rather offered a word of comfort, saying, "It's all right." This tender embracing motherhood was the most prominent characteristic of her leadership. With consistent love, the children and teenagers were gradually transformed. Later, these youngsters confessed to her, "If I had not had this church community and had not met the Kims, I would not be who I am today."

The turning point of her ministry came as she enrolled in a three-year M.Div. program in Korea during her sabbatical. These three years were crucial to her development as a missionary. During her studies, she worked as the director of children's ministry for two years. There she learned to embrace her pastoral identity. She now appropriately combined her tender and caring disposition with more active pastoral leadership. She had cultivated a spirit of service during all her years as a pastor's wife, and she naturally grew into the role of the healer and intercessor within the church community. She exercised a motherly leadership, characterized by sensitivity and empathy to those in pain, while she comfortably wore the mantle of spiritual authority when she preached.

When she finally returned to Indonesia after her completion of the M.Div. program, a new horizon opened in her ministry. A board of trustees elected her husband as the chair of an education foundation of more than eighty teachers and one thousand students, and Jeong-Im took up the position of treasurer. The foundation urgently needed to reduce the chronic budget deficit. Jeong-Im identified many areas of wasteful or dishonest expenditure as the treasurer, eradicating reckless spending, and systemizing the finances. Many principals of the schools and other local leaders protested the change. Some missionaries worried that the relationship between the missionaries and the local leaders would worsen. Yet, Jeong-Im was no longer docile and submissive. She aggressively pushed through the operation to achieve transparency in finances, even as she kept her tender personality.

The most dramatic change in her ministry happened after her ordination. Her teaching ministry greatly expanded in the seminary. Before, Jeong-Im would hold back and remain an assistant to her husband. Nevertheless, once she was ordained, she allowed herself to preach more often. The process of preparing and delivering sermons developed her identity and authority as an ordained minister. At this moment, while her husband is taking a sabbatical year as a visiting professor in Korea, she is taking up all the responsibilities as the senior pastor of the church as well as a professor of the seminary.

KOREAN WOMEN MISSIONARIES
AWAKENING WOMEN IN BOLIVIA

At this point of my essay, allow me to remind the reader that my goal is to explore how Korean women missionaries have contributed globally to the *missio Dei*. The next narrative in this series comes from Latin America. The PCK commissioned Lee Soo-Mi and her husband to Bolivia in 1995.[11] She started the Study Room Project for children in a slum area. Often, no one offered proper protection for the children in this community, and the cycle of poverty passed down through generations. Initially, these children were seriously neglected and open to all kinds of dangers. She set up the Study Room Project for the protection of the children in this area. Soo-Mi's Study Room Project was an extension of her past in Korea. Since her college years, she had worked as a teacher in Community Tutoring Center near the factory area where the poorest and the most vulnerable reside. Soo-Mi simply brought her previous Korean experience to a new missionary context. Gradually, the study room expanded its scale and size, and other ministries such as church planting, well digging, and a small medical clinic grew out of it. These various ministries became the contact point to reach the local people. As Soo-Mi's relationship with the locals grew, they asked the missionaries to help start an official school, which eventually grew to hold six hundred students from kindergarten to high school, and the Bolivia Department of Education accredited it.

Soo-Mi, a Bible study teacher for middle-school students, motivates the students to have a global vision and challenges them to serve the world. In her interview, she shared an episode of how her class became a channel of fresh hope for the children. When Soo-Mi was telling her students about India, one student, Claudia, unexpectedly approached her and said, "I want to be a missionary." Now the twenty-one-year-old Claudia is in a university preparing to become a medical doctor and working toward her calling in medical missions. Soo-Mi's efforts are finally bearing fruit, as evidenced in Claudia and others who are dedicating themselves to missions.

Besides educating children, Soo-Mi, with the mothers of the students, started a women's ministry. After realizing that unless the parents of these children

---

11. The author obtained the story of Lee Soo-Mi from an email interview on May 13, 2014.

changed their lifestyles she could not stop the cycle of poverty and the ensuing deficiencies, her central ministry became educating mothers with a Christian worldview. As Soo-Mi saw the needs of the mothers, she felt a specific call to serve this group of people. Their husbands had abandoned them, and they were raising their children alone, with no way to improve their destitute situation. Most of them were illiterate. For Soo-Mi, the best and easiest way to teach them about Christian motherhood was to start with the stories of women in the Bible. Through these stories, she taught not only the responsibilities but also the privileges of motherhood. The Bible study group gradually grew into a women's prayer meeting, and later became the women's gathering at the community church.

The turning point for Soo-Mi's interest in women's ministry occurred in 2006, when she took a sabbatical year and studied in a master's program in missiology. The program was a chance to evaluate her ministry more objectively. It also challenged her to see new possibilities for ministering to the women of Bolivia. Once she finished her degree in Korea and went back to Bolivia, she applied her theories in practice. Soo-Mi selected five women from the community in their mid to late thirties who had one or two children each. The highest education of the women was third grade of elementary school, so they were close to illiterate. They all spoke the Quechua language rather than Spanish; all of them worked as house cleaners or janitors or sold goods in the marketplace. Enrolling them in night school and holding a Bible study class on Genesis for a year, she shared a calling to help other women in similar situations. The training did not always go well. Three out of the five women were not always committed because of various family and financial reasons. After a year, Soo-Mi commissioned the remaining two women as leaders to another slum area. They received no monetary stipends, but only a few items needed for ministry. One of these two left for Argentina, initially with a missionary vision, but is now merely sustaining a Christian life.

Soo-Mi remains hopeful for Juana, now forty-one years old. She used to sell water in the streets and barely support herself and her daughter. She was not socially well adjusted and seemed belligerent at times. People often misunderstood her because she could not speak clearly. With a bit of trepidation and much prayer, she commissioned Juana to a church community in another slum area. About two months later, Juana contacted Soo-Mi asking her to come and preach to a women's gathering. Soo-Mi visited and observed a group of about twenty mothers in passionate prayer. From the time she arrived, Juana had visited daily to encourage villagers to come to the women's meeting. The result was a spirited community devoted to prayer, praise, and memorizing the Word of God. Juana continues to serve this church as a prominent leader. Her daughter, who is about to graduate from high school, is prayerfully preparing to become a medical missionary for the Muslims in northern Africa. Juana's case shows how God can choose and empower anyone to become God's partner in sharing the Good News.

THE STORIES ANALYZED: STRUGGLE
FOR FULL PARTICIPATION IN *MISSIO DEI*

The stories of these female missionaries indicate the ongoing quest for gender equality within the Korean missionary community. Despite her astonishing accomplishments, Song Kwang-Ok is still struggling within the missionary community to push for more gender equality. She often had to bear with others' discreet prejudices against unmarried women whom they regard as abnormal or distasteful. Kim Jeong-Im also had to continually cultivate and affirm her own identity as a missionary when other missionaries did not accept her independent role in the missionary community. In the case of Lee Soo-Mi, she had a clear missionary identity from the beginning, yet has to find true sisterhood in which she can share her feminist consciousness and her struggle for gender equality. These stories illustrate how they and many others struggle to find their identity as missionaries within their own communities.

In the last thirty years, the roles of female missionaries have greatly expanded. Not only do they outnumber male missionaries, but also the female missionaries are involved in almost every area of mission work. According to Jeong-Soon Lee, female missionaries are involved in various sectors, including church planting, women's ministry, education, health, broadcasting, Christian music production, Christian counseling, sports, social work, and administration.[12]

The Korean women in mission fields often experience pressure to work more than those back home because of the shortage of workers. The stories above illustrate the numerous accomplishments of female missionaries, but in a way, they are often in such situations where women must fill in and work harder than they might actually wish. As a result, many women often begin ministry without adequate preparation and missionary training. Pressured to jump into ministries they might not have prepared for, many still managed to flourish. In addition, female missionaries' tender, adaptable, and nonauthoritarian attitudes allowed them to adjust to cross-cultural ministry better than their male counterparts. In the case of married women with more than ten years of mission experience, they tended to be better adjusted to the culture than the unmarried and younger women since they were free from the burden of child care, and more active in their ministries.

Despite the active involvement and excellent performance of female Korean women in various missionary works, the PCK still relegates most female missionaries to the side to assist their male coworkers. It is still rare to find women on executive boards; and even if they are in high positions, they are simply there as tokens and not as individuals with leadership potential.

Considering this context, these three women's accomplishments and their struggles to find their role in God's mission are astounding. Doing their best to fulfill God's mission, they are true heroines as they use the best of their abilities and resources to participate in God's mission.

---

12. Lee, *Sae Ge Sun Gyo Wa Han Guk Yeo Sung Gyo Sa Deul* [World Mission and Korean Women Missionaries], 55-58.

CONCLUSION

The three female missionaries that I sketched above are the true descendants of Kim Soon-Ho. Their stories echo her life, and at the same time resonate with mine and that of other younger women in missions. Eventually, these stories become part of the grand narrative of *missio Dei*. As Charles E. Van Engen states,

> The *missio Dei* is God's mission. Yet the *missio Dei* happens in specific places and times in our contexts. Its content, validity, and meaning are derived from Scripture; yet its action, significance, and transforming power happen in our midst.[13]

Van Engen also emphasizes that theology of mission must "seek to understand God's mission, God's intention and purpose, God's use of human instruments in God's mission and God's working through God's people in God's world."[14] In the process of theologizing about mission, we also recognize that human instrumentality is a crucial component of the accomplishment of *missio Dei*. In another words, *missio Dei* occurs by the participation of *missiones ecclesium*. In addition, because this *missiones ecclesium* occurs in the midst of our daily lives, it often reveals its scars and wounds due to the weaknesses and failures of the church. Yet, this imperfect *missiones ecclesium* is the path that God chooses for *missio Dei*. Indeed, *missio Dei* continues through this fallible and imperfect instrument called the church.

Missio Dei, through the imperfect *missiones ecclesium,* is evident in the story of the Korean missionary movement. The church's error is most notable in its systematic and cultural gender discrimination that hinders women from fully participating in missions. Although errors and scars riddle the missionary movement of the Korean church, through these women as the agents of *missio Dei, missiones ecclesium*, it moves forward. As long as there are new stories of women who continue to testify how the gospel of Jesus Christ emancipated their lives, the *missio Dei* in the Korean missionary movement will continue.

---

13. Charles Van Engen, *Mission on the Way: Issues in Mission Theology* (Grand Rapids: Baker Books, 1996), 29.

14. Charles Van Engen, "The Relation of Bible and Mission in Mission Theology," in *The Good News of the Kingdom: Mission Theology for the Third Millennium,* ed. Charles E. Van Engen, Dean S. Gilliland, and Paul Pierson (Maryknoll, NY: Orbis Books, 1993), 23.

Chapter 21

Mission Theology and Postmodern Social Networks

Shawn B. Redford

The discipline of mission theology offers guidance to the missional role of Facebook, Google+, LinkedIn, Instagram, China's Qzone, Twitter, YouTube, and the ever-expanding postmodern social networks. At first glance, it would seem unusual to think that biblical theology of mission could offer insights for this modern technology. Even the most simplistic forms of these networks were not prevalent until the 1990s, almost two thousand years after the writing of the New Testament. Today nearly every facet of human communication has had some sort of virtual parallel, while electronic devices have become the convergence tools of countless areas of communication.

This analysis will examine the role that social networks have in affecting the nations, people of God, and mission of God with the goal of understanding how these systems influence allegiance toward God. Social networks are empowered by people, and they have the capacity to be helpful or destructive, wise or thoughtless, and godly or godless. Further, social networks that willingly give glory to God are more likely to engage in God's mission. The thesis of this chapter is that social networks can release human potential while diminishing levels of control, structure, resources, empowerment, and personal glory—allowing those engaged in God's mission to demonstrate human frailty, trust, and solidarity with the Holy Spirit's missional leadership, leading to innovative, resourceful, and God-directed mission practices.

To address the role of mission practice with respect to postmodern social networks, this chapter requires missional and thematic hermeneutics. Scripture has the capacity to speak to silent biblical topics such as this subject since there are social networks found in every sociocultural setting, including those in biblical times. Thus, the chapter will examine the missionary witness of Israel through the year of Jubilee, the oppressive social context of God's people in Babylon and resulting mission, and the notions of power versus witness influencing God's purposes during the time of Solomon. The last segment deals with God's missional call from the Gospel of Matthew in first-century Palestine, and concludes with a biblical guide for postmodern social networks.

THE MISSIONARY WITNESS OF THE JUBILEE

God's calling for Israel to live by the Jubilee standard was one of the most profound missional callings of the people of God. The Jubilee plan included internal checks and balances for both the poor and the wealthy, permitting a social context that crossed into the whole of Israel's socioeconomic life. The Jubilee had a mission to address poverty among the people of God. Additionally, a community of people who could successfully implement this type of corporate care for the poor would simultaneously develop a strongly attractive (centripetal) witness.

Leviticus 25 contains the instructions of the year of Jubilee. Within the passage the Hebrew word *toshab* (*tôšāb*, תּוֹשָׁב), meaning "sojourner" or "stranger," occurs seven times (vv. 6, 23, 35, 40, 45, 47 [twice]). Most often, this word refers to those outside the people of God, except for verse 23 where God likens the Israelites to the strangers or sojourners whom they encounter. God asserts that the land belongs to him, and all those in Israel are the "foreigners and tenant farmers working for" God (v. 23, NLT). Further, God reminds the Israelites that it was through God's own power that they were freed from one of the most powerful forces of the ancient world—Egypt (Lev. 25:38, 42, 55; cf. 26:13). God protected his people who were once strangers in the midst of their bondage, and they only found security through God (Lev. 25:18-22; cf. 26:1-12). Israel is now called to offer the same level of mercy and security to the stranger in its midst. These early Israelite "strangers" and "sojourners" may have played a role in shaping Old Testament missional thinking.

Through the Jubilee, God affirmed Israel in its purpose as a witness for the nations.[1] This is evident in Leviticus 25:18-19 through the claim that it would find "security" in the land by following God's commands. These commands would seem foolish to any nation observing Israel's practices. These actions, however, were a hallmark of a nation that God had called together for a missional purpose. If Israel had lived by God's standard it would have been a witness to the world—a group of people who had eliminated systemic poverty and where a minority did not have control of excessive wealth.

Systemic poverty can only take place when each new generation has limited options for economic growth, while the wealthy ignore the plight of the poor. Gerald H. Anderson echoes Leviticus 25 claiming, "Evangelization is humanization."[2] Societies bring about systematic poverty by unjust practices,

---

1. Lesslie Newbigin, *The Open Secret: An Introduction to the Theory of Mission*, rev. ed. (Grand Rapids: Eerdmans, 1995), 30-39, 66-90.
2. Gerald H. Anderson, "Theology of Mission," in *Concise Dictionary of the Christian World Mission*, ed. Stephen Neill, Gerald H. Anderson, and John Goodwin (Nashville: Abingdon Press, 1971), 594-95, 594.

whether corruption, stealing, enslavement, deceitfulness, or fraudulence. The Jubilee allowed the community to reset the playing field every fifty years to ensure that systemic poverty and excessive wealth could not spiral out of control. The poor had the opportunity to learn from their mistakes, and the wealthy could not persistently benefit from the reckless choices or the unfortunate circumstances of others. It was equally important that the poor of Leviticus 25 could not place unhealthy dependency on the wealthy. Ill-advised decisions by the poor affected their immediate family until the Jubilee year offered opportunity for correction.

The missional impact of the Jubilee was multifaceted as it allowed a new start for the poverty stricken, those who sold their labor for debt, and even for the land. Trusting in God for a bumper crop in the sixth year would have had immediate impact on Israel, and upon the servants, hired workers, and sojourners who lived with the people of God (see v. 6). This act portrays a faith dependence on God (vv. 54-56). Israel's lifestyle was a witness to the foreigners living among them, and the other nations. that Israel was on display, yet never subjugated to the nations (cf. Lev. 26:6-13). They were to be the people of God who redeemed their own in difficult times and who did not take advantage of one another.

WITNESS IN OPPRESSIVE SOCIAL CONTEXTS

In the book of Daniel is another Old Testament example of a social network releasing humanity to engage in God's mission. One of the most selfless acts in all of Scripture occurs in Daniel 3 in the midst of an oppressive social context. Shadrach, Meshach, and Abednego witness to the ancient Near Eastern world through their overwhelming allegiance to God. Nebuchadnezzar, the Babylonian king, has no understanding of the limits of his power. His response to these three men of threatening to cast them into the midst of a blazing furnace demonstrates his lack of understanding of the true God. Ronald H. Sack contends that Nebuchadnezzar "developed a considerable reputation as a [military] field commander," and was convinced that no foreign idols could stop his forces.[3] Conquering Judah was akin to defeating the God of Israel, as Nebuchadnezzar's forces overtook the Jewish temple. Shadrach, Meshach, and Abednego remained respectful, twice using the term "O King" (*melek*, מֶלֶךְ) during their rebuttal (3:16-18), yet confidently affirmed that their allegiance to God did not allow them to conform to social structures that place anyone over God, even if this might cost them their freedom or their lives.

This is an example of the formulation of theology in the midst of mission. Mission takes shape through their convictions as their mission theology clarifies

---

3. Ronald H. Sack, "Nebuchadnezzar," in *The Anchor Yale Bible Dictionary*, ed. David Noel Freedman, Gary A. Herion, David F. Graf, John David Pleins, and Astrid B. Beck (New York: Doubleday, 1992), 1058. Nebuchadnezzar established his gold statue or idol, yet it is difficult to know if this was a means of creating solidarity within his empire (cf. Dan. 2), or if Nebuchadnezzar had animistic/henotheistic tendencies. Nebuchadnezzar was impressed with the God of Daniel (Dan. 2:45-47), yet Daniel was already subject to Nebuchadnezzar's control.

their allegiance to the God of Israel, while indirectly addressing the extremes of Nebuchadnezzar and the Babylonian Empire. Their mission theology affirmed the following: (1) they respected the local authorities, yet they could not give humanity greater allegiance than their God; (2) the king held power over them, yet God holds a much greater power over all humanity; (3) any saving act is not summoned via human authority or through divination; and (4) their lives are ultimately in God's hands as any rescue must come through the power of God.

Nebuchadnezzar's remarkable response to the God of the three Israelite youths was "Elah illay," translated as "God Most High" (3:26; 4:2, Biblical Aramaic *'ĕlāh 'illāy*, אֱלָהּ עִלָּי). We do not know if Nebuchadnezzar had heard this phrase before, yet Daniel uses the same words in his later discussion with King Belshazzar (5:18, 21). This account has similar missional dynamics to Abram's repetition of Melchizedek's term "El elyon" (Hebrew *'ēl 'elyôn*, אֵל עֶלְיוֹן).[4] Abram's and Daniel's adoption of these indigenous Aramaic and Hebrew phrases is instructive. Both repeat the exact phrases without adding further theological amendments. In the case of Nebuchadnezzar, the use of his phrase was most likely henotheistic rather than monotheistic, demonstrating that one's missional concern should focus on the declared allegiances of others versus a concern for ultimate theological purity.

The missional witness found within the social network of Daniel 3 demonstrates that those with little political, military, financial, or social power have the ability to witness to figures of authority and the nations. Solely through God's empowerment were Shadrach, Meshach, and Abednego able to manifest any witness. Conversely, when God's people possess levels of authority, it is difficult for the nations to discern God's presence, since they can easily attribute successes to human endeavor. The next section explores this scenario through the First Testament narrative of Solomon.

GREAT POWER DOES NOT EQUAL GREAT WITNESS

During the reign of Solomon, Israel's social context was comparable to a modern superpower. In terms of missional vision, Solomon's dedication of the temple included concern for God's purpose with the other nations (1 Kgs. 8:42-43, 51-53). Yet, as Solomon's reputation grew in the ancient world, his social ideology shifted toward personal grandeur and subjugating the nations (1 Kgs. 9:20-23; 11:1-5; cf. Gen. 27:29). In particular, I will consider the case study of Solomon's intercultural encounters with the Queen of Sheba to support this idea.

The detailed accounts of the visit of the Queen of Sheba to King Solomon in 1 Kings 10 and 2 Chronicles 9 are nearly identical, with the exception of one phrase. The phrase "and the name of Yahweh" (לְשֵׁם יְהוָה) in 1 Kings 10:1 has caused some variations in biblical translations. Most of the translations,

---

4. In Genesis 14:17-24, Abram's reply in 14:22 combines Melchizedek's use of "God Most High" and "creator of heaven and earth": קֹנֵה שָׁמַיִם וָאָרֶץ (creator of heaven and earth); אֵל עֶלְיוֹן (God Most High); יְהוָה (YHWH).

however, associate this phrase with Solomon's relationship with Yahweh. The NRSV is one of the few English translations to treat the phrase as the author's comment. The Septuagint (LXX) chooses a simple reading, that she "heard about the fame/name of Solomon and the fame/name of the Lord" (ἤκουσεν τὸ ὄνομα Σαλωμων καὶ τὸ ὄνομα κυρίου).[5] The LXX also is the strongest missional translation, as it not only ascribes the phrase to the Queen of Sheba, but also that the name of Yahweh, which is known outside of Israel, independently of Solomon.

The missional challenge is that the Queen of Sheba gives a great deal of glory to Solomon, yet only some glory to Yahweh. It would be incorrect to assume that the queen's glory given to Solomon was in fact given to Yahweh. It was for this very reason that Israel was to operate differently than all the other nations, as a kingless nation led by God—a missional theocracy elected to redeem the nations. Solomon's fame brings forth some of the strongest attractive forces in Israel's history, yet it is difficult to determine if this was missional in nature since the level of glory given to Solomon clouds the glory given to God. It is much more difficult to discern God's actions when there are significant levels of human power. The personal glory given to Solomon is in contrast to the many witnesses in Scripture who consistently point to God as the source of their abilities (cf. Dan. 2:26-28). This essay will now move from examining the Old Testament role of social networks within Israel's Jubilee, Daniel in Babylon, and Solomon's encounter with the Queen of Sheba to the Gospel of Matthew to understand how these systems influence allegiance toward God and his mission in the early church.

CALLING HUMANITY TO GOD'S MISSION

This section considers a number of case studies from Matthew's Gospel in chapters 2, 10, 15, 24, 25, and 28 to view the mission to the nations, and shows the progressive social expansion of the missionary calling. The gospel writer purposed a missional admonishment to his Jewish audience, informing them that they had missed the coming of the Messiah. Those open to his message would need to adjust their preconceived conceptions, ultimately realizing that they were like the unprepared bridesmaids, the uncommitted servants, and the goats of Matthew 25. In Matthew's Gospel, with ever-increasing force, the author challenges those who remain entrenched in their misconceptions.

Near the beginning of Matthew's account he introduces us to the magi (*magoi*, μάγοι)—royal diviners from the East. God led these foreigners to be among the first to worship and present their offerings to the vulnerable Jesus. Here we see the infant Jesus in one of the first encounters with the nations. The magi are subsequently entrusted to protect Jesus from Herod, a brutal murderer despite being the leader of Israel (Matt. 2:11-12). The magi most likely

---

5. Randall Tan and David A. deSilva, *The Lexham Greek-English Interlinear Septuagint* (Bellingham, WA: Logos Research Systems, 2009), 3 Kgdms 10:1.

arrived with a limited understanding of the situation. Yet, mission experience would suggest that they shared their encounter with the Christ Child when they returned to their homeland. Only Matthew includes the magi who see the signs that lead them to the Messiah and the newborn king. By contrast, Israel fails to perceive God in their midst.

In Matthew 10, we find another missional account sometimes stripped of its context: "Jesus sent out the twelve apostles with these instructions. 'Do not go to the Gentiles or the Samaritans, but only to the people of Israel—God's lost sheep'" (Matt. 10:5-6, NLT). The twelve missionaries are confined to Israel; yet why the restriction? Some believe that Jesus is intending to eliminate mission to the nations. This command is not one of exclusion. Rather, Jesus is ensuring that the Twelve remain focused on the task before them. Jesus is challenging them to call Israel back to its roots. The appositional phrase, "God's lost sheep," supports this point. I believe that Jesus was saying, "I'm sending you to those who are convinced that they are following God. They are not. You will receive miraculous power, in the midst of your witness, yet this is going to be a very difficult mission. Don't try to avoid this mission by going to friendlier mission fields, such as the Gentiles or the Samaritans." Matthew 15 has another surprising turn of events regarding Jesus's mission to the nations.

In Matthew 15:21-28, Jesus's response is shocking—"It is not right to take food from the children, and throw it to the dogs" (Matt. 15:26, NLT). The Syrophoenician woman had been insulted by the disciples, and even by Jesus himself. No one came to her aid, yet she confronts the situation in the hope of her daughter's healing. It is difficult to know the tone of Jesus's words. William Barclay reminds us that Jesus's personal mannerism may have softened a seemingly harsh phrase claiming, "The tone and the look with which a thing is said makes all the difference. A thing which seems hard can be said with a disarming smile."[6] R. T. France believes, however, "In any culture [this] would be demeaning to those depicted as dogs over against children."[7] Either may be correct.

There is another missiological possibility. Jesus may have been testing his disciples and the Gentile woman to demonstrate who had the greater resolve. When Jesus insulted the woman, there is no indication that the disciples thought that Jesus has gone too far. They even encouraged Jesus to send her away. We would expect the woman to become angry or discouraged. Yet, she matches wits with Jesus, word for word. The image here is one of Jesus trying to rest in the midst of the nations, while the nations are begging for the smallest piece of the Messiah's attention. The woman's desperation annoys the apostles rather than moves them. They are not interested in acting as God's envoys. Jesus ultimately had compassion for the woman, and gives grace and healing to her daughter. Yet, Jesus seems to be the sole voice of grace for the nations.

---

6. William Barclay, *The Gospel of Matthew*, vol. 2, The Daily Study Bible, rev. ed. (Philadelphia: Westminster Press, 1976), 122.

7. R. T. France, *The Gospel of Matthew*, The New International Commentary on the New Testament (Grand Rapids: Eerdmans, 2007), 594.

Consider Matthew's later missional accounts of Jesus. In Matthew 24:9, 14 Jesus declares, "Then you will be handed over to be persecuted and put to death, and you will be hated by all nations because of me. . . . And this gospel of the kingdom will be preached in the whole world as a testimony to all nations, and then the end will come" (NIV). The overall tone of the passage is that the nations will be adversarial to the people of God (24:9). In Matthew 24:14, however, we find a precursor to Matthew 28 preparing the Jewish audience for God's missional concern of the nations.

Furthermore, in Matthew 25:31-33 Jesus affirms, "All the nations will be gathered before him [the Son of Man], and he will separate the people one from another as a shepherd separates the sheep from the goats" (v. 32). As we know from the remainder of Matthew 25, God will not automatically label the nations "goats" because of their "unclean" origins. Rather, the shepherd chooses the sheep because of their lifelong allegiance and faith in action, authenticating their relationship with God.

Finally, we encounter the Great Commission (28:16-20). In verses 19-20, Jesus says, "Therefore go and make disciples of all nations, baptizing them in the name of the Father and of the Son and of the Holy Spirit, and teaching them to obey everything I have commanded you" (NIV). Bearing in mind the Jewish audience, what would be the response of anyone who had not undertaken the missional training of Jesus's followers? For the average Jewish person, their response to the Great Commission might have been confusion: Make disciples of what, whom, the nations? Have you lost your mind? You are a Jew! You do realize that we grew up knowing that following God meant staying as far away from Gentiles as possible. Those people, the *ethnē*, are unclean! We do not even associate with the Samaritans since they are half-Jewish. Jesus has all authority, and this is his plan? Jesus is calling us to make disciples of "all the nations (*panta ta ethnē*, πάντα τὰ ἔθνη)"? We can certainly make disciples, yet from among "all the nations?" That is too much!

Throughout Matthew's writing, we see a challenge to the prevailing social network. Committed Jews are convinced that they have upheld God's standards for millennia, even though God's call to mission has often been ignored. Matthew challenges his audience to move from a place of national loyalty to one of allegiance to God's mission. Matthew gracefully admonishes the Jews to understand what Israel has mostly missed—that Jesus is the Messiah, the one whom the prophets foretold, and the Savior of all. For a Jewish audience, Matthew 28 would not have been the Great Commission. Rather it would have been the astounding, insane, and shocking commission.

Looking beyond Matthew 2, 10, 15, and considering Matthew 24, 25, and 28, are we to think that Jesus had some sort of missional paradigm shift halfway through his ministry, at which point mission to the nations suddenly became a part of Jesus's thinking? This is not likely. Rather, it is probable that the author wrote the gospel aimed toward a Jewish audience to deal with their obstinacy. Jesus knew that Israel's historical allegiance to God's mission was limited, and his earthly ministry seemed to have limited impact on any further missional allegiance.

God's mission could have taken place independently of humanity, yet God's chosen social network of mission was to involve human beings. God began with the nation of Israel, who often failed in its allegiance to God's mission because of a lack of allegiance to God. That said, why would not God give up on human engagement in mission? The thought of calling human beings again into mission would seem to be a quest of absolute despair. Yet, God persisted, calling those from the margins who were willing to engage. God empowered those who were willing to take a risk. God emboldened those who were willing to give their lives for his purposes.

BIBLICAL GUIDANCE FOR POSTMODERN SOCIAL NETWORKS

If social networks represent new opportunities for Christian witness, then our first step must be presenting our true selves. We cannot offer only the best pictures of our lives. Social networks can serve as a mixture of personal and godly goals; they can be a force to strengthen God's community or a medium that allows someone to project a false image of others. Israel was not immune to this tendency; the people of God wanted the attention of the nations in Solomon's day to show the nations their glory. The people of God, however, are most often capable of allowing others to see God when we are at our weakest. Let me illustrate this point.

One of Israel's greatest opportunities for mission occurred in the midst of the foreign conquest of Judah and subsequent captivity in Babylon, at which point they could boldly affirm, "If we are thrown into the blazing furnace, the God whom we serve is able to save us. He will rescue us from your power, Your Majesty. But even if he does not, we want to make it clear to you, Your Majesty, that we will never serve your gods." (Dan. 3:17-18, NLT). Likewise, Paul affirmed, "We ourselves are like fragile clay jars containing this great treasure. This makes it clear that our great power is from God, not from ourselves" (2 Cor. 4:7, NLT). As the people of God, we must learn to be appropriately caring and sensitive to have merit as one among many in the conversation.

Within Scripture, there are failures in mission because the people of God fail to become involved. Our response as Christians has a ripple effect, because the world is watching to see how the people of God respond to tragedy. How does the body of Christ become the family that we are called to be, on social media and beyond? Foremost, the people of God must be a people who hold allegiance to God and his mission without prejudice of the communication norms utilized by each generation.

Social networks such as the Internet provide opportunity for those who choose to act as agents of God's grace. For those who naturally utilize social media with the hope of healing, how does the Christian community speak and be present itself in the midst of a person's pain? When we do encounter someone suffering, we must demonstrate wisdom. The higher the level of severity of personal trauma the higher we must set our own missional commitment in terms of skill and training.

Should the people of God have a presence in the midst of a virtual world? Can virtual relationships affect real life? Just about everything we write has some sort of feedback loop, such as the interactive comments for an article. In these cases, we are interacting predominantly with people we have never met and never expect to meet except in the few-shared sentences. As the people of God, we must foremost be a people who care, love, and have genuine motives for the betterment of the lives of others.

Social networks offer a certain amount of egalitarianism, yet little in the way of knowing whether there is any movement toward genuine commitment and action. Moving from the virtual world to the real world most often requires greater levels of commitment. Social networks allow us to share fleeting moments of our lives in many forms that may influence family and close friends. The design of social media allows some level of integration between the real and virtual worlds. The people befriended in social media are real people whom we have somehow met. We need to look for ways to integrate these worlds, the virtual and real, and feel comfortable with both.

CONCLUSION

The chapter has examined the missionary witness of Israel's Jubilee celebration, Daniel's allegiance through the oppressive social context of King Nebuchadnezzar, the notions of power versus witness with Sheba's proclamation of King Solomon's glory, and Matthew's record of God's calling of believers into mission, together with biblical foundations for postmodern social networks.

One influence of postmodern social networks has been to dissipate the level of control held by television, radio, and publishing houses. This leaves us in relatively uncharted waters in which anyone and any story can gain overwhelming public interest, from unexpected social issues to relatively unknown artistic voices. This also offers unprecedented opportunity for Christians to share their journey among friends, in larger circles, and even among Internet mass media channels. For social networks to allow us to demonstrate our hope in Christ, the people of God must foremost be a people of overwhelming allegiance to God and his missional concerns. Only then will the world know us as the community of God, transformed by Christ, and transformative within our communities.

Part 8

Mission Theology and Ministry Formation

Chapter 22

Engaging the Nations in Los Angeles: A Spirituality of Accompaniment

Jude Tiersma Watson

"The nations are moving to the cities" is old news. This movement has been underway for decades, and in fact was also true during the time of Paul's missionary journeys. This move to the cities continues unabated, and is increasingly impacted by globalizing influences. When we speak of "engaging the nations," we must also address the nations and people groups that have moved into cities, both through internal migration and migration among countries.

This chapter looks specifically at one particular context of this larger movement, the nations that have moved to a neighborhood in central Los Angeles. The integrating theme is a spirituality of accompaniment, accompanying others as a means of mission in a globalizing world. If our means of mission is accompaniment, this will include the stories of those with whom we walk, as well as our own pilgrimages. God's big picture narrative embraces the people in my neighborhood as well as the story of the larger globalizing forces impacting urban neighborhoods.

Charles Van Engen has pointed out that within urban missiology we need new ways of seeing in the city. "We need to search for a theology of mission that will give us new eyes for perceiving our city, inform our activism, guide our networking, and energize our hope for the transformation of our city."[1] Accompaniment leads to new ways of seeing and being, as we embrace the awareness of the holy ground of encountering another culture. We accompany those from other cultures and places through listening, being neighbors, and walking alongside one another in and through the hard places and the joyful places. Accompaniment is not walking ahead with the answers or behind in servitude, but walking together to seek God's peace in and for the city. It does not mean a false humility that we have nothing to offer, but does include a true humility that we are learners on life's journey.

---

1. Charles Van Engen, *Mission on the Way: Issues in Mission Theology* (Grand Rapids: Baker Academic, 1996), 92-94.

Through accompanying we will find ourselves walking along the road and in the streets, not simply viewing the city from a balcony seat. This perspective gives us new eyes to see, as we see from another location, learning through the eyes and ears and hearts of those with whom we walk. When Jesus walked on this earth, he walked the dusty roads and streets. When we follow the way of Jesus, we too will walk the dusty streets. I learned this distinction in a class with Van Engen, who described this metaphor of how we read the gospel from John MacKay in *The Other Spanish Christ*.[2] When we choose accompaniment as a means of mission, we cannot stay sitting in the balcony, but walk the dusty, messy streets. Only when we are walking the streets have we made the choice that the Good Samaritan made to get off his donkey to serve his neighbor. If we are far away in the balcony, we may not even know the choice before us, making it that much easier to stay uninvolved.

With accompaniment as the integrating theme, this chapter begins with my own story as I enter the context of central Los Angeles and describe three lenses I have learned in my journey of accompaniment across borders and among the nations in LA. The first is the lens of belonging to one another; the second lens is the difference between change and transformation; and the third is the mission community, InnerCHANGE, which has been my own context of life in the city.

An underlying theme of this chapter is the lived-out practice of faith through pilgrimage. "In pilgrimage, a theology is not so much defined as lived."[3] This pilgrimage takes place in a particular context and place, yet so much of spiritual formation has been devoid of context. Christians have often avoided the cities as hard places, but through pilgrimage in urban contexts, God can form us and transform us into his people.

MY STORY IN URBAN LOS ANGELES

When I first moved into a marginal, under-resourced immigrant neighborhood in Los Angeles, I imagined it would be for a few years. LA was the "never" of my life, but God knew what I could not have known then—that this forgotten corner of the world, serving as an Ellis Island to many immigrants, would become my home for over two decades. It was a place I entered in obedience. Yet, it would become a place of deep connection and joy through participation with God's mission; there I would come to understand what it means to accompany people and let others accompany me, allowing God's transformation to work through our lives and in our neighborhood and city.

Jeremiah exhorts the exiles that have been carried into Babylon to build houses and settle down, plant gardens and eat, to seek the peace and prosperity of the city, pray to the Lord for it, for in the peace (*shalom*) of the city will be their peace (Jer. 29:5-7). The neighborhood where I moved is west of downtown Los Angeles. It is an area known (if known at all) for high crime rates, poor

---

2. John MacKay, *The Other Spanish Christ* (Eugene, OR: Wipf & Stock, 2001).

3. Mark R. Gornick, *Word Made Global* (Grand Rapids: Eerdmans, 2001), 221.

schools, and as the birthplace of two notorious gangs. Historically, Westlake was the first suburb of downtown LA. As affluence moved west along Wilshire Boulevard, the neighborhood became more neglected, and various immigrants began filling in the abandoned places. A famous Jewish deli and various historic buildings remain and serve as a reminder of the past.

During the 1980s, Central Americans caught up in civil wars within their countries arrived, fleeing torture, disappearances, and conscription into the army. When they first arrived, many worked in the garment industry. Clothing was made in LA and shipped to destinations in the United States and around the world. During the 1990s, the forces of the globalizing economy meant that many of these jobs would disappear from Los Angeles and move overseas. The effects of the globalizing world and economic restructuring that accompanied it have continued to impact and mold our cities.

During these early years, it did not take long to learn that my spirituality, formed in rural and mountain contexts, would not sustain me in this new environment. Raised on a dairy farm in a Dutch immigrant family, with the Sierra Nevada mountains near by, my early encounters with God took place while walking through fields and under pine trees. Although my theological belief was in a God who was everywhere, in my own practice this was not the case. The images on the covers of many of our devotional books reinforce the idea that we retreat to beautiful places devoid of people to meet God. The anti-urban bias that is an undercurrent of American society had impacted much spiritual formation literature, as well as my own formation.

Desperation led me to a journey of learning to see God through new eyes on city streets and in the many faces of the city. Since the Catholic Church seemed to have fared better in the city than Protestants, I turned to the Archdiocese Spirituality Center. Sister Ann became my guide on this journey. She encouraged me in the practices of being attentive in the midst of the city: paying attention to my own heart and mind, paying attention to where God was present around me, paying attention to what the city was saying. Over time and with these new practices, the city lost its sense as a place devoid of God's presence and became the place where I encountered God most readily.

"WE BELONG TO EACH OTHER"

Before I moved into my Los Angeles neighborhood, I spent a summer on the outskirts of Mexico City. Here I was first introduced to the value of accompanying others. My Mexican family lived in a "new town," in a small house made of concrete blocks and corrugated iron, with pirated electricity and water brought in with a truck. Also on the property was the very small hut the family had lived in for many years while building the one room concrete structure. During my time there, someone would always accompany me when I went out. Walking alone was not an option. This was a challenge to my independent ways, but I began to appreciate this way of being in the world, where we needed one another in ways I had not previously experienced. While this accompanying had a survival aspect, the people I was with also saw it as a way of being in the world and ministry. They accompanied others in the settlement also; for example, we visited a man who was invalid as a means of accompaniment, even though we only sat on the edge of his bed. Accompanying was a way of life and ministry, without distinction between the two. When I returned to Fuller Seminary, where Van Engen had just arrived, I sat in on one of Chuck's courses, and the value of accompaniment came up again in class discussions. When I moved into my neighborhood in LA, accompanying others had become something I had come to appreciate.

Josie and her two children welcomed me when I first moved into the Cambria apartment building in Los Angeles, affectionately called "the building." She spoke little English and my Spanish was limited, but laughter was our universal language. Josie had fled her native El Salvador during the civil war, although her reasons for coming alone as a teenager had more to do with her abusive stepfather. Josie and her small family gave me the gift of hospitality and belonging. They invited me over for plantains and beans and Salvadoran *crema* (cream). In missiology we talk of extending hospitality as part of mission. Many of those who have crossed boundaries to other cultures have experienced hospitality extended to us far beyond what we had imagined. Josie and her daughter and son had little of this world's resources, but they shared with me what they had, sharing their space, hearts, and lives. We would gather in their very small space, called a "bachelor," half the size of many suburban bedrooms. Josie cooked on a hot plate, and we ate at the two school desks she had been given and where her kids could do their homework. The bathroom was in the hallway. More than once they had to take cover as stray bullets from drive-by shootings broke through their window.

Josie shared her story with me, about why she had to leave her home in El Salvador, of arriving in Los Angeles without any connections, and the struggle of the first years. She also shared with me the feeling of shame associated with poverty in her new country. When growing up in El Salvador her family was very poor, but so was everyone. In El Salvador, she told me, it was not shameful to be poor. In the United States, she said, the hardest part of poverty was being made to feel that somehow it is your fault that you can't provide adequately for your children.

Josie's greatest gift was laughter. I have no idea anymore what we laughed about, but we laughed each time I was there. Josie and my other neighbors also taught me about celebration. Life was a struggle, *una lucha* (a fight), but there was always room to celebrate life as the gift given to us each day. I learned through Josie that cultures, like people, have gifts to give each other. Certainly help with English homework and translating documents was a useful gift to her. But equally significant were the gifts she gave me. Ours was a relationship of mutuality, or mutual transformation. We accompanied each other through the seasons of life.

Josie would become one of the leaders of *Comunidad Cambria*. When the owner increasingly abandoned the apartment building we called home, the tenants gathered and talked about what we could do. Over several years, we worked with many nonprofits, as well as the city of LA, until the entire building had been rehabbed. The Cambria building would win awards as the housing of the year, collectively owned by the tenants.[4] Coming upon Mother Teresa's quote, "if we have no peace, it is because we have forgotten that we belong to each other," I began to see how belonging is the gift that comes when we share life and accompany one another. Significant too is that we belong to God, together. We don't only belong to one another, but together we belong to God.

"Belonging to one another" grew deeper roots in my soul the summer John Watson came to be an intern with our InnerCHANGE team. Born in Philadelphia and raised in New Jersey, John was the first African American on our team. Through a relationship with John that moved toward marriage, all that I had studied and learned of intercultural communication became concrete and personal. When we belong to each other, "justice issues" are not a cause out there, but become woven into the fabric of our relationships, I would soon learn. During our engagement, I began to read the literature that was not part of my schooling—works by Langston Hughes, Frederick Douglass, and Martin Luther King, Jr., and John helped me understand that I was marrying him, but also marrying into a story, a history.

Shortly before our wedding, I was at the downtown public library, passing by a gallery of rotating photos. That month, the photos depicted the stories of lynching during the Jim Crow era. I wanted to walk by, but was stopped in my tracks. I knew I had to go in. As I gazed at the photo of a black man on a horse with a noose around his neck, I noticed that the man in the image was the spitting image of John's dad, Big John, my father-in-law. And then it hit me. This was not a horrible chapter in history that happened to "them," the other. This was my family. These were also my people.

Isn't this what the Scripture tells us? Christ has broken down the dividing walls. We are all one now in Christ Jesus. There are no platforms or dividing walls at the cross of Jesus. Followers of Jesus know these words, but it is not enough to theologically believe that Christ broke the dividing walls. We have to make choices daily to walk through and live the reality of the broken dividing walls. Accompanying others means we cannot close our eyes to the walls that divide us, but must live into a new reality. We have to walk through the walls that divide us. I do not pretend that I somehow can now understand the African American experience in this country. I do know that the journey is not separate, but tied up with mine.

Desmond Tutu, drawing from the African experience, calls this *ubuntu*, the essence and gift of being human. *Ubuntu* "speaks of the fact that my humanity is caught up and inextricably bound up in yours. I am human because I belong.

---

4. This story is featured in Jill Shook, ed., *Making Housing Happen* (Eugene, OR: Wipf & Stock, 2012).

It speaks about wholeness, it speaks about compassion."[5] A person with
ubuntu knows that when someone else is diminished or oppressed, they too are
diminished, since they are part of the greater whole.

Perhaps mission in a global world is in fact walking through these walls that
have divided us. Mission is the crossing of barriers from one culture to another,
stepping into the history of another. That history might include struggle, pain,
and oppression. These "issues" are no longer something abstract that we read
about on the news, but part of who we are as the human family.

What are the gifts of each people and nation in our global family? What are
the gifts of the African church for Los Angeles?

> Africa has a great gift to give the world that the world needs desperately,
> this reminder that we are more than the sum of our parts: the reminder that
> strict individualism is debilitating. The world is going to have to learn the
> fundamental lesson that we are made for harmony, for interdependence. If
> we are ever to prosper, it will only be together.[6]

CHANGE OR TRANSFORMATION

One of the characteristics of cities is continual change. In many emerging
world nations, large numbers of rural dwellers are moving to the cities. Violence
and loss of home lead to migration among countries. Within the United States,
after decades of "white flight" to the suburbs, millennials are moving to the
city while poverty is moving to the suburbs. This particular change, often called
gentrification, is a hot topic in many cities, as it raises the question of what
happens where former urban dwellers are displaced. The news media regularly
tell stories of what is called the transformation of downtown Los Angeles,
Echo Park, Highland Park, and many others. Transformation is quite the
buzzword these days. However, we need to be clear that not all change equals
transformation.

A few years ago I was talking to Chris, one of the young people from our
neighborhood. We were talking about the changes in LA, how our neighborhood
is getting squeezed between Koreatown and downtown Los Angeles. I used the
words "change" and "transformation" interchangeably. He looked at me and
said, "Jude, but they are not the same. Change is not always transformation."
He clarified with this metaphor:

> If I come home from school, and I change my clothes, I take off my school
> clothes and put on different clothes. The clothes haven't changed. They
> stay the same. If they had been transformed, the old clothes would have
> become new. That would be transformation.

---

5. Desmond Tutu, *God Has a Dream* (Colorado Springs: Image Books, 2004), 26.
6. Ibid., 28.

Indeed, the old made new, this would be transformation.

When I hear people use the word transformation related to our cities, I wonder, is that really transformation? If an area is cleared of all those living on the streets, and they are forced to move to another alley, that might look like transformation in one area, but a closer look will show us that in fact it is just moving people around. To transform our cities, then, we must not just move the problems around from one place to another place less noticeable to the privileged. Transformation occurs, as in Jeremiah 29, when we make a place our home and accompany one another on the journey toward transformation. City transformation in line with the kingdom of God does not exclude some to make room for others. We strive for all to sit at the table.

INNER**CHANGE: A CHRISTIAN ORDER AMONG THE POOR**

Mission in the city is always complex, and those complexities are fleshed out in daily life in concrete neighborhoods and cities. When we think of ourselves as individuals living in the city, we will always be overwhelmed. My life in LA is possible by being part of an order, InnerCHANGE/CRM. It has also given me a lens to understand the complexities of the city. As an order, we accompany those in our neighborhoods, as well as each other, as we move together in mission.

InnerCHANGE operates through three dimensions or currents: missionary, prophetic, and contemplative. These three dimensions provide a lens for how we do ministry and how we see the city.

InnerCHANGE begins as a missionary order. We move into neighborhoods and accompany those on the margins. We listen and pray and look for where God is already present. We want to "get off our donkeys" and be part of neighborhood life, not driving by or walking by the needs and assets already in place. Ministry grows out of this place of incarnation, of walking with our neighbors.

Once we begin this process of accompaniment, walking with those on the margins, sharing life together, we begin to notice the larger systemic issues that impinge on the lives of those on the margins. After getting off our donkey too many times on the Jericho road, some reflection on this repeated action causes us to ask questions. Why are so many wounded people lying on this particular road? This reflection leads to our prophetic dimension. As prophets we press for justice alongside those in our neighborhoods and cities. We recognize that individuals contribute to injustice, but that city systems often perpetuate the structures that keep the poor in their place. The spirituality of accompaniment recognizes that when one suffers, we all suffer. Besides prophetic action, our prophetic dimension also reminds us to live in prophetic ways in our world. How we live our lives on a daily basis matters. Thus as an order, we commit to simplicity, humility, service, purity, prayer, community, and celebration.[7]

---

7. See www.innerCHANGE.org.

Through our third current, contemplative, we seek to walk humbly with our God. Here we recognize the importance of entering a new location with a humble posture. We do not come to fix or save a place. We are called to accompany those already planted in a place. Walking humbly with God prepares us to accompany others, not walking ahead but walking with, knowing the agenda is not ours to set. This accompanying also needs to leave space for the work of the Holy Spirit.

As contemplatives, we seek God first, knowing that worship and prayer characterize our core being. We remind ourselves that unless we abide in God's presence, we can do nothing. We acknowledge that our call, in the words of Mother Teresa, is not to the poor, but to God who calls us to the poor.[8]

As contemplatives in the city, we have learned to take the pain and disappointments of life and ministry and bring them as laments to God. When we walk with people in difficult places, sorrow as well as joy will be our companion. Developing deeper spiritual practices helps us to find life in contexts of pain and struggle. Our order has developed weekly rhythms to sustain and encourage us, to bind us together across the globe. Weekly team prayer and learning community, Sabbath days, quarterly retreats, and developing our own life rhythms remind us that we depend on the Holy Spirit to guide and empower us.

These three dimensions also inform how we see transformation. True transformation has to happen in all three dimensions—as we show mercy, as we work toward the transformation of systemic injustice, and in the transformation of our own lives and families.

CONCLUSION

Local expressions of mission now are deeply impacted by larger global contexts. What might it look like to accompany one another as a means of mission, to remember that we belong to each other even if we are not physically present with each other? What might mission in a "glocal" context look like if God's people saw themselves as those who accompany others from other tribes and nations, not only in the world to come, but also in this one. A spirituality of accompaniment is needed in our fractured world, still suffering the effects of colonization, where we accompany others and allow them to accompany us as we move forward in mission in our global world.

---

8. Ann Petrie and Jeanette Petrie, *Mother Teresa*, DVD (Los Angeles: Petrie Productions, 1986).

Chapter 23

Carrying Heavy Stories: Discerning What the Body Carries

Mary Thiessen Nation

I carried a troubling assortment of physical, mental, and emotional disquiet after our family reunion in Canada. My anguish began when I learned of the brutal murder of my nephew's close friend. I struggled to understand why my body refused to release the bone-level shock and grief. I practiced truth telling, naming, lamentation, relinquishment, and openness to God's deep comfort. I tried to shake the lingering distress in my whole being by physical exercise and deep breathing, by praying and playing. The uneasiness clung.

Since I teach a seminary course titled "Ministry in Times of Trauma," I had the opportunity to apply the psychosocial, biblical, and theological materials to my unsettled body. After examining and demonstrating numerous theories and biblical insights, I invited my students, ministers-in-training, to minister to me. I began by sharing my nephew's story.

My nephew Afonso is Angolan. He is married to my niece, a long-term missionary in Angola. They minister and raise their family in Angola. Afonso is a flexible, bright, godly man, a welcome addition to our family. Although Afonso made several delightful and wise contributions to the conversations during our family reunion, I sensed something was weighing on him. My niece confided to me that Afonso has carried a painful heaviness since his good friend was murdered.

Afonso's friend was traveling in a car with three dignitaries when they accidentally struck a ten-year-old girl in a remote village. The villagers surrounded the car and stoned three of the men to death. The fourth barely survived. Afonso lost his friend and colleague, a recent fellow-graduate of the theological school they attended. I was shocked and horrified. I ached for Afonso. He has suffered innumerable traumas throughout his life. He lost both parents in Angola's protracted civil war that lasted from 1975 to 2002—that is over twenty-five years of war in a very poor country. He has known rejection, physical abuse, and near-starvation.

I admitted to my students that I wanted desperately to respond sensitively to my niece when she first shared Afonso's traumatic story. Yet, I experienced inner revulsion. I froze. I felt traumatized—speechless, powerless, threatened. I said little. I timidly suggested that Afonso should seek help to process this trauma while on sabbatical in Canada during the coming months. Upon my return home to Harrisonburg, Virginia, the stoning repeatedly distressed me. It was unnerving, threatening.

After sharing the story of the stoning and my subsequent struggle, I invited the students to serve as my counselors, to apply what they had learned in the course thus far. I suggested that we walk around the room to aid in releasing my body's stress. Walking or changing one's physical position can awaken new ways of accessing hidden information. I also confessed that sitting and facing the students felt too intense, too exposed. I asked the students to pray and listen, to courageously risk offering counsel. I assured them I was wide open and receptive, unafraid of what might surface. I trusted the Spirit's gifts, the community's role, the power of listening and receiving. I trusted the body's wisdom.

We walked in silence for some time. Then one of the students simply asked, "Mary, does this event relate to something that happened to you at some point?"

"Oh my God! Yes, yes, yes!" I blurted.

I had forgotten. I once hit a young boy with my car in an intersection. It happened during my third month in inner-city Los Angeles where I was serving as a missionary. The boy had darted out as I accelerated when the light changed. My car hit the boy. The boy did not fall. However, he appeared to be limping so I turned around and drove back to find him. I got out of my car to discern if he needed help.

I barely had time to kneel in front of him before screaming adults surrounded me: "Call the police!" "Sue her!" "Don't let her get away with this!" I focused on the boy: asking him to please let me see his leg, telling the crowd I needed to make sure the boy was okay, repeatedly asking them to allow me to care for the boy first. The boy refused to let me check his leg. I am not sure he understood. Eventually the crowd grew tired and dispersed. The boy remained unwilling and silent. I could not help him. I slowly returned to my car.

I drove home. The pastor of a three-thousand-member church had already arrived for a fund-raising dinner. As the director of our girls' home, I had to rush back. I became a focused host. I shared about our home and neighborhood ministries. I said nothing about the accident at the time, and recounted it flatly to my housemates after the guests left. And that was that. Or so I thought.

Now, forty years later, here in Harrisonburg, the students and I continued walking around the room. I responded to further questions. I admitted that I had been profoundly afraid of the crowd surrounding me. I had glimpsed what it is like to be a minority, a stranger. I had felt nakedly white. I had also felt confused and stupid at the time, unsure if I was at fault. I had determined back then to avoid imagining what could have happened. I had directed myself to move on and forget it.

As the students and I now continued to walk, I breathed deeply. I talked and walked the memory out of my body. After several laps plus a few more questions and details, peace and even laughter returned to my body. I was amazed that my body had carried a forty-year-old memory and that this body of believers participated in my healing.

This opening story explores our embodied experiences: bodies stoned to death, Afonso's bodily heaviness, the injured body of the boy I struck with my car, my body's unresolved memory of the accident, the body of believers who walked with me toward healing: bodies in Angola, Los Angeles, and Harrisonburg. Bodies. In subsequent months, I pondered the relationship of the Christian story to bodies inhabited by traumatic experiences. I began by asking what our bodies carry in times of trauma.

WHAT ARE OUR BODIES CARRYING?

Trauma affects the physical body, whether the trauma stems from intentional human harm, unintentional human harm, or natural tragedies. Each experience of trauma warrants attention to the whole person. I ignored my body's messages when I hit a child forty years ago. At the time, I determined to calm down, get my body under control, deny my feelings, and move quickly to other matters. This response is common, both because of cultural messages and because many of us fail to understand and respect how our bodies were created to respond.

The body's instinctual and natural responses aid human survival. The cascade of chemicals and hormones enables the body to react quickly. The accelerated heart rate ensures efficient use of blood and oxygen. The quickened and shortened routes and storage within the brain aid the rapid responses. However, when the intestinal contractions, muscle constrictions, and tightness in chest and shoulders born of hyperalertness and increased adrenaline remain trapped, there is a hindrance in the free flow of oxygen and nutrients. When the body does not discharge in a timely manner, this inner tornado wreaks havoc in the body, brain, mind, and emotions. It subsequently affects the victim's relationships, view of the world, and health. We can learn from animals that naturally shake and cavort after experiencing a traumatic event. We do well to eliminate this trapped energy as soon as possible. As the opening story illustrates, however, there is a hope in healing of the body's memories.

Failure to address the physical responses hinders the needed grieving process as well. The profoundly physical and time-consuming nature of grief tempts many victims to suppress the body's complex pain. Suppressed grief further traps the physical symptoms within the body and memory.

Historic, cultural, and communal trauma and grief, such as found in Afonso's experiences, create additional challenges. We wonder: Did the villagers resort to mob brutality due to unresolved accumulated communal grief? Had they never experienced full-bodied, physical release of the effects of their past horrors? Did unresolved trauma lead the villagers to traumatize others? Alas, hurt people tend to hurt people.

Additionally, traumatic events attack our sense of meaning and purpose. Judith Lewis Herman contends, "The traumatic event challenges the victim to become a theologian, philosopher, and jurist."[1] Theologian Thomas G. Long observes, "The inability to make some kind of sense of the actions and will of God in a world of suffering and evil puts pressure on people of faith . . . to abandon the biblical claim that God is a God of history, of time, of material embodiment and actual circumstances, in favor of a mystical God of nature and spirituality."[2] How should Christian narrative practices address the existential despair caused by trapped memories and unresolved grief?

LEARNING TO CARRY AND HOLD STORIES TOGETHER

Chuck Van Engen, my professor and mentor at Fuller Theological Seminary, embodied Christlikeness. I first met Chuck when my body carried far too many unresolved, painful memories. The daunting final assignment in my first course with Chuck required students to examine an unresolved ministry story. Chuck instructed us to allow any and all questions to surface, to bring these new questions to the Scriptures, to be attentive to related biblical narratives, to note recurring themes and fresh insights, and, finally, to apply our findings to future mission ventures.

Within that initial assignment, I allowed my troubling questions to surface: questions about the sickening and tenacious effects of incest, abuse, bestiality, murder, dismemberment, and rape. I leafed through the entire Bible in search of similar or related stories, searching desperately for hope, for good news for the victims, for the healing of bodies. God's response to dehumanization and shame became my driving theme.

My final paper was long. Chuck recognized I was clawing my way back to faith and hope—underneath my writing lay personal shame and my complicity in unhealthy organizational patterns and structures. Chuck heard and carried my stories. He listened, normalized, named, celebrated, wept, and invited me to connect anew to God's living story. Together we navigated the complex intersection of ministry stories, the city's stories, my life story, and the biblical story. Two subsequent group seminars with students from five continents expanded and sharpened my examination of these multiple stories. Van Engen's integrative summary of narrative theology has often provided the scaffolding I need when I encounter threatening questions.

I meet many discouraged and disillusioned Christian workers who need guides like Chuck who will listen deeply to their stories and join them in lifting up their questions to the living God. L. Gregory Jones advocates: "The first step in this narrative journey involves listening. Listening carefully to both stories (ours and God's) in order to learn and unlearn our shaping stories."[3] Jones

---

1. Judith Lewis Herman, *Trauma and Recovery: From Domestic Abuse to Political Terror* (London: Basic, 1992), 178.

2. Thomas G. Long, *What Shall We Say? Evil, Suffering, and the Crisis of Faith* (Grand Rapids: Eerdmans, 2011), 34.

3. L. Gregory Jones, *Embodying Forgiveness: A Theological Analysis* (Grand Rapids: Eerdmans, 1995).

observes that we cannot do this "unless we take the time to hear each other's stories, to know the particular pasts of people's joys and griefs, hopes and fears, sin for which they need to repent and grace that they need to claim and celebrate."[4] Curt Thompson, in *Anatomy of the Soul*, explains how sharing one's life story, being known and feeling understood, are the first steps in the healing of bodies that are carrying the wounds of trauma.[5] We need guides to connect our broken stories with the meaning offered by God's story. I turn now to what God's story provides in this healing journey.

WHAT DOES GOD'S STORY CARRY?

God's story assures us that the God who created humankind sustains, redeems, and carries us. God is profoundly aware of our bodily existence. He "knows how we were made, he remembers that we are but dust" (Ps. 103:14).[6] God carries us like a shepherd, lifts up all who fall, covers us with protective wings, and walks alongside us in the valley of the shadow of death. The Scriptures are replete with bodily salvation: rescue from slavery, dehydration, starvation, captivity, lions, fire, snakebites, extinction. The God who carries in love also judges justly those who oppress, harm, destroy, and kill.

Immersing ourselves in these stories is vital in our current climate. Tom Long rightly asks:

> If people in our day are "spiritual but not religious," could it be that this is not simply because they are individualistic narcissists or people who find "institutional religions" bland and confining, but because they have lost a meaningful way to speak and think about a God who acts in history, in institutions, in actual human relationships, in concrete circumstances?[7]

We trust God's love and these stories of salvation because God has come to us in Jesus. God has shared our humanity. "Since, therefore, the children share flesh and blood, he himself likewise shared the same things" (Heb. 2:14). Moreover, "Because he himself was tested by what he suffered, he is able to help those who are being tested" (Heb. 2:18). The physicality of Jesus offers hope for our body's largest challenges: death, suffering, and temptation. Cherith Fee Nordling warns:

> When we fail to take Jesus' humanity seriously, the consequences are dire. Such a Savior knows nothing about our broken, tempted humanity and our need for the Spirit's empowering presence. And we know little about

---

4. Ibid., 168.

5. Curt Thompson, *Anatomy of the Soul* (Carol Stream, IL: Tyndale, 2010).

6. All Scripture citations are from the New Revised Standard Version unless otherwise indicated.

7. Long, *What Shall We Say?*, 34.

his glorious cruciform power, authority, and renewed righteousness in our own experience. We have no new Adam, no mediating human high priest, no king with whom we participate in our final resurrected destiny as image-bearing children of God.[8]

The physicality of Jesus expresses grief. Matthew recalls Jesus's agony in the garden. Jesus "began to be grieved and agitated" (26:37), and "going a little farther, he threw himself on the ground and prayed" (26:39). Luke recalls, "Then Jesus shouted out at the top of his voice, 'Here's my spirit, Father! You can take care of it now!' And with that he died" (23:46).[9] Hebrews 5:7 declares, "In the days of his flesh, Jesus offered up prayers and supplications, with loud cries and tears. . . ." Agitation, prostration, yelling, wailing, tears . . . with Jesus our brother we need not censor our body's responses during times of trauma and loss.

Jesus is indeed our co-sufferer. Yet, solidarity in suffering and trauma is not sufficient. When all around us bodies are bruised and broken, beaten and burned, we need to hear Isaiah's assurance: "Surely he has borne our infirmities and carried our diseases . . . he was wounded for our transgressions, crushed for our iniquities; upon him was the punishment that made us whole, and by his bruises we are healed" (53:4-5). The body of Jesus fulfilled these prophesies: "He himself bore our sins in his body on the cross, so that, free from sins, we might live for righteousness; by his wounds you have been healed" (1 Pet. 2:24). God in Christ carries our suffering.

The promised outcome of God's story—the redemption of our bodies—defines both the direction and resolution of the sufferings of the present time. I welcome John Swinton's description of this assured future:

> Eschatological imagination is inspired and sustained by God's promises in scripture of how things will be. Such a position presumes that knowledge of Christ and his redemptive movement within history has practical implications for the present and that the ways in which we live in the present have eschatological rhythms and echoes. The church's practices bring into the present, if only partially, the possibilities of the eschaton.[10]

I turn now to the role of the church and its practices to uncover the eschatological rhythms and echoes, to discern what the body of Christ carries in times of trauma.

---

8. Cherith Fee Nordling, "Which False Teachings Are Evangelical Christians Most Tempted to Believe In? Hidden Heresies Come in Many Shapes and Sizes: That Jesus Isn't Human," in *Christianity Today*, April 15, 2015, 26.

9. Tom Wright, *Luke for Everyone* (London: SPCK, 2001), 285.

10. John Swinton, *Raging with Compassion: Pastoral Responses to the Problem of Evil* (Grand Rapids: Eerdmans, 2007), 55.

WHAT THE BODY OF CHRIST, THE CHURCH, CARRIES

The earliest followers of Jesus responded physically to the Good News Jesus taught and embodied. Christ redirected their actions, relationships, allegiances, time, money, and occupations. They shared their food and belongings; they cast demons out of wracked bodies; they confessed and forgave sins with their bodies. They carried the gospel in their bodies. The church's first task in times of trauma is to embody the gospel. Trauma isolates. The Christian body provides a relational home, a place of belonging. Herman notes:

> Traumatic events destroy the sustaining bonds between individual and community. . . . Trauma isolates; the group re-creates a sense of belonging. Trauma shames and stigmatizes; the group bears witness and affirms. Trauma degrades the victim; the group exalts her. Trauma dehumanizes the victim; the group restores her humanity.[11]

The body of Christ listens to both God's story and the story of victims and survivors. The traumatic event often fosters powerlessness, speechlessness, and the threat of annihilation; victims often feel alone and cut off from human care.

> The individual who has been damaged . . . must reclaim more than a voice and a sense that it is possible to have allies in this world; also needed is a belief in one's own value as a human being as a member of a community. The testimony, by retracing the thread of a life course until it was broken by the repression, and the survival skills that promoted life after the traumatic events, facilitates a recovery of personal and social identity, a mending of the life line.[12]

When the body of Christ speaks the truth against evil and oppression, victims are freed of false guilt and unmerited shame. By unpacking complex stories, the Christian body examines the complex contributors—systemic, structural, historic, contextual, and communal—within traumatic events, thereby freeing individuals of burdens that are not theirs to carry.

Herman assures, "A group as a whole has a capacity to bear and integrate traumatic experience that is greater than that of any individual member, and each member can draw upon the shared resources of the group to foster her own integration."[13] The church enables individuals and the community to seek justice together, to entrust vengeance to God, to wait for God's comfort, and to watch together for God's coming in the present and future. The community must receive God's comfort and love to share this with others (2 Cor. 1:4-6).

---

11. Herman, *Trauma*, 214.
12. Adrianne Aron, "Testimonio: A Bridge between Psychotherapy and Sociotherapy," *Women and Therapy* 13, no. 3 (1992): 184.
13. Herman, *Trauma*, 216.

Finally, the body of Christ engages in communal practices that encourage the releasing of bodily grief to the God who hears. The biblical practice of lament is vital.

By giving voice to lament one can intercept and work on his suffering within the framework of communication. The hopelessness of certain forms of suffering—whether it is grounded in conditions that are at present petrified or whether it is unalterable—can be endured where the pain can still be articulated.[14]

Healing the Wounds of Trauma offers a vibrant example of storytelling and communal lament. The material was first developed, experienced, and recorded in a community in Nairobi, Kenya, where the authors subsequently translated the volume into 150 languages.[15] The practice of biblical lament makes possible an experience of grace that in turn introduces God's enablement of forgiveness, mercy, and reconciliation.

Belonging, shared stories, biblical lament, forgiveness, and reconciliation are just a few of the practices that equip the body to carry the traumas of its members and neighbors. These practices carry the hope, love, and faith of the gospel.

THE PURPOSE OF OUR BODIES

God created our bodies to carry the gospel. The Spirit pours God's love into our bodies, making possible the fulfillment of our purpose: to love God with all our heart, mind, soul, and strength and to love our neighbors as ourselves.

Swinton names the significance of this overflowing love in times of trauma: "Loving God is the linchpin of the Christian life and a key to resisting evil and enduring suffering. Loving God is not simply something we do; it constitutes what we are and why we are here; it is what we are created to do."[16] Evil becomes a serious problem when it disables this reason for living: "In isolating us from God and leaving us to face our suffering alone, evil both depersonalizes and dehumanizes us. If a person does not have the resources to resist evil, then he or she moves from the natural states of a person-in-relation with God, self, and one another to a state of isolation, hopelessness, alienation, and death."[17]

The fulfillment of the body's purposes requires "learning to practice gestures of redemption that will enable faith in the face of evil and tragedy."[18] By reclaiming the essential practices of our faith, we "enable people to continue to love God in the face of evil and suffering and in so doing to prevent tragic

---

14. Dorothee Soelle, *Suffering*, trans. Everett R. Kalin (Philadelphia: Fortress Press, 1975), 74.

15. See Margaret Hill, Harriet Hill, Richard Bagge, and Pat Miersma, *Healing the Wounds of Trauma: How the Church Can Help* (Nairobi: Paulines Publications Africa, 2004).

16. Swinton, *Raging with Compassion*, 76.

17. Ibid., 77.

18. Ibid.

suffering from becoming evil."[19] Remaining intimately connected to God's love "does not take away the pain that [trauma] inflicts, but it *does* transform it."[20]

I recall tangible gestures of God's redemptive love in our inner city ministry, where I hit the boy with my car. We wept, held, washed, carried, and bandaged bodies. Ministry always involved bodies. We touched, sang, danced, played, fed, swam, hiked, and shared life with our neighbors. Additionally, we viewed each other's bodies as inhabited by God. When people treated bodies around us as commodities or violated and used them for personal gratification, we sought instead to protect and define our relationships by God's sacrificial love. God's foundational love found daily expression. There is an integral relationship of word, deed, and life. Along with many other Western Christians, however, the relationship of soul and body when speaking of salvation or spirituality failed to name this integration.

Rob Moll's studies of neuroscience and spirituality aid in restoring this integration: "Spirit and flesh, it turns out, are intimately intertwined. . . . And understanding how things work—how our bodies are designed to commune with God—can enhance our faith and give us a fuller picture of God's work in the world and in our lives."[21] Warren S. Brown and Brad D. Strawn expose the temptations toward inwardness and individuality when people separate the care of the soul from the body and social relationships.[22] Matthew Lee Anderson agrees, "The body is a social reality, which means there is no such thing as a spiritual discipline that does not transform our relationships."[23] The physicality of spirituality makes it unthinkable to claim to be spiritual apart from particular behaviors and relationships.

The spiritual theology of Eugene H. Peterson and pastoral theology of Ray S. Anderson offer definitions of the soul that overcome the separation of soul and body. Peterson suggests, "The term 'soul' is an assertion of wholeness, the totality of what it means to be a human being."[24] Anderson states:

> I use the term "soul" to denote the inner core of the whole person, including the body. By "soul" I mean the personal and spiritual dimension of the self. Thus, the phrase "body and soul" is not intended to suggest that the soul is something that is merely "in" the body, or separate from the body, but the whole person with both an interior and an exterior life in the world.[25]

---

19. Ibid., 85.

20. Ibid., 75.

21. Rob Moll, *What Your Body Knows about God: How We Are Designed to Connect, Serve and Thrive* (Downers Grove, IL: InterVarsity Press Books, 2014), 16.

22. Warren S. Brown and Brad D. Strawn, *The Physical Nature of Christian Life: Neuroscience, Psychology, and the Church* (New York: Cambridge University Press, 2012).

23. Matthew Lee Anderson, *Earthen Vessels: Why Our Bodies Matter to Our Faith* (Bloomington, MN: Bethany House, 2011), 192.

24. Eugene H. Peterson, *Christ Plays in Ten Thousand Places: A Conversation in Spiritual Theology* (Grand Rapids: Eerdmans, 2005), 36.

25. Ray S. Anderson, "On Being Human: The Spiritual Saga of a Creaturely Soul," in *Whatever Happened to the Soul? Scientific and Theological Portraits of Human Nature,* ed. Warren Brown, Nancey Murphy, and H. Newton Malony (Minneapolis: Fortress Press, 1998), 177.

Peterson adds, "Spirituality is not immaterial as opposed to material; not interior as opposed to exterior; not invisible as opposed to visible. Quite the contrary; spirituality has much to do with the material, the external, and the visible. What it properly conveys is living as opposed to dead."[26]

Christian philosopher Nancey Murphy's examination of body and soul in conversation with philosophy and neuroscience offers the term "spirited-bodies" in her attempt to avoid the separation of soul and body.[27] She names the inherent problems within this separation as follows: "Christians have oscillated back and forth between an inwardly oriented devotional piety that tends to slip into a withdrawal from the world, or an emphasis on social action that is constantly in danger of minimizing the specific revelation of Jesus Christ and the empowering presence of the Holy Spirit in its pursuit of social justice."[28] I find that descriptors such as "spirited-bodies," "embodied souls," or "en-souled bodies" may help to overcome the unfaithful separation of soul and body.

What is the purpose of spirited-bodies? As dwelling places of the Spirit, our bodies serve as living sacrifices, instruments of righteousness (Rom. 12:1-2). "The Holy Spirit, his empowering presence, lives in the very sinews and bones of our mortal bodies, reshaping them and reforming our members into instruments of righteousness."[29] In addition, "the more we are aware of the body, the more we recognize just how much care and attentive love people require for their health and well-being."[30] Anderson reminds us that it was the Samaritan's care of the body that made him a good neighbor.

> Our en-souled bodies carry Christ's suffering love. Our humanity before God is determined not by whether our lives are free from bodily harm or suffering, but whether the love of God himself, dwells within and rebuilds the ruins of the temple. . . . The cross is the shape of a life that is in the world, but not of it. And when we know the power of the resurrection, we shall find ourselves wanting to participate in the sufferings of Christ, to manifest the same love that he poured out for us to a world that is desperate for hope and joy.[31]

As together we are carried by and carry others within the cross-shaped life, we trust that "the sufferings of this present time are not worth comparing with the glory to be revealed" (Rom. 8:18) and that nothing can separate us from God's love (Rom. 8:39). A friend of mine in London lives and waits at the intersection of this unfathomable glory and immeasurable love where creation groans, we groan, and the Spirit sighs (Rom. 8:22-27).

---

26. Peterson, *Christ Plays*, 30.
27. Nancey Murphy, *Bodies and Souls, or Spirited Bodies?* Current Issues in Theology 3 (New York: Cambridge University Press, 2006).
28. Ibid., 67.
29. Anderson, *Earthen Vessels*, 126.
30. Ibid., 99.
31. Ibid., 98, 230.

WHAT ARE WE CARRYING ABOUT IN OUR BODIES?

My friend and her husband adopted a boy whom people had sexually molested as a child. During his teenage years, his memories of abuse and ongoing struggles of acceptance manifested itself in periods of uncontrollable rage. All my friend and her husband could do during these times was to restrain their chosen son. They held him tightly. As they wrestled with and cradled their son, they gently and sadly repeated: "I love you! I love you! I love you!"

After one such exhausting struggle that lasted for over an hour, my friend wrote the following reflections. She gave me permission to share them. Her son's name is changed.

As I lay restraining Kevin with spit on my face and him pulling my hair, I realized how Jesus' love was just like that. He loved us to enable us to know love and forgiveness—he let others spit on him; swear, jeer at him, and he said "I love you." And last night I knew in my heart of hearts that somehow Kevin's future ability to forgive his abusers was bound up with me being covered in spit, with a bruised and aching back.

My friend's life displays Paul's words in 2 Corinthians 4:10, "Always carrying in the body the death of Jesus, so that the life of Jesus may also be made visible in our bodies." Kevin's mother is able to do this because she is not alone. Her community bears these burdens with her. She cares for her body through physical exercise and full-bodied spiritual disciplines. The body and blood of Christ nourish her each week.

The final resurrection beckons and infuses our embodied souls, our spirited bodies. We do not await a disembodied resurrection. The Spirit will animate our future "spiritual bodies" fully. Until then, I pray that Afonso and I will trust the God who carries us. I pray that we will discern both the humanity and the glory that our bodies and Christ's body carry. I pray that our bodies will always carry the death of Jesus so that the life of Jesus is visible in our bodies.

Chapter 24

Reaping Missionary Leaders in the College Years

Christina Tellechea Accornero

A starting point in my discussion of how to reap missionary leaders might be to seek clarity and understanding of the meaning of the concept of "reaping." At least this is a beginning point that addresses the foundational assumptions that we make about who, how, and what contributes to the preparation of people in their college years. With any "reaping," there is an assumed planting of sorts—a metaphorical soil has been prepared for the planting. Further, there is the continuing notion that a certain feeding, nurturing, weeding, and protection have happened before the "reaping" of the missionary leader. Thus I begin this chapter with the view that a convergence happens, during the college years, that connects the dots of leadership training, preparation, and launching for those who will be the future leaders of our missional enterprises. In that convergence, what development, inner change, growth, and nurturing takes place in the college years to prepare new missionary leaders? Before I answer these questions, first allow me to share my academic journey.

The 2013–2014 academic year was the last of my forty-year journey in higher education. I spent the first fifteen years at public universities, teaching, and coaching undergraduates. I took a four-year break to do my doctoral work at Fuller's Pasadena campus, continued for another fourteen years of teaching and administrative work at seminaries and graduate schools, and have now closed out my academic career back with undergraduates. It has been a privilege to serve both undergraduate and graduate students, helping to develop people from the young age of sixteenh to those in their later years of growth, well into their fifties.

For my own growth and development, it was significant that I met the Van Engen family mid-career when Chuck, Jean, and their children traveled through the San Francisco Bay area on a vacation. A year later, I was beginning my doctoral studies at Fuller Theological Seminary, and Chuck became my encourager, helping me to develop my missiological voice. Through open dialogue with me and other developing missionary leaders, he modeled, taught, and mentored. In reflection, I can see the intention in his work and life: the components of how he invested in us. Chuck poured daily life-giving water on all of us as he connected us to the *missio Dei*, walking with us on the road of life as we discovered and strengthened our voice of leadership. It was very evident from my first encounters with him that he was an ecumenical and missional leader, yet not at all typical. He had all of the credentials in education, experience, talent, languages, publications, and titles to exercise leadership and theology "from above"—from the power chair—yet he chose instead to be among us.

One of the most transformative times of my development was in the middle of a Van Engen lecture. We were taking our evening break when someone asked Chuck to explain the comments he had made the hour before on leadership development. In this particular lecture, he gave us a picture of leadership development that I still pass on to my seventeen- to twenty-year-old students today. I have used it as a model for these young ones to give them a glimpse of the essential components of their development. It is a model that might serve us well as we think about engaging our potential leaders during their college years.

Chuck painted a picture for us that day of a stadium with the stands full of people. They were in various stages of preparation as leaders of mission communities around the world. These people looked like us—people of various ages, life experiences, ethnicities—women and men who were eager to learn about their place in leadership. On the field in the middle of the stadium were a number of current and past mission leaders, each with a cup of coffee or tea in hand. Each leader's cup was a different size, color, and shape, filled with a beverage that they fixed exactly to their liking and taste. I am sure that Chuck was one of those leaders, and that he had a cup of coffee: café con leche y azúcar, or was it azúcar con leche y café?

I cannot remember whether this was an original metaphor or one he had heard elsewhere, yet the word picture that Chuck painted for us is what I see today when I consider how we might "reap" mission leaders during their formative college years. It is a model of sorts for leadership development that has been so valuable in my work with undergraduate students. In essence, I think this is what the editors of this volume had in mind when asking me to write on the topic of reaping missionary leaders. They have both worked with college-age people and would probably not see their work as "reaping" but as opening doors—doors that provide choices and possibilities. In other words, although they gave me the topic, I do not think they really meant "reaping." My reasoning goes back to Chuck's story, and the invitation to come down on the field. He asked us to envision bringing our cup—getting up from our seats and coming to the field with our beverage of choice. Through the intentional act of moving out of the role of observer and spectator, we shift and move forward, out of our current engagement and thinking about mission, into a new place that converges with current mission praxis and the historical concepts of mission.

A POSSIBLE MODEL FOR THE COLLEGE YEARS

We might use this "field" as a prototype for a way to work with people in their college years, with the possible components of *invitation, storytelling, convergence, and transformation.* These four components came to mind as I reread Van Engen's October 2005 article in *Global Missiology,* "Toward a Missiology of Transformation," that challenges us to think together about how we might "transform" mission praxis and missiological analysis.[1] Nine years later, as I consider how I might develop a model of transformation for working with students in their college years, I remember the stories and conversations around the conference table. Chuck gave us many challenges that helped us re-read Scripture with missiological eyes, and engage historical and current mission praxis, while allowing our own definition of "mission" to develop.

INVITATION

The invitation is to come to the stadium, no matter your condition or background—come and watch, listen and learn. Chuck was saying that it does not matter what degree or training one pursues. Many undergraduates have a sense of God's calling for their future work, and that work can be in any field or specialty–the "invitation" is open to all. The idea is to come to the stadium to meet others who are also preparing for their future work and place in the kingdom of God. This type of preparation, in the college years, looks a lot like what Chuck did for us during our seminary years. There was a different depth of conversation and understanding, but he was still laying a solid foundation for leadership development:

- He instilled confidence at our core level with this invitation.
- He affirmed our voice, heard us, and invited us to bring our voices to the field.
- He saw us and opened the door to honest dialogue.
- He said, "Come, we need your view, your thoughts, and opinions."
- He helped us launch out into our future work and ministries.

The invitation should be to come to the university, and join others who are wondering about their future as well. It should be a call of sorts that identifies a safe place for growth and learning without judgment—a "let's see what God has in mind for you" open door. Just writing this reminds me of the many times over the last forty years that I have "judged" a student at first encounter—first year, even first semester. I have been most surprised four years later by those I was so quick to label. They are now serving around the world as God's change agents. So let us invite these young ones in, listen, encourage, affirm, and instill core confidence, no matter what degree path or faith tradition.

---

1. Charles Van Engen, "Toward a Missiology of Transformation," *Global Missiology,* vol. 3 (October 2005), available at www.globalmissiology.org/english/archive/vanengen_missiology_transformation_4_2005.html.

STORYTELLING

Storytelling in the imaginary stadium involved watching and listening to those on the field as they wove historical conversations into current theologies and theories of mission. It was like watching God weave a tapestry. I have used the tapestry image along with the stadium story to support my undergraduate students as they weave and tell their own stories. I'm sure we can think of many ways that life stories are told around the world—through symbols, pictures, music, drawings, paintings, weavings, collages and written words— all contextually and culturally influenced. This creative contextuality was a hallmark of Van Engen's classes:

- Chuck is an amazing storyteller—infusing life, love, and energy into each one.
- He would not let us leave a conversation or class without having voiced our stories.
- He taught us how life giving it is to have our story voiced and valued.

The task of developing leaders requires a firm foundation in the history and experience of those who have gone before us. The stadium story implies that we find our strength and fullness of self as we carry our cup, intentionally walk down the steps, onto the field, and walk among a cloud of witnesses. God adds our stories to theirs.

In the college years, what if, in the first semester, the first assignment for students was to start a journal, an electronic portfolio, where they collected pieces of their college years? A coach or mentor could be a consistent, encouraging voice alongside for the four or five years, helping the students grow their portfolios. These potential leaders could fill their cups with experiences, writings, and memories, and get ready to move out of the stands, onto the field. They might even record a video or audio piece that would chronicle their journey through the college years—possibly like a Facebook timeline.

CONVERGENCE

Convergence happens as we see God's mission from the long view, the inclusive view that takes in the various theologies from above, below, with, beyond, and among God's people. This idea of convergence, in my opinion, has been at the core of Fuller Theological Seminary's mission from the beginning— for theologies to converge and strengthen each other. Students come to Fuller Theological Seminary from a global community, numerous countries, and cities, to converge on deeper understanding and preparation. They have all grown and developed during their college years and in various ministry contexts that bring a richness of experience. Many never had the "stadium" experience, however, and influencers never invited them to the field during their college years. How amazing it was for me when my convergence happened in a Luke–Acts course with Chuck Van Engen. During a lecture on healthy leaders and mission organizations, I instantly saw my place among those on the "field."

During my college years, at secular universities, I was not a Christian and had no connection to a church, mission organization, or understanding of this God who calls us. I became a Christ follower at the age of twenty-five, yet had no understanding of how my chosen profession connected with the *missio Dei*. Convergence for me was realizing that God uniquely prepared me for a particular part of his mission enterprise.

How can we help those in their college years move toward convergence? Can we develop and grow the unique person, chipping away at the awkward stone block to reveal what God has created? Can we polish and smooth out the rough edges without changing the uncut gem inside? It occurs to me in a new way, here, that the invitation and storytelling incorporate each unique, individual cup. The cups remain the same, with their individual character, as they join the others on the field to expand the circle and transform their surroundings.

TRANSFORMATION

God asks us to join the conversation on the field: to get up from our seats and bring our own cups to the circle. In 1992, twelve of us took a course with Chuck on urban ministry, now called Encountering the City. We did not know when we started the class, but Chuck had in mind that we might write a book together. He and Jude Tiersma-Watson had wondered if we might be able to sit around a table each week, talk about our contexts of ministry, and each write a chapter. We brought our cups to the field. We wrote *God So Loves the City* because Chuck saw the power of the collective urban story. We witnessed a model develop out of the voices raised around the table. He gave us encouragement and support for our academic work and our personal development. When Los Angeles burned during the 1992 race riot, Chuck allowed us to work out our ethnographies by crying, talking, and laughing together. He was our emotional net and created a safe place. We found that we could succeed at little things when life became difficult.

What Chuck taught then and continues to teach, to all who walk with him, is a "missiology of transformation." A missiology that involves "trans" and "formation," "discontinuity and change coupled with continuity and recreation."[2]

When I first read Van Engen's 2005 article, I was teaching a course in Cross Cultural Leadership and having conversations with church leaders about "incarnational ministry." Those of us who contributed to *God So Loves the City* talked at length about transformation. Now those conversations come back to mind along with Van Engen's view that a missiology of transformation calls for "incarnational contextuality," for wrestling with the relationship of gospel and culture in thousands of different contexts worldwide. Van Engen states,

---

2. Ibid.

This transformation is not merely a change of religious affiliation, not merely a matter of new church membership. This is not merely civilization or education, or a change of ethical behavior; it is not merely socio-economic and political betterment. Rather, a missiology of transformation entails the *new formation*, the *re-creation* of whole persons—of all and every aspect of their lives, each in their particular context in terms of knowing, being, doing, serving, and relating to one another. It has simultaneously personal, social, structural, and national implications. It involves reconciliation with God, self, creation, others, and the socio-cultural structures.[3]

CONCLUSION

The day I met Chuck, we talked non-stop from the SFO airport to the mission conference where he was to speak. I was the conference planner and administrator for the hosting organization, yet knew nothing about God's mission, mission organizations, mission education, or the mission leaders who were coming. I was on a fast track of soaking it all in when Chuck arrived. Starting with his teaching that evening and through the weekend, he invited me into the conversations with my weird cup from the world of business and athletics. By the next summer, I was on my way to Fuller Theological Seminary with a new view of my part in God's mission enterprise; my life transformed and recreated. J. Samuel Escobar summarizes this calling and creativity that lead to the wide open doors of the global initiative of mission:

Rather than a speculative exercise, missiology is a reflection of God's people as they engage in acts of obedience to God's missionary call, under the light of God's word. Romans . . . [15:11-33] is permeated by an intense personal tone. . . . This is not the dry, institutional, impersonal language of time charts, job descriptions, and management schemes, which in some circles today constitute . . . the image of the missionary enterprise. . . . Paul does not need to use marketing techniques to prove that his own call is the best and the most urgent in order to attract donors from competing agencies. . . . His missiological creativity is a good example for the kind of creativity that our times demand as we look to a future of missionary partnership on a global scale.[4]

It was at Fuller Seminary that I first heard of the "already, not yet" kingdom of God, a view of mission that has kept me moving forward on the streets, in the cities, in the noise of an ever-changing and hurting world. From this kingdom

---

3. Ibid.

4. J. Samuel Escobar, "A Pauline Paradigm of Mission: A Latin American Reading," in *The Good News of the Kingdom*, ed. Charles E. Van Engen, Dean S. Gilliland, and Paul E. Pierson (Maryknoll, NY: Orbis Books, 1993), 57, 59, 64.

vantage point, I have taught, trained, mentored, coached, and launched many students out of their college years. They are now working around the world, living among the people they love, speaking life-transforming words of a God whom they love. What a privilege to have a place of ministry that has allowed me the opportunity to pour my life into these young women and men. It has been humbling at the same time, knowing that I am a trusted advisor and mentor, that these young ones come, sit in my office, bring their cup, and join the conversation. The doors are wide open.

Conclusion: Seeking Ways Forward in Mission Theology

Charles E. Van Engen

When Rob and Paul graciously offered me the honor of writing the conclusion to this volume, I thought it would be an easy task. After years of thinking and teaching about mission theology (MT), I did not think it would be difficult to suggest "ways forward."[1] As I approached the writing of this chapter, however, I discovered that this was a much more daunting task than I had first envisioned. The wonderful group of colleagues who participated in this project represents a veritable "who's who" in MT. Their thinking, writing, and teaching over the past decades has shaped this fledgling subdiscipline of missiology. This book offers us a snapshot of thinking about MT. Therefore, to suggest "ways forward" seems somewhat presumptuous. At the risk of over-simplification, let me offer some broad observations concerning our call to engage the nations in this new century.

What is mission theology? Although there were notable precursors to MT, we might describe the field as follows. Theology of mission as a subdiscipline of missiology with its own parameters, methodologies, scholars, and foci began in the early 1960s through the work of Gerald H. Anderson, who compiled what I consider to be the first primary text of the discipline as a collection of essays entitled *The Theology of Christian Mission.*[2] Ten years later, in the *Concise Dictionary of the Christian Mission*, Anderson defined theology of mission as, "Concerned with the basic presuppositions and underlying principles which determine, from the standpoint of Christian faith, the motives, message, methods, strategy, and goals of the Christian world mission."[3] He considered there were "three points [that were] especially important for understanding contemporary Theology of Mission: The Basis: The source of mission is the triune God who is

---

1. Over the years, I have tended to use "Theology of Mission" and "Mission Theology" interchangeably. Of late, encouraged by my students, I have begun to use "Mission Theology" more often to follow the lead of J. Andrew Kirk, who has emphasized the fact that missiology is theological reflection and that we need to transform theology through missiology. See J. Andrew Kirk, "What Is Mission?," *Theological Explorations* (London: Darton, Longman and Todd, 1999).

2. *The Theology of Christian Mission,* ed. Gerald H. Anderson (London: SCM, 1961).

3. *Concise Dictionary of the Christian Mission*, ed. Stephen Neill, Gerald H. Anderson, and John Goodwin (London: Lutterworth, 1971), 594.

himself a missionary. . . . The Scope: In this 'post-Constantinian' age of church history, mission is no longer understood as outreach beyond Christendom, but rather as 'the common witness of the whole church, bringing the whole gospel to the whole world . . .'; (and) the Task: Evangelization is humanization. . . . Through witness and service to humanity, assisting them in struggles for justice, peace and dignity, Christians share in God's mission of restoring men and women to their true, God-intended nature."[4]

> Theology of Mission is simultaneously missiological action-in-reflection and theological reflection-in-action. In 2007, Inter-Varsity Press published what is to my knowledge the first *Dictionary of Mission Theology* (John Corrie, edit.). Corrie (J. Corrie, edit.: 2007, xv) explained the purpose of the dictionary. "In recent years, the integral nature of the relationship between theology and mission has been increasingly recognized. . . . It is acknowledged that missiology should not be seen merely as an outpost of theological investigation, compartmentalized in the curriculum, and tacked on alongside biblical theology, hermeneutics, ecclesiology, and so on. It is rather that all theology is intrinsically missiological since it concerns the God of mission and the mission of God. This means that all theological categories are inherently missiological and all missionary categories are profoundly theological.[5]

Over time, missiologists have shaped and reshaped MT by the issues facing the church in its mission practices. David J. Bosch suggested the idea of "paradigm shift" as a way to understand these changes. Building on the work of Hans Küng, who drew earlier from Thomas Kuhn and David Tracy, Bosch described the transformation over time of the church's perceptions of mission.[6] Paradigm shifts involve a continuing process of reconceptualization of theory that builds on, but does not eliminate or discard, previous knowledge. Thus, paradigm shift involves both continuity with the past and new perspectives and theories into the future: ways forward in mission theology. In the last chapter of *Transforming Mission,* Bosch challenged all of us to consider thirteen issues of MT awaiting further discernment.

Many of the chapters in this volume interface with Bosch's list of issues. In the intervening years many of us have come to recognize that MT has shifted from being predominantly a Western reflection on mission practice to become a glocal conversation (simultaneously global and local) whereby we all together seek to learn from one another in an effort to reformulate mission theory, theology, and practice. This involves a major shift from monocentric, mostly Western theorizing to polycentric glocal reflection, a shift we have been aware of for some time but are still struggling to understand and incorporate into our

---

4. Ibid.

5. Charles E. Van Engen, "Mission, Theology of," in *Global Dictionary of Theology,* ed. William A. Dyrness and Veli-Matti Kärkkäinen (Downers Grove, IL: InterVarsity, 2008), 550-51.

6. David J. Bosch, *Transforming Mission: Paradigm Shifts in Theology of Mission,* 25th Anniversary Edition, American Society of Missiology Series 16 (Maryknoll, NY: Orbis Books, 2011).

mission thinking and action. Standing fifteen years into this new century, where and how may we seek ways forward in mission theology?

One way to perceive the paradigm shift we are presently experiencing is to take the long view and compare this one with others in the past. Focusing on Protestant mission thought since William Carey, and at the risk of over-simplification, we might describe the shifts of "engaging the nations" as involving five significant reorientations of mission theory and practice.[7] Please keep in mind that paradigm shifts do not erase earlier perceptions but rather draw from them, build upon them, and often mix with them. Elements of earlier paradigms often remain a part of new paradigms. Such is the case with mission theology. However, a review of past conceptualizations of mission may help us better to understand our present shift from "then" to "now."

The first paradigm I would call exploration. Especially from the 1770s through the 1850s, Protestant mission thinking focused on discovering new cultures, new peoples, and new languages outside Western Europe. Three hundred or so years after Roman Catholic missioners had already been similarly involved, Protestant missionaries from Western Europe and North America went all over Africa, Asia, Oceania, and Latin America meeting new cultures and creating biblical justification and theological understanding of what they found. Sadly, the cultural arrogance and self-perceived superiority that many of those Westerners tended to assume blinded them to the theological and missiological richness of the new civilizations and cultures they encountered.[8] In this first engagement with them, Protestants learned that the existence of peoples, tribes, and nations was important data for mission.

I would call the second paradigm the era of expansion. Especially evident from the 1850s to the 1930s, Western Protestant mission agencies and denominations began to found, form, and disseminate their denominational theologies, histories, polities, and structures. They even gave the new churches their own names (Anglican, Baptist, Congregationalist, Presbyterian, Methodist, Lutheran, etc.).[9] Western missions and denominations subdivided continents and countries through carefully crafted comity agreements, trying not to compete with one another in their expansion efforts. Rufus Anderson and Henry Venn articulated the "Three-Self Formula," which stated that the primary goal of mission should be to create churches that were self-propagating, self-governing, and self-supporting. The formula became a nearly unquestioned and

---

7. The five "paradigms" described here are not meant to be historically accurate periodi-fications. Rather, they summarize a broad category of mission thinking. I owe Andrew F. Walls an immense debt of gratitude for teaching me how the historical development of mission practice over time brings about the transformation of the theories and perceptions of mission. See Andrew F. Walls, *The Missionary Movement in Christian History: Studies in the Transmission of Faith* (Maryknoll, NY: Orbis Books, 1996) and *The Cross Cultural Process in Chrisitan History: Studies in the Transmission and Appropriation of Faith* (Maryknoll, NY: Orbis Books, 2002).

8. There were many notable exceptions, of course, yet in the interest of brevity, I need to avoid the temptation to list them here.

9. A remarkable exception was the Reformed Church in America, which already in the late 1850s decided to collaborate with national church groups in India and China and not form satellites of its own denominational name and polity.

unchangeable law for many churches and missions.[10] Along with educational, medical, and agricultural mission activities, the European and North American missions and denominations also began training leaders around the world to replicate church and mission structures of the West. One might make a case that the great mission conference of Edinburgh 1910 (where Western mission practitioners and executives were in the vast majority) was a kind of apex of this era. Jan A. B. Jongeneel has pointed out, "The first stage in the history of [Protestant international] cooperation may be described as *inter-mission co-operation* [especially true of the nineteenth century]."[11] For both good and ill, this engagement with the nations involved incorporating them into Western colonial church structures.

A third paradigm began to take shape after World War II and extended into the 1970s. I have called this the era of enculturation. This was a decolonization time of the rise of the nation-states around the globe. From 1948 to 1970 more than fifty independent nations were born, including many African nations and others such as Israel, India, and Indonesia. With the birth of nations there came also an emphasis on "national churches," a movement that spawned the "moratorium" debate about mission partnerships. This was a time when national churches began to determine their own structures, leadership, priorities, and destinies. This era also gave rise to thinking about the indigenous church as well as contextualization and the relation of the gospel to the cultures of immersion.[12] "Engaging the nations" took on a new meaning due to the new reality of new nations and cultures actively working out their self-determination.

A fourth paradigm of mission theology arose in the 1960s and extended into the new century. I have called this the exodus paradigm. During this era, the search for liberation was a major concern. Liberation theology became the topic of missiological reflection in Latin America as well as in Africa, in South Korea (*minjung* theology), India (*dalit* theology), the Philippines (theology of struggle), and North America (black and feminist theologies). Most of those movements drew in one way or another from a rereading of the Exodus story and sought to reformulate the role of the church in seeking the liberation of oppressed peoples within their own nations. This search and struggle continue today. This paradigm of MT generated new theological, hermeneutical, and missional perspectives articulated in a large body of new literature. Engaging

---

10. For example, see Van Engen, "Working Together Theologically in the New Millennium: Opportunities and Challenges," in *Working Together with God to Shape the New Millennium*, ed. Gary Corwin and Kenneth Mulholland (Pasadena, CA: WCL, 2000), 82-122. I grew up in the National Presbyterian Church of Mexico, where the formula reigned supreme.

11. Cf. Jan A. B. Jongeneel, 1997:182, quoting Alexander McLeish, *Co-operation in Planned Evangelism* (London, 1948). See Jan A. B. Jongeneel, *Philosophy, Science and Theology of Mission in the 19th and 20th Centuries: A Missiological Encyclopedia—Part II: Missionary Theology*, 2d ed. (Frankfurt am Main: Peter Lang, 1997). See also John R. Mott, *Cooperation and the World Mission* (New York: International Missionary Council, 1935), and James A. Scherer, *Gospel, Church and Kingdom: Comparative Studies in World Mission Theology* (Minneapolis: Augsburg, 1987), 19.

12. Beginning in 1965, Donald A. McGavran and his colleagues in the School of World Mission at Fuller Theological Seminary were at the forefront of the development of these missiological perspectives.

the nations called for a liberating engagement of the socioeconomic and political realities of nation-states.

This brings us to a fifth paradigm, which is beginning to take shape in this new century. I call it the exile paradigm of MT. This involves a paradigm shift in which Christian persons, people groups, churches, and mission agencies engage one another and their contexts as pilgrims in a foreign land. In the midst of the largest mass migration of peoples in the history of the earth, Christian leaders, mission agencies, and churches are seeking to understand their missionary role of being a transforming presence in the midst of multiple cultures and multiple religious affiliations. Africans and Latin Americans are evangelizing Europe. Korean missionaries are evangelizing Europe, North America, Africa, China, and Latin America. Missionaries from India are evangelizing the globe. The number of mission agencies sending missionaries around the world from India, Africa, Asia, and Latin America has now outstripped mission sending from Europe and North America combined. Soon the Chinese church will join in this massive missionary movement to the whole earth. Simultaneously, the largest missionary movement in this century is the migration of Christians from everywhere to everywhere. The Chinese, Korean, African, and Latin American diasporas are now a significant global missionary movement in its own right. With more than 70 percent of world Christianity in Asia, Africa, and Latin America, Christianity is no longer a Western religion. Of course, it was not originally a Western religion. It was originally a Middle Eastern, North African, and Near Asian religion. This is a global reality that Wilbert R. Shenk has referred to as "poly-centric."[13] This also means that in this new century, Christians are exiles everywhere. In addition, the reevangelization of the West is now part of the reality that MT is just beginning to comprehend. Engaging the nations now involves Christian mission from everywhere to everywhere by everyone to everyone around the globe. Although we have known this for some time, we have not done well in integrating this new reality into the essence of our MT.

In the rest of this chapter, I will refer to this fifth paradigm as "now," as compared with "then" of past paradigms and offer a brief summary of some broad categories that I believe are part of this latest paradigm shift in MT.

SOURCES OF MISSION THEOLOGY

What are the sources, the foundational data, that MT draws from to do its work? From where do the ideas, methodologies, and presuppositions of MT derive?

Then

In the past, MT drew primarily from four fountains of mission theory: the Bible, mission history, philosophy and theology, and mission strategies or

---

13. Wilbert R. Shenk, "Mission in Transition: 1972–1987," *Missiology: An International Review* 15, no. 4 (1987): 419-30, 429. Bryant Myers wrote, "Proportionally the Christian church is now non-Western, and its theology and mission practice are following suit." Bryant Myers, *The New Context of World Mission* (Monrovia, CA: MARC/World Vision, 1996), 12.

policies. As David Bosch, Christopher J. H. Wright, and Michael W. Goheen have pointed out, missionaries have mostly used the Bible to provide a "biblical basis" or "biblical foundations" that would justify the mission activities they examined. MT would then go on to discuss and analyze mission practice from the perspectives of mission history, philosophy, and theology. Large Protestant congresses and conferences saw gatherings of folks trained in this way of thinking and resulting in documents and publications that drew predominantly from these same sources for their MT.

Now

The sources mentioned above continue to be important. Without them MT loses its direction and orientation. In this new century and in a new paradigm, however, MT is discovering that there are other wells from which the water of missiological reflection may be drawn. As the authors of Part 3 of this book demonstrate, mission theology must now draw its methodologies and data from particular cultural contexts, from the arts and the sciences, and from socio-economic and political analysis. Business-as-mission is teaching us new ways of thinking about mission derived from the world of corporations. Mega churches and small congregations alike are now doing their own MT reflection drawing from their particular mission activities and experiences. Globalization has changed everything. MT is now multifaceted, multicultural, multilingual, and glocal in its engagement with the multiple peoples and cultures of the globe.

AGENTS OF MISSION THEOLOGY

This being the case, who are the agents, the protagonists, and interlocutors, the ones who do MT?

Then

In the past, the analysts, thinkers, writers of MT were mission executives, some thoughtful mission practitioners, and professors of mission. Many leaders of denominational mission programs and sodality-type mission agencies contributed to MT. A survey of mission journals such as *Evangelical Missions Quarterly, Missiology,* and *International Bulletin of Missionary Research* would result in a list of names of folks who do MT.

Now

Although we are deeply grateful for, and are indebted to, the past thinkers and writers of MT, many others have joined the conversation. As the authors in Part 4 of this volume remind us, MT is an activity of the whole church of Jesus Christ. The church itself is now the primary agent of MT. So Christian leaders in all walks of life now weigh in on issues of MT. Church members, pastors of local churches, young people through the Internet, Christians everywhere are offering their perspectives regarding the mission of the church. This trend can be seen with reference to large mission congresses like Lausanne III in Cape Town, South Africa, where the vast majority of the participants were not missiological specialists but were rather church members and Christian leaders who represented a multiplicity of perspectives and experiences in mission. In this new century, Christian exiles all over the world are now the mission theologians.

METHODOLOGIES OF MISSION THEOLOGY

The paradigm shift I am seeking to describe has dramatically changed the way missiologists now do MT.

Then

In the past, MT depended on specific theoretical methodologies to do its work. Historical analysis, philosophical presuppositions, systematic theology, and description of mission strategies and issues provided the methodologies that guided the reasoning of those of us doing MT.

Now

Because the sources and agents of MT have begun to change, the methodologies of MT are now in flux. The former methods are essential. Now linguistics and hermeneutics suggest new readings of the Bible concerning God's mission in God's world. Sociocultural analysis is an important element in MT's methodologies. Issues of spiritual power and spiritual discernment of spirits is now a critical aspect of MT. As the authors of Parts 1 and 5 of this volume would remind us, we are to consider narrative theology, personal experience, and the methods of the social sciences as equally valid methods of MT. All the gifts of the Holy Spirit are being encouraged in the doing of mission theology. This affects how MT is carried out, changing also the topics and objectives of MT.

TOPICS OF MISSION THEOLOGY

The topics that thinkers and writers of MT discuss have changed.

Then

In the past, MT dealt with topics such as the structures and unity of the church, the three-self-definition of a mature church (as discussed above), the growth and decline of local congregations and denominations, socioeconomic and political issues of liberation of oppressed peoples, and matters pertaining to education, medicine, and agriculture. The relation of church and mission demanded much attention. Cross-cultural workers considered the formation and support of missionaries and mission endeavors as an important topic. The effects of colonialism, paternalism, postcolonialism, and independence were major issues. How was one to understand the *missio Dei,* God's mission in the world?

Now

All of the above remain important topics for anyone involved in doing mission theology. They continue to be relevant to doing mission in this new century. However, the world church that is now located mostly in the East and South of the globe is calling for MT to reflect on other issues. A list of all of these would be too long and complicated for this essay. Nevertheless, the authors of Part 6 of this volume helped me remember many other topics that are crucial for MT to consider in this new century. These would include, by way of example, the church's mission in the exploding cities of our world today. It would include discussion of polygamy, ancestors, and the spirit world. MT would examine issues of religious freedom in the midst of religious militancy and persecution. It would continue to explore conversations concerning, and the means of co-existence of, Christians with people of other faiths. It would reexamine assumptions and methodologies regarding biblical hermeneutics. In addition, it would explore how we can do MT in the midst of global and local violence. It would reflect on urgent issues like population explosion, human trafficking, and the care of creation. Moreover, as a "theology of exile," MT would devote much thought to the matter of immigration, the unprecedented movement of peoples around the globe, and the implications of that for the church's mission today. Essential topics going forward would include the reevangelization of the West; the evangelization of the children of believers: the second, third, and fourth generations; the evangelization of nominal Christians everywhere; and the missiological issues facing immigrant churches in the cities of the globe. These last issues will call for a recontextualization of the gospel in constantly changing cultures. Engaging the nations will challenge us all to reexamine what it means to be followers of Jesus in this new world.

CONCLUSION

As we seek ways forward in MT, it behooves us to remember and draw from past paradigms of MT and seek to live into new ones. We are in the midst of a major paradigm shift in MT. Our way forward is unpredictable. Therefore we must reexamine our goals: One of them involves clarifying the definition of mission. The other is understanding the motivations for mission. There is today much confusion as to the nature of mission itself. Many churches and even mission agencies no longer even use the word. Why should the church engage in mission at all? There are contextual realities in thousands of different situations around the globe that are in constant flux and challenge MT to continual reexamination and rethinking of its calling. The authors of this volume would also call us to remember that there are certainties that do not change. Our call to participate in God's mission in God's world does not change. My own way of saying this is as follows: It is God's will that the church proclaim in word and deed the coming of the kingdom of God in Jesus Christ, inviting women and men, in the power of the Holy Spirit, to become followers of the Lord Jesus Christ, active participants in Christian faith communities, and committed agents of the transformation of their contexts. May the Holy Spirit grant us insight and wisdom as together we seek ways forward in mission theology.

Index

297

Previously Published in
The American Society of Missiology Series